Remembering Paul

Remembering Paul

Ancient and Modern Contests over the Image of the Apostle

BENJAMIN L. WHITE

OXFORD

UNIVERSITY PRESS

OXFORD

UNIVERSITY PRESS

Oxford University Press is a department of the University of Oxford.
It furthers the University's objective of excellence in research, scholarship,
and education by publishing worldwide.

Oxford   New York
Auckland   Cape Town   Dar es Salaam   Hong Kong   Karachi
Kuala Lumpur   Madrid   Melbourne   Mexico City   Nairobi
New Delhi   Shanghai   Taipei   Toronto

With offices in
Argentina   Austria   Brazil   Chile   Czech Republic   France   Greece
Guatemala   Hungary   Italy   Japan   Poland   Portugal   Singapore
South Korea   Switzerland   Thailand   Turkey   Ukraine   Vietnam

Oxford is a registered trade mark of Oxford University Press
in the UK and certain other countries.

Published in the United States of America by
Oxford University Press
198 Madison Avenue, New York, NY 10016

© Oxford University Press 2014

First issued as an Oxford University Press paperback, 2017

CIP data is on file at the Library of Congress

978-0-19-937027-6 (hardcover); 978-0-19-066957-7 (paperback)

For Melissa

γνησία σύζυγος

Contents

Preface

I WANT TO preface this book with a confession. While this might seem odd, it is necessary for avoiding what Michel de Certeau noted of Michel Foucault's work—that in the attempt to historicize ideas, he was remarkably obscure about the history of his own (cf. Chapter 7). The confession is this: though I study and write about Paul, I have to admit that "Pauline Studies" as a discipline isn't that much fun anymore. Let me explain. I began serious study of the Pauline Epistles at Gordon-Conwell, where "exegetical" courses on the Greek text of Romans and 1 Corinthians sparked my interest in Pauline theology. The so-called "New Perspective on Paul" was at its height of influence and, while I had read quite a bit of the literature on either side of the debate about how to understand justification "apart from works of the Law," it all seemed rather arcane and technical to me until I then went off to Duke Divinity School to study Paul with Richard Hays and Ed Sanders, the latter of whom of course is the godfather of the "New Perspective." Ed Sanders forced me for the first time to think *seriously* about the social and historical location of Paul's interpreters. What if the Paul that had been traditioned to us by Luther, through F. C. Baur and other prominent German Protestant scholars of the nineteenth and twentieth centuries, wasn't the "real" Paul? What if Paul's main concern with Judaism was its ethnocentrism, to put it in James Dunn's language, not its dependence on "works righteousness"? All of the sudden Pauline Studies involved so much more than following words on an epistolary page. Reading them as if they described reality "wie es eigentlich gewesen," to use the famous dictum of Leopold von Ranke, seemed altogether naïve. I became convinced that the discipline had been overly concerned with *exegesis*, or at least the deployment of the rhetoric of *exegesis*, and required a fundamental reorientation toward traditions of *eisegesis*— toward exploring the ideological frameworks within which the apostolic past becomes an object of knowledge.

I began thinking about this in two distinct, but now connected, ways. First, the doctoral program in Early Christianity at the University of North Carolina at Chapel Hill provided the perfect incubator for thinking about "New Testament Studies" within the context of the production and reception of the New Testament in "Early Christianity." Bart Ehrman, my *Doktorvater*, became a model in this regard as I began to work on topics related to "Paul in the Second Century." In particular, I became interested in the contestation over the "real" Paul in the second century—places in the literary evidence where disputes over the authorship and interpretation of Paul and Pauline texts seemed to signify larger clashes within the process of early Christian culture-making. Second, I conducted this work with one eye constantly trained on the modern distinction between the "real" Paul and the Paul of "tradition," or the "historical" Paul versus the "ecclesiastical" Paul, or "authentic" and "inauthentic" Pauline epistles. The two discourses, ancient and modern, seemed remarkably connected.

Exploring the ways in which ideology and tradition shaped what seemed to be "natural" receptions of Paul to writers like Irenaeus of Lyons helped to clarify the most important question that I believe should now confront all of Paul's interpreters, ancient and modern: Which Paul? While it is true that Pauline Studies has evolved in interesting directions in the past several decades, wherein sensitivities to a number of ideologies have exposed certain dominant reading traditions within our discipline, I fear that something fundamental has been missed along the way. What if the "New Perspective on Paul" and the "Paul and Politics" movements haven't gone far enough? What if they haven't come close to touching the *prolegomena* of Pauline Studies: discourses on the "real" Paul as they have played out in the determination of Pauline pseudepigrapha since the nineteenth century? What counts for "Paul" in the first place? The "New Perspective," for example, did not address the Lutheran biases in the elevation of the *Hauptbriefe* (Rom, 1–2 Cor, Gal) as quintessentially Pauline, and thus authorially unquestioned, but rather focused its energy on the interpretation of particular letters that had already been fixed in critical tradition as being self-evidently Pauline. I wonder whether or not the seven-letter "authentic" Paul, the "given" of our discipline, whose core is really the *Hauptbriefe*, is like the Titanic, heading unknowingly toward the iceberg of a *rigorous* sociology of knowledge, upon which we continue to look at the same deck chairs, rearranged in different ways, without ever bothering to ask why it was *these* deck chairs (and not some others) upon which we're seated.

This is what I mean when I lament the state of Pauline Studies. We're not really engaged with the *prolegomena* of our discipline any more.

This book, a revised version of my doctoral dissertation, is the first part of the argument that Pauline Studies, as a discipline with its own self-perpetuating institutions, is due for a creative reorienting—a reorienting away from discourses on the "real" Paul, which presently still trade in a nineteenth-century positivist historiography while masking the ideological preferences that they support ("what I want Paul to be"), toward a historiography, along the lines of what Certeau urged, that gives fuller consideration at its very foundation to the interplay of the historian's "social *place*, 'scientific' *practices*, and *writing*" (cf. Chapter 7). The entry points here are twofold: a narration of Paul's reception in the second century, with particular emphasis on the proto-orthodox "Paul" of *3 Corinthians* and Irenaeus's *Adversus haereses*, and an exploration of the role of collective memory in producing meaningful pasts for the present. Inasmuch as the raw data for modern Pauline Studies continues to be Greek manuscripts of "authentic" Pauline letters from the second and third centuries, some understanding of the polemical discourses over Paul's legacy during that period is important. The manuscripts, their texts, and their producers were already part of contestations over the Apostle. Our Paul is necessarily theirs. Ultimately, however, the category that modern Pauline Studies is missing is "tradition"—or at least an appreciation for its ubiquity. Closely related to tradition is "memory," which, for some reason, every other humanities discipline has embraced, including increasingly Historical Jesus Studies, except for Pauline Studies. This book fills that void and strongly urges our discipline to understand the nature and practices of commemoration within the historiographical process.

For some of my readers, a second confession will be even more important for heeding Certeau's warning that "by moving discourse into a non-place, ideology forbids history from speaking of society and of death—in other words, from being history" (cf. Chapter 7). I have remained, ecclesially, a Protestant. Thus, while the "*solas*" no longer make sense to me and much of my work is an attempt to defamiliarize Paul as he has been traditioned to us by Luther, through Baur and nineteenth-century German Protestant scholarship on Paul, I hope that the reader will understand that this book is more of a critique of my own tradition and its scholarship than anything else. It is an attempt, through a rigorous sociology of knowledge, to become a better historian.

At the editorial level, I have translated all lengthy block quotes from German and French sources into English and have provided the original languages in the corresponding endnotes. I have also provided English translations of many of the ancient sources quoted in this book. In some instances, however, the Greek and Latin are untranslated. This has been the case when I want the reader to appreciate particular verbal parallels in the original languages.

Acknowledgments

WHILE I HOPE that this book is a reflection of my participation in the species *homo sapiens*, I believe, with Berger and Luckmann, that "*Homo sapiens* is always, and in the same measure, *homo socius*" (*The Social Construction of Reality*, 51). To a large degree, then, this project is a reflection of the various communities within which my own interest in the figure of Paul developed. As I have noted in the Preface, it is a work of tradition, for which I am thankful. Thanks to Donald Penny, my undergraduate New Testament professor at Campbell University, for writing a dissertation on "The Pseudo-Pauline Letters of the First Two Centuries" (1979, Emory) of which I was unaware when I was his student but which has since become an important part of my thinking about the story of "Paul in the Second Century." Little did I know at the time, when I was 19 years old, that my first book (or that I would even write a book) would be so heavily indebted to his language of "Pauline Fragmentation." Thanks to Ed Sanders, Richard Hays, and now Douglas Campbell, Pauline scholars *extraordinaire* at Duke, for helping me in various ways with this project. Ed, as I have mentioned above, got me to ask the right questions. Richard was helpful on matters of intertextuality in Irenaeus. He pointed me to Gérard Genette and Jörg Helbig for Chapter 6. Douglas, whom I got to know only after moving to UNC-CH, has helped me to clarify further what is at stake in how we read Paul. He also provoked me to read Michael Polanyi on tacit knowledge and Alasdair MacIntyre on tradition.

Thanks to a number of generous souls in the Religious Studies Department at UNC-CH who helped to advance my historical-critical work on early Christian texts within the context of more theoretically driven questions. Jonathan Boyarin, who has since moved on to Cornell, was an important dialogue partner on the issues of memory and culture. Zlatko Pleše provided innumerable suggestions over the years on issues as broad as intertextuality and Hellenistic anthropology. Thanks to both. I'm sure

that I have fallen short of their suggestions in several places. Most important, thanks to Bart Ehrman, who has contributed to this project and to my
young career in innumerable ways. Working with Bart has convinced me
that, in the end, it is not enough to be a scholar of the New Testament. We
are all, knowingly or unknowingly, scholars of Early Christianity. We only
have access to the initial decades of Christianity (Christian origins)
through communities that lived a century or more later. Their later concerns have shaped much of what we know about the earliest years of this
new religious movement. Through constructive criticism, a consistent example of hard work, a healthy dose of humor, and a zeal for clarity, Bart
has exemplified what it means to be an educator: a scholar who is both
rigorous with the data and generous in sharing his results. Thanks to Bart
for allowing me the freedom to explore the initial ideas for this book in
seminar papers and CIA (Christianity in Antiquity) meetings and for
wearing out his red pen on everything that I do.

Thanks to a number of other consistent dialogue partners. Several
friends have listened to and helped to clarify my thinking on this thesis,
including Jason Staples, T. J. Lang, Hans Arneson, David Eastman, and
too-numerous-to-count members of the UNC-Duke CIA Reading Group.
Thanks to all. Other dialogue partners I don't personally know. They are
from another generation and I have had to encounter them through their
books: Edward Shils and Hans-Georg Gadamer, in particular. I feel a bit
closer to Shils on account of his student, Steven Grosby, being my col-
league in the Department of Philosophy and Religion at Clemson University. Steve has consistently prodded me over the past several years to "get
that book done." He deserves thanks for looking out for me as a junior
faculty member. This book would also not have been completed without
course-release support from the Faculty Research Development Program
in the College of Architecture, Arts and Humanities at Clemson.

Parts of earlier versions of Chapters 5 and 6 have appeared in article
form: "Reclaiming Paul?: Reconfiguration as Reclamation in *3 Corinthians*," *Journal of Early Christian Studies* 17 (2009): 497–523; and "How to
Read a Book: Irenaeus and the Pastoral Epistles Reconsidered," *Vigiliae
christianae* 65 (2011): 125–149. I thank Johns Hopkins Press and E. J. Brill
Publishers for permission to reprint some of that material here. Thanks to
Marcela Maxfield, editorial assistant at OUP, and especially Theo Calder-
ara, my editor, for their expeditious and thorough work on behalf of this
manuscript and for finding anonymous readers at the beginning of the
process who suggested numerous ways to turn my dissertation into a book.

Last, but not least, thanks to my family: my parents, Lester and Marlene White, and my sister and brother-in-law, Leslyn and Josh Benfield, for their patience with and encouragement to me over the years; and my wife, Melissa, for her marriage both to me and to this project to which I have given too much time and energy. This is an arrangement that has worked only because of her love and devotion through periods when my work has been all-consuming. The book is dedicated to her.

Abbreviations

ABBREVIATIONS OF ANCIENT texts follow the *Society of Biblical Literature Handbook of Style* (Peabody: Hendrickson, 1999).

AARAS   American Academy of Religion: Academy Series

AARSR   American Academy of Religion: Studies in Religion

AB   Anchor Bible

ABRL   Anchor Bible Reference Library

AcOr   *Acta orientalia*

ACW   Ancient Christian Writers

AGJU   Arbeiten zur Geschichte des antiken Judentums und des Urchristentums

ANF   Ante-Nicene Fathers

ANT   Arbeiten zur neutestamentlichen Textforschung

ARGU   Arbeiten zur Religion und Geschichte des Urchristentums

ATANT   Abhandlungen zur Theologie des Alten und Neuen Testaments

AThR   *Anglican Theological Review*

ATR   *Australian Theological Review*

BAC   Biblioteca de autores cristianos

BBR   *Bulletin for Biblical Research*

BDAG   Bauer, Danker, Arndt, and Gingrich = Danker, Frederick W., ed. *A Greek-English Lexicon of the New Testament and Other Early Christian Literature*. 3rd ed. Chicago: University of Chicago Press, 2000.

BETL   Bibliotheca Ephemeridum Theologicarum Lovaniensium

BGBE   Beiträge zur Geschichte der biblischen Exegese

BHT   Beiträge zur historischen Theologie

Bib   *Biblica*

BibInt   Biblical Interpretation

BJRL	*Bulletin of the John Rylands University Library of Manchester*
BZ	*Biblische Zeitschrift*
BZNW	Beihefte zur Zeitschrift für die neutestamentliche Wissenschaft
CBQ	*Catholic Biblical Quarterly*
CBQMS	Catholic Biblical Quarterly Monograph Series
ConBNT	Coniectanea biblica: New Testament Series
CTJ	*Calvin Theological Journal*
CTM	*Concordia Theological Monthly*
CTQ	*Concordia Theological Quarterly*
Di	*Dialog*
Enc	*Encounter*
ETS	Erfurter theologische Studien
EvT	*Evangelische Theologie*
FoiVie	*Foi et vie*
FRLANT	Forschungen zur Religion und Literatur des Alten und Neuen Testaments
Greg	*Gregorianum*
HBT	*Horizons in Biblical Theology*
HDR	Harvard Dissertations in Religion
HNT	Handbuch zum Neuen Testament
HNTC	Harper's New Testament Commentary
HTR	*Harvard Theological Review*
HvTSt	*Hervormde teologiese studies*
ICC	International Critical Commentary
Int	*Interpretation*
ITQ	*Irish Theological Quarterly*
JAARSup	*Journal of the American Academy of Religion Supplements*
JAC	Jahrbuch für Antike und Christentum
JBL	*Journal of Biblical Literature*
JECS	*Journal of Early Christian Studies*
JETS	*Journal of the Evangelical Theological Society*
JFSR	*Journal of Feminist Studies in Religion*
JR	*Journal of Religion*
JSNT	*Journal for the Study of the New Testament*
JSNTSS	Journal for the Study of the New Testament: Supplement Series
JSOT	*Journal for the Study of the Old Testament*
JTS	*Journal of Theological Studies*

KD	*Kerygma und Dogma*
LCL	Loeb Classical Library
LD	Lectio divina
LNTS	Library of New Testament Studies
LTP	*Laval theologique et philosophique*
LTQ	*Lexington Theological Quarterly*
NA	Nestle-Aland (Novum Testamentum Graece)
NedTT	*Nederlands theologisch tijdschrift*
NHC	Nag Hammadi Codex
NHS	Nag Hammadi Studies
NICNT	New International Commentary on the New Testament
NIGTC	New International Greek Testament Commentary
NovT	*Novum Testamentum*
NovTSup	Novum Testamentum Supplements
NTAbh	Neutestamenliche Abhandlungen
NTOA	Novum Testamentum et Orbis Antiquus
NTS	*New Testament Studies*
NTT	*Norsk Teologisk Tidsskrift*
NTTS	New Testament Tools and Studies
OLA	Orientalia Lovaniensia Analecta
PMS	Patristic Monograph Series
PTS	Patristische Texte und Studien
QD	Quaestiones disputatae
R&T	*Religion & Theology/Religie & teologie*
RB	*Revue biblique*
RBén	*Revue bénédictine*
RHPR	*Revue d'histoire et de philosophie religieuses*
RHR	*Revue de l'histoire des religions*
RivB	*Rivista biblica*
RSR	*Recherches de science religieuse*
SAQ	Sammlung ausgewählter kirchen- und dogmengeschichtlicher Quellenschriften
SBLDS	Society of Biblical Literature Dissertation Series
SBLSP	*Society of Biblical Literature Seminar Papers*
SBLTT	Society of Biblical Literature Texts and Translations
SBS	Stuttgarter Bibelstudien
SC	Sources chrétiennes
SD	Studies and Documents
SecCent	*Second Century: A Journal of Early Christian Studies*

SemeiaSt	Semeia Studies
SHR	Studies in the History of Religions
SNTSMS	Society for New Testament Studies Monograph Series
SNTSU	Studien zum Neuen Testament und seiner Umwelt
SP	Sacra Pagina
SPCK	Society for Promoting Christian Knowledge
SR	*Studies in Religion/Sciences religieuses*
STAC	Studien und Texte zu Antike und Christentum
STDJ	Studies on the Texts of the Desert of Judah
StPatr	*Studia patristica*
SUNT	Studien zur Umwelt des Neuen Testaments
TAPA	*Transactions of the American Philological Association*
TB	Theologische Bücherei
TBT	*The Bible Today*
TLZ	*Theologische Literaturzeitung*
TQ	*Theologische Quartalschrift*
TUGAL	Texte und Untersuchungen zur Geschichte der altchristli-chen Literatur
TynBul	*Tyndale Bulletin*
UBS	United Bible Society
VC	*Vigiliae christianae*
WBC	Word Biblical Commentary
WMANT	Wissenschaftliche Monographien zum Alten und Neuen Testament
WTJ	*Westminster Theological Journal*
WUNT	Wissenschaftliche Untersuchungen zum Neuen Testament
ZHT	*Zeitschrift für historische Theologie*
ZKG	*Zeitschrift für Kirchengeschichte*
ZKT	*Zeitschrift für katholische Theologie*
ZNW	*Zeitschrift für die neutestamentliche Wissenschaft und die Kunde der älteren Kirche*
ZPE	*Zeitschrift für Papyrologie und Epigraphik*
ZRGG	*Zeitschrift für Religions- und Geistesgeschichte*
ZTK	*Zeitschrift für Theologie und Kirche*
ZWT	*Zeitschrift für wissenschaftliche Theologie*

Remembering Paul

I

Introducing "Paul"

> Every historical book worthy of the name ought to include
> a chapter, or if one prefers, a series of paragraphs inserted
> at turning points in the development, which might almost
> be entitled: "How can I know what I am about to say?"
> MARC BLOCH, The Historian's Craft[1]

The "Real" Paul

At some point in the late-second century C.E., according to Tertullian (*Bapt.* 17.5), a nameless presbyter was confronted with questions about the origins of a certain "Acts of Paul" (*Acta Pauli*). Confessing to having written the work, the presbyter explained that he had produced it "for love of Paul" (*amore Pauli*).[2] What the presbyter considered a chance to memorialize his hero, Tertullian viewed negatively as "adding of his own to Paul's reputation." For Tertullian, Paul needed no reputational entrepreneurs, particularly not ones whose portrayals of the Apostle went against his own letters.[3] Paul would have never authorized a woman (Thecla) to teach in the Church, as the *Acts of Paul* narrates. The North African apologist knew of women who pointed to its stories as inspiration for their own teaching and baptizing ministries. He quickly corrects this popular Pauline tradition, citing 1 Corinthians 14.35: "'Let them keep silence,' he [Paul] says, 'and ask their husbands at home.'"

We see in this short episode an example of the kinds of sociopolitical ramifications that the contestation of Paul's legacy had and continues to have for Christianity and for the cultures that have been shaped by its various manifestations. As with Tertullian, these kinds of debates about the Pauline tradition, whether ancient or modern, have often hinged on whether or not the authority of the "real" Paul can be invoked in favor of one's side.[4] Tertullian's strategy was to unmask a particular Pauline text as a fabrication. By doing so, he could marginalize its contents.[5] He sidelined

the *Acts of Paul*, whole-cloth, while many modern scholars dismiss 1 Corinthians 14.35 as a non-Pauline interpolation into an otherwise authentic
text, robbing Tertullian of his preferred comeback line.[6] One cannot
escape this latter kind of distinction in New Testament scholarship—a
distinction that trades on differences between the "real" or "historical"
Paul and some other Paul, designated variously as the Paul of "tradition,"
the "ecclesiastical" Paul, the "canonical" Paul, or the "legendary" Paul,
among others:

> Alongside this image of Paul, to which the ecclesiastical future be-
> longed, there is, however, the *real Paul* as well. This Paul remains
> confined in seven letters and for the most part unintelligible to pos-
> terity, not only to the ancient Church and the Middle Ages.[7]

> . . . the *real Paul*, as he himself admits, was anything but a master of
> the improvised speech [contra Acts] . . . as a speaker he was feeble,
> unimpressive (II Cor. 10.10).[8]

> Catholicism can convincingly appeal to Ephesians, but Protestant-
> ism draws its ecclesiology and much of its practice from the *real
> Paul* reflected in his authentic epistles.[9]

> . . . a kinder and gentler Paul will become visible. But, equally im-
> portant, he will be simpler and more coherent. He will also be less
> like his modern Western readers, and so ultimately more able to
> help them. Hence, modernity may yet benefit from the abandon-
> ment of an essentially modern reading of Paul. It seems that beyond
> our European conceits, the *real Paul* awaits us.[10]

The "real" Paul in much of this kind of modern discourse signifies the
Paul of the seven "undisputed" letters: Romans, 1 and 2 Corinthians, Galatians, Philippians, 1 Thessalonians, and Philemon. He should be differentiated from the "Paul" of tradition, largely represented by the
pseudonymous Ephesians, Colossians, 2 Thessalonians, and the Pastoral
Epistles, as well as by his portrayal in Acts. These texts stand at some distance from what Paul was *really* like and what he *really* believed. Beginning in earnest with F. C. Baur in the mid-nineteenth century, this kind of
categorical division of Pauline materials has helped to resolve the problem
of conflicting material in the canonical Pauline letter corpus and in Acts,

as well as to fill a historical void between Paul's own life and his legacy in the second century. The "disputed" letters and Acts are then evaluated on how distant they are from the "historical" Paul. The "real" Paul, as he is normally described in this scheme, was Protestant, liberal, dialogical, feminist, and/or anti-imperial. The Paul of "tradition" was and is Catholic, conservative, rigid, homophobic, and fixated on power. The former was "domesticated" by the latter.[11] Yet despite the deployment of such a confident discourse on the "real," the ideologically evaluative language that often accompanies it is but one indicator, in the end, of the close relationship between the two (history-telling and ideology).

The seven-letter "historical" Paul (which is ultimately the two-letter Paul of Romans and Galatians) is now, ironically, its own tradition. A rather fixed image of the "real" Paul now permeates our academic institutions and is the tradition within which neophytes to the study of early Christianity come to understand the Apostle. Take, for instance, the distribution of papers on particular texts in "Paul" or "Pauline" sections of the Society of Biblical Literature during the last five annual meetings (2009–2013).[12] During this period, 47 papers were delivered on Romans, while only 7 were given on Colossians and 22 on the group of three Pastoral Epistles. None of the papers on Romans was presented in the "Disputed Paulines" section, while all but one of the papers on Colossians and the Pastoral Epistles were delivered under that category (cf. Appendix 1). Major commentary series also reflect differences in the way that some texts are privileged as quintessentially Pauline over others. In five of the leading English-language commentary series (Hermeneia, International Critical Commentary, Anchor Bible, Word Biblical Commentary, and Sacra Pagina), only one page (total!) is given to the issue of the authenticity of Romans, whereas 48 total pages are provided for Colossians and 184 for the Pastoral Epistles (cf. Appendix 2). Long and torturous cases are made for and against the Pauline authorship of the Pastoral Epistles, whereas commentaries on Romans provide such uncritical and short statements as are found in the opening of James Dunn's two-volume, nearly 1,000-page commentary on Romans: "No doubt is today entertained regarding the author of this letter (see, e.g., Cranfield, 1–2). He identifies himself with his first word, 'Paul,' and is clearly the one known more or less from the beginnings of Christianity simply as 'the apostle Paul.'"[13] This is all the space Dunn gives to the issue of authenticity in Romans, while the two-volume, nearly 1,000-page commentary written by Cranfield to which Dunn sends his readers for more information provides little more by way of argument. A short paragraph ends: "Since Paul's authorship is not now questioned, it is unnecessary to set out the evidence here."[14]

What counts for "Paul," then, is now reinforced in numerous ways for the academician. Small groups of individuals who stand in a tradition organize conferences and edit commentary series that largely secure the tradition, making certain constructions of "Paul" seem natural and self-evident, whereas the ideologically driven practices that produce the so-called real Paul continue to remain hidden. All the while, the "Paul" of his reputational entrepreneurs diffuses into the wider cultural imagination. The turn toward Paul as apocalyptic world-denier in contemporary philosophy, for example, is largely the Paul of F. C. Baur's *Hauptbriefe* (Romans, Galatians, 1–2 Corinthians), as any read through the works of Agamben, Taubes, Badiou, and Žižek clearly shows.[15]

I raise here the current state of Pauline Studies, its foundation on the distinction between genuine and disputed Pauline texts, and the subsequent elevation of some texts over others as hermeneutically important for understanding the "real" Paul as a way of highlighting that Pauline Studies has come full circle since the second century. Discourses on the "real" Paul, so apparent in modern Pauline Studies, were already alive and well in the second century, as Tertullian's *De baptismo* and numerous other texts attest.[16] We see in that period all three of the modern rhetorical strategies for discerning and deploying the "real" Paul. First, one could deny the Pauline origin of an entire text, as we find not only in Tertullian's dismissal of the *Acts of Paul*, but also in his claim that Marcion "rejected" the Pastoral Epistles:

This epistle [Philemon] alone has so profited by its brevity as to *escape Marcion's falsifying hands.* As however he has accepted this letter to a single person, I do not see why *he has rejected (recusaverit) two written to Timothy and one to Titus* about the church system. I suppose he had a whim to meddle even with the number of the epistles. (Tertullian, *Marc.* 5.21.1)[17]

So then, shipmaster out of Pontus, supposing you have never accepted into your craft any smuggled or illicit merchandise, have never appropriated or adulterated any cargo, and in the things of God are even more careful and trustworthy, will you please tell us under what bill of lading you accepted Paul as apostle, who had stamped him with that mark of distinction, who commended him to you, and who put him in your charge? . . . From now on I claim I shall prove that no other god was the subject of the apostle's profession, on the same terms as I have proved this of Christ: *and my evidence will be Paul's epistles. That these have suffered mutilation (mutilates) even in number, the precedent of that gospel, which is now the heretic's, must have prepared us to expect.* (Tertullian, *Marc.* 5.1.2, 9)

Second, as the latter of these two passages suggests, one could accuse another of "adulterating" a Pauline text through interpolation, deletion, or alteration. Tertullian had already made this accusation against Marcion's *Apostolikon* in Book Four of *Adversus Marcionem*, while also noting that Marcion himself might have been the first to make the "adulterating" accusation against someone else's Pauline text (although surely not Tertullian's, given their dates):

So we must pull away at the rope of contention, swaying with equal effort to the one side or the other. *I say that mine* [Pauline text] *is true: Marcion makes that claim for his. I say that Marcion's is falsified (adulteratum): Marcion says the same of mine.* Who shall decide between us? Only such a reckoning of dates, as will assume that authority belongs to that which is found to be older, and will prejudge as corrupt that which is convicted of having come later. (Tertullian, *Marc.* 4.4.1)

Finally, if the number of texts and their actual wording were not in dispute, one could contest the interpretation of particular Pauline passages:

Just as our beloved brother Paul wrote to you according to the wisdom given to him, speaking about these things as he also does in all his letters, *in which certain things are hard to understand, which the ignorant and unstable distort to their own destruction,* as they also do with the rest of the Scriptures. (2 Pet 3.15b–16)[18]

Certain persons are afraid that they may arise [from the dead] naked: therefore they want to arise in the flesh. And they do not know that those who wear the flesh are the ones who are naked. Those who [. . .] to divest themselves are not naked. *"Flesh [and blood will not] inherit the kingdom [of god]."* [1 Cor 15.50] *What is the flesh that will not inherit it? The one that we are wearing.* And what, too, is this flesh that will inherit it? It is Jesus' flesh, along with his blood. (*Gospel of Philip* 56.26–57.3)[19]

But it is necessary to subjoin to this composition, in what follows, also the doctrine of Paul after the words of the Lord, to examine the opinion of this man, *and expound the apostle, and to explain whatsoever [passages] have received other interpretations from the heretics*, who have altogether misunderstood what Paul has spoken, and to point out the folly of their mad opinions; and to demonstrate from that same Paul, from whose *[writings]* they press questions upon us, that they are indeed utterers of falsehood, but that the apostle was a preacher of the truth, and that he taught all things agreeable to the preaching of the truth. (Irenaeus, *Haer.* 4.41.4)[20]

For let us *pay attention to the meaning of his* [Paul's] *words,* and the purpose of them, and *[your] falsification of scripture* will become evident. (Tertullian, *Marc.* 5.3.3)

The language of the "real" Paul is absent from these ancient sources, but we find in each of them the same concern for who and what represents the true Pauline legacy. Like its modern counterpart, the second-century discourse on the "real" Paul was birthed in the conflicting variety of theologies and praxes that are found in the earliest layer of the "Pauline" tradition, by which I mean (1) the broad stream of written material that circulated in Paul's name during 50–100 C.E., without prejudging the authorship of any particular text; (2) the oral traditions about the Apostle that circulated in his former communities and elsewhere during this same period, whether they eventually made their way into literary form (Acts of the Apostles and the various *Acts of Paul* literature) or not; and (3) the stories in the canonical Acts of the Apostles itself, whether they came from prior sources or were the literary creation of the author of Acts.[21] On account of this early variety, from which individual elements were later combined in a number of differing ways, an increasingly rich assortment of additional Pauline texts and traditions was available by the end of the second century. The concomitant diversity of Christian authors who wrote about Paul or interpreted his texts for their communities was palpable. Canonical and non-canonical pseudepigrapha, various *Acts of Paul* traditions, Pauline apocalypses, martyrdom legends, theologically redacted Pauline letter collections, and a wide variety of exegetical traditions abounded. More than for any other apostolic figure, Paul's second-century reputational entre-preneurs received, shaped, created, and passed on a wide variety of Pauline traditions. With variety and competition, of course, comes the attempt to control and limit, as is evidenced in the ancient and modern students of Paul quoted above, each of whom needed the "real" Paul for the sake of larger theo-political contests.

"The *Apostle*"

Within a century and a half after his death, Paul had become "*the* Apostle" for an entire range of ideological adversaries—not *an* Apostle, but *the* Apostle. His widespread and developing charisma as the figure par excellence of the apostolic age can be seen in the various epithets with which he is characterized in Christian literature from the late-first to the late-second centuries (cf. Table 1.1).

Table 1.1 Epithets for Paul in the Second Century

Title	References
"*The* Apostle (Paul)" ὁ ἀπόστολος/*apostolus*	· Basilides (Clement of Alexandria, *Strom.* 3.2.1; Origen, *Comm. Rom.* 5.1)
	· Theodotus (Clement of Alexandria, *Exc.* 22.1; 35.1; 48.2; 49.1; 67.1; 85.3)
	· Ptolemy (*Epistle to Flora* 33.5.15; 33.6.6)
	· Heracleon (fr. 24 in Völker)[a]
	· *Treatise on the Resurrection* 45.23–27
	· *A Prayer of Paul the Apostle* (flyleaf of NHC I)
	· Athenagoras (*Res.* 18)
	· Irenaeus (81x)[b]
	· Tertullian (294x)[c]
	· Clement of Alexandria (214x)[d]
"*The* Apostolikon" τὸ ἀποστολικὸν	· Marcion's Pauline canon (Epiphanius, *Pan.* 42.10, 12)

(*continued*)

Table 1.1 (continued)

Title	References
"His (Christ's) Apostle" *Apostolus ejus*	· Irenaeus (*Haer.* 4.34.2; 5.2.2)
"The Apostle of the Lord" ὁ ἀπόστολος τοῦ κυρίου	· Clement of Alexandria (*Protr.* 9.87.4)
"The Apostle of the Resurrection" ἀναστάσεως Ἀπόστολος	· Theodotus (Clement of Alexandria, *Exc.* 23.2–3)
"The great Apostle" ΠΝΟϬ ⲚⲀⲠⲞⲤⲦⲞⲖⲞⲤ	· *Reality of the Rulers* 86.20
"The Divine Apostle" ὁ θεῖος ἀπόστολος	· Clement of Alexandria (*Strom.* 1.1.10; 2.2.8; 2.20.109; 3.3.18; 4.12.87; 4.16.101; 4.21.132; 5.5.1; 5.9.57; 6.11.95; 7.14.84)
"The divinely inspired Paul/ Apostle (of the Lord)" ὁ θεσπέσιος Παῦλος/ἀπόστολος	· Clement of Alexandria (*Strom.* 1.19.94; 5.10.60; *Protr.* 1.7.2)
"The fair Apostle" ὁ καλός ἀπόστολος	· Clement of Alexandria (*Strom.* 5.2.15; 5.6.34)
"The noble Apostle" ὁ γενναῖος ἀπόστολος	· Clement of Alexandria (*Strom.* 1.8.40; 2.2.136; 3.8.61; 5.3.18; 5.4.25; 5.12.80; 6.1.1; 6.16.147; 7.9.53)
"The blessed Paul/Apostle (of the Lord)" ὁ μακάριος Παῦλος/ἀπόστολος ὁ μακάριος ἀπόστολος Παῦλος *beatus apostolus Paulus*	· *1 Clement* 47.1 · Polycarp (*Phil.* 11.3) · *Muratorian Canon* 48 · Irenaeus (*Haer.* 4.41.4; 5.2.3) · Clement of Alexandria (*Paed.* 2.10.98; 3.3.20; *Protr.* 9.83.3; *Strom.* 1.10.49)
"The holy Apostle (Paul)" ὁ ἅγιος ἀπόστολος	· Clement of Alexandria (*Protr.* 8.81.2; *Strom.* 5.10.65)
"The most holy Apostle" *sanctissimus apostolus*	· Tertullian (*Bapt.* 17.2)

(continued)

Table 1.1 (continued)

Title	References
"The sanctified, the martyred, the most worthy of blessing" ὁ ἡγιασμένος, ὁ μεμαρτυρημένος, ἀξιομακάριστος	· Ignatius (*Eph.* 12.2)
"The blessed and glorious Paul" ὁ μακάριος καὶ ἐνδόξος Παῦλος	· Polycarp (*Phil.* 3.2)
"Our blessed brother Paul" ὁ ἀγαπητὸς ἡμῶν ἀδελφὸς Παῦλος	· 2 Peter 3.15

[a]Walther Völker, ed., *Quellen zur Geschichte der christlichen Gnosis* (SAQ 5; Tübingen: J. C. B. Mohr, 1932).
[b]Cf. the data in David H. Warren, "The Text of the Apostle in the Second Century: A Contribution to the History of its Reception" (Th.D. diss., Harvard University, 2001), 308.
[c]Cf. the data in Mark A. Frisius, "Interpretive Method and Theological Controversy: Tertullian's Use of the Pastoral Epistles, Hebrews, James, 1 and 2 Peter, and Jude" (Ph.D. diss., The Catholic University of America, 2009), 283–300. Frisius shows that 99.3% of the time that Tertullian uses *apostolus* in the singular, he is referring to Paul.
[d]ὁ ἀπόστολος in the singular appears 252 times in Clement, but 12 of these occurrences do not refer to Paul, and 26 of them add some additional qualifier. Cf. the data in the rest of this table for these 26 occurrences.

From where did this widespread Pauline charisma come? Furthermore, why does the "real" Paul carry so much authority in Christian polemics? For modern scholars, the answer to the latter question is clear. Paul is our earliest window into developing Christianity. How we describe that movement in its nascent form provides rhetorical payoffs in the authorization of various modern forms of Christianity through a kind of archaizing argument: "We ought to be 'x' because Christianity in its earliest genius was 'x.'"[22] But how did he become known as *"the* Apostle" for an entire range of ideological adversaries in the *second century*? Moreover, who, if any, got Paul right? To complicate the matter, given the diversity of the first-century Pauline material, which "Paul" are we talking about? These questions, expanded below, encompass a wide range of disciplinary concerns (methodology, exegesis, theory, ideology, and history) and strike at the heart of issues related to the *prolegomena* of Pauline Studies. As the presenting meta-questions of this study on the use of Paul in second-century Christian polemics, they arise out of careful consideration of Stanley Stowers's warning that "determining what is Pauline and what unpauline is an extremely difficult task that most of us do without much critical reflection."[23]

Practicing "Paul in the Second Century"

A number of lengthy studies on "Paul in the second century" already exist. One thinks immediately of the three near-comprehensive works of Andreas Lindemann, Ernst Dassmann and David Rensberger, each authored a little over three decades ago and described in subsequent chapters.[24] These studies helped overthrow the long regnant scholarly narrative of Paul's captivity to the "Gnostics" in the second century. Each argued that Paul's legacy grew steadily among a variety of second-century Christian groups, "orthodox" and "heretical" alike, which competed over him as *their* Apostle. In providing a new narrative for the rise of Paul, Lindemann, Dassmann, and Rensberger also set out the full range of data on the use of Paul in the second century. Two very recent volumes, one authored by Richard Pervo and the other edited by Michael Bird and Joseph Dodson, also described in subsequent chapters, do little to advance the methodological and theoretical conversation about Paul in the second century beyond those works of the late 1970s.[25] Pervo, for example, follows their basic conclusions and lays out much of the same data, but updates the discussion in light of the so-called "New Perspective on Paul" and the concomitant decentering of justification by faith as the *sine qua non* of Pauline theology. He begins to raise some of the same methodological and ideological critiques of previous scholarship on "Paul in the second century" that will be found here, but neither offers a theoretical justification for these critiques nor is able to escape his own dependence on the very interpretive traditions that he seeks to criticize (particularly his attempt to decenter the "Lutheran" Paul, upon whom he is ultimately reliant in his judgments about the authenticity of various canonical Pauline letters).

This book in no way attempts to rehash this prior work. Rather than a compendium of uses of Paul in the second century (the data are now widely available), or a declaration of which second-century writers and communities preserved the "real" Paul, it explores how Pauline traditions (written and oral) develop and make their way into early Christian rhetoric about the "real" Paul. It asks about the arrangement and interpretation of "Pauline" materials with an eye toward the conditions and practices whereby Paul became an object of knowledge in early Christianity. While Michel Foucault's name rarely appears in the following pages, his specter is nonetheless present throughout. I am interested in defamiliarizing claims about the "real" Paul and exploring the exclusionary practices whereby something is labeled "non-Pauline," or "not-naturally-Pauline," and then is marginalized and/or forgotten.[26] Five broad, interrelated questions drive the inquiry that follows:

1. What interests stand behind discourses on the "real" Paul? (ideology);
2. What is meant, from a theoretical standpoint, by tradition and memory—concepts often invoked by Pauline scholars, but hardly ever defined or explored? (theory/historiography);
3. How do we measure Pauline influence? (methodology);
4. How did various second-century writers imagine Paul and what resources were employed to produce a given interpretation of the Apostle? (exegesis); and
5. How did Paul become "*the* Apostle" for so many different kinds of Christian communities in the second century? (history).

The connection between these questions is not ultimately logical or sequential. Each is part of a larger "hermeneutical conversation," in which they inform and transform one another.[27]

Forgetting and remembering are at the heart of constructing portrayals of the past; thus this book provides a historiographical critique of positivist, Rankean attempts to fix a "historical" Paul and then to narrate this Paul's influence (or lack thereof) in the second century.[28] That project is part of the nineteenth- and twentieth-century reception-history of the Apostle. Admittedly, the ancient and modern discourses on the "real" Paul are related in several ways. Generally, they display similar rhetorical maneuvers, as we have already seen. More important, the manuscripts that modern scholars use to establish "what Paul actually said" are products of this early period when Paul's legacy was a contentious matter. The manuscripts are not innocent. They belong to the ancient discourse.[29] For these reasons, many of the methodological and theoretical discussions here may serve as a foundation for contemporary work on the "historical" Paul. To be clear, then: we are not interested in the question, Who got the historical Paul right in the second century? but rather in What is at stake in asking this question? What does it mean? and Can it be answered? The first question has dominated discussions of "Paul in the second century" for far too long. It presupposes that we know the "historical" Paul (as op-posed to the Paul of "tradition") and that the Apostle was a static individual—a motionless historical target that one can either hit or miss.[30]

Like the quest for the "historical Jesus," which has had its heyday at various periods in the nineteenth and twentieth centuries but is now somewhat waning, F. C. Baur's quest for the historical Paul is cracking, along with the epistemic certainty that attends the language of the "real" Paul.[31] While we wait for a full-scale deconstruction, some have already pointed in this direction. Wayne Meeks has famously tabbed Paul the "Christian Proteus" (cf. 1 Cor 9.19–23):

> Where among these multiple pictures of Paul and his influence is the *real Paul* to be found? Or is the question itself, when posed against this history of "strong misreading" (as the literary critic Harold Bloom might call them), not itself naïve?[32]

He urges historians of early Christianity to become immersed fully in postmodern forms of historiography.[33] Several others have sounded a sim-ilar tune.[34]

Such a trend in modern Pauline Studies, if it in fact exists, should have implications for the ancient (and modern) polemical discourse on the "real" Paul, as Calvin Roetzel has noted:

> But, which is the *real Paul*—the Paul of the letters or the Paul of later tradition? That is a very difficult question to answer for many reasons. In our discussions of Paul's theologizing we suggested that Paul himself changed over time as he faced new situations that forced him to think through his gospel and its application in new ways. . . . If we cannot locate a single archimedean point from which to measure Paul himself in the letters, how shall we do the same with a later tradition?[35]

In order not to import an increasingly contested nineteenth- and twentieth-century reception of Paul (the seven-letter "authentic" Paul) into an explo-ration of Paul's legacy in the second century, as Pervo has fatally done, I have had to make several methodological decisions about issues con-cerning Pauline pseudepigraphy and the so-called "Pauline School." The Pastoral Epistles, for instance, which have often been viewed since the early-nineteenth century as second-century Pauline pseudepigrapha, will

be lumped together here in an undifferentiated layer of texts and traditions that I call, for better or for worse, "the earliest layer of the Pauline
tradition," without prejudging actual authorship.[36] So much of what we
"know" about Christianity in the first century is dependent upon the
modern discourse on Paul versus "Paul," and until that discourse is probed
more critically (particularly with respect to the ideology that stands behind
the uneven application of more "scientific" criteria in determining authorship), I have limited this work to texts and authors that are almost univer-
sally placed in the last decade of the first century up to the end of the
second century. For this reason, the first generation or two after the death
of the Apostle will have to go without narration here. There is no discussion here of the "Pauline School," a product of modern debates about Pauline pseudepigrapha.[37]

Much of the "proto-orthodox" reception of Paul in the third century is
dependent on Irenaeus's use of the Apostle, so, for all practical purposes,
I have in mind the reception of Paul from *1 Clement* to Irenaeus, across
the ideological spectrum from within that period, although Tertullian's
work *Against Marcion* should also be included. The second century
marks the several generations of Pauline reception after which the Pauline epistles had been gathered, circulated, and mixed together with a
variety of oral traditions about the Apostle to produce a variety of "Pauls"
that in some ways outdoes those that we find in the modern Christian
imagination.

Re-membering Paul's Image

Weaving the above concerns together, this book argues that by the second
century Paul had become a traditioned figure. His role as the individual
who was responsible for the largest social shift in the history of the early
Church, moving it out from under the auspices of Judaism and opening
up the gospel to the Gentiles *qua* Gentiles, fixed a permanent place for his
memory as *the* Apostle in Christian communities across the ancient Mediterranean world. Paul's charisma, though, did not develop in a straight
line. A number of increasingly complex and diverse traditions were widening into full view of one another in the second century, producing rhetorical discourses on the "real" Paul. These traditions involved both the
production of Pauline images as well as the development of particular
lines of textual interpretation; the two evolved together. Pauline traditions
in the second century employed and deployed various pieces of the earlier

layer of the Pauline tradition while forgetting others. Appeals to particular combinations of texts and stories from this earliest layer, along with the elevation of some pieces above others, were the means of producing second-century Pauline image traditions. These images of the Apostle were not constructed out of thin air, but were part of the developing cultural and social memory of early Christianity. As such, each exhibits a unique mixture of continuity with and change from the past. Earlier interpretive traditions made their way into the second century, but, when combined with the ideological and social needs of developing Christian communities, evolved in time and place. Consequently, ancient discourses on the "real" Paul, like their modern counterparts, are problematic. Through a whole host of exclusionary practices, the "real" Paul, whose authoritative persona as "the Apostle" possessed a certain authority, was invoked as a wedge to gain traction for the conservation of ideology.

Ideology

Christian culture-making was a highly contentious activity in the second century as communities with diverse backgrounds and traditions assimilated Christ and his Apostle into their prior ideological networks, producing the ancient discourses on the "real" Paul noted in the preceding section. Ideological discourse is by nature conservative (cf. Chapter 4). It springs into action when the status quo is threatened. While this study is certainly interested in questions like How has x author read y Pauline text? and Is his reading faithful to earlier Pauline texts?, it is equally invested in the discourses that surround individual readings of the Pauline tradition. A *"total* conception of ideology," according to Karl Mannheim:

> does not criticize thought on the level of the assertions themselves, which may involve deceptions and disguises, but examines them on the structural or noological level, which it views as not necessarily being the same for all men, but rather as allowing the same object to take on different forms and aspects in the course of social development.[38]

Foucault agreed:

> The notion of ideology appears to me to be difficult to make use of, for three reasons. The first is that, like it or not, it always stands

in virtual opposition to something else which is supposed to count as truth. Now I believe that the problem does not consist in drawing the line between that in a discourse which falls under the category of scientificity or truth, and that which comes under some other category, but in seeing historically how effects of truth are produced within discourses which in themselves are neither true nor false.[39]

All language occurs in social contexts that are infused by power relations. Individual claims to "get Paul right" are situated within larger power structures (social and institutional). In recognition of this, several important questions arise for Pauline Studies. What does such rhetoric about "getting Paul right" preserve? What does it produce/effect?[40] Can such categorical language about the "real" Paul bear up?

Chapters 2 and 3 of this work provide the first substantial *Forschungsgeschichte* on the reception of Paul in the second century since Rensberger (1981). Chapter 2, in particular, explores the work of F. C. Baur, the father of modern Pauline Studies, and sets his conclusions about the "real" Paul and the subsequent deformation of this Paul in the second century into their proper historical and ideological context. Baur wrote within a burgeoning tradition of historical positivism that severed the historian (subject) from his or her data/facts (objects) in an attempt to narrate the past, in the language of Leopold von Ranke, "wie es eigentlich gewesen." As I will show in that chapter, however, Baur's claims about the "real" Paul were often undergirded by little more than ideological preference, lightly papered over in the language of objectivist historiography. From the outset, narratives about Paul's fate in the second century were ideologically situated, despite claims to the contrary. The foundation of the "Pauline Captivity" narrative, which dominated scholarship on "Paul in the second century" for more than one hundred years after Baur, will then come under particular scrutiny in Chapter 3. According to this narrative, Paul's radical, apocalyptic theology of divine grace had been most naturally appropriated by Marcion and the "Gnostics," who trumpeted Paul as their Apostle. For much of the second century the proto-orthodox either largely disregarded Paul and his theology or were too embarrassed, in light of his popularity on the other side, to utter his name. Only at the end of the second century, after the Pastoral Epistles and Acts had circulated widely, could Irenaeus finally assimilate Paul into the wider theology of the burgeoning Catholic Church.

Theory/Historiography

Pauline scholars, rightly, are quick to deploy historiographical language. But while the categories of "history" and "tradition" are often used, they are almost never clarified, and the pertinent theoretical literature often lies by the wayside. Chapters 2 and 3, then, are more than just a simple history of scholarship. The *Forschungsgeschichte* is placed alongside wider developments in historiographical theory and practice. As Chapter 2 situates F. C. Baur within the context of historical positivism, Chapter 3 explores early twentieth-century philosophical shifts in historiography that increasingly acknowledged the role of the author in prefiguring his or her historical field, as well as late twentieth-century presentist/postmodern concerns over historical representation. Chapter 4 then fully engages with theories of tradition and social memory and their relationship to the telling of history as a means of teasing out the particularly complex relationship between traces of the past and the present social location of the interpreter as it relates to developing constructions of the Apostle in the second century.

Social memory and the practices deployed in its maintenance have become an increasingly useful historiographical category in the humanities over the last two decades. Scholarship on the "historical" Jesus has already moved in this direction. Studies that apply theories of social remembering to the early Jesus tradition are now ubiquitous.[41] The Gospels are memorializations of Jesus that provide meaningful representations within particular social contexts. Social memory theory has provided a fruitful alternative to prior discussions on memory in the Jesus tradition (Bultmann vs. Gerhardsson vs. Bailey), encompassing the strengths of each. Yet there is still no full-scale study that applies these theoretical materials to the early memory of Paul. This study fills that gap. Paul, like Jesus, was a remembered figure in early Christian communities.[42] As with the Evangelists, each of Paul's second-century reputational entrepreneurs was interested in fixing a particular image of the Apostle for memorialization. These kinds of traditioned images were an important part of the Christian "culture-making" process, as Elizabeth Castelli has argued.[43] Christian identity was and is wrapped up in the representation of its apostles.

A broad and consistent sociological approach to the production of knowledge (and thus, memory), along the lines advocated by Mannheim, drives Chapter 4. In particular, the social constraints on individual memory are explored at length. Every early Christian writer who interpreted Paul for his or her community did so as a member of that community. While I draw on the work of Maurice Halbwachs, who pioneered the strong presentist approach to social memory, I ultimately side with those like Barry Schwartz and Patrick Hutton, who show how memory is not *just* a product of present needs, though it certainly is this, but is also constrained by the past—molded by the force of tradition.

Methodology

Various ways of measuring Paul's influence ("Paulinism") on early Christian communities have been proposed: identifiable dependence on Pauline letters; discernable adherence to a particularly Pauline theology; and/or recognizable admiration/imitation of Paul as a person. Disagreements about these matters divided two of the major studies from the late 1970s. Andreas Lindemann was concerned both with "Das Bild des Apostels" as well as the "Aufnahme und Verarbeitung paulinischer Theologie."[44] By the former he meant "how Paul was viewed": What images of the Apostle do we find in various texts, apart from the use of his letters? By the latter he meant the discernible continuities and discontinuities between Paul's theology and second-century appropriations of his epistles. David Rensberger, on the other hand, dealt only with the use of Pauline letters in the second century, deciding that concerns over Paul's image were "of so little moment to most second-century writers that its usefulness is difficult to see."[45]

In near totality, scholars have followed Lindemann over Rensberger, recognizing that the perceived influence of Paul on the Church was multifaceted. Various schemas for categorizing the data have been suggested: Lindemann = "Bild" and "Theologie"; De Boer = "legendary" and "epistolary"; Bovon = "monument" and "document"; Aageson = "image," "theology," and "use of letters"; and Marguerat = "documentaire," "biographique," and "doctoral" (cf. Chapter 3). While these scholars have highlighted the importance of discerning the image of Paul in a given text, none explores the nature of images and how they encode information and transmit meaning. Chapter 3, in addition to narrating the demise of the Pauline Captivity narrative and describing shifts in historiographical theory toward issues of representation, describes the natural explosion of studies on the *Paulusbild* of individual early Christian texts in the wake of these two considerations.

Chapter 4, then, among other things, grounds discussions of textually mediated images of Paul in theories of cognition and perception, both ancient
and modern, as a way of highlighting how controlling images of the Apostle
shaped the interpretation of Pauline texts within the second century and
vice versa. In the explicitly polemical contestations over Paul's legacy found
in 2 Peter, Irenaeus, Marcion, the *Gospel of Philip*, and Tertullian's *On Baptism* (cited earlier), one gets the sense that Pauline texts were pawns in the
defense of particular images of the Apostle—images that encoded the ideologies of individual communities. Irenaeus, for example, promises to "expound the Apostle," while at the same time showing that Paul was a
"preacher of the truth and that he taught all things agreeable to the preaching of the truth." The image of Paul as "preacher of the truth" was at stake
in the interpretation of his texts.

Exegesis

Chapters 5 and 6 offer "thick descriptions" of the constructed image of
Paul in *3 Corinthians*, a proto-orthodox pseudepigraphon from the late-
second century C.E., and Irenaeus's *Adversus haereses*, the earliest surviving heresiological tome, also dating from the last quarter of the second
century C.E. A "thick description," as opposed to a "thin description," to
use the language of Gilbert Ryle as popularized by Clifford Geertz, attempts to describe individual performances within larger networks of
meaning.[46] These two early Christian texts provide strikingly similar
portrayals of the Apostle and are representative of one particular stream
of the Pauline tradition in the second century. They serve as test cases for
two important theses of this book: first, that image construction stands
at the heart of textual interpretation, and second, that developing tradi-
tions/memories retain a complex mixture of continuity with and change
from the past. Irenaeus is of particular interest because of his explicit
claim to "expound the Apostle" in the face of those who have "misunderstood what Paul has spoken." The opportunity arises to explore Irenaeus's reading of key Pauline texts in light of his rhetoric on the "real" Paul
and to ask how he arranged, selected, and interpreted Pauline materials
to fit his "rule of truth" and produce an image of the Apostle that was
consonant with the rule. Paul, as he says, was a "preacher of the truth."
Many other second-century texts, of course, need to be explored in due
time. Chapter 7 provides some suggestions for further work in this
regard.

History

While not interested in the so-called historical Paul, this study is deeply interested in history: the history of Paul's interpreters, especially those of the second century. Once theories have been applied and individual data have been thickly described, we are still left with the histori(ographi)cal task: How can we *narrate* Paul's developing charismas in the second century? How did he go from Paul to "Paul"? What *story* best makes sense of the available data? The convergence of the aforementioned studies in the late 1970s by Lindemann and Rensberger, among others, brought an end to the hegemony of the Pauline Captivity narrative and opened up creative space for alternative stories (cf. Chapter 3). The current regnant narrative posits a number of developing, fragmented trajectories of Pauline tradition throughout the second century. Often these trajectories were in competition with one another, while at other times these competing traditions were so close to one another (despite the rhetorical discourses of their tradents) that they are now hard to distinguish, substantially. This now favored narrative, however, still needs a theoretical engine—a description of its foundation in the traditioning process and the practices of social memory. Chapters 4, 5, and 6 do that. Chapter 7 summarizes the case and then looks forward by offering eight suggestions for a more sophisticated historiography for Pauline Studies. These final considerations are aimed particularly at those presently engaged in discourses on the "real" Paul.

Capturing Paul: F. C. Baur and the Rise of the Pauline Captivity Narrative

A vigilant epistemology will guard here against the illusion of believing that what we call a fact coincides with what really happened, or with the living memory of eyewitnesses, as if the facts lay sleeping in the documents until the historians extracted them.

PAUL RICOEUR, Memory, History, Forgetting[1]

HISTORY-TELLING IS A landscape portrait. It is a narrative. It is a rhetoric.[2] Few scholars of early Christianity doubt that Saul of Tarsus was a (if not *the*) seminal figure among the Christ-believers of the mid-first century C.E. Likewise, none can deny that Paul was "*the* Apostle" for a wide-ranging set of Christian communities by the end of the second century (cf. Table 1.1 in Chapter 1). The passage of time between point A and point B, however, requires a narrative. It requires a portrayal of the landscape of early Christian memory-making. It requires an argument for how Paul, one of the most controversial figures of nascent Christianity, became revered by so many. This chapter explores the rise, development, and influence of the "Pauline Captivity" narrative, the dominant story about "Paul in the second century" from the mid-nineteenth century until the late 1970s. Beginning with F. C. Baur, the father of historical-critical approaches to Paul, the proponents of this prevailing narrative envisioned a second-century Pauline Captivity to Marcion and the "Gnostics" (often undifferentiated), whose apocalyptic dualism made them the natural receptors of Paul's radical theology of divine grace (in opposition to Law). The dearth of references to Paul or to his letters in several important proto-orthodox writers of the second century, according to this narrative, are indicative of

their embarrassment of or outright opposition to P
particularly in light of his appropriation by their t
More important than just describing the narrativ
Pauline Studies, this chapter examines its portray
the foundation of its particular image of the histc
ical preferences of nineteenth-century radical G
pered over by a burgeoning positivist historiography.

F. C. Baur, the "Objectivity of History," and the Historiographical Move to Separate Paul from "Paul"

The specter of Ferdinand Christian Baur (1792–1860) continues to haunt Pauline Studies.[3] Baur was the first historical-critical systematician of early Christianity and father of the so-called "Tübingen School."[4] His work on Paul was and still remains influential in a number of ways. He is most famous for his dialectical reading of early Christian history, which posited an initial division between two theological camps: a Jewish-Christian faction under Peter and James and a pro-Gentile faction under Paul. The entirety of early Christian literature (at least into the late-second century) can be assigned to one of these two sides or to the later "Catholic" synthesis of the mid-second century (cf. the harmonizing tendencies of Acts).[5] Many, even in Baur's own generation (cf. Albrecht Ritschl and Adolf Hilgenfeld), were unable to accept such a rigid schematization of early Christian history and literature, dependent as it appeared to be on Hegel, whom Baur began to read in the early 1830s.[6] Baur's emphasis, however, on conflict in the nascent church predated any known references to Hegel's work in his own and was ultimately rooted in the Pauline letters themselves, particularly 1 Corinthians 1–4 and Galatians.[7] And even without the Hegelian superstructure, most New Testament scholars today still follow Baur in preferring these letters over Acts for the naked truth about tensions among Jesus of Nazareth's earliest followers.

Before examining Baur's understanding of the Pauline legacy in the second century, we must describe how he understood Paul. Baur opened his monumental *Paulus, der Apostel Jesu Christi* (1845) with this proclamation: "That Christianity, in its universal historical acceptation, was the work of the Apostle Paul is undeniably an historical matter of fact." Paul was responsible for a Christianity that "asserted itself as a separate, independent principle . . . and took its stand as a new enfranchised form of

..s thought and life, essentially different from all the national pe-
..rities of Judaism."[8] For Baur, the only certainly authentic Pauline
..ts were Romans, 1–2 Corinthians, and Galatians, the *Hauptbriefe*, a
series of letters that most scholars now think represent a single two- to
four-year period of Paul's ministry in the mid-50s when the circumcision
question was at its height and Paul was making a "collection for the
saints" in Judea as a way of smoothing over the relationship between his
churches and the mother church in Jerusalem (1 Cor 16.1–4; 2 Cor 8–9;
Gal 2.10; Rom 15.25–28).[9] For Baur, all the other canonical Pauline letters
could be questioned as later tendentious forgeries in the name of the
Apostle due to their lack of theological insight, emphasis on the institutions of the church, and/or traces of Gnostic influence or anti-Gnostic
polemic.[10] Baur was not the first to question the authenticity of certain
Pauline letters. Friedrich Schleiermacher, one of Baur's early theological
influences, had already argued against the authenticity of First Timothy
in 1807.[11] In this pioneering work (not for its methods, but for its application of linguistic and literary tests in the determination of authorship
for the first time to the Pauline letters), Schleiermacher argued that First
Timothy was a forgery of the authentic Second Timothy and Titus that
was designed to elevate the role of deacons under the guise of the Apostle. The argument was based on "non-Pauline" elements within the
letter: unique phrases, numerous *hapax legomena*, and a disjointed
style.[12] "Non-Pauline," of course, presumes a "Pauline" Archimedean
point from which to launch an inquiry, and one early review of Schleiermacher's argument by W. M. L. De Wette hinted at its methodological
problem: Could not the authenticity all of the Pauline letters, when scru-
tinized this way, be questioned?[13]

When Baur began to publish on Paul in the 1830s, the debate over the
authenticity of the Pastoral Epistles, as a group, was several decades old.
Increasingly technical linguistic and historical arguments about individual letters were wielded on behalf of particular ideological commitments.
Using the same methodologies, most Catholic scholars came down on the
side of authenticity for all 13 letters, while German Protestants of the "radical" tradition like Baur largely embraced the free-thinking critical approaches of the Enlightenment and increasingly denied the apostolic
authorship of some New Testament texts.[14] The Idealism of Hegel and
Schleiermacher, devoid of dogma and creed, provided a way for these
"free" and "radical" Protestants to remain within the larger evangelical
fold, which was often apprehensive that the faith might be overturned by

such historical criticism.[15] Baur, in a letter to his brother, praised Schleier-macher's *The Christian Faith* and its emphasis on the feeling of absolute dependence:

> One can consider the work from its philosophical and theological side. With regard to its philosophical side the basic view is certainly pantheistic, but one can just as well say, idealistic. . . . Idealistic is above all the constant development of all the principal doctrines from the self-consciousness; pantheistic is especially the treatment of the doctrine of God which, certainly, sets God as the Absolute in the purest sense, but at the same time in such an abstract way that not just the essence of God but even the most general attributes . . . are taken into consideration; and in order to exclude every finite antithesis in the divine essence there can be no more talk of God as an actual personality. . . . It is impossible for me to view his system, as it is here set forth, as a purely self-contained one; indeed, he himself always points out that his representation appears in this form only with reference to the feeling of dependence. . . . I know of no representation of Christianity in which the peculiar essence of Christianity is so acutely comprehended and made so thoroughly the middle point of the whole system, none which could be held as being more Christian and orthodox.[16]

Despite the quasi-scientific back and forth between scholars over the authenticity of individual Pauline epistles, it was ultimately Baur's Protestant upbringing and eventual commitment to Hegelianism that caused him to assign texts with greater "Catholicizing" tendencies (e.g., Ephesians and the Pastoral Epistles) to the later synthesis of Petrine and Pauline factions. Baur found in the *Hauptbriefe*'s emphases on justification by faith and possession of the Spirit of God a version of Christianity that most closely aligned not only with his Lutheranism, but also with his Hegelian commitment to history as the unfolding of Absolute Spirit.[17] The other Pauline letters:

> stand below the originality, the wealth of thought, and the whole spiritual substance and value of [Rom, 1–2 Cor, Gal]. They are characterized by a certain meagerness of contents, by colourlessness of treatment, by absence of motive and connexion, by monotony, by repetition, by dependence, partly on each other, and partly on the

Epistles of the first class. . . . It is clear that the point of view from which these letters are written is not that of one seeking to make good, and to develop a general principle which has still to vindicate itself, and on which the Christian consciousness and life are to be formed. . . . The authentic Pauline Epistles have a true organic development; they proceed from one root idea which penetrates the whole contents of the Epistle from the very beginning, and binds all the different parts of it to an inner unity, through the deeper relations in which it holds them, even though they appear at first sight to be only outwardly connected. . . . Hence they exhibit a genuine dialectic movement.[18]

Paul could never be monotonous or repetitious! Nor a theological lightweight! The rather bald ideological preferences that ultimately drive his historical conclusions cannot escape one's notice. A Romantic and Protestant attachment to Paul has been wedded to strong theological and philosophical commitments.[19] As Baur began his work in the early 1830s on Paul and his Jewish Christian opponents, he was also in the midst of a public dispute with the Catholic scholar Johann Adam Möhler over the differences between Protestantism and Catholicism.[20] Ideology and history became comingled in his work.

The *Hauptbriefe*, then, were Baur's Archimedean point for imagining the historical Paul. Since then, the authorship of these four epistles, which in the wake of Luther had become polemical weapons against both the Catholic Church and Judaism, has rarely been rigorously questioned. Though most have agreed that Baur went too far in eliminating 1 Thessalonians, Philippians, and Philemon, it is the *Hauptbriefe* that continue to shape Pauline Studies and provide its institutional structure (cf. Chapter 1). They represent the "real" Paul. Bruno Bauer, from the same era as F. C. Baur, stands as the figurehead for the few radically skeptical scholars who had the methodological honesty to scrutinize equally each of the canonical Pauline letters.[21] The relationship between continued theological affinity for the *Hauptbriefe*, in general, and Romans and Galatians, in particular, among Paul's interpreters and the lack of critical attention given to the question of their authorship can be seen, for example, in an anecdote described by the late Harold Hoehner. In one of Hoehner's last published pieces, he playfully marshals together a number of arguments normally made against the authorship of the "disputed" Pauline epistles and shows how these same arguments, if administered fairly, would lead to the conclusion that Galatians was also a forgery. In this same piece he narrates how he was met with ire after explaining his transgressive project to an un-named German scholar who responded, "Don't do that, I like Galatians."[22]

F. C. Baur theorized and wrote in the midst of a trend in Western his-toriography that increasingly viewed narrations of the past as objectively attainable (once stripped of the accretions of tradition). The proper con-ceptual framework for doing history in the nineteenth century was sci-ence.[23] The former had a newfound "physics envy."[24] Archaeology, philology, and the other tools of the historian were pitted against ancient manuscripts in an attempt to describe the past "wie es eigentlich gewe-sen," to use the famous dictum of Leopold von Ranke (1795–1886), the standard-bearer of increasingly positivist approaches to historical work.[25] Forgeries and imposters were being exposed, whether they were found among the Platonic or Pauline corpora.[26] Historiography was "rigorously inductive."[27]

Ranke's historiographical philosophy and methodology, which became the model for Western university seminars on history for over a century, was rooted in archival work and the painstaking study of manuscripts.[28] He implored the historian to "'extinguish himself' before the facts" that presented themselves in these texts, arguing that they could provide a gen-uine and unobstructed window into history, if they could first pass histor-ical-critical muster.[29] Frederick Beiser has recently characterized Ranke's work as operating on four principles:

1. Criticism: "The first task of the historian is to ascertain the credibility of his sources."
2. Impartiality: "As far as possible, the historian should attempt to lay aside his own moral principles, political agenda, and religious beliefs, and he should try to understand the past in its own terms."
3. Primacy of induction over deduction: "[the historian] must never begin from general principles."
4. Individuality: "The historian should treat each person, action, and epoch in history as an end in itself."[30]

Yet Ranke was still a historical Idealist in the philosophical tradition of Hegel, despite his attempts to distance himself from what he viewed as Hegel's universalizing and deductive tendencies.[31] He was no total philo-sophical positivist. Once past events had been objectively described and ascertained with epistemological certainty, they must be understood within a larger metaphysical framework in which God reveals himself through them. The historian was to grasp "something infinite . . . something eternal, something deriving from God."[32]

The same was true for Baur. He believed that he was operating inductively from the data, and that the spiritual and dialectical framework behind the events only became clear, necessarily, afterward.[33] The influence of Ranke's teacher, Barthold Georg Niebuhr, whose *Römische Geschichte* consistently employed advances in source-critical methods, was evident in Baur's early career as he taught classics in Blaubeuren.[34] Later, Baur's affinity for Rankean historiographical methods can easily be seen in *Die Epochen der kirchlichen Geschichtschreibung*.[35] He preferred Ranke's "objectively maintained historiography" of the Reformation over that of G. J. Planck, whom he accused of imposing on the historical material a "systematic arrangement of events."[36] He offered the titles of these two works as signifying their different approaches. Planck's volume was entitled *Geschichte des Lehrbegriffs*, while Ranke's bore the name *Deutsche Geschichte im Zeitalter der Reformation*.[37] Baur's praise of Ranke's inductive rather than deductive methods sounds rather ironic now, given the former's Hegelian superstructure for reading early Christian history and his rather subjective comments about the authenticity of the *Hauptbriefe*. As Hayden White has argued, the objectivists of the nineteenth century could not avoid the constraints of rhetoric in their own work, despite their claims to the contrary. They merely switched from one rhetoric to another: "they failed to recognize that their own plain style was itself a rhetorical strategy."[38] Their ideologies hid behind the promotion of rigorous and transparent methodologies.[39] The "objective" and "secure" data about apostolic conflict in the *Hauptbriefe* were the starting point for Baur's work. He never questioned, though, whether or not they were actually *representative* of a nearly three-decade apostolate, such that other letters were necessarily *unrepresentative* of Paul. Why? "Opposition" between Spirit and Law, Protestantism and Catholicism, and Christianity and Judaism was the ideological frame through which he already read Paul. The other letters, of lesser religious authority and import in Baur's tradition, could now be distanced from the Apostle through the guise of positivist historiography.

In this burgeoning historiography, "tradition" was a dirty word. Niebuhr had advocated an "eternal war of criticism against tradition."[40] The eminent twentieth-century sociologist Edward Shils, among others, has narrated the demise of tradition and traditional societies in both the new social arrangements of the eighteenth and nineteenth centuries as well as the intellectual movements of that period, which elevated empiricism, rationality, industry, individuality, creativity, the present, and, most important, the open future as the *sine quibus non* of the modern experience.[41] For Thomas Aquinas and other Scholastic figures in the thirteenth century, tradition (*auctoritas* or *consuetudo*) had been equal in authority with *ratio* and *Scriptura*.[42] But already in the Renaissance, Reformation, and Romantic movements—though still "traditional" inasmuch as they looked backward for their inspiration (to the pristine eras of the classical and apostolic periods)—one can see the initial fuel for the intellectual tradition that led, finally, to Karl Marx's proclamation that "[t]he tradition of all the dead generations weighs like a nightmare on the brain of the living" and to Nietzsche's direct attack on self-evident "truths":

> What then is truth? A movable host of metaphors, metonymies, anthropomorphisms: in short, a sum of human relations which have been poetically and rhetorically intensified, transferred, and embellished, and which, after long usage, seem to a people to be fixed, canonical, and binding. Truths are illusions which we have forgotten are illusions; they are metaphors that have become worn out and have been drained of sensuous force, coins which have lost their embossing and are now considered as metal and no longer as coins.[43]

Tradition, like religion, provided a false-consciousness according to Marx, who yet acknowledged the progress made by Luther against this external bondage.[44] Reality was something altogether different. For Baur and many of Paul's interpreters in his wake, the "canonical" Paul had completely obscured the "real" Paul of the "authentic" letters.[45] Rankean historiography, in this way, still holds sway in Pauline Studies. Discerning the "real" Paul was and continues to be an act of liberation from the canonical tradition. For Baur, historical-critical work was a Protestant principle.[46] Once the wisdom of the fathers or any other "given" was shown to serve the needs of those in power and the institutional control necessary for suppressing the contestation of such traditions collapsed, modernity was born.[47] Hans-Georg Gadamer described this project as the attempt to rid society of all prior prejudices.[48]

The Rise of the Pauline Captivity Narrative

Once Baur had established the *Hauptbriefe*, with their emphasis on the Spirit and justification by faith, as the only authentically Pauline artifacts

in the canon, subsequent Christian literature could be measured against
them and slotted into his dialectical reading of early church history. Any
text that ignored Paul or exhibited anti-Pauline elements was deemed
"Jewish Christian," while texts that contained elements of Paulinism *and*
Jewish Christianity were assigned a place in the burgeoning Catholic tradition, the latter of which distorted Paul inasmuch as justification by faith
was not a fundamental aspect of its reception of the Apostle. Many
German scholars of the late-nineteenth and early-twentieth centuries
were happy to follow Baur in this last assertion, independent of their feelings about his dialectical reading of early Christianity.[49] The prime example of this is the two-volume *Der Paulinismus* (1873) by Otto Pfleiderer,
who had been one of Baur's students at Tübingen.[50] In the first volume,
he charts the psychological development of Paul's theology from Sin/Law,
through the person and work of Christ, to justification by faith. This
volume is dominated by references to the *Hauptbriefe*. The second volume
traces the development of "Paulinism" in new directions in the late-first
and early-second centuries (Alexandrian, proto-Catholic, and Catholic),
noting both continuities with and differences from the center of Paul's
theology (justification by faith alone). But the influence of Baur's Paul extended well beyond Germany into the English-speaking world. Stewart
Means, in his *Saint Paul and the Ante-Nicene Church* (1903), offered a similar framework. With respect to the "historical" Paul, he says, "There
seems to have been no other Jewish mind bold enough to grasp this idea
of a religion independent of law, and consequently the establishment of
the heathen Christianity is due to St. Paul."[51] Means then characterizes
second-century Catholic theology as developing a sense of Christ as the
"New Lawgiver" and an understanding of piety as the "New Law." This
meant, then, that most authors of that period had decisively departed
from Paul's theological genius.

Baur's distancing of Paul from "Paul" provided the framework for a
narrative about Paul's legacy in the second century, now commonly
called the "Pauline Captivity" narrative, that would hold sway into the
1970s. Its most evolved form eventually detailed how Paul had been
latched onto by Marcion and the "Gnostics," who wrestled substantively
with the heart of his theology, while the proto-orthodox continued to
develop in directions that were either anti-Pauline or had at least cor-
rupted Paul's theology. Any invocation of Paul by the latter would have
risked association with the "apostle of the heretics" (cf. Tert., *Marc.* 3.5.4:
haereticorum apostolus), the theological champion of the wrong side of a

remarkably diverse second-century Christianity. It was only with the pseudonymous authorship of the Pastoral Epistles, as well as the production of Acts, that Irenaeus could finally reclaim Paul for the proto-orthodox—a Paul that was now in line with their wider tradition. Hans von Campenhausen, writing in the 1960s, represents the mature form of the Pauline Captivity narrative:

> Around the middle of the second century there was a falling-off in esteem for Paul in orthodox circles. This is connected with the fact that he was held in such high esteem by the heretics and especially by Marcion, and was treated by them virtually as one of themselves.[52]

And:

> Only when combined with these inauthentic letters [the Pastorals] could the genuine legacy of the apostle be tolerated by the Church and made "canonical."[53]

This narrative was based largely on a Pauline "silence" in Justin Martyr, Papias, and Hegesippus. Justin is particularly important because he would have certainly known the Pauline letters, living in Rome at the time of Marcion and Valentinus, both of whom, according to later proto-orthodox writers, considered themselves to have been devotees of the Apostle. Papias and Hegesippus are less consequential. Little of their work remains, and Papias's *Expositions of the Sayings of the Lord*, on the basis of its genre, would not have given room to Paul.

A variety of nineteenth-century attempts to explain Justin's silence concerning Paul were offered. Karl Credner (1832), writing before Baur's views on the matter had solidified, tied Justin to a Jewish Christianity that remained leery of Paul.[54] Credner viewed Justin's aversion to eating meat sacrificed to idols as being closer to James and Peter in Acts 15 than to Paul in 1 Corinthians 8–10. He was vigorously refuted about a decade later by Carl Semisch (1842), who noted similarities between Justin and Paul on the Jewish Law, while denying any connection between Jewish sensitivities and Justin's position on sacrificial meat.[55] Semisch's rebuttal, however, was overshadowed by the rising influence of Baur and the "Tübingen School" on the imagination of German higher-critical scholarship.

Like Credner before him, Baur argued that prominent proto-orthodox authors of the second century (Justin, Papias, and Hegesippus) were the ideological heirs of the Jewish Christianity that had opposed Paul during his own lifetime. While these three were less radical in open opposition to Paul than either the Ebionites or the communities that produced the *Pseudo-Clementine* literature, their Pauline silence suggested an opposition to the Pauline gospel.[56] Baur's assertion, however, that Justin was associated with Jewish Christianity was tortured. He thought, on the one hand, that Justin's predilection for the Old Testament, his benign attitude toward Jewish Christians (cf. *Dial.* 47), and his aversion to meat sacrificed to idols were indications of an affinity for Jewish Christianity. On the other hand, Baur found some similarities between Justin and Paul, especially their common dislike for the Jewish ceremonial Law.[57] Despite this ambiguity, he remained adamant that Justin did not want to be associated with Paul. Ultimately, as Semisch had done with Credner, Baur's links between Justin and Jewish Christianity were resoundingly refuted by Albrecht Ritschl and J. B. Lightfoot, among others.[58] Yet the weight of Baur's larger historical reconstruction of a continuing Jewish Christian opposition to Paul in the second century opened up a wide-ranging conversation about the Apostle's legacy during the middle of that period, with patristic references to the Ebionites' rejection of Paul as the solid anchor point for envisioning some degree of anti-Paulinism in the second century.[59]

As proponents of a strong Jewish-Christian (however weakly defined that term remained) connection for Justin became less numerous as the nineteenth century progressed, other explanations for his Pauline silence were offered.[60] The common denominator for these was the simple observation that *silence about* does not necessarily mean *rejection of* or *antipathy toward* Paul. Johann Otto, writing during Baur's heyday (1842–1843), saw numerous traces of Pauline language in Justin and argued that the absence of overt Pauline citations was due solely to Justin's rhetorical contexts: the Jewish audience of the *Dialogue with Trypho* and Marcion's influence in Rome made arguing from Paul counterproductive.[61] Justin's occasional deployment of Pauline language, however, indicates that he was not antagonistic toward the Apostle. Theodor Zahn would later agree (1888).[62] By the late-nineteenth century, Marcion, in particular, began to take center stage in explanations for Paul's absence in some second-century proto-orthodox circles. For a time these explanations were sometimes still combined with theories about Justin's Jewish-Christian affinities. Justin read Paul as congenial to Marcion and thus identified more with Jewish Christianity, even if he betrayed knowledge of Paul in some of his language and arguments.[63]

What we find in seed in Otto became a fully blossoming flower by the early-twentieth century. Adolf von Harnack and Walter Bauer were among those who placed Marcion and other "heretics" front and center.[64] Together, they provided a powerful and influential narrative of Paul's "captivity" in the second century. Harnack (1909) argued that the proto-orthodox (Justin in particular) faced a certain embarrassment over (though having no lack of fondness for) Paul because of the ease by which their opponents made use of him. The Apostle was, in this sense, held captive by the other side. Harnack's Marcion, about which we will have more to say below, was chiefly a Pauline theologian. In fact, Marcion was the first Reformer, since he, like Luther, Baur, and Harnack himself, understood justification by faith alone as the center of Paul's theology. On account of Marcion's appropriation of the Apostle, Justin was wary of invoking him in public discourse. In the long run, though, the use of Paul's letters within larger proto-orthodoxy prevented a wholesale abandonment of him. Irenaeus, in the late-second century, through his elevation of Acts and the Pastoral Epistles, was eventually able to win Paul back from the heretics. According to Harnack, then, both the initial embarrassment over Paul *and* the subsequent canonization of Acts and the Pauline letters (inclusive of the Pastorals) were due to Marcion.[65]

Walter Bauer's now famous and ground-shifting thesis (1934)—that an originally diverse Christianity was snuffed out by the growing proto-orthodox church of Rome—took over much of Harnack's position (minus the *philo*-Marcionism).[66] Christian thinkers like Marcion, Valentinus, Basilides, and the Montanists were actively engaging Paul, while Papias, Justin, and Hegesippus stood on the sidelines and watched. They had no choice until the Pastoral Epistles were forged to reclaim Paul from those with "myths and endless genealogies" (1 Tim 1.4), who proclaimed a "falsely-called knowledge" through the use of "antitheses" (1 Tim 6.20). Irenaeus was the first to fully incorporate the Paul of the Pastoral Epistles into the wider Pauline tradition.

The heart of the Pauline Captivity narrative was the frequent claim that none in the early Church, except for possibly Marcion and Valentinus, understood Paul's dialectical theology or his doctrine of justification by faith. Paul's earliest readers were, in essence, accused of not having identified a limited set of passages in Romans and Galatians as the heart of his theology. Those few proto-orthodox authors who dared to invoke Paul thus misconstrued him. Walter Bauer found no significant loyalty to Paul in the early church after the Apostle's death, even among the congregations that he established.[67] Eva Aleith (1937), while conceding that most everyone in the second century had access to and had read Pauline epistles, concluded that no one actually understood Paul. By the time that his letters were circulating as a corpus, they had already been collected together with pseudo-Pauline literature, making it nearly impossible to get at the heart of Paul's theology.[68]

The force of Harnack and Bauer and their Pauline Captivity narrative held sway into the second half of the twentieth century. In addition to Campenhausen's conclusions (cf. earlier discussion), Wilhelm Schneemelcher (1964), among others, argued that Paul's letters were little used in nascent Catholicism.[69] 1 Clement knew only 1 Corinthians. Ignatius of Antioch had not read any of Paul's letters. The Apologists do not mention Paul's name. If Paul's letters were not cited by a particular author, Schneemelcher assumed that they were either being ignored or were unknown.[70] He had been "intentionally shoved aside" ("als würde er absichtlich beiseite geschoben").[71] The Apostle had been appropriated so thoroughly by the "heretics" that the Roman church would have preferred to omit his letters from the developing New Testament canon, but the force of tradition would not allow it.[72] Those who did cite Paul, like Polycarp and Irenaeus, were not true Paulinists (read: justification by faith alone was not what they derived from his letters).[73]

Kurt Aland (1979) directly challenged Schneemelcher's position on the Apostolic Fathers, while still retaining the Pauline Captivity narrative in broad outline. He argued that the Pauline corpus had been assembled and had circulated widely by the end of the first century, as evidenced by 1 Clement (who knew 1 Cor, Eph, and Heb), Ignatius (who knew 1 Cor and Eph), Polycarp (who knew Phil and the Pastorals), and 2 Peter 3.16. A more sophisticated method of determining literary dependence on Paul in the Apostolic Fathers allowed for the identification of more echoes than Schneemelcher had admitted.[74] Aland disagreed with Schneemelcher's assertion that if a text was not cited, it was unknown to an author. He also balked at the thought that the proto-orthodox were uninterested in Pauline theology. 1 Clement, for instance, borrowed its seed imagery for the resurrection from 1 Corinthians 15 (1 Clem. 24.5). One might also point to the constellation of terms from 1 Corinthians 15 in Justin's First Apology:

τὸν αὐτὸν τρόπον λογίσασθε ὅτι διαλυθέντα καὶ δίκην **σπερμάτων** (cf. 1 Cor 15.38) εἰς γῆν ἀναλυθέντα τὰ ἀνθρώπεια **σώματα** (cf. 1 Cor 15.35-44) κατὰ καιρὸν προστάξει θεοῦ ἀναστῆναι καὶ **ἀφθαρσίαν ἐνδύσασθαι** (cf. 1 Cor 15.53) οὐκ ἀδύνατον (1 Apol. 19.4).

Nevertheless, for Aland, Marcion and the Gnostics *best* understood Paul.[75] The proto-Catholic Fathers often got him wrong, despite their interest in various aspects of his theology. Irenaeus's reading of Paul was, for example, a reactionary engagement with his opponents' use of the Apostle, not a genuine wrestling with Paul's writings on their own terms. Aland did, however, insist that the question, Who got Paul right? is unimportant for doing work on the second-century reception of the Pauline corpus.[76] This was a rare admission from within this larger tradition.

Paul and the "Heretics": Marcion

As has been mentioned, the flip side of the proto-orthodox silence about and misinterpretation of the Apostle in the Pauline Captivity narrative was his more careful reception among the "heretics." Marcion and the Valentinians were viewed as the true inheritors of Pauline theology. They understood the radical nature of Paul's dialectical theology and apocalyptic faith in Christ; a faith that was reckoned solely on the basis of God's grace, apart from participation in traditional religious institutions and their necessary "works." Tertullian was right to call Paul the "apostle of the heretics" (*Marc.* 3.5.4).

Harnack had been captivated by Marcion from his teenage years until his death.[77] The title of his recently edited and published Dorpater Preisschrift, written at the age of nineteen, clearly indicates his favorable reading of Marcion: *Marcion: Der moderne Gläubige des 2. Jahrhunderts, der erste Reformator* (1870).[78] His *Marcion: Das Evangelium vom fremden Gott*, published 51 years later (1921), became the standard work on Marcion's Paulinism for over half a century.[79] Harnack saw a line of theological succession running from Jesus to Paul to Marcion to Augustine and finally on to Luther.[80] His love for Marcion's reading of Paul (as an opponent of Torah) is seen in two now-famous passages:

> Marcion was the only Gentile Christian who understood Paul, and even he misunderstood him: the rest never got beyond the appropriation of particular Pauline sayings, and exhibited no comprehension especially of the theology of the Apostle, so far as in it the universalism of Christianity as a religion is proved, even without recourse to Moralism and without putting a new construction on the Old Testament religion.[81]

... the rejection of the Old Testament in the second century was a mistake which the great church rightly avoided; to maintain it in the sixteenth century was a fate from which the Reformation was not yet able to escape; but still to preserve it in Protestantism as a canonical document since the nineteenth century is the consequence of a religious and ecclesiastical crippling.[82]

Disagreeing with the portrayal of Marcion by the early Church Fathers, Harnack distanced the "Pontic Wolf" from the syncretism of the "Gnostics" and rendered him as a consistent and simple reader of Paul, mediated chiefly through Galatians, which stood at the front of Marcion's *Apostolikon*.[83] In addition to finding in Galatians a forceful statement of Paul's superiority to the Jerusalem Church, Marcion discovered there a complete antithesis between Law and Gospel, extrapolating from this an absolute antithesis between the ethnic God of the Jews (the Creator) and the universal God of Jesus and Paul (the Unknown God of Love).[84] Much like Harnack for the Protestantism of his day, Marcion tried to relieve the burgeoning Catholic Church of its *complexio oppositorum*—its attempt to hold the Old and New together in harmony.[85]

Proto-orthodox Church Fathers frequently accused Marcion of editing out elements of the Pauline letter corpus that were inconvenient for his oversimplified reading of Paul (cf. Irenaeus, *Haer.* 1.27.2, 4; Tertullian, *Praescr.* 38; *Marc.* 5.3.3; 5.21.1), whether individual words or whole texts (the Pastoral Epistles). Marcion, on the other hand, saw himself as restoring the pristine condition of Paul's letters, which had been interpolated by Judaizing influences in the early Catholic Church (Tertullian, *Marc.* 4.4.1). Despite this rhetorical back and forth, recent studies have shown that Marcion's *Apostolikon* represented (for the most part) the common Greek text of an already gathered *Corpus Paulinum* in Rome in the early-second century.[86] His supposed changes were much less numerous than the proto-orthodox imagined, and many of them can be found throughout the *Vetus Latina* manuscript tradition. He likely deleted some passages that were favorable to Abraham and Israel or that portrayed Christ as having a share of the creation, but even this limited editorial work was not consistent (Tertullian, *Marc.* 4.43).

Harnack's reading of Marcion, which dominated liberal Protestantism for over half a century, has been challenged in a variety of ways by numerous scholars during the last several decades.[87] Barbara Aland,

among others, has argued that Marcion, theologically, was much closer
to the Gnostics than Harnack wanted to admit. While gnosis, election,
allegorical interpretation, and a complicated cosmogony were not primary features of Marcion's thought, other emphases, including cosmo-
logical dualism and a separation between the Jewish and Christian
gods, were quite consistent with classical "Gnosticism."[88] This particular question about Marcion's relationship to Gnosticism, of course,
hinges on how broadly one wants to apply the term "Gnostic." More
recent studies on "Gnosticism" by Michael Williams and Karen King
have alerted us to the ethical and historical problems of this term, and
its cognate, "Gnostics."[89] Gerhard May has sustained a similar argument to Aland, while also emphasizing that Marcion's unique contributions in early Christianity were his prophetic (ethical) critique of
burgeoning Catholicism and his radical dualism at a time when most
Roman thinkers, including other Christians, sought philosophical
unity.[90] For both Aland and May, Marcion was neither pure Paulinist
(contra Harnack) nor pure Gnostic (contra the Heresiologists), but, like
all of Paul's interpreters, brought certain philosophical and existential
concerns to Paul's texts.[91]

Sebastian Moll (2010) has recently attempted to re-envision Marcion
in the wake of these studies.[92] Moll argues that Marcion began not with
Paul, but with the Old Testament. His "fanatical hatred of the world" led
him to the problem of theodicy and the Creator God of the Old Testament.[93] Unique among early Christian thinkers, Marcion came to loathe
the capricious God that he found there, and only subsequently found religious justification for his feelings in Luke and Paul, whose writings were
edited to conform to his reading of the Old Testament. Moll concludes,
"Marcion does not understand the Old Testament in the light of the New,
he interprets the New Testament in light of the Old."[94] Paul, then, was not
the primary lens of Marcion's theology. Pride of place went, rather, to the
Old Testament.

Many of these more recent studies argue that Harnack's romantic
portrayal of Marcion as a second-century Reformer was too colored by
his own historical location in the heart of Protestant Germany in the
early-twentieth century.[95] That is not to say, most of them clarify, that
interpreters of ancient texts can ever finally overcome their own subjec-
tivity. But prior conclusions can always be checked by later generations
who are better situated to see the biases of their forebears. None disagree
with Harnack that Marcion was the first known Christian to develop a

consistent theological reading of the entire Pauline corpus (*sans* the Pastorals).[96] But, as May concludes, as with Harnack's reading of Marcion:

> his [Marcion's] exegesis is dependent on massive dogmatic presuppositions. One calls him a biblical theologian only inasmuch as for him his scripture canon represents the only standard of faith. He is not one in the sense that he had brought the originality of the "Gospel" and Pauline theology to bear against speculative interpretations.[97]

Whether proto-orthodox readings of Paul were "closer to the biblical texts" than Marcion's, as May claims, remains a contested matter.[98] Judith Lieu has recently argued that neither side was "closer" to Paul than the other. Rather:

> Tertullian, it might be said, is more attuned to a "salvation-historical" reading of Paul, sensitive to the over-arching purpose of God, Marcion to a more "apocalyptic" one, alive to the radical in-breaking of the new.[99]

Paul and the "Heretics": The Valentinians

Valentinus was present in Rome at the same time as Marcion. An Alexandrian Christian, Valentinus became the father of a large and extensive movement of churches that came to threaten proto-orthodox identity.[100] According to Clement of Alexandria, the Valentinians claimed a direct line to Paul's *pneumatic* teaching through Theudas, disciple of Paul and teacher of Valentinus (*Strom.* 7.17; cf. also Hippolytus, *Haer.* 6.35.5). Valentinus and his followers appealed to 1 Corinthians 2.6 ("But we speak wisdom among the mature"), arguing that Paul possessed secret wisdom from God the Father and in turn passed it down to those who were "mature" (Irenaeus, *Haer.* 3.2.1). This wisdom stood over and against the earthly traditions of the Apostles. Theodotus, a representative of eastern Valentinianism, states (programmatically):

> In the type of the Paraclete, Paul became the Apostle of the Resurrection (ὁ Παῦλος ἀναστάσεως ἀπόστολος). Immediately after the Lord's Passion he also was sent to preach. Therefore he preached the Saviour from both points of view: as begotten and passible for the sake of those

on the left, because, being able to know him, they are afraid of him in this position, and in spiritual wise from the Holy Spirit and a virgin, as the angels on the right know him (Clement, *Exc.* 23.2–3).[101]

Some of the language of the Pauline corpus was fertile ground for the Valentinians and their middle-Platonic thought.[102] Passages such as Romans 8.3 ("God sent his own son in the *likeness* of human flesh") and Romans 7.5 ("When we were *in the flesh,* sinful passions, which came about through the Law, worked in our members in order to bear fruit for death") were particularly important (cf. Tert., *Carn. Chr.* 16–17; Clem., *Exc.* 67.1). The most suggestive was 1 Corinthians 15.50, concerning which Irenaeus laments:

> Among the other truths proclaimed by the apostle, there is also this one, "That flesh and blood cannot inherit the kingdom of God." This is the passage which is adduced by all the heretics in support of their folly, with an attempt to annoy us, and to point out that the handiwork of God is not saved (*Haer.* 5.9.1).

Appeals to these Pauline texts and others by the Valentinians eventually forced the hand of proto-orthodox defenders of the faith. They needed to reclaim these particular Pauline passages for their own side. Two of these responses were *3 Corinthians* and Irenaeus's *Adversus haereses,* which will be explored at length in successive chapters below.

Thanks to the discovery of the Nag Hammadi library, we now have, among other things, an extensive hoard of Valentinian primary sources that use and appropriate Pauline material, including the *Apocalypse of Paul* (NHC V, 2) and the *Prayer of Paul the Apostle* (NHC I, 1).[103] These texts helped fill out what was already known through the Church Fathers about Pauline exegesis in Ptolemy (cf. Irenaeus, *Haer.* 1.1.1–1.8.5, and Epiphanius, *Pan.* 33.3.1–7.10), Heracleon (cf. Origen, *Comm. Jo.*), and Theodotus (cf. Clement, *Exc*).[104] For many scholars of early Christianity, however, the Nag Hammadi texts only confirmed half of the proto-orthodox testimony. The "Gnostics" did use Pauline texts to substantiate their theology, including the pesky 1 Corinthians 15.50. Like Marcion, they made use of all of the Pauline epistles except for the Pastorals.[105] Much to the chagrin, though, of the Fathers, their opponents, according to these scholars, appear to have gotten Paul "right" more often than not, particularly with respect to the resurrection and the historical triumph of spirit over flesh.

Space does not permit a full analysis of the Pauline material in the Valentinian texts from Nag Hammadi.[106] Their use of 1 Corinthians 15.50, however, deserves a brief note. A passage from the *Gospel of Philip*, cited in Chapter 1 as an example of early Christian interpretive disagreement over Paul, offers the only preserved Valentinian citation of this Pauline verse:

> Certain persons are afraid that they may arise (from the dead) naked: therefore they want to arise in the flesh. And they do not know that those who wear the flesh are the ones who are naked. Those who [. . .] to divest themselves are not naked. "Flesh [and blood will not] inherit the kingdom [of god]." What is this flesh that will not inherit it? The one that we are wearing. (*Gos. Phil.* 56.26–57.1)

Was Irenaeus wrong, then? Was 1 Corinthians 15.50, with this single attestation in the surviving Valentinian literature, a prominent interpretive site for their theology? While appearing only here in the Nag Hammadi texts as a full citation, the language of 1 Corinthians 15.35–58 permeates several other Valentinian texts, and we should not easily dismiss the testimonies of Irenaeus or Tertullian about its importance among their opponents.[107] Paul was, according to Theodotus, "the Apostle of the Resurrection" (Clement, *Exc.* 23, 2–3). Moreover, a relatively small percentage of "heretical" texts from antiquity have survived, and the use of this verse in literary texts is only one of the ways Irenaeus would have encountered his opposition's invocation of 1 Corinthians 15.50.

For many proponents of the Pauline Captivity narrative, the Valentinian emphasis on non-fleshly resurrection was truly Pauline. 1 Corinthians 15.50, when read with the "spiritual body" (σῶμα πνευματικόν) language of 15.44 and the surrounding dichotomies of "perishable/imperishable" (1 Cor 15.42, 50, 52–54), "mortal/immortal" (1 Cor 15.53–54), and "earthly/heavenly" (1 Cor 15.47–49), most naturally aligned with the Platonic tradition of the Valentinians and not with the millenarianism of the proto-orthodox. Robert McL. Wilson's conclusion about the above passage from the *Gospel of Philip* is typical:

> From the passage as a whole it would appear that he looked for a resurrection of the body, after which the Gnostic would strip off the garment of the flesh in order to be clothed upon with his heavenly robe. Which is a sufficiently faithful reproduction of the Pauline doctrine to explain why in the second century the Church departed

from Paul and emphasized, with such writers as Justin and Tertullian, the resurrection of the flesh. Paul's teaching lent itself too readily to adaptation in a Gnostic interest.[108]

Similar statements have been made by others about Pauline theology in other Valentinian texts.

On the *Gospel of Truth*:

This picture allows us to see how profound Pauline influence is on the *Gospel of Truth*. The mutuality of the knowledge between God and the Elect . . . is a typically Pauline doctrine.[109]

On the *Treatise on the Resurrection*:

Now, in fact, this interpretation of the form of the resurrection body seems a more faithful interpretation of the Pauline conception of such a body than does the interpretation of many of the early Heresiologists.[110]

Dissenting voices to this part of the Pauline Captivity narrative could be heard all along the way in the work of Theodor Zahn, Carola Barth, and others, who argued that the Valentinians were *not* close readers of Paul. Rather, like their proto-orthodox counterparts, they brought their philosophy and mythology to the New Testament texts.[111] These studies, unfortunately, were too often swept away in the twentieth century with a simple rhetorical move: to agree with the estimation of the Church Fathers that the Valentinians twisted Paul's letters was to be complicit with their nasty polemic, to "have adopted from them certain value judgments and interpretations of the gnostic material."[112] Any cursory look at the data, however, shows that Valentinian interpretations of Paul, aside from the occasional literalistic interpretation, as in the case of 1 Corinthians 15.50, were largely allegorical, like the rest of their Scriptural exegesis.[113] This allowed them, possibly in reaction to Marcion, to preserve the Old Testament as a witness to spiritual truth.[114] Ptolemy's *Epistle to Flora* provides the most poignant insider description of Valentinian Scriptural hermeneutics:

Now, once the truth had been manifested, the referent of all these ordinances [the Jewish Law] was changed, inasmuch as they are images and allegories. As to their meaning in the visible realm and their physical accomplishment they were abolished; but as to their spiritual meaning they were elevated, with the words remaining the same but the subject matter being altered (Epiphanius, *Pan.* 33.5.9).[115]

Ptolemy then substantiates this hermeneutic with an allusion to Romans 2.29, "And he [the savior] wished us to perform circumcision, but not circumcision of the bodily foreskin, rather of the spiritual heart" (33.5.11), and a direct citation of 1 Corinthians 5.7: "Christ our Passover has been slain" (33.5.14).

Conclusion

The Pauline Captivity narrative in its numerous variations held sway from F. C. Baur until the late 1970s as the dominant portrayal of "Paul in the second century." While it contained a number of moving parts, it was ultimately erected on a single historiographical foundation from the Rankean era: the separation of objectively attainable historical truth from the accretions of tradition through the application of higher-critical methodologies. The historiographical climate in which F. C. Baur wrote opened up rhetorical space for Baur and others to talk about the "real" Paul, as opposed to the ecclesiastical "Paul" of later Catholic tradition. Inasmuch as this discourse on the "real" Paul still dominates Pauline Studies as a discipline, Ranke's ghost continues to haunt it. This positivist historiographical foundation has often covered over a more deeply set ideological foundation just below: nineteenth- and twentieth-century Protestant theology and its attachment to a particular conception of Paul. The Paul of Romans, Galatians, and the Corinthian correspondence has rarely been on the operating table, thereby being protected from the scalpel of historical-critical doubt over their authorship. While the so-called "New Perspective on Paul" has asked us to re-envision the Paul of these letters, positioning itself against a "Lutheran" reading of them, it has failed to recognize that a largely Lutheran image of Paul persists in the very selection of the texts in the first place.

Once the Paul of the *Hauptbriefe* had been established (or assumed) as the "real" Paul, he became the measure of all subsequent receptions of the Pauline tradition, whether in the second century or the nineteenth or the twentieth. According to the Pauline Captivity narrative in its most developed form, Paul's theology had been distorted, forgotten, and/or suppressed by the proto-orthodox in the second century. He had become the "apostle of the heretics" (Tertullian, *Marc.* 3.5.4). Marcion and the Valentinians were the more authentic and faithful interpreters of the Apostle. Sporadic challenges, as we have seen, had been registered against various pieces of the narrative, including Harnack's Marcion. By the late 1970s, however, the account as a whole began to undergo serious and sustained scrutiny. The next chapter describes the challenges that it ultimately faced, its decline in influence, and the *status quaestionis* concerning "Paul in the second century," while placing more recent narratives about Paul's influence in that century within the context of the shifting historiographical theories of the twentieth century.

3

Re-Imagining Paul: Recent Portrayals of "Paul in the Second Century"

> But more importantly, I would argue, by concentrating on
> history writing as rhetorical exercise, we can identify more
> clearly the ideological biases or perspectives which inform
> the discourse.
>
> HAYDEN WHITE, "Rhetoric and History"[1]

THE PAULINE CAPTIVITY narrative and its supporting discourses on the "real" Paul and "who got Paul right in the second century," made influential by Harnack, Bauer, and Campenhausen, and undergirded by early work on the Nag Hammadi literature, was at its height in the 1970s.

An important essay by C. K. Barrett (1974), however, signaled that a shift in thinking about the post-apostolic Pauline tradition was afoot.[2] Barrett advanced the notion of multiple Pauline "legends"—developing portrayals of Paul that were to some degree independent of the reception of his letters. Ultimately, Irenaeus's "orthodox" or "good" legend (to use Barrett's language) of Paul as martyr, Apostle to the Gentiles, and subject to the apostolic teaching eventually overcame the "Gnostic" (inclusive of Marcion) or "bad" legend of Paul as otherworldly, apocalyptic visionary because it had already been sufficiently developed and accepted by the end of the first century, as can be seen in the pseudonymous Ephesians and Pastoral Epistles, Acts, and 1 Clement. The "good" legend was cemented in too many communities for the proto-orthodox to do away fully with its Paul. The mixture of the early "orthodox" legend with the "historical" Paul in the New Testament canon was the "price we pay," according to Barrett, for reclaiming Paul from the Gnostics.[3] However noticeable Barrett's personal commitment to the Protestant Paul of the *Hauptbriefe* as the "historical" Paul and his evaluative positions on the two Pauline legends might be, his basic approach to Pauline traditions would become important for more recent accounts of the reception of Paul in the second century in two ways. First, as will become plain, Barrett was an early proponent of the thesis that developing Pauline images often controlled the fate and interpretation of Pauline epistles in the early Church. Second, Barrett saw lines of continuity between earlier and later Pauline legends. As we will argue in Chapter 4, any model for understanding the Pauline tradition in the second century should give due weight to the force of tradition. While Justin may have avoided using Paul for several understandable reasons, his theological successors could not. The proto-orthodox Pauline legend during the second century was already too widespread in too many communities to ignore.

What one could see in part in Barrett came into full focus in 1979–1981 in major works by Andreas Lindemann, Ernst Dassmann, David Rensberger, and Donald Penny, each of which contributed to what would become an important re-narration of "Paul in the second century." Covering much of the same material, but with unique emphases, their combined argument reset the study of the early reception-history of Paul. This chapter describes their historical and exegetical work, as well as the twentieth-century shifts in historiographical theory that were beginning to problematize overly objectivist accounts of the past, including the Pauline Captivity narrative. It ends by exploring developments in the description of "Paul in the second century" at the end of the twentieth century and into the twenty-first in the wake of the demise of the Pauline Captivity narrative and these larger theoretical shifts.

Narrative Iconoclasm: The Fall of the Pauline Captivity Narrative

In a period of three years (1979–1981), four book-length studies appeared that would bring an end to the long-standing dominance of the Pauline Captivity narrative. Among the four, Andreas Lindemann's *Paulus im ältesten Christentum* (1979) was the most important, though the others provided key additions to Lindemann's basic thesis.[4] A near comprehensive study of Paul in the late-first to mid-second centuries, Lindemann's monograph directly challenged the Pauline Captivity narrative by exploring a number of indications that Paul continued to be revered by proto-orthodox groups in the second century and by re-evaluating the Apostle's role among the "Gnostics."[5] Ernst Dassmann, whose book *Der Stachel im Fleisch: Paulus in der frühchristlichen Literatur bis Irenäus* appeared the same year, took a similar tack, but was more openly concerned with modern theological norms than Lindemann. Dassmann asked about the weight that should be given to Pauline theology in the modern church (in relationship to other early Christian authorities) and used the examination of Paul's early influence in the burgeoning Catholic Church as a way of helping illustrate his thesis that while Paul was an important ground for Christian theology in the first two Christian centuries, he was never the only ground. The Church has always determined what portions of the Pauline legacy are important at a given time, though his *theologia crucis* has served as a constant "Stachel im Fleisch" for it from its inception.[6]

Lindemann and Dassmann proceeded cautiously with the data. Lindemann, in particular, was reticent to assign intertextual dependence on Paul unless a citation formula was present, although allusions to Pauline material could be reasonably assumed when the content and wording was Pauline and could not be assigned to the wider Christian tradition. The certainty of an allusion increases if knowledge of Pauline letters could be shown elsewhere in a given author.[7] Lindemann found early and extensive interest in Paul among the proto-orthodox. The existence of a wide-ranging pseudo-Pauline literature, in combination with the redaction (cf. 2 Cor), collection, and circulation of Pauline letters toward the end of the first century, was sufficient to establish continued proto-orthodox attention to Paul into the second century.[8] Several of the "Apostolic Fathers" invoke both Paul's persona as well as his letters (cf. the honorific references to Paul in *1 Clement*, Ignatius, and Polycarp, for example, cited in Chapter 1).[9] Methodologically, Lindemann was concerned both with "Das Bild des Apostels" (the propagation of Pauline images) as well as the "Aufnahme und Verarbeitung paulinischer Theologie" (the interpretation of Paul's letters) in the second century. The reception of Paul, for Lindemann, as well as for Dassmann, was a multifaceted process.[10] From the textual side, for example, the author of *1 Clement* certainly knew 1 Corinthians and Romans.[11] Ignatius knew 1 Corinthians, Ephesians, and possibly other Pauline letters.[12] Polycarp, like *1 Clement* and Ignatius, drew freely on Paul whenever he felt the need.[13] The Corinthian correspondence, in particular, according to Dassmann, was not only influential on *1 Clement*, Polycarp, and Melito of Sardis, but was normally interpreted by them in ways that were faithful to the letters' original intention.[14] The use of Paul by these authors was the initial phase of a trend whereby Paul would end up becoming the most frequently cited early Christian authority among second-century writers. He was always, according to Lindemann, a "fundamentaler

Bestandteil ihrer eigenen Tradition."[15] While justification by faith alone—
the identified center of Paul's legacy from the Reformation through his
reception in the historical-critical scholarship of the twentieth century—
was absent from the proto-orthodox reception of Paul in the second century, more than a few authors were interested in aspects of his theology,
even if they might have misunderstood it at times (cf. Aland in Chapter 2).[16]
Both Lindemann and Dassmann further argued, in line with Barrett, that,
at least among the proto-orthodox, Paul's image retained a large degree of
continuity from the early pseudo-Pauline literature into the mid-second
century. Paul was, throughout, the Apostle to the Gentiles, the founder of
churches and the opponent of heresy.[17]

When assessing Paul's absence from certain second-century authors,
Lindemann, like Baur's early detractors, argued that any number of factors ought to be considered, including a writer's geographical location and
the genre of his particular text. Embarrassment over the Apostle was
merely one possible cause.[18] No solid evidence exists for a widespread
anti-Pauline movement continuing into the second century, outside
maybe the Epistle of James and some later pockets of marginal Jewish-
Christian groups.[19] Furthermore, the texts from Nag Hammadi show no
real predilection for Paul over other Christian authorities. His theology,
Lindemann concluded, was not "konstitutiv" for the Valentinians.[20] Ptolemy, for instance, exhibits only a superficial use of Paul's letters.[21] Dassmann argued similarly, successfully showing how Johannine rather than
Pauline traditions were most important in shaping "Gnostic" thought.[22]

The work of Lindemann and Dassmann was seismic for at least two
reasons. First, they convincingly showed the varieties of engagement with
the Pauline tradition in both proto-orthodox as well as Marcionite and
"Gnostic" forms of early Christianity. There was a robust Pauline influence among the proto-orthodox leading up to and through the second century. While that influence might not have looked like what modern
Protestant scholars have identified as the heart of Pauline theology, there
is no evidence of a shying away from either Pauline literature or thought
within burgeoning proto-orthodox circles.[23] Furthermore, the "Gnostic"
use of Paul was much less impressive than what supporters of the Pauline
Captivity narrative had made it out to be. This latter claim would be most
comprehensively defended by David Rensberger two years later. Second,
Lindemann's decision to outline both developing Pauline images as well
as invocations of Pauline theology partially laid the groundwork for a near
cottage industry of articles and monographs on the "Paulusbild" of

particular texts, a trend that also seems indebted to wider developments in twentieth-century historiographical theory, which we will consider later in this chapter.

David Rensberger's dissertation (Yale, 1981), "As the Apostle Teaches: The Development of the Use of Paul's Letters in Second-Century Christianity," was completed on the heels of these two German monographs and largely confirmed their conclusions, while making a number of other important contributions. Though never published, it became the standard English-language resource for the use of Paul's letters in the second century for three decades. Like Lindemann, Rensberger sought to displace the Pauline Captivity narrative through a close examination of the full range of use of Pauline letters during this period.[24] From the outset, he was particularly concerned with understanding Justin's Pauline silence, inasmuch as this served as the linchpin for the narrative. His work differed, however, from his immediate predecessors in two methodologically important ways. First, like Aland, Rensberger sidelined questions about who "rightly understood" Paul's theology in the second century.[25] He was concerned with the reception of Pauline letters, not the influence and proper reception of a reconstructed Pauline theology, which was a preoccupation for both Lindemann and Dassmann. Second, Rensberger concluded that concerns over Paul's image were "of so little moment to most second-century writers that its usefulness is difficult to see."[26] Paul's persona, then, factors little in his work.

Like Lindemann, Rensberger posited a number of alternative explanations for why some second-century authors made little to no use of Paul's letters. After meticulously exploring the varieties of engagement with Paul's letters in the Apostolic Fathers, Pauline pseudepigrapha, the apocryphal Acts, apologetic literature, Gnostic and Valentinian writers, Marcion, martyrological literature, encratite sources, Irenaean sources, and finally Irenaeus himself, Rensberger concluded that where reactions to an opponent's use of Paul can be sensed, the response was always alternative exegesis, not avoidance.[27] Rather than widespread distrust of the Apostle, or outright rejection of him (only visible in the Ebionites and *Pseudo-Clementines*), the dearth of direct references to Pauline letters in some early to mid second-century Christian texts is likely attributable to the fact that Paul's letters had not yet attained that much authority.[28] The same was also true of other literature bearing the apostolic stamps of Peter, James, and John. Paul was only one of several potential sources of Christian teaching in this early period, little of which was ever directly cited.[29]

Considerations of genre should also be taken into account. Rensberger noted that apocryphal gospels made very little use of Paul's letters, regardless of theological bent.[30] Apologies, directed toward outsiders, never invoked the name of Paul and sometimes never even mentioned the name of Christ.[31] Yet several of the Apologists also wrote texts for their communities. Tatian freely used Pauline literature among believers. Rensberger found that intra-community texts, including "commentaries, doctrinal treatises, and polemical tracts," evidence much earlier and wider engagements with Paul, regardless of their theological stripe.[32] Finally, with respect to Justin, the *Dialogue with Trypho* did not need Paul's authority; in fact, to invoke him might have been counterproductive. He only needed the Jewish Scriptures and the life of Jesus (mediated through his apostles) to argue his point.[33]

Rensberger, like Lindemann and Dassmann, also found little evidence of special regard for Paul (above other early apostolic figures or literature) in either classical Gnosticism or Valentinianism.[34] This was a conclusion that has continued to be substantiated by studies like Jacqueline Williams's work on the *Gospel of Truth*, an important Valentinian text in which only a third of the 73 potential allusions to texts that would become part of the New Testament come from the Pauline letters.[35] If fact, Rensberger shows that just as many "Gnostic" texts "avoid" Paul as those from proto-orthodox circles.[36] Tertullian's characterization of Paul as the "apostle of the heretics" (*Marc.* 3.5.4) seems to go unsupported from the available literature of such groups, although we should be cautious here, given what little remains of the "heretical" literature. Only Marcion, in the end, seems to have had a particular affinity for Paul.[37] While not wanting to get into arguments over "who got Paul right," Rensberger was deeply suspicious, like Zahn, Barth, and Lindemann before him, and now others, of those who vaunted the Valentinians as the true inheritors of Pauline theology.[38]

A little noticed but important dissertation at Emory University (1979) by Donald Penny entitled "The Pseudo-Pauline Letters of the First Two Centuries" was completed during this same period (1979) and should also be mentioned here, briefly, because it provides nice conceptual language for the emerging story about Paul's reception in the second century that was developing out of the shattered pieces of the Pauline Captivity narrative.[39] Penny's work was the first comprehensive appraisal of Pauline pseudepigraphy in early Christianity to appear after the pioneering work of Wolfgang Speyer and Norbert Brox on literary forgery in antiquity.[40] It addressed the pseudepigraphical techniques and motives of the authors of the Pastoral Epistles, II Thessalonians, Ephesians, *3 Corinthians*, and *Laodiceans*, who deceptively authored texts in Paul's name to reclaim him from other competing construals of the Apostle.[41] These texts, in response, provided their own "tendentious images of Paul."[42] Drawing from Speyer and Brox, Penny denied that pseudepigraphy was a generally accepted practice in antiquity.[43] Rather, careful distinctions must be made between pseudonymous literature whose guise was adopted for purely literary reasons (speeches in histories, school exercises, etc.) and those whose guise served extra-literary purposes (most Christian pseudepigrapha).[44]

Penny saw the divergent images of the Apostle struck in each of the pseudo-Pauline letters serving as ciphers for a variety of early theological positions. They developed in the midst of conflict and competition in early Christianity, with each side trying to wrest the Pauline tradition in their own direction. Each attempt to reclaim the Apostle "preserves something of the genuine Paul and distorts him, with the result that the Pauline heritage is fragmented."[45] Eschewing earlier construals of the fate of "Paul" after Paul's death (including the "Pauline Captivity" narrative), Penny argued rather for a story of "Pauline Fragmentation," whereby Paul's authority was invoked by various Christian groups from the beginning, and trajectories of Pauline tradition developed around theological concerns that were in constant tension with one another, none of which held greater claim to preserving the "genuine Paul" than the others.[46]

By the end of the 1980s, in large part due to the work of these four studies, the Pauline Captivity narrative had been displaced with another story, a different landscape portrait, an alternative rhetoric about Paul in the second century. To use Penny's language, a narrative of "Pauline Fragmentation" was developing, which saw Paul's image (except in the case of Rensberger), as well as the use of Pauline letters, evolving in different directions among a variety of often competing Christian communities, none of which had a monopoly on Paul.[47] A meeting convened at Southern Methodist University in 1987 under the title "Paul and the Legacies of Paul" marks the symbolic end of 150 years of thinking about Paul's reception in the second century. The meeting aimed at consolidating and building upon the foundation set by Lindemann and Dassmann, who both contributed papers, particularly as it related to the constructive appropriation of Paul in various proto-orthodox groups and texts.[48] The conference's organizers sought to destroy further the "distressingly stereotyped pattern" of the Pauline Captivity narrative among twentieth-century Protestant scholarship.[49] William Babcock, its organizer, opined that we "must

be willing to acknowledge both that there may be other ways to construe Paul and that there may be other ways to interpret the patristic evidence."[50] What influence the Pauline Captivity narrative might still have after the 1980s is best seen in its continued presence in some introductory textbooks, which, as a genre, are typically and painfully out of date, yet at the same time powerfully formative.[51]

Historicizing the Historian: The Fall of Historiographical Positivism

Even though Lindemann and others argued aggressively and successfully against the Pauline Captivity narrative, their basic historiographical assumptions remained largely conservative, tied to the historical positivism of the nineteenth century. Lindemann and Penny, in their division of the canonical Pauline corpus along now-traditional lines (the seven "authentic" Pauline letters), used the discourse on the "real" Paul versus the Paul of "tradition" to establish a robust pseudepigraphical interest in the Apostle among the proto-orthodox during the late-first and early-second centuries. A full break from a tradition, including a historiographical tradition, is difficult, if not impossible, in just one generation. At the wider level, however, shifts in historiographical theory in the twentieth century were beginning to provide new resources for scholars of early Christianity. The French *Annalistes*, British Marxist historians, and literary critics like Hayden White emphasized that history-writing always involves the interests of the historian. The past is not reconstructed "wie es eigentlich gewesen," but is always constructed anew from present concerns. It is not surprising, then, that by the 1970s, as the Pauline Captivity narrative was being challenged, numerous scholars were becoming interested in the Pauline images that second-century authors had constructed. Christian writers of various stripes rendered the apostolic past in ways congenial to their present needs. I will first briefly describe the historiographical shifts of the twentieth century and then the new lines of inquiry that developed in the study of the early reception of Paul.

Several factors ultimately led to the loosened grip of an overly positivist historiography. First, two World Wars shook the foundation of European confidence in the discernment of causal connections between events. How could one explain such massive bloodshed?[52] Hegel's teleological historical philosophy in the hands of European nation-states took a battering. Second, conceptual frameworks in the physical sciences were shifting.

Newtonian physics gave way to Einstein's theory of relativity, while the Heisenberg uncertainty principle eventually unsettled aspects of the entire field.[53] "Paradigm shifts," to use the language of Thomas Kuhn, were coming fast and furious, though prior conceptions of reality did not go down without a fight.[54] Science was being exposed as tradition-driven and often resistant to change.[55] The Hungarian philosopher of science Michael Polanyi argued that the practice of science differs little from art or theology in this regard, requiring faith in a series of givens that have no hope of verification: "This is the way of acquiring knowledge, which the Christian Church Fathers described as *fides quarens intellectum*, 'to believe in order to know.'"[56] All of this meant that history as a discipline needed to rethink its scientific idol, as Marc Bloch noted:

> The generations just prior to our own, in the last decades of the nineteenth century and even in the first years of the twentieth, were as if mesmerized by the Comtian conception of physical science. . . . We find it far easier to regard certainty and universality as questions of degree. We no longer feel obliged to impose upon every subject of knowledge a uniform intellectual pattern, borrowed from natural science, since, even there, that pattern has ceased to be entirely applicable.[57]

Third, increased attention was given in the early- to mid-twentieth century to the role of the historian in prefiguring his or her subject matter. They were increasingly seen as stakeholders in their projects. E. H. Carr summarized this turn toward the historian in his 1961 George Macauley Trevelyan lectures:

> In the first place, the facts of history never come to us "pure," since they do not and cannot exist in a pure form: they are always refracted through the mind of the recorder. It follows that when we take up a work of history, our first concern should be not with the facts which it contains but with the historian who wrote it.[58]

Descartes was giving way to Kant in twentieth-century historiography. Unmediated access to reality was increasingly considered impossible. The limitations of language and the social location of the historical interpreter were ultimately determinative of how the past looked. For a period of time, though, this sensitivity to the role of the historian in shaping the past was wed to a continued and robust positivism. R. G. Collingwood, in his posthumously published *The Idea of History* (1946), for instance, acknowledged the contemporary concerns found within all narrations of the past.[59] Yet he still upheld that the task of history was to get inside the minds of figures of the past, describing accurately and objectively their perceptions about the world.[60]

The French *Annales* School, represented early on by Lucien Febvre and Marc Bloch and more recently by Jacques Le Goff and Pierre Nora, also strongly criticized nineteenth-century German event-history as epitomized by Ranke. The *Annalistes*, whose work often appeared in the *Annales d'histoire économique et sociale*, deployed social-scientific methods to produce micro-history. Still operating within a largely positivist historiography, they were concerned with describing the general conditions of average people, whose lives were often obscured by the narration of major events, as recounted by cultural elites.[61] Economics, agriculture, and climate were studied as a way of understanding the history of the voiceless. Febvre and now Le Goff also sought to describe *mentalités*, or the mental regimes that limited what could be thought in the past. They tried to expose the "social, economic, and political embeddedness of ideas."[62]

Historiography, for the *Annalistes*, started with the present. The historian poses her questions to the past and then sets out for answers. Bloch noted that "every historical research supposes that the inquiry has a direction at the very first step. In the beginning, there must be the guiding spirit."[63] And, "[i]n the last analysis, whether consciously or no, it is always by borrowing from our daily experiences and by shading them, where necessary, with new tints that we derive the elements which help us to restore the past."[64] The past is always in the service of the present. Concern for giving visibility to the "other" in the French historiography of the twentieth century was just one indication that the historian had become as much an ethicist as an antiquarian.

British Marxist historians like E. H. Carr and Eric Hobsbawm proceeded similarly, advocating for both presentist (activist) concerns and positivist historiographical methodologies.[65] For Howsbawm, for instance, the historian should look for evidence "from below" that would shatter the hegemonic "invented" histories of the cultural and political elite. The importance of securing indubitable evidence from the past lies in its ability to provide present and future liberation from dominant and legendary accounts of the past.[66] Thus, not all constructions of the past can be equally valid:

it is essential for historians to defend the foundation of their discipline: the supremacy of evidence. If their texts are fictions, as in
some sense they are, being literary compositions, the raw material
of these fictions is verifiable fact. . . . If history is an imaginative art,
it is one which does not invent but arranges *objets trouvés*.[67]

By the 1960s, more radical presentist approaches to historiography
could be found in the work of Michel Foucault and Hayden White. Foucault, as a historian of ideas, worked to expose the power structures latent
in the unconscious formation of ideas, whether notions of insanity (*Mad-
ness and Civilization, The Birth of the Clinic*), sexuality (*The History of Sexuality I, II, III*), criminality (*Discipline and Punish*), or man himself (*The
Order of Things*). Paul Veyne, with tongue in cheek, declared Foucault
"the first completely positivist historian," inasmuch as Foucault argued
that *all* knowledge develops within historical conditions dominated by
power relations.[68] Everything has a history, and thus nothing is fixed. The
historian gazes not upon natural and plain objects from the past, but
upon prior ideological constructions of reality now refracted through his
or her own present situation. "History, he argued, should not be con-
strued as a repetition of what the sources 'said,' but as a discourse that
'rewrites.'"[69] In the preface to the English version of *Les Mots et les choses*,
he opined:

> If there is one approach that I do reject, however, it is that (one
> might call it, broadly speaking, the phenomenological approach)
> which gives absolute priority to the observing subject, which attri-
> butes a constituent role to an act, which places its own point of view
> at the origin of all historicity—which, in short, leads to a transcen-
> dental consciousness.[70]

Foucault's history of ideas was largely built upon post-structuralist literary
theory, wherein the referential link between words and things (or language and reality) had been shattered. He was concerned with "defamiliarizing" the past.[71]

For Foucault, history was a constructive, not an archival, act. It proceeded along the lines of rhetorical discourse in the form of narrative.
Historiography was finally taking the "linguistic turn" and firmly distancing itself from positivist and scientific rhetoric—in short, from its "physics envy." Historical causation was out; language, discourse, narrative, and

power were increasingly *en vogue*.[72] "Representation" was becoming and now is the watchword of historians in the post-structuralist tradition. Hayden White has been the most vigorous defender of history-telling as enthymeme (rhetoric), not syllogism (logic).[73] In his foundational *Metahistory* (1973), White argued that there are strong poetic and rhetorical foundations to the narration of the past. Every history is written with a particular "historiographical style," which consists of choices that must be made about emplotment (romance, comedy, tragedy, and satire), formal argument (formism, organicism, mechanism, and contextualism), and ideological implication (anarchism, conservatism, radicalism, and liberalism). These choices are not made in a vacuum, however, but reflect *tropological* constraints, or modes of consciousness that provide linguistic protocols for prefiguring the historical field. These constraints are poetic in nature, producing histories that turn on metaphor (representation), metonymy (reduction), synecdoche (integration), or irony (skepticism/relativism). Discrete events from the past can and should be narrated in any number of ways, depending on the social and philosophical location of the historian.[74]

White narrated the transitions from the ironic mode of Enlightenment and early nineteenth-century historiography to the synecdochic style of Hegel and mid nineteenth-century historians, among whom F. C. Baur belongs, back to the ironic mode at the turn of the century as practitioners became disillusioned by the numerous "scientific" ways to represent the same events.[75] If there is a prescriptive aspect to White's work, it is his final plea to see irony and skepticism as only one of several ways to narrate the past. It is not the "necessary perspective" from which historians must operate.[76] The adoption of a particular narrative form is a deeply ethical task, and historians should be conscious of the shape of their histories and the potential consequences of their tropological choices:

> When it is a matter of choosing among . . . alternative visions of history, the only grounds for preferring the one over another are moral or aesthetic ones. . . . One must face the fact that, when it comes to the historical record, there are no grounds to be found in the record itself for preferring one way of construing its meaning rather than another. . . . We can tell equally plausible, alternative, and even contradictory stories . . . without violating rules of evidence or critical standards. . . . One can imagine not only one or two but any number of alternative stories of . . . any . . culturally

significant event, all equally plausible and equally authoritative by virtue of their conformity to generally accepted rules of historical construction.[77]

Since *Metahistory*, White has continued to try to destroy the wall that was erected between history and rhetoric/poetry/art in Greek antiquity (cf., e.g., Thucydides, *Peloponnesian War* 1.21; and Lucian, *The Way to Write History,* 7–8) and then later reinforced in eighteenth- and nineteenth-century Europe. The interpretive process cannot be separated from the discovery of neutral "facts." Rhetorical, poetic, and thus interpretive frameworks prefigure how we see the data in the first place.[78] They function as what we might call, colloquially, "common-sense."[79] Form (structuralism) leads to content. Narrative provides meaning to the past; it is not found there.[80] Chronicles and annals differ from narratives at this very point. The logic for advancing from event to event must be supplied by the historian to form a coherent narrative, a history.[81] Events take place, but facts, or literary presentations of events, are completely constructed by the historian.[82] White encourages historians to write eloquent and engaging prose, full of rhetorical flourish. To do so is to recognize that "the differences between a history and a fictional account of reality are matters of degree rather than of kind."[83]

Competing Images of Paul

Changes in historiographical theory and practice in the 1970s, combined with the deconstruction of the Pauline Captivity narrative during that same period, have given rise to the now widespread focus on the images or portrayals of Paul (*Paulusbilder*) constructed in various early Christian texts.[84] These texts portrayed Paul in tendentious ways that were productive for their authors' communities. The question Who got Paul right? was becoming less of a concern (although not absent) than How is Paul constructed in a given text and why?

Martinus de Boer, in an important article entitled "Images of Paul in the Post-Apostolic Period" (1980), picked up where C. K. Barrett and Hans-Martin Schenke had left off in the 1970s, arguing that the common portrayal of Paul in Colossians, Ephesians, Acts and the Pastorals stood at the beginning of a "trajectory" of Pauline reception into the second century.[85] De Boer identified six aspects of this received image, showing continuities and developments between first- and second-century texts: (1) Paul, the

Apostle; (2) Paul, the Apostle to the Gentiles;[86] (3) Paul, the Evangelist of the Whole World;[87] (4) Paul, the Sufferer;[88] (5) Paul, the Redeemed Persecutor;[89] and (6) Paul, the Authoritative Teacher of the Church.[90] These six elements "were starting-points from which the authors of these works were able to appropriate Paul in a way meaningful and useful for their own time and situations."[91] De Boer found a "dynamic interplay," a "backward" and "forward" movement, between an older, received image of Paul and later "variations on common themes and concerns."[92]

This complex, developing image of Paul predated, in most cases, the influence of Paul's letters. The Paul of the Apostolic Fathers was not the "epistolary Paul," but the "legendary" or "ecclesiastical" Paul (as in Acts).[93] Some places where Lindemann had identified knowledge of Pauline letters are just as easily explained by knowledge of particular Pauline legends, caricatures, and catchwords, according to de Boer (cf. *1 Clem.* 5; 30–33; Polycarp, *Phil.* 3.1, 3; 9.2).[94] It is the "ecclesiastical Paul" who is raised to check the divisions produced by upstarts in Corinth in *1 Clement*, not the "epistolary Paul."[95] Even those early second-century writers who show knowledge of Paul's letters each have a different "epistolary Paul," depending on which of the letters they know.[96] Which Paul? then, is the first question we must ask of each invocation of the Apostle. Is it the legendary Paul? If so, which legend? Is it the epistolary Paul? If so, which epistle(s)?

A number of others have since argued similarly.[97] Karlfried Froehlich (1996) concluded, "It seems that the tradition of a Pauline legend glorifying the great preacher, missionary, and miracle worker antedates the epistolary collection by a considerable margin . . . the legendary Paul had a life independent of such material."[98] Froehlich noted, however, that this was not the only set of images of Paul in the second century. On account of the "general versatility of Paul's own theologizing in the surviving remnants of his correspondence," a "plurality of 'Pauls,' all of whom had their supporters and detractors in various circles of Christians," developed.[99] For example, Michael Kaler (2004) has explored the images of Paul found in the Nag Hammadi literature, concluding, "'Gnostics' (I use the term loosely), like other early Christians, created and used legendary images of Paul, and these legendary images may not have been so different from those created and used by the proto-orthodox."[100] Kaler's work is self-consciously positioned in the stream of work culminating in the *Paul and the Legacies of Paul* volume, which signaled the end of the hegemony of the Pauline Captivity narrative. He explores: (1) Paul, the Apocalyptic Hero

(Coptic *Apocalypse of Paul*); (2) Paul, One of the Apostles (*Exegesis of the Soul*); and (3) Paul, the Image of Christ (*Testimony of Truth* and *Silvanos*). Kaler wants those who study "Gnosticism" to "expand [their] understanding of Paulinism" beyond the strict reception of Pauline letters or theology as those who study proto-orthodox receptions of Paul have already done.[101] His extensive work on the Coptic *Apocalypse of Paul*, for instance, has gone a long way in teasing out the image of Paul as apocalyptic mediator in various second-century texts.[102]

In addition to Froehlich and Kahler, the work of several others should be mentioned briefly here, if only to provide a sense of the number of ways in which early Pauline traditions could be pulled. Calvin Roetzel has traced several less-explored images of Paul into the second century: Paul as celibate and Paul as miracle-worker.[103] Margaret Y. MacDonald has compared the relationship between Paul and women as it is constructed in the Pastoral Epistles and in the *Acts of Paul and Thecla*.[104] On this count, she emphasizes that "it is important not to view development in Pauline Christianity as monolithic."[105] MacDonald's work builds on the influential book on the same subject by Dennis R. MacDonald, *The Legend and the Apostle: The Battle for Paul in Story and Canon* (1983). Dennis MacDonald emphasized, as had Penny, that images of the Apostle were often being constructed in reaction to and against other Pauline images. Disputes over the "real" Paul found in 2 Peter, Irenaeus, Tertullian, and the *Gospel of Philip* (cf. Chapter 1) certainly suggest that his texts and legacy were contested entities from all sides of the competitive second-century Christian world.

Writing in the midst of the narrative turn from Pauline Captivity to Pauline Fragmentation, MacDonald posited sociological tension between two particular trajectories of the Pauline tradition: one represented by the Pastoral Epistles and the other by the *Acts of Paul*.[106] MacDonald argued that the narratives that eventually made up the *Acts of Paul* (written 150–190 C.E.) had a lengthy oral prehistory.[107] The presbyter of Tertullian's *De baptismo* 17 was more of a chronicler than an author, and the stories that he preserved followed the traditional folkloric patterns identified by Axel Olrik.[108] These stories about Paul, Thecla, and other women involved in their ministry were prized and preserved in south-central Asia Minor among Christian women who found liberation in them.[109] They display "a sensitivity to the concerns of women that is extremely rare in early Christian writings" and functioned as a *hieros logos* among groups of once or still marginalized Christian women.[110] These stories were the "old wives' tales" (1 Tim 4.7; cf. 2 Tim 3.6) to which the author of the Pastoral Epistles responded: "Let a woman learn in silence with full submission. Now I do not permit a woman to teach or to have authority over a man; but she is to be silent . . . she will be saved through childbearing" (1 Tim 2.11–12, 15). The Pastor's knowledge of the legends accounts for the numerous narrative and onomastic similarities between the *Acts of Paul* and the Pastoral Epistles.[111]

MacDonald saw in the *Acts of Paul* an apocalyptic, world-denying strain that more closely resembles the "historical" Paul than do the Pastoral Epistles, which is one reason that both of the former evidence a greater role for women in early Christian ministry than do the latter.[112] While the *Acts of Paul* and the Pastorals both lay claim to the Pauline tradition, MacDonald concluded:

> we are obligated to decide which of the interpretations of Paul we shall prefer . . . although the New Testament does not contain the *Acts of Paul*, it does contain two competing images of Paul to which we must respond: the Paul of the genuine epistles and the Paul of the Pastorals. . . . I choose the Paul of the genuine epistles.[113]

Here we have competing early Christian images of the Apostle. MacDonald's ideological preference is clear. He sees his work as both historical and ethical. By undergirding his preference for the Paul of the *Acts of Paul*, however, with an archaizing appeal to "the Paul of the genuine epistles," one does wonder which came first: MacDonald's predilection for a particular image of Paul or his supposedly neutral and scientific decision about the authorship of the Pauline epistles?[114]

While many contemporary interpreters might find MacDonald's fondness for the *Acts of Paul* commendable, numerous studies have shown that his historical reconstruction of the text and its relation to the Pastorals cannot bear up under scrutiny.[115] Many now recognize the deep ambiguity toward women in the *Acts of Paul and Thecla*. In its final form, at least, it still has a patriarchal edge.[116] Regardless of the details of MacDonald's case—and I do think that he has over-argued it—Tertullian's *De baptismo* is an indication that MacDonald rightly conceives of the Pauline traditions in the second century as diverse and often competing. He recognizes that what was at stake was claiming "the Apostle" for one's own side. To do this required narrative and interpretive strategies that shaped earlier pieces of the Pauline tradition into suitable images of Paul.

MacDonald highlighted what was at stake for gender relations in the construction of Pauline images. Elaine Pagels has drawn attention, on the other hand, to the theological competition over Paul in the second century. Weaving together texts from Nag Hammadi with evidence from the early Church Fathers, Pagels (*The Gnostic Paul*, 1975) argues that two divergent readings of Paul developed in the second century: one that read Paul *anti-gnostically* (e.g., Irenaeus), while the other read him *gnostically* (e.g., the Valentinians, in particular).[117] "Gnostic" exegesis of Paul forced a response from his "anti-Gnostic" readers. Perhaps it was the "Gnostic" reading of Paul that engendered the "anti-Gnostic" reading in the first place.

Pagels's study has been maligned both for its fanciful Valentinian readings of Paul (many of which actually do not appear in the primary sources to which she refers) and for its lack of nuance in distinguishing between Valentinian schools.[118] History-telling, however, requires imagination. The historian, out of necessity, must fill in large gaps between small shreds of evidence. Pagels has helped us envision what *a* consistent Valentinian reading of Paul *might* look like. She has also highlighted, as Rensberger would do shortly after her, the responsiveness of different Christian groups to each others' readings of Paul. The Valentinians took up Paul's texts, recognized that they could be read one way (dealing with Jews and Gentiles), and chose to read them in another (as referring to *psychics* and *pneumatics*). The pre-Gnostic Paul became the Gnostic Paul, who then had to become the anti-Gnostic Paul. But which of these readings of Paul was "right"? Pagels concluded, correctly:

> Each of these opposing images of Paul (and each of the hermeneutical systems they imply) to some extent distorts the reading of the texts. To read Paul either way—as hypergnostic or hyperorthodox— is to read unhistorically, attempting to interpret the apostle's theology in terms of categories formulated in second-century debate.[119]

Several aspects of her conclusion are pertinent here. First, like Barrett before her and Lindemann, de Boer, and others after, Pagels saw "images of Paul" at stake in the wrestling over Pauline texts. Second, she adequately recognized that to interpret the past is always to "distort." The role of the reader/observer always enters into the hermeneutical task, despite the attendant rhetoric over "true" and "real" readings. Pagels, then, was more thoroughly in line with some of the key shifts in twentieth-century historiography than was MacDonald. Third, her measure of comparison was not ultimately with the "historical" Paul, a reconstructed figure of the nineteenth and twentieth century, but with Pauline texts of the first century. How were particular Pauline texts received and read? Theoretically and methodologically, Pagels has pointed in the right direction.

Social-Scientific Approaches to the Image of Paul

Within the widening stream of studies on early Pauline images, several have attempted to ground the discussion in social-scientific theories. Anthony Blasi's *Making Charisma: The Social Construction of Paul's Public Image* (1991) draws on Weberian concepts of charisma to describe how Paul went from being a person to a persona after his death.[120] Blasi goes beyond Weber, however, by arguing that charisma is not just a quality that inheres within certain individuals, but is also socially projected:

> We are social beings with our language, imagery, and expectations. We transform public persons so that they become items of our vocabulary, figments of our collective imagination, and fulfillments of our societal needs. Charisma comes from us as much as it is projected by the personages.[121]

For an individual persona to endure through time, it must be "constructed anew" in successive generations, always resulting in a change to the public image of the individual.[122] The initial, remarkable impression that an individual makes on others will not attain beyond the first generation unless it is updated for new situations and needs.[123] At the same time, a "charisma cannot represent a total break with what went before it; it appears to need to stand in some organic relationship with past beliefs and practices."[124]

Blasi, assuming a seven-letter "actual" Paul, charts the developing charisma of Paul in Acts and the "disputed" Pauline Epistles in the New Testament, touching briefly as well on *1 Clement*, Polycarp, 2 Peter, the *Acts of Paul*, and Marcion. He argues that Pauline charismas can be charted along two axes (relationship to tradition and communal orientation to the world), providing four different "Pauls":

1. Paul as Founder (Acts): Invoking Tradition/Outward Orientation;
2. Paul as Legitimator (Pseudo-Paulines): Invoking Tradition/Inward Orientation;

3. Paul as Martyred Innovator (*Acts of Paul*): Breaking Tradition/Outward Orientation;
4. Paul as Criterion for a New Canon (Marcion): Breaking Tradition/ Inward Orientation.[125]

There is much to quibble with here, from the lack of nuance in his rigid categories, to his comparisons with the wooden, seven-letter "actual" Paul, to the placement of particular texts in individual slots. On the other hand, Blasi should be commended for bringing theoretical tools to the discussion of Paul's early legacy and for describing the construction of Pauline images within the context of social forces and needs. And like Pagels and de Boer, he holds a balanced position, where the "backward" and "forward" dialectic of tradition (to use the language of de Boer) is at work in each of these developing strains.

Bruce Malina and Jerome Neyrey (*Portraits of Paul: An Archaeology of Ancient Personality*, 1996) discuss constructions of Paul through the lens of "modal or typical personality."[126] By exploring encomium, forensic defense speeches, and physiognomy, Malina and Neyrey argue that Paul himself, the author of Acts, and the author of the *Acts of Paul* produced portrayals of the Apostle that were set within the framework of socially negotiated expectations for ancient personality. They show how "first-century Mediterranean persons were strongly group-embedded, collectivist persons . . . they were 'socially' minded, as opposed to 'psychologically' minded."[127] 1 Corinthians 4.7 serves as a theme for their inquiry: "What do you have that you did not receive? But if you did receive it, then why do you boast as if you did not?"[128] Malina and Neyrey argue, correctly, that even the texts of the so-called real Paul (Gal 1–2; Phil. 3.2–11; and 2 Cor. 11.21–12.10) are socially conscious self-constructions. While self-constructions, they are still constructions.[129] The encomiastic elements of these passages highlight "everything a person has received from others or that has befallen a person, features that lay beyond the control of the individual."[130] Lists of Pauline accomplishments display concern for "the group's well-being, integrity, solidarity, and health."[131] The argument is strained for Galatians 1–2, where the rhetoric seems to work in the opposite direction, but from a methodological standpoint their exploration of "undisputed" Pauline texts together with Acts and the *Acts of Paul* when discussing images of Paul is evenhanded and compelling.

Numerous interpreters in addition to Malina and Neyrey have taken up physiognomic studies of the *Acts of Paul* 3.2, wherein Paul is described as "a man small in stature, bald, bow-legged, well-built, uni-browed, hook-nosed, full of grace, sometimes appearing as a man, at other times having the face of an angel."[132] Malina and Neyrey, in particular, build on Robert M. Grant's brief study, which concluded that Paul is described here as the ideal general.[133] Grant's conclusion seems to accord well with some of the anti-imperial themes in the *Martyrdom of Paul*, but what he did not explain is why these particular physical descriptions were ascribed to generals in Archilochus and Herodes in the first place. Malina and Neyrey show how the individual elements of the list, when combined, signal the presence of an "ideal male," someone who is "masculine, fearless, pious, virtuous, truthful, benevolent, but above all, fit for public life."[134] These qualities, then, are secondarily applied to ideal generals in antiquity (including Paul, the great spiritual general).

Status quaestionis

Wide agreement now exists on the propriety of talking about diverse, textually mediated images of Paul in the late-first and early-second centuries. Some have teased out a particular image as it developed in a cluster of texts.[135] Gregory Sterling (2008), for instance, argues that Ephesians and Acts, both written toward the end of the first century, provide similar images of Paul through different approaches (Ephesians = *vita contemplativa*; Acts = *vita activa*): he was the primary apostolic figure upon whose revelatory experiences the church was built.[136]

Others, like Daniel Marguerat, chart various Pauline images across numerous early Pauline texts, showing how multifaceted methodologies for discerning Pauline influence are required. Marguerat (2008) proposes a three-pronged typology: "documentaire" (the collection and use of Paul's letters); "biographique" (the use of Pauline narratives); and "doctoral" (the use of Pauline theology in later Pauline pseudepigrapha).[137] Each of these elements must be taken into account in order to provide a comprehensive description of Paul's early influence, which was "complexe et multiforme."[138] The letters of the historical Paul (seven) are only a (small) part of the ongoing Pauline influence at the end of the first century. Acts, then, can justifiably be called "Pauline," despite its apparent lack of interest in Pauline letters. The author of Acts, like the author of the *Acts of Paul*, was privy to communally traditioned stories about the Apostle.[139] Many of these stories were birthed in the very *ekklesiai* that Paul had founded. Marguerat, for instance, places the Pauline miracle stories in Acts alongside

Paul's own cryptic statements about "signs and wonders" within his ministry (cf. 2 Cor 12.12; 1 Thess 1.5; Rom 15.18–19; Gal 3.5). The portrayal of Paul as a healer, then, was not invented by Luke (contra Vielhauer).[140] Community traditions about the Apostle share many similarities with the "undisputed" Pauline letters, but also exhibit differences in focus and characterization. This is an important aspect of Marguerat's work, because it sets the stage for his more general comments about reception, which he claims always exhibits "cohérence *et* déplacement, continuité *et* rupture face à l'origine."[141] Using three images, Paul as Apostle, Paul as Sufferer, and Paul as Teacher, Marguerat explores lines of continuity between Acts, the canonical "pseudo-Paulines," and the "undisputed" Pauline letters. While Acts and the Pastoral Epistles portray two divergent images of Paul's relationship to the wider apostolic tradition, Marguerat finds that both are ultimately rooted in Paul's own letters. Paul falls in the line of apostolic witnesses in Acts and 1 Corinthians 15.5–11. He is independent from them in the Pastorals and Galatians 1–2. The image of Paul in his own letters, then, is neither "lisse" nor "uniforme."[142] Furthermore, the intertextual overlay of Jesus and Paul in Luke's Gospel and Acts provides a biographical witness to Paul's theology of suffering with Christ. This narrative identification is clearer in the *Martyrdom of Paul*, where Christ predicts Paul's death as a new co-crucifixion with the Lord.[143]

The two most recent monographs on Paul's early legacy also emphasize Pauline images and the developing persona of the Apostle. James Aageson's *Paul, the Pastoral Epistles, and the Early Church* (2008), like the work of Marguerat, offers a methodologically multi-pronged account of the reception of Paul in the second century. In a brisk and quasi-popular fashion, Aageson examines the reception of Pauline images, theology, and letters from the Deutero-Paulines to Origin through the lens of one important piece of the Pauline tradition itself: the Pastoral Epistles. Proto-orthodox texts are given pride of place over "heretical" receptions of Paul. Aageson pursues a "bifocal approach" by positioning the Pastorals "on a continuum that reflects and passes on the earlier Pauline tradition, as well as shapes and directs the subsequent Pauline legacy."[144] He sees in the Pastoral Epistles an early canonizing of the Pauline tradition. Paul is already being connected with the apostolic tradition at large. He assumes seven "authentic" letters of Paul and apparently places the Pastoral Epistles (likely written by two different authors, given the differences in theological pattern between 2 Tim and 1 Tim/Titus) toward the end of the first century, although no firm dates are ever given.

Aageson grounds his work theoretically in Blasi's aforementioned distinction between "person" and "personage," describing the particular Pauline "charismas" that developed in the course of his sacralization in the second century. This is the book's major methodological strength. Aageson states:

> If the image of Paul and the theology of his letters were thoroughly interwoven in the early church, as they undoubtedly were, the adaptation of Paul and his words by the early Christians was more than an issue of simple textual reinterpretation. It was also a matter of an evolving Pauline image merging with the developing concerns of the day, where the words and ideas of the apostle came to bear on the circumstances and conflicts of the church.[145]

In the Pastorals, Paul is heresy fighter and caretaker of the household of God.[146] He is inwardly focused on the *ekklesia*. For Luke, Paul is public speaker and missionary.[147] His mission is to the world.[148] For Ignatius, Paul is the great martyr. For *1 Clement*, Paul is the writer to a factious Corinthian congregation. He is the wise teacher for Polycarp. In the *Acts of Paul and Thecla*, which Aageson views, like Dennis MacDonald, as a set of traditions in direct competition with the Pastoral Epistles, Paul is the challenger of traditional society.[149] Each of these authors/texts presents an image of Paul that not only "conforms to [the author's] needs and circumstances," but also reflects the "social situation" in which the author shapes the Pauline tradition.[150]

Aageson stands in the line of more recent interpreters who see the Pauline legacy in the second century as "complex, diverse, and uneven."[151] He believes that the "Pauline legacy displays a regional stamp, as different traditions, issues, and movements developed in different parts of the church," and that we can talk about "lines of development" (à la James Robinson and Helmut Koester's *Trajectories Through Early Christianity*) in addition to "identifiable tensions between competing elements" (à la Pagels above).[152]

A more recent account of the reception of Paul in the first two centuries of the Church may also be the most robust English-language project on this topic since Rensberger's dissertation. Richard Pervo's *The Making of Paul: Constructions of the Apostle in Early Christianity* (2010) tracks the influence of the "historical" Paul from his early pseudepigraphers (the six "disputed" Pauline epistles in the New Testament) to Irenaeus. Unlike

Aageson, who is particularly attuned to the influence of the Paulinism found in the Pastoral Epistles and consequently leaves out whole swaths of early Christian literature (Marcion, "Gnostics," etc.), Pervo's account is both comprehensive and a self-conscious attempt to update Lindemann, Dassmann, and Rensberger in light of the decentering of justification by faith in modern Pauline Studies (cf. the "New Perspective" on Paul and its critique of the "Lutheran" Paul).[153]

The results of *The Making of Paul* are mixed. From a methodological (and theoretical) standpoint, there are strengths. Its title hints at the historiographical shifts of the twentieth century described above. Paul in the second century was a figure created by his historical interpreters. Like Aageson and Marguerat, Pervo works with the use of Pauline letters in the early Church as well as with developing images of the Apostle, though sometimes these two features are not tightly intertwined in his textual analyses. His constructive goal is to show how "[t]he portraits of Paul that emerge in early (and subsequent) Christianity . . . seek to address the problems of those churches in their own times."[154] He correctly claims that "Letters contain or, more often, presume a story," following de Boer and others who find that developing Pauline images and narratives lie behind later pseudepigraphic Pauline texts.[155] This conclusion, however, should also be extended to texts that Pervo thinks are "genuine" Pauline letters, as Malina and Neyrey have argued. Presumed narrative worlds exist in all communication. The "Paul" of Galatians and Corinthians, for instance, presumes/creates a narrative about his relationship with these congregations as he implores them to stay aligned with his gospel.

Like Penny and Aageson, Pervo sees the Pauline tradition in this period as a mixture of "trajectories and common threads," displaying a range of "variety and creativity."[156] The Pauline tradition did not develop in a straight line but exhibited tensions as various groups interpreted Paul for their own needs.[157] Each of these "Pauls" retained some elements of "Paul's own thought" while neglecting others.[158] The "historical" Paul was "a master of polyphony," providing the kind of diverse material with which his early interpreters could work.[159] The basic rudiments of the proto-orthodox and canonical Paul that Irenaeus would defend toward the end of the second century (Paul as Martyr, Apostle to the World, and Teacher of Righteousness) was already in place by the end of the first century as can be seen in *1 Clement* 5.5–7, which Pervo dates to the 90s C.E., before the Pauline letter collection, before Acts, and before the Pastoral Epistles.[160] He finds "some basis" for these images in the ministry of the historical

Paul, though the entire snapshot develops in the Church's production of the Pauline canon (Acts + 13 letters).[161] All of these aspects of Pervo's work are to be heartily commended.

The book, however, has a deep historiographical flaw—at least if we take seriously Pervo's insistence on not privileging the Paul of the Reformation and later German Protestant scholarship as the "real" Paul.[162] The rather confident narrative that Pervo draws from the "real" Paul (of the seven "undisputed" letters) through the "pseudepigraphic Pauline letters" to the Apostolic Fathers, for instance, presupposes many of the decisions on Pauline authorship that originated among German scholarship of the nineteenth century. But these decisions were often (if not always) made out of theological preference (cf. Chapter 2).[163] He never connects the fact that the "real" Paul discourse of the nineteenth century is part and parcel with the Lutheran reading of Paul. This is regrettable. The standard historical narrative that moves from Galatians (Paul) to Ephesians and Acts (pseudo-Paul) to the Pastoral Epistles (really pseudo-Paul) is ultimately built upon Luther being read through Baur. Until we begin to treat the seven-letter "genuine" Paul versus the "pseudepigraphical" Paul discourse as part of a much later era of Pauline reception, yet still driven by the same kinds of ideological concerns as were already present in the second century (i.e., Who was the "real" Paul?), the early history of the Pauline tradition will continue to be narrated in our own image. Pervo pushes the "disputed" Pauline letters into the "Pauline School(s)," which he places in Ephesus (quite confidently), and lumps the phenomenon of Pauline pseudepigraphy under the singular title "Deutero-Paulinism."[164] His picture of the Pauline School(s) becomes even more speculative when he claims that they "were more like rival faculties of theology located within the same metropolis, inimical to each other, but reading one another's literary output."[165]

The methodological problem not only makes for an ideological narrative of Pauline democracy devolved into institutionalism, but also produces some waffling back and forth about whether or not the "real" Paul is of relevance for discussions of "Paul in the second century." Pervo tips his hat quite early on to the "dual impact of Christian ecumenism and postmodernism" on our ability to know the "real" Paul and suggests that "the only real Paul is the dead Paul" (i.e., Paul had to die before his true impact could be felt). But his continued practice of comparing the historical or "real" Paul with the "Paul" of Acts as well as of the letters authored in his name betrays his initial sentiment.[166]

Pervo's book also pulls in both directions on the second-century "Pauline Captivity" narrative. He delivers a very cautious statement about the silence of Justin, Hegesippus, and Papias: "Those who neither name Paul nor appropriate aspects of his theology *may* have had negative views of the apostle, but this thesis cannot be assumed."[167] He finds, in the end, no anti-Paulinism in these authors. In fact, the *Epistle to Diognetus*, Justin, and Tatian each betray, at times, a rather deep Pauline (theological) influence. Pervo's conclusion about Irenaeus's Paulinism is also on target:

> Like every other interpreter of Paul, he brought to his construction presuppositions and goals that differed from those of the historical Paul, but these do not automatically amount to a betrayal. Irenaeus should be ranked among the creative and insightful exponents of Pauline theology. He provided stimulus for the subsequent Greek interpretation of Paul. Irenaeus did not "rescue" Paul from the clutches of the heretics, but he did show one path to a positive theological use of the apostle's words.[168]

Pervo also claims, however, that "the major exponents of Pauline theology belonged to the heretical side of the eventual division. The proto-orthodox stressed his moral message."[169] He raises the Household Codes in Colossians and Ephesians as an early witness to proto-orthodox ethical interest in Paul, failing to mention the cosmic theology of each of these letters, which, of course, Pervo thinks are proto-orthodox receptions of Paul. Furthermore, this characterization of the proto-orthodox use of Paul does not square with his conclusion that Ignatius was "the first creative Pauline theologian to find an eventual home in proto-orthodox circles." Paul was his inspiration and model.[170] Nor does it square with his attempt to show Pauline *theological* influence on *Diognetus* and Justin; unless by "major exponents of Pauline theology" Pervo means those whom he believes prefigured Reformation theology, which, if so, signifies that he has not moved that far from Harnack and Campenhausen.

Toward a New Historiography of Pauline Studies

Recent scholarship on "Paul in the second century" has produced, then, several trends. First, a broad consensus has emerged that views Paul's legacy in the second century as a complex set of fragmented trajectories. From the beginning, the Pauline tradition developed neither in a singular and straight line, nor in a hot-potato style handoff from one group to another (contra the Pauline Captivity narrative), but along a variety of trajectories among a variety of communities, each of which incorporated Paul's letters, as well as stories about the Apostle, into their prior network of theological authorities.

As a result of twentieth-century shifts in historiographical theory, a second important trend involves the increasing interest in textually mediated Pauline images. Where data are sufficient, how has an individual author imagined the Apostle? In what narrative about the Apostle has a given image become situated? Moreover, how are these Pauline images related to the interpretation of Pauline texts? Most important, what ideology does each image preserve?

Third, the notion of "Paulinism," once defined as the adherence to a singular Pauline *theologoumenon*—justification by faith alone—has broadened.[171] As several have reminded us, including Marguerat and Pervo, the "historical" Paul was at times complex and inconsistent. He provided no singular image for successive generations. There is good reason, then, to decenter questions about the "real" Paul and about "who got Paul right" in the second century, at least from a historical perspective. Such questions are normally loaded with too much ideological freight. Scholars are increasingly marking out elements of both continuity and change from the earliest layer of the Pauline tradition across *all* subsequent receptions of the Apostle.

Despite these positive developments, a theoretical tension still lies at the heart of the study of the *Wirkungsgeschichte* of Paul. On the one hand, a number of scholars seem to have taken seriously the presentist and poststructuralist historiographical shifts of the twentieth century. Judith Lieu, for instance, has recently adopted the language of the "Remembered Paul," who in the course of second-century theological struggle became a "'hero from the past' through whom different patterns of practice, of communal structure, of confrontation with contemporary society and ideas, of authority, could be explored and negotiated."[172] Appeals to the "real" Paul are, in her mind, misguided.[173] The same sentiment can be found Glenn Snyder's recent book on the *Acts of Paul*:

> To reread the *Acts of Paul and Thekla* as hagiography—that is, to reread the text as a hagiographic work *about and for Paul*—would open a range of interpretive possibilities. Among other things, it would encourage us to continue studying the literary portrayal of characters in the text, understanding them as less historical and

more symbolic of the author's contemporary circumstances and/or interests. . . . The *Acts of Paul and Thekla* is a story that tells us at least as much about its author's ideology and practices as it does about Paul and Thekla. Using not only Thekla but also Paul "to think with," the text portrays an enkratic Christian life that is founded on a love for Paul.[174]

Other studies, while signaling these theoretical shifts, pull back and seek to preserve some appeal to the "real" Paul in their discussions of his legacy. Work on the second-century reception of Paul, then, is prejudged by the nineteenth- and twentieth-century reception of Paul. Two recent edited volumes exhibit this historiographical tension. Joseph R. Dodson, in his introductory essay to *Paul and the Second Century*, states that "it is wise to discern whether or not these blended portrayals of Paul *faithfully* reflect his New Testament legacy."[175] Dodson approvingly cites Kenneth Berding's assertion that in the various second-century portrayals of Paul there is a "historical move away from Paul's understanding of unmerited grace toward a theology where human action eventually takes a more central role."[176] Buried in a footnote, unfortunately, on the same page is the confession that "this assumes that there is an understanding of what a faithful reflection of Paul actually looks like."[177] Kenneth Liljeström's introductory essay to *The Early Reception of Paul* falls within the same lines. While the authors in the volume assume, unanimously, the distinction between seven "authentic" letters of Paul and six pseudo-Pauline letters, Liljeström begins the volume with a warning:

The vantage point from which we approach the objects of our study, temporally and culturally distant as they are, may easily be a treacherous one. The perpetual risk of allowing the present to project itself on the past is especially acute when the subject of our study occupies an especially prominent place in our time. This risk is especially acute when one intends to study the earliest reception of Paul from a qualitative viewpoint. It is highly dubious to posit any single aspect of Paul's theology from a merely nominal or even fallacious one. To be sure, this should not lead the scholar to an exaggerated relativism but rather to an acknowledgment of the role that hermeneutics play in any process of interpretation, to say nothing of interpreting texts potentially carrying religious or existential importance to the interpreter.[178]

What is now needed in Pauline Studies is a full-scale shift away from the continued impulse to deploy positivist and Rankean historiography in the service of the "real" Paul of the *Hauptbriefe*. A more hermeneutically sophisticated approach is required if we are to take seriously the epistemological challenges of the twentieth century. And in the attempt to historicize discourses on the "real" Paul, exposing their social and ideological situatedness, we must come to the place where we can concede that an "Archimedean point" for reconstructing the "real" Paul may never be possible, particularly if this language is intended to freeze the Apostle in time and treat him as an ahistorical figure incapable of change.

By invoking "memory," Lieu, in particular, has indicated the proper direction for a new historiography of Pauline Studies. As mentioned in Chapter 1, Historical Jesus scholarship has already moved down this road, as have the humanities in general. Markus Bockmuehl has now published widely on Simon Peter as a figure of early Christian memory.[179] In the following chapter, I will describe the disciplinary shift in the late-twentieth century toward "memory" as a foundational historiographical category and I will argue that theories of social remembering can provide a particularly useful set of tools for conceiving of and talking about the reception of Paul—tools that are sufficiently sensitive to the twentieth-century critique of Ranke and that ultimately expose the vacuity of language about the "real" Paul, whether ancient (cf. 2 Peter, Irenaeus, Tertullian, and the *Gospel of Philip*) or modern (cf. Baur et al.). At the same time, when tethered to a proper understanding of the force of tradition, social memory theory can help us to understand the important lineages that exist between past and present. Memory, in this way, is never a pure "invention," contra Hobsbawm. The following chapter, then, provides a framework for narrating the emergence of Paul as a traditioned figure of memory among various Christian communities in the second century.

4

Remembering Paul: Pauline Memory
Traditions into the Second Century

Nothing called tradition is a simple thing.
EDWARD SHILS, Tradition

The concept of memory is close to the concept of tradition
and associated with it.
JOSEF PIEPER, Tradition[1]

THE PAULINE "TRADITION." In modern scholarship, as we saw in Chapters 1 and 2, such language has often been used to distinguish between the "real," "actual," or "historical" Paul and the later encrustations and interpretive frameworks that were added to and now surround such a pristine corpus as the "undisputed" Pauline letters. Such accretions to and changes of the "real" Paul are often characterized as producing a "domesticated," "ecclesiasticized," and/or "canonized" Paul. Sometimes this language is offered with a twinge of disappointment. In the historiography of the nineteenth century, and in its continued influence over much of Pauline Studies even into our day, tradition was the enemy of the science of history. No one doubts that Paul had become a traditioned figure by the second century. Three generations, whose length and boundaries differ in each social context, are needed to establish a *traditum*.[2] Much like the portrayals of Jesus in the canonical Gospels, communally traditioned narratives of Paul's relevance for the early Church were becoming solidified in a variety of Christian locales throughout the Mediterranean world some 40 to 60 years after his death. Dissimilar to Jesus, however, there was a broad swath of Pauline letters that influenced these developing Pauline traditions.

The more interesting question, historiographically, is whether or not an uninterpreted "real" Paul can ever appear in view, beyond the framework of tradition. Though ever-present in the language of the scholarly literature on first- and second-century Paulinism, "tradition" has been used more often as an ideological weapon than as a carefully deployed concept. The historiographical challenges to positivist and scientific conceptions of history in the second half of the twentieth century have yet to sensitize Pauline Studies fully to the inescapability of tradition and to the ever-present social mechanisms through which things become the objects of knowledge. "Common sense" is always prefigured by interpretive frameworks that conserve, rhetorically, ideology. In arguing for a *"total* conception of ideology," Karl Mannheim, like Foucault after him (cf. Chapter 1 and later discussion in this chapter), pointed out that all individual perceptions of the world (of "reality"), of smaller communities within it, and of members inside the community (including ourselves), both past and present, are shaped by human environments. None is excluded from the clutch of social forces. Epistemology must reckon with the social fact.[3]

Many historians, particularly of early Christianity, have been reticent to adopt a strict presentist approach to our knowledge of the past for fear that there would be no way of discriminating between various constructions of reality. One could point to Hayden White, for example, who ultimately conceded, in light of the claims of Holocaust deniers, that the historical imagination comprised "both the real world from which one has launched one's enquiry into the past and the world that comprises one's object of interest."[4] This chapter explores the nature, benefits, and limits of tradition and cultural memory, a related category, for contemporary historiography and begins to lay out a new theoretical and methodological program for Pauline Studies. The first part of the chapter examines the nature of tradition. It addresses the relationship between past and present in the traditioning process and argues that developing authoritative Pauline image traditions, which encoded the meaning and significance of the Apostle for various Christian communities, were the context within which wrangling over the interpretation of Pauline texts took place. The second part of the chapter explores the relationship between tradition and memory. Sustained discussions of the latter have been all but absent from accounts of the Pauline tradition in the second century, despite the utility of memory studies in Jesus scholarship and most other fields in the humanities. I am particularly interested in the social and ideological constraints of memory as they relate to the developing reputation of key historical figures. Rooted in these explorations of tradition, social memory, and image construction, the end of the chapter offers a brief narration of how Paul became "Paul" in the second century, as well as a further developed critique of positivist discourses on the "real" Paul. The discussions throughout the chapter will be, by and large, theoretical. At various spots I make suggestive comments about how these matters might affect our understanding of Pauline traditions in the second century, but a full-scale application of theories and methods will have to wait for Chapters 5 and 6, where I begin to work much of this out in an extended way for *3 Corinthians* and Irenaeus's *Adversus haereses*, two late second-century texts.

Tradition

The eighteenth- and nineteenth-century signification of tradition as something unitary, static, all-encompassing, and perpetuated by elites (cf. Chapter 2) ended up being the necessary creation of modernity itself.[5] To position itself as the bearer of progress, the Enlightenment, including its positivist and Marxist strains, eviscerated all progressive elements from its conception of tradition.[6] It also constructed a vision of authority that meant nothing more than "blind obedience."[7] The hermeneutic philosopher Hans-Georg Gadamer, in his influential critique of the Enlightenment (*Truth and Method*, 1960), argued, alternatively, that tradition is the necessary means by which all subjects in the present make sense of the past as it relates to the future: "*The prejudices of the individual, far more than his judgments, constitute the historical reality of his being.*"[8] More important, for Gadamer, the present necessarily transforms what it receives, making tradition a progressive rather than a static phenomenon. Living within a living tradition, for Gadamer, is a fundamental aspect of being human.

In what follows, I want to tease out Gadamer's basic theses on tradition in light of Edward Shils's important work on the same subject (*Tradition*, 1981), as well as the work of several more recent theorists. Shils, like Gadamer, espoused a rather totalizing conception of tradition. He identified a "tradition," or *traditum*, as "anything which is transmitted or handed down from the past to the present," notably including, for our purposes, "images of persons."[9] More recently, Delwin Brown has reminded that traditions contain not only ideas, but also include "communal symbols and stories, institutional structures, moral practices, ritual actions, aesthetic sensibilities, personal feelings, etc. . . . they are a *mélange* of these discursive and non-discursive practices, social and individual activities, spontaneous and formalized actions, analytical and affective processes."[10] Tradition, then, includes both conscious and unconscious features, though it is often characterized by its more tacit elements.[11] Even in the sciences, as Michael Polanyi has argued, *"we can know more than we can tell"* (cf. Chapter 3).[12] The theoretical roots of this "inflationary use" of tradition can already be seen in Karl Mannheim's *Ideology and Utopia* (1929), which challenged the givenness of Marxist critiques of ideology and untethered "tradition" to serve as a broadly applied heuristic for cultural analysis.[13] Like Husserl's "life-world" and Wittgenstein's "forms of life," "tradition" now functions as an "overarching concept for cultural theory."[14]

When we say that Paul had become a "traditioned" figure by the second century, we mean that certain increasingly complex traditions about the Apostle were handed down early on from one generation to the next, including the transmission of particular Pauline images. As we will see in subsequent chapters, these complex Pauline traditions, though often presented as obvious and coherent wholes, are, in fact, amalgams of smaller traditions that, when fashioned together in particular combinations at particular times, produced further unique traditions in particular social locations. As Shils states, "A tradition of belief contains constituent beliefs about many particular things."[15] Or further:

> The [religious] tradition is usually put forth by learned believers as homogenous in composition and unilinear in interpretation. These self-interpretations are however incorrect. Every major tradition is a product of the confluence of contributory traditions, not only at its origin but in the course of its history.[16]

A tradition, then, is not only a thing in itself, but is also the "chain of transmitted variants of a tradition," stretching from the present both backward and forward.[17]

The links of the chain are held together by events/processes/actions (Latin: *tradere*).[18] Gadamer understood tradition as both *Erfahrung* ("integrative process") and *Geschehen* ("event").[19] Each subject of the chain is an actor/actress in history. Tradition is the "back-and-forth movement between the claims of the past and our appropriation of it (meaning our action in the world) . . . the human mode of being historical."[20] The process is a continuous and simultaneous handing down "from" and handing down "to." It assumes three locative and temporal places. Moreover, the traditioning process is always situated in history, and thus contingent on a variety of exigencies.[21] It is a constant negotiation of "two horizons," to use the language of Gadamer—"the movement of tradition and the movement of the interpreter." Each chain of the tradition "participate[s] in the evolution of the tradition, and hence further determine[s] it [himself/herself]."[22] Thus, despite the attempts of early Christian heresiologists like Irenaeus to protect the apostolic deposit (cf. Chapter 6), traditions are subject to a variety of kinds of pressures to change over the course of time. This is how they ultimately endure through time and space.

Traditions, then, are not fixed, hegemonic entities against which progress can be positioned. Jürgen Habermas's criticism of Gadamer as a loyalist to present conditions and as unable to provide a rational basis for the criticism of tradition (and thus for emancipation) falls short for this reason. This is not the place to rehash the Gadamer-Habermas "debate" of the 1970s over the possibility of transcending the hermeneutical situation, but it should be said that Habermas consistently undersold Gadamer on this point.[23] For Gadamer, it was through the process of dialoguing with Others, who are situated in different traditions, that one comes not only to appreciate their own hermeneutical situation, but finds resources for responding to, criticizing, and altering it, if needed. Traditions confront other traditions.[24] He insisted, as did Shils, that self-identified progressives and defenders of modernity, who often see their contributions as breaking entirely new ground, free from the constraints of older traditions, are often blind to their own dependence on earlier progress and to the tradition of progressivity itself.[25] Gadamer reminded us, "the perspectives that result from the experience of historical change are always in danger of being exaggerated because they forget what persists unseen."[26] David Gross has more recently asserted that "*[w]herever* there is enculturation or socialization there is some element of tradition, and *wherever* there is a store of background information that people draw upon as tacit knowledge, some amount of tradition is present."[27] Only those who are attuned to "substantive traditionality"—which, according to Shils, is "the appreciation of the accomplishments and wisdom of the past and of the institutions especially impregnated with tradition, as well as the desirability of regarding patterns inherited from the past as valid guides"—can see and understand the lineages of the progressive tradition.[28] Shils's "substantive traditionality" is comparable to Gadamer's notion of the "historically effected consciousness" (*wirkungsgeschichtliches Bewusstsein*), which understands the human experience as helpfully marked by both finitude and historicity.[29] "Hermeneutical experience," in the end, "is concerned with *tradition*."[30]

By making tradition progressive and progress traditional, new sets of questions become relevant for understanding the early reception of Paul.

For example, Marcion might no longer be seen as an isolated and radical innovator. Rather, we should ask about how Marcion received Paul. In what kind of Pauline tradition did he stand such that Galatians could become the hermeneutical lens through which Paul should be read? Moreover, from where did this tradition develop? John Knox argued long ago that Marcion was reared on a collection of Paul's letters, interpreted without reference to the LXX.[31] Whether or not he was right, Knox offered the kind of historical reconstruction that takes the force of tradition seriously.

Traditions, though prone to progress and evolution, are resistant to *wholesale* alteration and preserve a traceable core through the traditioning process.[32] They are particularly resistant to blanket change within short periods of time.[33] This is due to their utility in the construction of meaning. Shils rightly points out that "[b]eliefs which have been known to work are generally not lightly discarded."[34] They have not been "arbitrarily accumulated."[35] Rather, they are the prejudices that provide, according to Gadamer, the "common meaning" necessary for social and cultural cohesion.[36]

Initially, only the outsider to a particular tradition can see its unique mix of continuity and change over an extended period, whereas the adherent normally conceives of himself or herself as standing within something that is ancient and unchanged. As Shils observes:

> what makes it a tradition is that what are thought to be the essential elements are recognizable by an external observer as being approximately identical at successive steps or acts of transmission and possession. . . . Conversely, tradition might undergo very great changes but its recipients might regard it as significantly unchanged. What they are experiencing is rather a sense of filiation with a lineage of prior possessors of a tradition which, in any two successive generations, changes by variations so small as not to be perceived as significant changes.[37]

Irenaeus, as we will see in Chapter 6, constructs an image of Paul that he deems "natural." He views his own reading of the Apostle as largely continuous with the Apostle himself. The heresiologist has a "sense of filiation" with his Paul, to use Shils's language. He is unaware, as an insider, that his reception of the Pauline tradition has been shaped in the century after Paul's death by a number of external social forces and that he has made his own contributions from within this developing Pauline tradition.[38]

While traditions do not die easily, some have argued that they can be invented without difficulty, particularly when perpetuated by elites to serve their own ends. Eric Hobsbawm (cf. Chapter 3), whose edited volume with Terence Ranger, *The Invention of Tradition*, has become quite influential among some theorists of tradition, describes an "invented tradition" as "a set of practices, normally governed by overtly or tacitly accepted rules and of a ritual or symbolic nature, which seek to inculcate certain values and norms of behaviour by repetition, which automatically *implies* continuity with the past."[39] They are traditions that "appear or claim" antiquity, but in the end "are often quite recent in origin and sometimes invented."[40] Hobsbawm, offering a typically Marxist view, understands tradition as inflexible, whereas custom exhibits a "combination of flexibility in substance and formal adherence to precedent."[41] As an example, Hobsbawm calls what a judge does "custom," while "the wig, robe and other formal paraphernalia and ritualized practices" are invented traditions—an attempt to give a sense of historical invariance to the process of adjudicating legal disputes.[42] They are the authorizing elements of the judicial custom. Because for Hobsbawm traditions do not flex and change over space and time, invented traditions are the necessary products of rapid and robust social change. They replace older traditions that are no longer useful and/or sustainable.[43]

Hobsbawm's thesis has been criticized in a number of ways. First, the rhetoric of the "invention of tradition" only retains power when one posits a particularly inflexible notion of tradition, as have Hobsbawm and numerous others since the Enlightenment.[44] In this view, tradition does not evolve to fit the needs of new social realities. Hobsbawm seems to have confused the rhetoric of staunch loyalists within a tradition with how tradition actually works.[45] Second, Hobsbawm glosses over the fact that traditions are complexes of prior traditions, which, like tributaries, provide the momentum for subsequent streams of tradition. To take an example of this from early Christianity, even the Ebionites' maliciously "invented" story (according to Epiphanius, *Pan.* 30.16.8–9) about Paul's Gentile birth in Tarsus, subsequent conversion to Judaism to win the love of the high priest's daughter, and eventual preaching against Judaism because of love unattained, is constrained by the early and broad tradition of Paul as Apostle to (and really "among") the Gentiles. The past is always present in varying degrees.

Hobsbawm was right, however, in claiming that for those inside a particular tradition, including the progressive, the tradition has normative power.[46] Replication across time is not enough to identify something as a tradition. The replication must occur for the sole reason that it was previously enacted.[47] This normative power often takes the form of belief. Invoking Augustine of Hippo's "Unless you believe, you shall not understand," Michael Polanyi noted that all traditions of knowledge, including the scientific, are grounded in trust:

> It appears then that traditionalism, which requires us to believe
> before we know, and in order that we may know, is based on a
> deeper insight into the nature of knowledge and of communication
> of knowledge than is a scientific rationalism that would permit us
> to believe only explicit statements based on tangible data and de-
> rived from these by a formal inference, open to repeated testing.[48]

This tacit belief in the tradition's authority holds both for its origin as well as its transmission over time and space and is what distinguishes it from a custom, which normally lacks the full-scale "prescriptive power" of a tradition.[49]

Delwin Brown has recently argued that traditions act within a canonical structure. They survive within a process of constant "reconstruction of a canonical inheritance."[50] Like most canons, traditions are "internally diverse" and "never fully coherent," and thus are susceptible to change from within.[51] *Endogenous* changes to the tradition, to use Shils's classifications, are the result of some perceived inconsistency within the tradition itself, provoking improvements through rationalization, correction, and imagination.[52] While these kinds of changes "proceed from a state of satisfaction with much of the tradition," they are changes, nonetheless.[53] These changes include "minor reformulations, clarifying definitions, differentiating categories or grouping them under more general categories, resolving apparent contradictions, and restoring the unity of the body of belief, which had been diminished by critical analysis."[54] Like culture itself, as James Clifford has shown, tradition is not a coherent whole, but possesses various pieces of different ages and origins in "continuous negotiation."[55]

Endogenous changes are often provoked by and are hard to distinguish from *exogenous* changes, the latter of which result from traditions being locatively and temporally transposed and encountering other traditions with which they need to become synthesized.[56] The circumstances that once made the traditions useful no longer obtain, so they are updated.[57] This updating allows them to survive as living traditions through time and space.

Regardless of the cause, changes in tradition normally find as their resources aspects of the tradition itself, particularly elements of the tradition that were not as useful in the past. A newly positioned piece of the tradition, as Brown argues, causes the once privileged elements to be "reinterpreted through the lens provided by the new center."[58] The variegated canon is rearranged in order to provide greater "efficacy" for its new social and cultural environment.[59] The morphology of traditions, then, normally proceeds as an act of "recovery and reconfiguration of elements internal to the tradition."[60] There is, in the end, little difference between tradition and interpretation, as Michael Fishbane has shown, for example, with respect to the Hebrew Bible:

> each solidification of the *traditum* was the canon in process of its formation; and each stage of canon-formation was a new achievement in *Gemeindebildung*, in the formation of an integrated book-centered culture. The inner-biblical dynamic of *traditum-traditio* is thus culturally constitutive and regenerative in the most profound sense.[61]

As I will argue at the end of this chapter and in Chapters 5 and 6, understanding the canonical nature of tradition is particularly helpful for describing the reception of Paul in early Christianity. The highly diverse nature of what I have called the "earliest layer of the Pauline tradition" (cf. Chapter 1) provided the kind of variegated canon whereby second-century communities could easily shift forward and backward the necessary pieces from within the tradition to provide updated readings of the Apostle that were more amenable to new cultural locations.

Finally, for our purposes, apparently competing traditions often display family-like characteristics, despite the claims of their adherents.[62] This is mainly due to the fluid boundaries and composite nature of traditions. Smaller elements of larger, competing traditions sometimes exhibit remarkably consistent features, regularly leading to "embarrassment when such an overlapping is discovered."[63] Rather than give ground, however, the devoted often dig in their heels and deny these similarities.[64] In Chapter 6 we will explore, for instance, Irenaeus's frustration that his opponents also laid claim to 1 Corinthians 15.50. Since this text had made its way into the Pauline tradition of both the Valentinians and the proto-orthodox, skirmishes over the Pauline tradition had to operate at the level of interpretation, requiring reorganization of canonical Pauline materials to suit the preferred reading.

Pauline Traditions in the Second Century: Image, Text, and Tradition

Inasmuch as Paul was a traditioned figure in the second century, the various developing complex Pauline *tradita* that we find in a variety of early Christian texts comprised multiple kinds of smaller *tradita*. As we saw in Chapter 3, a majority of scholars now hold that the various Pauline traditions of the second century must be discerned by measuring both their use of Pauline letters as well as their invocations of developing Pauline images. While in broad agreement with this trend, I want to push it a bit further here by arguing that images of the Apostle are *foundational* in the use and interpretation of Pauline letters.[65]

Our earliest evidence suggests that we cannot separate the tasks of trying to understand the variety of developing authoritative images of Paul (remember, "images of persons," according to Shils, are traditions) and of exploring the use of his letters in the Christian literature of the second century. A number of texts at the end of the first and the beginning of the second centuries already commingle honorific titles for Paul with references to his letters:

1 Clement 47.1–4[66]

Ἀναλάβετε <u>τὴν ἐπιστολὴν τοῦ μακαρίου Παύλου τοῦ ἀποστόλου</u>. [2] τί πρῶτον ὑμῖν ἐν ἀρχῇ τοῦ εὐαγγελίου <u>ἔγραψεν</u>; [3] ἐπ' ἀληθείας πνευματικῶς <u>ἐπέστειλεν ὑμῖν</u> περὶ ἑαυτοῦ τε καὶ Κηφᾶ τε καὶ Ἀπολλώ, διὰ τὸ καὶ τότε προσκλίσεις ὑμᾶς πεποιῆσθαι. [4] ἀλλ' ἡ πρόσκλισις ἐκείνη ἥττονα ἁμαρτίαν ὑμῖν προσήνεγκεν· προσεκλίθητε γὰρ <u>ἀποστόλοις μεμαρτυρημένοις καὶ ἀνδρὶ δεδοκιμασμένῳ παρ' αὐτοῖς</u>.

Take up *the epistle of the blessed Apostle Paul.* [2] What did he *write* to you at first, at the beginning of his proclamation of the gospel? [3] Truly, he *sent you a letter* in the Spirit about himself and Cephas and Apollos, because even then you were divided into parties. [4] But that partisanship brought you to a lesser sin, for you were inclined toward *approved apostles and a man recognized by them.*

2 Peter 3.15b–16[67]

καθὼς καὶ <u>ὁ ἀγαπητὸς ἡμῶν ἀδελφὸς Παῦλος</u> κατὰ τὴν δοθεῖσαν αὐτῷ σοφίαν <u>ἔγραψεν ὑμῖν</u>, [16] ὡς καὶ <u>ἐν πάσαις ἐπιστολαῖς</u> λαλῶν ἐν αὐταῖς περὶ τούτων, ἐν αἷς ἐστιν δυσνόητά τινα, ἃ οἱ ἀμαθεῖς καὶ ἀστήρικτοι στρεβλοῦσιν ὡς καὶ τὰς λοιπὰς γραφὰς πρὸς τὴν ἰδίαν αὐτῶν ἀπώλειαν.

Just as our *beloved brother Paul wrote to you* according to the wisdom given to him, [16] speaking about these things as he also does *in all his letters*, in which certain things are hard to understand, which the ignorant and unstable distort to their own destruction, as they also do with the rest of the Scriptures.

Ignatius, *Ephesians* 12.2[68]

πάροδός ἐστε τῶν εἰς θεὸν ἀναιρουμένων, <u>Παύλου συμμύσται, τοῦ ἡγιασμένου, τοῦ μεμαρτυρημένου, ἀξιομακαρίστου</u>, οὗ γένοιτό μοι ὑπὸ τὰ ἴχνη εὑρεθῆναι, ὅταν θεοῦ ἐπιτύχω, ὃς <u>ἐν πάσῃ ἐπιστολῇ</u> μνημονεύει ὑμῶν ἐν Χριστῷ Ἰησοῦ.

You are a passageway for those condemned to death for God; *you are fellow initiates of Paul, the sanctified, the martyred, the most worthy of blessing*, at whose feet may I be found when I attain to God, who *in every letter* mentions you in Christ Jesus.

Polycarp, *Philippians* 3.2[69]

οὔτε γὰρ ἐγὼ οὔτε ἄλλος ὅμοιος ἐμοὶ δύναται κατακολουθῆσαι τῇ σοφίᾳ <u>τοῦ μακαρίου καὶ ἐνδόξου Παύλου</u>, ὃς γενόμενος ἐν ὑμῖν κατὰ πρόσωπον τῶν τότε ἀνθρώπων ἐδίδαξεν ἀκριβῶς καὶ βεβαίως τὸν περὶ ἀληθείας λόγον, ὃς καὶ ἀπὼν <u>ὑμῖν ἔγραψεν ἐπιστολάς</u>, εἰς ἃς ἐὰν ἐγκύπτητε, δυνηθήσεσθε οἰκοδομεῖσθαι εἰς τὴν δοθεῖσαν ὑμῖν πίστιν.

For neither I, nor another like me, can approach the wisdom of the *blessed and glorious Paul*. When he was among you, he carefully and reliably taught the word of truth before those alive at that time. When he was absent, *he also wrote you letters*, in which, if you look closely, you will be able to be built up in the faith given to you.

Polycarp, *Philippians* 11.2–3

Qui autem non potest se in his gubernare, quomodo alii pronuntiat hoc? Si quis non se abstinuerit ab avaritia, ab idolatria coinquinabitur et *tamquam inter gentes iudicabitur, qui ignorant iudicium domini. Aut nescimus, quia sancti mundum iudicabunt? <u>Sicut Paulus docet</u>.* ³ *Ego autem nihil tale sensi in vobis vel audivi, in quibus laboravit <u>beatus Paulus</u>, qui estis <u>in principio epistulae eius</u>. De vobis etenim gloriatur in omnibus ecclesiis, quae deum solae tunc cognoverant; nos autem nondum cognoveramus.*

For if one cannot govern himself in such things, how will he proclaim this to others? If one does not abstain from covetousness, he will be defiled by idolatry and will be judged among the peoples who are ignorant of the judgment of the Lord. Or do we not recognize that "the saints will judge the world?," *as Paul teaches.* ³ But I have neither sensed nor heard of any such thing in your midsts, among whom *the blessed Paul* labored and who are mentioned in *the beginning of his Epistle.* For he magnified you among all the churches, which alone knew God at that time; but we had not yet known Him.

Behind each of these honorific titles—"our beloved brother," "the blessed [Apostle]," "the most worthy of blessing," "the approved Apostle," "the sanctified," "the martyred," and "the glorious"—stands a mental image of the Apostle, an image that is part of a particular narrative about the Apostle's significance for early Christian history and identity formation. These titles, like all of those outlined in Table 1.1 in Chapter 1, are descriptive handles for a larger set of traditions, mostly oral, about the Apostle that were developing into the second century. These traditions, however, were apparently already in contact and being combined with Pauline letters, as each of the texts above suggests. Even the hagiographical *Acts of Paul and Thecla,* which provides the earliest detailed attempt to provide a fixed image of Paul (*Acts Paul* 3.2), also appears to be in dialogue with earlier Pauline texts (e.g., the Pastoral Epistles and 1 Corinthians).[70]

The data suggest that the reception of the Pauline Epistles was closely bound up with developing, authoritative images of Paul. For scholars of early Pauline traditions, both aspects—text and image—must be held together and brought into dialogue in order to provide a thick description of Paul as a persona in the second century.[71] We must do for the second century what Margaret M. Mitchell has done for the fourth in *The Heavenly Trumpet* (2002), her exploration of John Chrysostom's reception of Paul.[72] Through an analysis of John's homily *De laudibus sancti Pauli apostoli*, in combination with his homilies on the Pauline letters, Mitchell convincingly argues that "[e]xegesis of Paul, as Chrysostom practices it, is exegesis of the author as well as of the words enshrined in his writings."[73] What she finds in Chrysostom's hermeneutics can be said of all of Paul's interpreters:

> each reader of Paul's letters, to the present day, formulates a por-
> trait of the soul of the author of these letters in the act of his or her
> reading, even if not so artistically or imagistically as John. Quite
> often the bricolage from which these mental images have been
> formed is unexamined, and represents not only the biblical sources
> in a range of configurations, but also contacts with Christian art,
> hymnody, popular traditions and media forms.[74]

Already in the second century, innovative readings of authoritative Pauline literature worked to undergird particular preconceived constructions
of Paul, but given their early collection and dissemination, the Pauline
epistles were also an important vehicle for carrying "the Apostle" into
Christendom.[75] The processes of image construction and textual reception and interpretation were and continue to be synthetically related. We
cannot divorce, then, the earliest written Pauline traditions from the earliest orally traditioned images of the Apostle. Nowhere is this clearer than
at the end of Book Four of Irenaeus's *Adversus haereses* (4.41.4; *ll.* 86–89,
91–93), where he laments that "heretics . . . have altogether misunderstood what Paul has spoken" (*et quaecumque ab haerticis in totum non intel-
legentibus quae a Paulo dicta sunt alias acceperunt interpretations explanare*).
In his assessment there were egregious misinterpretations of Pauline
texts that had gone unchallenged and that needed refutation. In this same
passage, Irenaeus promises to "expound the Apostle" (*Apostolum expo-
nere*) and to show that, in fact, Paul was a "preacher of the truth and that
he taught all things agreeable to the preaching of the truth" (*Apostolum
vero praedicatorem esse veritatis et omnia consonantia veritatis praeconio do-
cuisse*). The image of Paul as "preacher of the truth" was at stake in the
interpretation of his texts. More important, providing an image (*Bild*) of
the apostle that fit within the bounds of the received "rule of faith" (cf.
Chapter 6) played a critical part in preserving proto-orthodox tradition/
culture (*Bildung*).[76] It appears, at least in the case of Irenaeus (and argu-
ably others), that defending an image of the Apostle that fit within perceived theological norms was primary, while textual interpretation then
served to achieve this desired end. This latter suggestion pushes beyond

the current consensus by ordering the various comingled elements (theology, image, text) of a given Pauline tradition in an attempt to place the wrangling over particular Pauline texts within the larger contexts in which the hermeneutical task occurs.

Each of the developing Pauline traditions of the second century, whether simple or complex, whether based in oral or textual materials or both, ultimately provides a particular image of Paul. These images of the Apostle were the primary means through which his significance was transmitted in early Christian cognition. In what follows, I survey both modern as well as ancient theoretical works on orality, textuality, and mental imagery as a way of informing this claim about the priority of images in the early contestation over Paul's legacy.

In exploring the production of traditioned images, it will be helpful first to dissolve any particularly dichotomous understanding of the relationship between (written) texts and (oral) tradition.[77] Despite the rhetoric of fundamentalist communities, which view texts as inspired points within the flux of human tradition, texts reflect wider communal traditions at the time of their writing (in addition to the innovative contributions of their authors).[78] They function as materially fixed communicative expressions of tradition, or what Gadamer, citing Johann Gustav Droysen, called "enduringly fixed expressions of life."[79] Yet even as objectified and "fixed expressions" of a community's traditions, authoritative texts can only continue to communicate through a *"hermeneutical conversation"* with later interpreters, whose own subjectivity/historicity is the decisive factor in understanding.[80] This fusion of horizons between text and interpreter, to use Gadamer's language, results in the destruction of rigid boundaries between text and tradition, between something fixed and something in flux. The text is part of the tradition and, as experience teaches us, is open to updated readings within the community. Concerning the Judeo-Christian tradition, in particular, Michael Fishbane reminds us:

> Indeed, it is a commonplace in traditional Judaism and Christianity (Roman and Orthodox) to affirm that revelation is comprehensible only through the authoritative tradition of interpretation. To the historically minded, this transformation—and it occurred early—is nothing short of remarkable. The protest of the Reformers, *"sola scriptura,"* stands out in sharp relief against this background.[81]

On the other side of the false dichotomy, oral traditions are often informed by written texts. The introduction of written texts into oral/aural communities does not cause oral traditions to cease. "Rather," according to Jan Vansina, the prominent ethnographer of Africa, "people incorporated them [texts] into their traditions just as some literate persons incorporated traditions into writings."[82] Brian Stock, the social historian of late antiquity, has argued that "textual communities" arise when populations formerly dominated by oral/aural media begin to grapple with the increasing presence of authoritative, written texts in their midst.[83] Whereas previous studies on this issue posited a linear, evolutionary development from orality (fixed, resistant to change) to literacy (progressive, open to change), Stock argues that even in largely literate societies there exists a symbiosis between writing and orality, linked together by a more broadly conceived vision of "textuality."[84] He understands a text to be the culture constructed through the objectivizing of a community's self-reflection. Oral performances, then, including the public reading of written texts, contribute to the construction of textual communities through aural reception. Stock conceives of culture as "more like a game, in which a central place is reserved for interactive play" and demonstrates the interdependence between oral and written texts in the construction of medieval culture, which has often been mischaracterized as a predominantly oral culture.[85] The introduction of written traditions into a society is a technological advance, but Stock insists that "societies that lack writing nonetheless record, remember, and transmit verbal texts whose grip on norms, values, and traditions is no less tenacious than that of writing."[86]

Mary Carruthers has argued similarly. For Carruthers, the premodern West was a "memorial culture." While books (*written* texts) were important, "in a memorial culture, a 'book' is only one way among several to remember a 'text,' to provision and cue one's memory with 'dicta et facta memorabilia.'"[87] She reminds that the Latin *textus* comes from a verb meaning "to weave" and argues that "it is in the institutionalizing of a story through *memoria* that textualizing occurs."[88] The *mode* of memorializing, whether written or oral or some combination of the two, matters little. Carruthers's project is concerned with the *praxes* whereby memory was trained in the Middle Ages. She is particularly interested in deconstructing the oft-held position that the rise in literacy meant a concomitant decline in the importance of memory within a given culture. Rather, she shows how written texts (books) work to train memory in a variety of ways.[89]

Carruthers's work is indebted to classical theories of memory and cognition. Beginning as early as Plato and Aristotle, but extending through the Roman era, the mind and its perceptions were viewed as a wax tablet upon which the senses impressed images:

> Imagine . . . that our minds contain a block of wax, which in this or that individual may be larger or smaller, and composed of wax that is comparatively pure or muddy, and harder in some, softer in others, and sometimes of just the right consistency. . . . Let us call it the gift of the Muses' mother, Memory, and say that whenever we wish to remember something we see or hear or conceive in our own minds, we hold this wax under the perceptions or ideas and imprint them on it as we might stamp the impression of a seal ring. Whatever is so imprinted we remember and know so long as the image remains; whatever is rubbed out or has not succeeded in leaving an impression we have forgotten and do not know. (Plato, *Theaetetus* 191D–E)

> The change that occurs marks [the body] in a sort of imprint, as it were, of the sense-image, *as people do who seal things with signet-rings*. (Aristotle, *De memoria et reminiscentia* 450a)

> [M]emory . . . is in a manner the twin sister of written speech [*litteratura*] and is completely similar to it [*perisimilis*], [though] in a dissimilar medium. For just as script consists of marks indicating letters and of the material on which those marks are imprinted, so the structure of memory, like a wax tablet, employs places [*loci*] and in these gathers together [*collocate*] images like letters. (Cicero, *Partitiones oratoriae* 26)[90]

The inscription of sensory stimuli upon the mind brings writing and memory quite close together from a conceptual standpoint.[91] For these Greek and Roman authors, the senses impress a "mental picture" on the brain.[92] Vision, being the keenest of the senses, causes all sensory impressions, whether visual, aural, or otherwise, to be stamped as images on the mind for later recall.[93] In Cicero's *De oratore* 2.86–87, Antonius declares that the mind best retains oral/aural experiences or other impressions about the world if "also conveyed to our minds by the mediation of the eyes." In the event that visual impressions are not also available, the mind registers these stimuli for recall by transforming them into "a sort of image or figure" (*quasi et imago et figura*).[94] In the Greek tradition these mental pictures were called *phantasmata* ("representations") or *eikones* ("images").[95]

These mental images could be produced by any number of media, whether literary or graphic, oral/aural or visual. Through the rhetorical exercise of *ekphrasis*, orators and authors could make distant persons or works of art present to their audiences through vibrant description.[96] Verbal iconography, or literary portraiture, was sometimes considered a more enduring medium than that of sculpture or painting (cf. Isocrates, *Evag.* 73–75; and Lucian, *Imag.* 23).[97] This classical tradition was carried forward into late antiquity through works like Eusebius's *Vita Constantini*, which, as Margaret Mitchell reminds us, begins with an argument against the durability of the visual arts (1.3) and then positions itself as a "portrait through words, to the memory of this man so loved of God," in "imitation of the art of mortal painting" (1.10).[98] Carruthers notes that, in the High Middle Ages, Richard de Fournival's *Li Bestiaire d'amours* (a picture-book of animals) combined both *painture* (painted images for the eye) and *parole* (written descriptions for the ear) for the aid of memory.[99] In its introduction Richard writes, "And it is the same thing with hearing a text, for when one hears a story read aloud, listening to the events one sees them in the present."[100] Both reading, whether silent or aloud, and hearing, whether one's own voice or the voice of another, produce *painture* in the mind's eye. Carruthers concludes:

> *Painture*, as Richard de Fournival's comments make clear, is a function of words themselves, not only of what we think of as painting. Through ekphrasis and related figures, one could paint with words alone, making imaginary pictures that never seem to have been realized in what we would consider to be a pictorial way. . . . The author is a painter, not only in that the letters he composes with have shapes themselves, but in that his words paint pictures in the minds of his readers.[101]

These classical, late ancient, and medieval conceptions of mental imagery have been supported in recent years by modern theorists and practitioners of cognitive psychology, who assert the foundational nature of mental imagery in human cognition.[102] Stephen Kosslyn, William Thompson, and Giorgio Ganis, for instance, have shown how neuroscientific data support the theory that the cortex has particular areas "that are spe-cifically designed to depict patterns. These areas are *topographically orga-nized*—they preserve (roughly) the geometric structure of the retina."[103] Against their critics, who make the careless assumption that mental images are nothing but mental photographs, Kosslyn, Thompson, and Ganis, clarify:

> a mental image occurs when a representation of the type created during the initial phases of perception is present but the stimulus is not actually being perceived; such representations preserve the perceptible properties of the stimulus and ultimately give rise to the subjective experience of perception.[104]

They understand mental images to be "quasi-pictorial," though this in no way diminishes their ability to "depict information," particularly spatial information.[105] Carruthers, while using the misleading phrase "mental pictures" on occasion in *The Book of Memory*, clarifies that mental images are only "*quasi*-pictures, "representations" in the sense that the informa-tion stored causes a change in the brain that encodes (the modern word) or molds (the ancient one) it in a certain way and in a particular "place" in the brain."[106] As Cicero carefully claimed, sensory stimuli impressed "a *sort* of image or figure" (quasi *et imago et figura*) upon the mind. This sig-nifying aspect of mental images seems to have been recognized as early as Aristotle, who described mental images as having two features. They are both objects in their own right as well as representative images:

> Once more, if what is retained is like the original in the fashion of an impression or a copy, why is the perception of this very thing the memory of some other thing and not of it itself? It is the modifica-tion of consciousness which one engaged in remembering has present to the mind, and it is this that he perceives. How then can one remember what is not present to one? One might as well see or hear what is not present. But perhaps there is a way in which this can occur and it does really come about? That is so, for, as the animal depicted on the panel is both animal and representation, and, while remaining one self-identical thing, is yet both of these, though in aspect of existence the two are not the same, and we can regard it both as animal and as copy, so too the image in us must be considered as being both an object of direct consciousness in itself

and relatively to something else an image, so far as it represents something else it is a copy and a souvenir. (*De memoria et reminiscentia* 450b)[107]

Like language, images function as signs and are not identical with the objects they represent.[108] Aristotle seems concerned not to commit the "intentional fallacy" that modern anti-depictivists try to pin on defenders of mental imagery. Mental images, like all images, are frustrating to those who desire immediacy. From a Foucauldian perspective, W. J. T. Mitchell, the noted art historian and critical theorist, has argued:

> instead of providing a transparent window on the world, images are now regarded as the sort of sign that presents a deceptive appearance of naturalness and transparence concealing an opaque, distorting, arbitrary mechanism of representation, a process of ideological mystification.[109]

Mental imagery, then, like language, should be understood "functionally rather than mimetically," according to Carruthers.[110] It does not offer an unmediated picture of reality, but encodes complex information into schemes whereby simpler pictograms and/or ideograms function as a synecdoche or metonymy for a particular subject, object or scene. W. J. T. Mitchell uses the example of a man.[111] Various kinds of signs can represent "man." On the one end of the spectrum (say, on the farthest left) is a photograph of a man (best case scenario) or at least a detailed drawing and/or painting of a man. Further to the right is a common stick-figure drawing of a man (a pictogram). Further to the right still is the common ideogram for a man (♂). In this case, the phallus represents what it means to be "man." We have a synecdoche. On the farthest right-hand side of the spectrum is the word "man." What each of these means as a signifier and as an image of a man is socially negotiated and is part of a complex web of cultural "practices, disputes, and agreements," or, what we might call in the context of this chapter, "tradition."[112] Proponents of mental imagery do not deny that language is inherent to this signification process. "In fact, each point in the depiction may be accompanied by a set of propositions that codes additional information. . . . Rather, the issue is whether *only* propositional representations are used in imagery, or whether depictive representations also play a role."[113] Each mode of internal representation works with the others to "make different sorts of information explicit and accessible."[114]

Mental images, then, give us simple ways of characterizing complex realities. While neither the amount of data stored in a mental image nor the total storage capacity of the brain can be measured, experience teaches us that vast quantities of unprocessed information cannot stay in the mind for very long. "Perception," then, "is a process of information reduction whereby a welter of sensations is reduced into a simpler and more organized form."[115] Mental images, as signs, are "composed from highly processed perceptual encodings" and thus are efficient in storing information.[116] They allow us to envision quickly and remember long term. They are the biological and cognitive *ars memoria*. So while mental images do obscure, they are necessary for the meaningful representation of the outside world.

In the second century, written and oral Pauline texts and traditions participated in and contributed to the process of constructing and transmitting in memory mental images of the Apostle. Pauline letters were just beginning to circulate widely as collections of texts and enter into the larger Pauline tradition. Ostensibly from Paul himself, they gained authoritative status quickly. But oral forms of the Pauline tradition carried just as much weight as, if not more weight than, these Pauline (written) texts. This was certainly the case for the author of the Acts of the Apostles in the late-first century, as well as the authors of the various second-century *Acts of Paul* traditions. Some of the "oral histories" of members of the Apostle's communities were still alive in this period as well.[117] Like Papias's preference for "a living and abiding voice" (ζώσης φωνῆς καὶ μενούσης) over "books" (τῶν βιβλίων) in the construction of his *Expositions of the Sayings of the Lord* (frag. 3; Eus., *Hist. eccl.* 3.39), authoritative, orally transmitted stories about the Apostle continued into the second century.

Each of the images retained in and produced by these early Pauline traditions encoded information about his *particular* significance for the early Church. They were synecdochic or metonymic in nature, providing handles for grasping his primary importance in the midst of a sea of Pauline material. They were the more complex sets of tradition that stood behind the epithets for Paul outlined earlier and in Chapter 1. These textually mediated images of the Apostle (in the broad sense of textuality) should not be viewed as completely transparent portrayals of Paul, but rather as traditions that helped provide meaning and stability for early Christian communities as they negotiated their early histories and cultures—histories and cultures that were intimately bound up in communal memories of the apostolic age. In subsequent Christian centuries, full-blown "Lives" of the saints would provide this same sort of identity-forming and discipline-regulating function as "verbal icons" and "imaginal histories."[118] Already bearing an interpretive framework, these images frustrate access to the "real" Paul, if by that rhetoric one means a Paul denuded of tradition. On the other hand, as traditions, images of persons always retain some significant degree of continuity with the past, so that the rhetoric of "invention" also loses some of its power. Finally, from a methodological standpoint, given the explicitly polemical contestations over Paul's legacy found in 2 Peter, Irenaeus, Marcion, the *Gospel of Philip*, and Tertullian, scholars of early Christianity need to give considerably more attention to the way that controlling images of the Apostle shape and then are shaped by the interpretation of Pauline texts, with which they connected.

Memory, Tradition, and Society

At the same time that Paul was taking on specific images within individual communities, he was also becoming "*the* Apostle," in a broader sense, not just for Marcion, the Valentinians, and the authors of classical Gnostic texts like the *Reality of the Rulers*, but for proto-orthodox thinkers like Irenaeus and Tertullian (cf. Chapter 1). Peter, James, John, Thomas, and others were certainly apostles in the early Christian tradition. Paul, however, was "*the* Apostle." The second half of this chapter connects this hagiographical elevation of Paul above the other apostles with the specific, meaningful images of the Apostle that appear in the various Christian groups by situating our discussion of the development of Pauline image traditions within the purview of memory as a historiographical category. In discussing the nature of tradition as well as the image-producing power of written and oral texts, we have begun to approach what is really at stake in the construction of Pauline images: early Christian memory-making. Memory, in all of its social and cultural complexities, provides the necessary framework for tying together these developments into a plausible narrative of the rise of "Paul" among the fragmented trajectories of tradition that carried him to any number of Christian communities and for describing how particular synecdochic Pauline image traditions are constructed within the bounds of perceived authoritative norms.

As a normative version of the past, memory is, conceptually, quite close to tradition.[119] The contemporary focus on memory and its construction among psychologists, sociologists, historians, anthropologists, artists, philosophers, and theologians suggests that, like tradition, it has become, according to Patrick Hutton, "the quintessential interdisciplinary interest" in the social sciences and humanities.[120] Anyone who is interested in "habit, recollection, commemoration, image-making, representation, and tradition" must consider the role of memory.[121] Of particular interest for this study are the social forces that shape individual memories. As members of Christian communities, those who wrote about Paul and/or interpreted his texts for their communities were aided by the formative memories/traditions of those same communities.[122]

All memory is socially conditioned. This was the great contribution of Maurice Halbwachs, the father of collective memory studies.[123] Halbwachs, writing in the first half of the twentieth century, was part of the burgeoning field of the sociology of knowledge. As a realm of inquiry, Karl Mannheim described the sociology of knowledge as the attempt "to analyze the relationship between knowledge and existence."[124] It has "set itself the task of solving the problem of the social conditioning of knowledge by boldly recognizing these relations and drawing them into the horizon of science itself and using them as checks on the conclusions of our research."[125] Mannheim observed that "it is not men in general who think, or even isolated individuals who do the thinking, but men in certain groups who have developed a particular style of thought in an endless series of responses to certain typical situations characterizing their common position."[126] Humans are not just *homo sapiens* but, more fundamentally, to use the language of Peter Berger and Thomas Luckmann, *"homo socius."*[127]

As we have noted already on several occasions, Mannheim advocated a strict sociology of knowledge—a *"total* conception of ideology"—void of moralizing inferences (contra Marx).[128] As with traditions in general, ideological change occurs when one's social realities shift either horizontally (physical location) and/or vertically (social class).[129] The "symbolic universes" that once legitimized reality no longer obtain in light of these new conditions.[130] Clean breaks from prior networks, however, are rare, creating situations in which multiple versions of reality exist, symbolic universes clash, and changes to regnant constructions of reality must occur to ensure meaningful survival. For Mannheim, this tension between ideology (conservatism) and utopia (progressivism) increases as societies begin the democratization process, resulting in the presence of diverse interpretive traditions of reality as groups compete for power.[131] This last observation helps explain, for example, the diversity of the Pauline traditions in the second century. As long as Christians were an assorted, yet growing, web of minority cultures in the Ancient Mediterranean world, the Apostle was sure to be a contested figure. There was not yet an institutionalized mechanism whereby his image could be controlled. These developing, shifting, and sometimes intermingling Pauline image traditions were products of communal memories of the Apostle. By "communal memories," I mean, like Halbwachs, that individual memories (as evidenced in texts) are formed within the frames of social interaction. Communities, technically, do not remember. Individuals do. Yet the content of individual memory is collectively shaped.[132] It is born in the midst of mnemonic communities and reinforced through story-telling, communally sanctioned commemorative events and rituals, material reminders (*lieux de mémoire*), and other elements of the *ars memoria*.[133] Neophytes, whether through birth or conversion, must go through the socialization process of learning the community's authoritative myths and traditions.[134] As such, memory has identity- and culture-forming power.

Largely influenced by Kant and Durkheim, Halbwachs held that memory is organized by the frames (or conditions) of time and space (plus language), and that these frames are not just matters of individual cognition, but are socially constructed.[135] Time and space are the pegs for hanging our communally shaped mental stuff:

> But if a truth is to be settled in the memory of a group it needs to be presented in the concrete form of an event, of a personality, or of a locality. A purely abstract truth is not a recollection; a recollection refers us to the past. An abstract truth, in contrast, has no hold on the succession of events; it is of the order of a wish or of an aspiration.[136]

Memories, like traditions and ideologies, their conceptual cousins, are reflections of social realities, which are almost always in flux.[137] The alteration of social frameworks, then, results in the alteration of memory. For Halbwachs, this meant that memory tells us more about our present social situation than it does about what really happened in the past.[138]

Autobiographical memory and historical memory are little different in this regard.[139] The ways in which we remember and narrate our own past, come to understand our individual identity, and construct mental representations of our lives, are shaped, to a large degree, by social forces.[140] The first and most influential of these mnemonic communities into which our own story is mapped is the family.[141] In most cases the autobiographical and episodic memories of our childhood are formed in the context of this primary social relationship and without continued rein- forcement from the outside (through looking at pictures and home movies, listening to others tell stories about us, etc.), memories of our own past will fade.[142] A variety of studies have shown that, over time, indi- vidual recollections of events become increasingly schematized to reflect elements of the past that were significant for all group members. These are the elements that are continually voiced and shared within the community.[143]

The same is true for the memory of events that we have not experi- enced and of people with whom we have had no contact. In his *La Topog- raphie légendaire des évangiles en terre sainte* (1941), Halbwachs analyzed the account of Jesus' life found in the writings of the fourth-century Pilgrim of Bordeaux, concluding that the Pilgrim's memory of the life of Jesus had been largely shaped by his visit to Jerusalem in 333 C.E.—a Jerusalem that now, in time and space, distorted the Jewish environment in which Jesus had actually lived and breathed.[144] The canonical Gospel accounts, as products of Christian communities many decades after the actual life of Jesus, had already begun this process of telling the life of Jesus with an eye to their present situation.[145] The Gospels, birthed in anonymous commu- nities, contain only a portion of the memories of Jesus' original follow- ers—those relevant to community needs at the end of the first century—and were shaped in their final form to give the impression that Jesus' ministry was nothing but an inevitable march to the cross.[146] Only the original fol- lowers of Jesus could have correctly identified the places where Jesus had performed miracles. By the time that the Gospels had been written, Jeru- salem had been destroyed (in 70 C.E.) and his original followers were long gone. When the Pilgrim from Bordeaux visited the Holy Land some 250 years later, Jerusalem had been completely reconfigured as *Aelia Capito- lina*. For Halbwachs, this change in space meant a change in memory.[147] Thus the life of Jesus as portrayed in the Pilgrim's account exhibits mul- tiple layers of community memory from various periods, stretching from the trace elements of the earliest memories of Jesus' original followers in the first century C.E., through the memories of Jesus communities crystal- lized in written gospels at the end of the first century, and ultimately fil- tered through fourth-century visits to Jerusalem.[148]

Histories, as accounts of the past, are necessarily selective, dependent on the present needs and biases of their authors and their communities (cf. Chapter 3). As a corollary, whatever is not selected for narration is consigned to oblivion.[149] All historical memory, then, like imagery, is a distortion of the past—it obscures what actually happened in favor of what is useful for present circumstances.[150] At what point, though, can memories be labeled "false"? The phenomenon of false memory, particularly as it relates to personal autobiography, has been well documented among a variety of disciplines (cognitive psychology, psychiatry, neurobiology, and sociology).[151] "Distortion," however, like "invention," operates on a sliding scale and is thus hard to define. Not even eyewitnesses provide the sort of information about "what exactly happened in the past" that historians would like.[152] Frederic Bartlett, in the same era as Halbwachs, showed that cognitive *schemas*, or mental representations of "x" or "y" based on previous experience, shape the way that we encounter the world. Much like pictograms or ideograms, *schemas* represent what has been essential to a particular set of situations in the past and prejudice what we see in any new event that appears similar.[153] Inasmuch as all memory contains elements of distortion, then, all memory is false memory. Yet to position "invention," "distortion," and "false memory" against "real," "historical," and "true" conceptions of the past covers over the complexity of the issue, as I am afraid has become the case in both ancient and modern contestations over Paul.

Halbwachs in no way disparaged the social frames of memory or the present interests that undergird preservations of the past. Since Halbwachs, however, a prominent strain of memory studies, known alternatively as the "politics of memory" or "presentist" and/or "strong constructionist" theories of memory, has brought attention to the way that elites and majority cultures program memory for the sake of their own power.[154] The constant wrangling over US history textbooks, for example, and how much attention should be given to Christopher Columbus and George Washington, on the one hand, and the Native Americans and Crispus Attucks, on the other, highlights this connection between the training of memory and politics.[155] A more immediately relevant example is the strong institutional bias since at least the era of F. C. Baur, described in Chapter 1, toward the Paul of the *Hauptbriefe* over numerous other Pauline texts of the first century for envisioning the "real" Paul. We have argued that the foundation of this bias is ideological preference for one religious culture over another. The "politics of memory" is concerned with "rhetoric about the past mobilized for political purposes."[156] Presentist theories of memory rely heavily on Halbwachs in combination with the social and economic theories of Marx, the denigration of tradition found in Nietzsche, and the concern for power relations expressed by Foucault.[157] While all communities (from the family to the nation-state) are mnemonic in constitution and provide narrations of the past for the sake of identity and cohesion, only a few members of the community control the commemorative mechanisms necessary for perpetuating a given set of narratives.[158] In an attempt to expose the hegemony of official memory, historians like Hobsbawm and Ranger comb the material record for evidence "from below," or for the "hidden transcripts" of the past.[159] They write, in line with many of the concerns of the *Annalistes,* "social history as an alternative to political history; the history of collective mentalities (attitudes toward everyday life) to that of the history of ideas (elite culture); women's history to that of men's history; non-Western history to that of European history; global history to that of national history."[160]

The French historiographer Pierre Nora has been the most prolific chronicler of how *lieux de mémoire,* or "sites of memory," such as textbooks, monuments, museums, archives, and holidays, function to shape communal and national memories.[161] Nora has shown how French identity and memory in the nineteenth and early-twentieth centuries were created out of the memorial practices of the winners of the democratic Revolution. Various attempts to "record" the history of the Revolution were in effect attempts to shape a normative memory of the past.[162] Nora sees a deep chasm between *milieux de mémoire* ("real environments of memory") and *lieux de mémoire.* The existence of the latter point to a "collapse of memory" and a shift toward "history" in the face of radical social breaks with the past (e.g., the industrial and democratic revolutions in France bringing an end to peasant culture).[163] "Real memory" has been replaced by "nothing more in fact than sifted and sorted historical traces." Elite memory is a mere "representation of the past," subject to the commemorative practices of those in charge of helping us remember such things.[164]

In cultures that no longer have a living connection to the past through tradition and memory, *lieux de mémoire,* according to Nora, function as handles for the appreciation of the past in the midst of change. They are the "archive" of modern memory—material sites that prod us to remember the past.[165] They are intended to "stop time, to block the work of forgetting, to establish a state of things."[166] As *lieux de mémoire,* monuments, museums, archives, and the like must serve symbolic and functional roles.[167] They encode formative narratives about the past as a means of socializing group members into the community's identity-forming myth.[168] They are sites where communities go to hear the sacred story, to remember their origins, and to reinforce mental images of the past.[169] For our purposes, we should emphasize that normative texts, as sacred and canonical indicators of authoritative tradition, function as *lieux de mémoire*. They are material sites to which a community returns over and over again to hear one particular version of the past, rather than another. Margaret Mitchell has helpfully reminded us on this score that Chrysostom referred to the Pauline epistles as "pillars" or "monuments":

> And not only did you [Paul] publicly disgrace him [Peter], but also, as though on a monument, you engraved the battle in words, and made the memory of it immortal, so that not only those who were present then, but also all the inhabitants of the world might learn through the epistle what happened (*hom. in Gal. 2:11*).[170]

As I will argue later, continued appeals to certain Pauline texts over others in second-century Christian writers were part of a larger phenomenon of remembering the Apostle *rightly*. Without the ability to read written Pauline texts, most Christians were at the mercy of the literate elite to provide for them a meaningful and coherent portrayal of the Apostle.

The politics of memory, however, tells only half of the memory story. Much like Gadamer and Shils for tradition, and Mannheim for ideology, several have now offered more holistic approaches to memory.[171] Jan and Aleida Assmann, for example, have argued extensively that the enculturation/traditioning process, in which the concept to memory should be placed, has an "enabling aspect, which does not just mutilate people and knock them into shape, . . . but which also (and we would like to say above all) develops forms of life, opens up possibilities in which the individual can invest and fulfill himself."[172] They describe this as the "bonding" element of memory, which involves "cultural efforts that aim to establish connections and consolidate togetherness." Memory is not just "collective," but "connective."[173] Cultural memory connects us synchronically and diachronically with those on whom we are dependent through meaningful symbol systems, thereby connecting the past with the present, with an eye to the future.[174] Contra Nietzsche, socially and culturally determined identities allow us to be "rescued from oblivion."[175]

Jan and Aleida Assmann also emphasize that culture, as part of the traditioning process, is constantly evolving and possesses at any given time strata of memory from various periods of time.[176] Memory is a storehouse of the past, just as much as it is a reflection of the present. It has two horizons—the ancient text (broadly understood) and its modern reception. Linking the two is a history of interpretive tradition. There is thus no *perfect* homeostatic congruity between tradition/memory and society.[177] Like Rome, which is "an inextricable tangle of old and new, of obstructed and buried material, of detritus that has been reused or rejected," memory, as Jan Assmann reminds, is a complex web of cultural negotiations between the past and the present, between social realities that are constantly in flux.[178] He likens it to Derrida's "archive" and to the more broadly construed understanding of tradition found in Gadamer. Both Jan and Aleida Assmann describe cultural memory as the interaction between "canon" and "archive."[179] Cultural forms of memory store not only elitist visions of the world (canon), but also "the age-old, out-of-the-way, and discarded," as well as "the noninstrumentalizable, heretical, subversive, and disowned" (archive).[180] Material resistance from below (marginalized texts and archaeological finds) eventually challenges the dominant memory of the past.[181] Others have also criticized the "politics of memory" theorists on this very point. Patrick Hutton has argued that the crux of social memory is the constant tension between "repetition" ("the presence of the past") and "recollection" ("present efforts to evoke the past").[182] Strong presentist theories of memory often downplay or ignore memory's lineages with the past:

> Commemoration acknowledged the limits of memory's restorative powers. But in appreciating the reality of a discrete past, what one wanted to remember were connections with it. The present might be different from the past, yet remained linked to it through developmental lines of continuity.[183]

The sociologist Barry Schwartz further reminds: "Given the constraints of a recorded history, the past cannot be literally constructed; it can only be selectively exploited."[184]

Reputation and Image: Excursus on Abraham Lincoln in American Collective Memory

Schwartz's work on Abraham Lincoln's place in American memory offers a particularly compelling example of how images of an authoritative individual develop among various (and often competing) communities. These images of Lincoln reflect not only the present concerns of a given community, but also exhibit strong elements of continuity with the past. Images of persons, it should be remembered, are traditions.[185] They are the visual and mental images that typify and encode information about individuals from the past whose reputation has been viewed worthy of remembrance by particular groups. In wrestling with the nature of social and cultural memory and the data on Paul in the second century, particularly where polemical contestations over Paul's legacy are apparent and it is clear that his literary legacy is wrapped up in the larger attempts to preserve particular images of the Apostle, I have found that Schwartz's work provides a heuristic tool for thinking about Paul's own early reputational entrepreneurs.

Schwartz's first book on Lincoln, *Abraham Lincoln and the Forge of National Memory*, charts the developing images of the sixteenth president among various social and political groups from the date of his assassination in 1865 to the dedication of the Lincoln Memorial in 1922.[186] Some 50 years after his death, Lincoln's persona was invoked by immigrants, progressives, capitalists, socialists, African Americans, white Southerners, and women's rights advocates. He went from being one of the most controversial figures in American politics in his day to a charismatic totem for nearly every interest group of the early twentieth century.

Schwartz convincingly shows that, despite Lincoln's contentious tenure as president, his tragic death on Good Friday, just days after Robert E. Lee had surrendered and ended a protracted and costly war, provided an initial narrative of martyrdom for the sake of the Union. According to Schwartz, "his assassination was an occasion for ritual acts of national affirmation and national communion."[187] Abraham Lincoln was immediately keyed to George Washington, the father of the Union. Lincoln was the great preserver of Washington's legacy.[188] Keying, according to Schwartz, "transforms the meaning of activities understood in terms of one event by comparing them with activities understood in terms of another . . . [it] arranges cultural symbols into a publicly visible discourse that flows through the organizations and institutions of the social world."[189]

Yet even a tragic death and an attempt to tie Lincoln to Washington could not overcome years of entrenched opposition. Only at the beginning of the twentieth century, when most of his political antagonists had passed on, were the conditions right for broad and diverse memorializations of Lincoln. The initial emotional outpouring over his death was strong and widespread enough to bridge the decades of the late-nineteenth century.

The outcomes of the Civil War had also become settled results: the Union had been preserved and the slaves had been emancipated. Lincoln was responsible for both. Moreover, the stronger the linkage between Washington and Lincoln was pushed by his later supporters, the greater his reputation became.[190]

As a new cult of America began to grow in the wake of the Spanish-American War (1898), the status of the presidency was elevated and Lincoln, as protector of the union, continued to gain prominence in the early-twentieth century. The centennial celebration of Lincoln's birth in 1909 became a widespread "occasion not only for expressing feelings about his personal accomplishments but also for performing ritual acts of national affirmation and national communion."[191] It was during this period that divergent groups took up Lincoln for their cause. Immigrants touted an inclusive Lincoln; progressives portrayed the sixteenth president as the strong hand of the state pushing against subhuman economies; capitalists invoked Lincoln as a defender of the free market; socialists understood him to be a friend of labor; African Americans and women viewed the former president as an advocate for minority rights; Jews read Lincoln in light of Moses and the prophets.

These preferred Lincolnian images were propagated by "reputational entrepreneurs."[192] The role of the reputational entrepreneur, according to Schwartz, is "to make an ordinary person great, or, more commonly, to bring the person's greatness to public attention."[193] Such apologists, however, do not work on deserted islands. Each of Lincoln's eulogists, biographers, sculptors, and political defenders, among others, reflected as well as contributed to the line of Lincolnian traditions in which they stood. As members of communities, reputational entrepreneurs offer "collective representations—images that existed in the mind of the entrepreneur because they first existed in certain segments of the society."[194] They are unable to escape the force of tradition. Furthermore, individual entrepreneurs and their communal interests were kept from having a corner on the Lincolnian image market by the decentralized character of Lincolnian memory-making in the early-twentieth century.[195]

Schwartz challenges strict "politics of memory" approaches by showing how each of the images that Lincoln took on during the early-twentieth century was a mixture of elements, rooted in both the historical record of Lincoln's own day and the present situation/needs of communities that required him as authentication for their ideologies.[196] The historical Lincoln could not control these images, but his life and writings did partially constrain them. The images of Lincoln as the "Man of the People," "The Great Emancipator," the "The Savior of the Union," or the "Father of Civil Rights," were not invented out of thin air.[197] Schwartz understands collective memory as "a representation of the past embodied in *both* historical evidence and commemorative symbolism."[198] Lincoln's later reputational entrepreneurs, those who had something to benefit from a particular image of Lincoln, offered constructions of the past that were both domineering *and* desired; "domineering" in the sense that commemorations of Lincoln were often stages for political and social influence, and "desired" in the sense that any commemoration must provide compelling continuities with earlier forms of widely accepted tradition. To use the language of Clifford Geertz (which Schwartz does), Lincoln was both a "model *of*" as well as a "model *for*" society.[199] Images of Lincoln reflected (as a mirror) the mores of various communities, while also serving as a light for further illumination (as a lamp).[200] Shils reminds, "It is not within the powers of any single active generation to replace most of what it has begun with . . . no generation, even those living in this present time of unprecedented dissolution of tradition, creates its own beliefs, apparatus, patterns of conduct, and institutions."[201]

Selection from the Lincolnian corpus was the art of public memory.[202] What was not selected was forgotten—that is, until some competing interest, through the act of retrieval, brought the forgotten elements of the Lincolnian tradition into view.[203] Like all traditions, which evolve through a reorganization of the canon, Lincolnian texts provided material resistance for other Lincolnian texts. I highlight here just one example from Schwartz of the kind of ambiguity that existed in Lincoln's record, thereby allowing him to become "a conductor through which these conflicts were expressed rather than a fuse that muted them."[204] On the one hand, socialists pointed to statements in the record where Lincoln seemed to support their efforts to mitigate differences between labor and capital distribution:

> [It] has so happened in all ages of the world that some have labored, and others have, without labor, enjoyed a large proportion of the fruits. This is wrong and should not continue. To secure each laborer the whole product of his labor, or as nearly as possible, is a worthy object of any good government.[205]

On the other hand, the capitalists could point to other kinds of statements:

If any continue through life in the condition of the hired laborer, it is not the fault of the system, but because of either a dependent nature which prefers it, or improvidence, folly, or singular misfortune.[206]

Appeals to Lincoln's words, then, functioned within larger networks of ideology, each of which tried to establish, through various forms of media, an image of Lincoln that was amenable for their own purposes, yet still tied, rhetorically, to Lincoln himself.[207]

These kinds of disparate statements in the Lincolnian record raise larger questions. Was Lincoln "really" a socialist or a capitalist? Was he "really" a civil rights advocate or a supporter of the Southern status quo? What about memory distortion? Was the log-cabin Lincoln of the Progressives a figment of their imagination—a distortion, a politically expedient Lincolnian self-construction during his own election that was exploited again by a later movement?[208] In order to talk about image "construction," as if it is significantly different from historical "reality," one must believe that "reality" can be known.[209] Is it possible to talk about the "real" Lincoln, and what do we mean when we use this kind of language? On the former, Schwartz thinks so:

> Diverse images of Lincoln appears [*sic*] as different "utterances" of the same language. They refer to different aspects of the *real* Lincoln, matters of liking or disliking him in different degrees, of emphasizing different parts of his life.[210]

In this final statement, Schwartz is dependent on the distinction between *langue* (language) and *parole* (speech) in Saussure. He continues:

> As different sentences enact the unseen reality of a single language, so different depictions of Lincoln enact one of the many sides of the same man. This does not mean that some groups were more justified in identifying with Lincoln than others; it means that Lincoln himself was ambiguous, complex, and many-sided, and that different communities, according to their experiences and interests, saw one side more clearly than others.[211]

The "real" Lincoln, then, was not a fixed entity. His views and goals developed over years of controversy and contestation. On the issue of slavery and emancipation, for instance, Lincoln moved over the course of four years from (1) wanting a constitutional amendment whereby slavery would be protected in Southern states that rejoined the Union; to (2) seeking a "gradual, compensated emancipation of slaves accompanied by the emigration both of former slaves and free blacks from the United States"; to (3) finally, issuing the Emancipation Proclamation and supporting the framework of what would become the Thirteenth Amendment.[212] After emancipation, he readily admitted that the accompanying plan for black colonization of Central America (or Texas, or Florida) was "wrong."[213] In his final public address, just four days before his assassination, Lincoln promised "to make some new announcement to the people of the South."[214] We can attribute each of these positions, despite their differences, to the "real" Lincoln. This, however, flattens the rhetorical advantage of using such language. In the end, we can only talk about the Lincoln of particular texts at particular times (i.e., Which Lincoln?). To speak of the "real" Lincoln, as if he were some static entity, is to blur history. The textual and historical evidence lends itself to any number of "Lincolns," as his early twentieth-century reputational entrepreneurs so acutely show.

"The *(Polymorphic) Apostle*"

The idealizations of Lincoln in the first 50–75 years after his death are a constructive lens for understanding Paul's charisma in the early-second century. The early development of Pauline traditions was *similar* to the early development of Lincolnian traditions in a number of ways. I want to think here *about* Paul *with* Lincoln. While granting the limits of such a historical comparison, I do want to insist that all knowledge innovations are produced on recognizable patterns from elsewhere and turn on the power of metaphor.[215] First, and most generally, we see Lincoln being invoked by nearly every interest group in the Progressive Era, in the same way that Paul became "*the* Apostle" for the proto-orthodox, the Valentinians, the Marcionites, and various Gnostic and Encratic groups of the second century.

Second, Lincoln and Paul were instigators of the most dramatic social shifts of their day. Lincoln not only preserved a fragile Union, but delivered the Emancipation Proclamation (intentions aside), while Paul was the key figure in moving a predominantly Jewish sect toward a Gentile-dominated religion (intentions aside here, as well). This guaranteed that he, like Lincoln in American cultural memory, would be secured a place of commemorative importance for later generations of Christians.[216] The most dominant and unifying aspect of the early layer of the Pauline tradition appears to have been that Paul engaged in a wide and far-flung mission to the Gentiles. The Pauline Epistles (cf. 2 Tim 4.17: "But the Lord stood by me and strengthened me, in order that through me the message might be fully accomplished and that *all the Gentiles* might hear it"), the canonical Acts of the Apostles (cf. Acts 13.47 : "For thus the Lord has commanded us, 'I have set you as a light for the *Gentiles*, in order to bring salvation to the *ends of the earth*'"), *1 Clement* 5.7 ("Paul . . . taught righteousness to the *whole world*"), and the *Acts of Paul* 11.3 ("we enlist soldiers . . . from the *whole world*"), among others, reflect an image of a Paul who was in and out of numerous communities across a broad geographical expanse, often staying in an individual city for only a short period of time.[217] This "broad impression" about Paul, which is "recurrently attested" throughout the sources (applying Dale Allison's categories for the Jesus tradition to the Pauline tradition), does not require us to fill it in with any more specificity in order to posit that, within the complex, multilayered Pauline traditions of the late-first and early-second centuries, this element has the greatest likelihood of correspondence with Paul of Tarsus.[218]

His martyrdom was eventually connected to this role as a "herald in both the east and the west":

> On account of envy and discord, Paul displayed the reward for endurance, having been bound seven times, made to flee, and stoned. After becoming a herald in both the east and the west, he received the suitable fame for his faith. He taught righteousness to the whole world (ὅλον τὸν κόσμον), came to the boundary of the west and suffered martyrdom before the rulers. In this way he was released from the world and taken up to the holy place, having become the greatest example of endurance. (*1 Clem.* 5.5–7)

In the trial scene in the *Acts of Paul* (11.3), Nero, just before beheading the Apostle, asks, "Man of the great king, but (now) my prisoner, why did it seem good to thee to come secretly into the empire of the Romans and enlist soldiers from my province?" Paul responds, "Caesar, not only from thy province do we enlist soldiers, but from the whole world (ἐκ τῆς οἰκουμένης πασῆς). For this charge has been laid upon us, that no man be excluded who wishes to serve my king."[219] Paul was remembered as "*the* Apostle" in the second century because of his decisive and active role in this social shift in the Church.[220] A martyr's death in the capital of the

Roman Empire only solidified this image of the Apostle in the commemorative space of early Christian hagiography and memory.[221] Moreover, in
Paul's ministry there was what historian John Lewis Gaddis calls a
"sensitive dependence on initial conditions," a "point at which small shifts
at the beginning of a process produced large consequences at the end of
it."[222] His ubiquitous memorialization in early Christian communities reflects his role at a sensitive moment.

Third, like Lincoln, Paul evidently had numerous enemies during his
own lifetime. Several of the Pauline Epistles (esp. Gal and 2 Cor) depict
the Apostle on the brink of losing his congregations to various "false apostles" (2 Cor 11.13), some of whom preached "another gospel" (Gal 1.7) or
"another Jesus" (2 Cor 11.4). The ethnic unity that these texts try to forge
between Jew and Greek in the Pauline *ekklesiai* was fragile, at best. Paul's
apostleship was often questioned or denied. He had not known the earthly
Jesus. He had previously been a persecutor of the church (1 Cor 15.9; Gal
1.13; Phil 3.6; 1 Tim 1.13; Acts 7.58; 8.1–3; 9.1–2; 22.4, 19; 26.9–12). After
his death, a small element of anti-Paulinism continued to exist into the
second and third centuries (cf. Chapter 2).[223] But none of this could keep
him from being memorialized among communities across the Mediterranean. Further, if there is any truth to the image of Paul as missionary to
the world—and, again, I believe that beyond all of the problems that we
have in uncovering the "real" or "historical" Paul, this is the most probable aspect of his ministry—then it is understandable how remembrances
of the Apostle were not controlled by any one community, region, or ideology. In the diverse and unorganized world of second-century Christianity
there were "no precise rules and no custodianship" for the transmission
of the Pauline traditions, whether oral or written.[224] Each community that
encountered Paul had a different experience with him, needed different
things from him, and passed on different stories about Paul's apostolic
interactions with them. As "group accounts," narrative portrayals of the
Apostle were woven into the foundation stories of early Christian communities.[225] These early oral traditions would have lacked "a single line of
transmission . . . most oral tradition is told by many people to many
people. . . . Hence the transmission really is communal and continuous.
There are no neat lines of communication reserved for all oral traditions."[226] In almost all cases, multiple versions of a particular tradition
exist and often interpenetrate one another.[227]

Fourth, the apparent complexity of Paul's own views (regardless of how
many letters we now want to attribute to him) and the variety of images

that he would have had to self-construct to meet his rhetorical goals, as with Lincoln, meant that he could be idealized by a variety of reputational entrepreneurs.[228] The seven so-called undisputed letters of Paul alone provide a bewildering assortment of perspectives that often defy systematization.[229] When "Pauline" epistles combined with Acts and the oral traditions standing behind the *Acts of Paul*, this large and early layer of Pauline tradition provided the kind of initial variety that aided and abetted the developing trajectories of Pauline image memory in communities throughout the Mediterranean world.[230] Traditioned Pauline images and texts worked together to provide "collective representations" of the Apostle.[231] Until institutions developed that could control how the diverse early tradition was to be interpreted, memories of the Apostle were almost always handed down tacitly.[232] Some constellations of tradition achieved dominance over others, but dominance never guarantees the ability to enforce uniformity.[233] As we have noted, traditions are like canons, "internally diverse" and "never fully coherent," and thus are susceptible to change.[234] The early Pauline traditions of the second century were no exception. Rhetorical attempts to provide a fixed image of Paul, to freeze the "real" Paul on the basis of one or several passages from this corpus of material, were always "subject to challenge and revision" from within the corpus itself.[235] John Lewis Gaddis reminds us:

> The megalosaurus you see modeled in a museum, for example, is a static representation. Biographers can't content themselves with this, because biography must not only flesh out bones but animate them. It's like time-lapse photography: our sources are our snapshots; but the sequence in which we arrange them and the significance we attach to the gaps between them are as important as what any one of them shows. We rerun whole lives, not single moments in them.[236]

It is not possible, at least here, to scratch the "historical" Paul itch beyond what we have suggested. Categories like tradition and memory, as complex and nuanced as they are, are often pitted against the would-be certainties of "history."[237] As we have seen, positivist historians often want to know what the "historical" Paul was *really* like and who best represented the Apostle and his thought in the second century. While I would argue that the basic contours of Paul's ministry that I have just outlined in exceedingly general terms provide some *adequate* frameworks for talking about Paul of Tarsus, I do not think that the critical first step of ideological self-reflection (the consistent application of the sociology of knowledge as Mannheim has suggested) has become fully integrated into the historical methods of modern scholars of Paul (cf. Chapter 7 for some brief comments on the future of Pauline Studies). It was certainly not in view for Irenaeus, Tertullian, Marcion, and the authors of 2 Peter and the *Gospel of Philip*. For them, the "real" Paul was self-evident and unproblematic. The historiographical trends of the twentieth century, however, in combination with the rise of the sociology of knowledge, should force us to become scholars of Pauline traditions first (including those traditions that birthed the present "historical" Paul in nineteenth-century Protestant Germany). After that, I suspect that we will never arrive at the measure of certitude that ideologies require for their rhetoric of the "real" Paul to have a significant degree of power.

Rooted in ideology, and equipped by a positivist historiography, much of the scholarship on "Paul in the second century" has been dominated by concerns over the question Who got Paul right? Nineteenth- and twentieth-century scholars, as we will see in Chapter 6, thought that Irenaeus had misinterpreted Paul. Questions like Do the Pastoral Epistles or the *Acts of Paul and Thecla* better represent the "historical" Paul? suggest that there is some Archimedean point from which we as twenty-first-century scholars can reconstruct an untraditioned Paul. We are confronted, however, by the fact that already in the second century the Apostle had become "all things to all people" (cf. 1 Cor 9.22). In our own period, it has taken a prophet or two to deconstruct the lenses through which Paul has seemed "natural" to us. These prophets normally have an elevated perspective, with at least one foot outside the tradition. The so-called "New Perspective" on Paul, for instance, has sensitized us to what it calls "Lutheran" readings of Paul. It has disabused the field of Pauline Studies of a regnant image of the Apostle, but must also be introspective enough to acknowledge its own "Post-Holocaust" reading of Paul. Methodologically, we must be rigorists like Mannheim. In doing so, several more nuanced questions can be asked of Paul's interpreters, whether Tertullian, Marcion, or us: Which Paul? What communal rules of faith have shaped this reading of Paul? Which Pauline texts have been invoked to substantiate this image of the Apostle? How have they been interpreted? and What is the precise mixture of past and present in a given memorialization? These are the questions that Margaret Mitchell has asked of Chyrsostom, and about which she has concluded:

Pauline interpretation is fundamentally an artistic exercise in conjuring up and depicting a dead man from his ghostly images in the ancient text, as projected on a background composed from a selection of existing sources. All these portraits are based upon a new configuration of the surviving evidence, set into a particular, chosen, framework. The images they produce, ekphrastic monuments to real persons in the past with (necessarily) freshly imagined faces, and verisimilitudinous lines scripted from a single, one-sided report about them, become the *dramatis personae* in the docudrama that is exegesis.[238]

And these are the questions that we will now submit to *3 Corinthians* and Irenaeus's *Adversus haereses* as a way of tracing the relationship between discourses on the "real" Paul and the nature of tradition and memory in one prominent trajectory of the Pauline tradition of the second century.

5

Reclaiming Paul: The Image of Paul in 3 Corinthians

*Words and images seem inevitably to become implicated
in a "war of signs" (what Leonardo called a paragone) in
which the stakes are things like nature, truth, reality, and
the human spirit.*

W. J. T. MITCHELL, Iconology[1]

IN THE MIDST of a process whereby a number of fragmented and sometimes overlapping trajectories of Pauline reception were developing in the
second century, several of his reputational entrepreneurs appear to have
written specifically in order to "reclaim" the Apostle from some other
stream of interpretation (cf. Chapter 3). Irenaeus laments that his opponents trumpeted 1 Corinthians 15.50 in support of their anthropology:
"This is the passage which is adduced by all the heretics in support of their
folly, with an attempt to annoy us, and to point out that the handiwork of
God is not saved" (*Haer.* 5.9.1).[2] The heresiologist then sets out an interpretation of the text that is amenable to his position: that flesh and blood
can inherit the kingdom of God. This process of reclaiming Paul and his
texts for the proto-orthodox, however, was not limited to long apologetic
defenses of the faith like that of Irenaeus. A letter authored in the name of
the Apostle himself, such as *3 Corinthians*, could correct any number of
perceived mis-readings of Pauline texts.[3]

This chapter and the next explore *3 Corinthians* and Irenaeus's *Adversus
haereses* as windows into one particular stream of collective memory of
Paul that allowed for his assimilation into the burgeoning proto-orthodox
theology of the late-second century. The interplay between image construction and textual interpretation in the Pauline traditions of these two
texts can be shown by examining several shared features of their portrayals
of Paul: each works with earlier Pauline materials to mitigate differences

between Paul and the other apostles, providing an image of Paul that is keyed to the wider "apostolic" tradition; each programmatically invokes the language of the Pastoral Epistles, which serve as framing *lieux de mémoire* for this apostolic tradition; and each displays similar hermeneutical moves in its readings of 1 Corinthians 15.[4] None of these elements of the reception of Paul *has* to be linked with the others. As Edward Shils reminds us, "A tradition of belief contains constituent beliefs about many particular things."[5] These constituent pieces:

> are parts of interconnected sets of traditions of judgments of particular objects. They were heterogeneous in the past, and their diversified lines of development linking and separating them from each other over time makes the pattern of effectively accepted beliefs at any one time extraordinarily differentiated.[6]

The specific combination of these elements in *3 Corinthians* and *Adversus haereses*, however, *does* work to form a more complex Pauline tradition and to memorialize an image of Paul that was both a "model *of*" ("mirror") as well as a "model *for*" ("lamp") proto-orthodox receptions of Paul.[7] This chapter explores the resultant image of Paul in *3 Corinthians*. The next chapter moves to Irenaeus. These chapters, taken together, offer an example of the kind of "thick description" of Pauline traditions that is necessary for understanding how and why the Apostle was memorialized as he was in the second century.

3 Corinthians: *Introduction*

3 Corinthians, a second-century pseudepigraphon extant in Latin, Armenian, Coptic, and Greek manuscripts, has received relatively less interest from twentieth-century scholars than have many other early Christian apocryphal texts.[8] This may be due to its proto-orthodox viewpoint, which has not provoked as much scholarly interest as other forms of early Christianity in the past century. More likely, however, is the fact that since the publication of *Papyrus Bodmer* (*P. Bodm.*) X by Michel Testuz in 1959, a certain scholarly consensus on *3 Corinthians* has emerged: it is a second-century pseudepigraphic refutation of either "Gnostic" or Marcionite thought; its origin must be sought outside the *Acts of Paul*, in which it is found in several of the manuscript traditions; and *P. Bodm.* X (our single Greek version) is not only the earliest witness (ca. third century C.E.), but also the closest witness to the original text of the letters.[9] *P. Bodm.* X, unlike the later Syriac, Coptic, Armenian, and (part of the) Latin traditions, contains only a set of paired letters from the Corinthians to Paul and his response, without any preceding or intervening narratives (cf. Appendix 3 for my translation of *P. Bodm.* X).[10] It also lacks some of the later textual expansions that elevate Mary and the Church even more than are already the case in *P. Bodm.* X.[11] At some point in the third or fourth century, *3 Corinthians* was absorbed into the expanding *Acts of Paul* literature, only to be later extracted, but with some of the surrounding narrative of the *Acts of Paul* still intact. I take these positions as a settled starting point and will not address them here.[12]

As a paired set of letters, the first provides the context for the second. Stephanus and the presbyters of Corinth (Daphnos, Euboulos, Theophilos, and Zenon) write to Paul for advice on how to deal with the recent arrival of Simon and Cleobius, who are "upsetting the faith of some with destructive statements" (*3 Cor.* 1.2).[13] The Corinthians describe six facets of their teaching (*3 Cor.* 1.10–15):

> They say
>> that we ought not use the prophets; and
>> that God is not Almighty; and
>> that there is no resurrection of the flesh; and
>> that the formation of humanity is not from God; and
>> that the Lord did not arrive in flesh nor was he born from Mary; and
>> that the world is not from God, but from the angels.

They request that Paul either visit or write so that the influence of these two might be checked. Paul, of course, replies with a letter, addressing the various false teachings and reminding the Corinthians of what he had originally passed on to them as the proper standard of doctrine.

The significant remaining historical questions about *3 Corinthians* revolve around the determination of a more precise location for its polemic (provenance, date, and opponents). Typical approaches to these questions have tried to identify the particular "heresy" against which the author is writing. Assuming that the letter from the Corinthians to Paul reflects the positions of a single, targeted individual or group, standard treatments have mined the Fathers for evidence that might help whittle down the potential candidates.[14] Proposals have included the Marcionites, Valentinian or Ophite groups, Saturnilus, and Simon Magus.¹⁵ Others view the polemic as directed toward "Gnostics" in general because the teachings mentioned are quite common among the various systems.¹⁶

Rather than trying to reconstruct the identity of a particular opponent in *3 Corinthians*, this chapter analyzes its portrayal of Paul, as well as its interpretive tendencies toward earlier Pauline materials, in particular its reading of 1 Corinthians 15. This approach will allow us to explore and to emphasize the *general* polemical thrust of the work, to situate its portrayal of Paul within the context of other similar, firmly datable, construals of Paul, and to understand the ways in which the proto-orthodox were attempting to reaffirm Paul as their own at the end of the second century. I will argue that *3 Corinthians* is a *late* second-century, proto-orthodox invocation of the "Pastoral" Paul (i.e., the Paul of the Pastoral Epistles), who stands as the defender of apostolic teaching (διδασκαλία) in the face of "deviant views" (ἀστοχήματα) of a *generally* "Gnostic" variety.¹⁷ Yet in this pseudepigraphic attempt to re*claim* Paul, we encounter a re*configuration* of the Pauline tradition wherein, among other things, Paul ironically becomes a defender of σάρξ. This last conclusion stands in contrast with Vahan Hovhanessian, one of the few recent major commentators on *3 Corinthians*, who asserts, "The similarity of the author's message to that of the apostle Paul, affirmed in 3 Cor, supports the author's intention."¹⁸

Paul and His Opponents

The two letters that make up *3 Corinthians* present a single, targeted picture of Paul. He is the quintessential defender of apostolic teaching (διδασκαλία) against "heresy." Absent are the ethical and cultural issues, as well as the eschatological urgency, that are so prevalent in 1 and 2 Corinthians, Galatians, and 1 Thessalonians, for instance.¹⁹ The letter from the Corinthians functions as a list of "destructive statements" (φθοριμαίοις λόγοις) that have been proffered by the arch-heretics Simon and Cleobius and that stand in contrast to the apostolic "statements" (λόγους) of Paul and others (1.2, 4). Paul responds as if he had anticipated the letter, stating that he is "not astonished (Οὐ θαυμάζω) at how quickly the doctrines (δόγματα) of the Evil One are advancing" (2.2) through the ones who are "counterfeiting his [Jesus'] words (τὰ λόγια αὐτοῦ)" (2.3). This is in marked contrast to the rhetorical strategy of Galatians 1.6: "I am astonished (Θαυμάζω) that you have so quickly deserted the one who called you by the

grace of Christ for another gospel." Paul calls on the Corinthians to "flee
from their [Simon and Cleobius's] teaching (διδασκαλίας)" (2.21) and to
"remain in the standard (κανόνι) that you received through the blessed
prophets and the holy Gospel" (2.36). These admonitions are sprinkled
throughout Paul's paratactic refutation of the heresies.

The "destructive statements" of Simon and Cleobius and the attendant rhetoric over sound teaching should be viewed as a defense of apostolic teaching over and against heresy in the most general sense. Simon
and Cleobius appear together as the first heretics in both Hegesippus
(Eus., *Hist. eccl.* 4.22.5) and the *Didascalia Apostolorum* (23.6.8).[20] While
little is known of Cleobius, Simon Magus emerges as the father of the
"Gnostics" and the foil for proto-orthodox dogma throughout early Christian literature. He is listed first in the genealogy of early Christian heresy
as early as Justin's now lost *Syntagma* (1 *Apol.* 26).[21] Irenaeus, likely drawing from Justin, commences his catalogue of the history of heresy with
Simon (*Haer.* 1.22–23) and later calls him "the father of all heretics"
(*Haer.* 3.pref.1).[22] Hippolytus likewise calls Simon the "starting point" of
heresies that later masqueraded under other names (*Haer.* 6.2–15; cf.
Origen, *Cels.* 6.11). The author of *3 Corinthians*, by positioning Paul
against the supposed father of heresy and his sometime sidekick, portrays his response as a definitive uprooting of the various claims at their
source.[23]

That Paul's words are to be viewed as a panacea to all varieties of theological error can be understood from the description of his situation at the
beginning of his letter: "Paul, the prisoner of Christ Jesus, in the midst of
many deviant views (ἐν πολλοῖς ὢν ἀστοχήμασι)—to the brothers in Corinth—
Greetings" (2.1). Previous translations have not satisfactorily rendered the
Greek ἀστόχημα. Schneemelcher and Rordorf read "tribulations."[24] J. K.
Elliott provides "afflictions."[25] More recently, both Vahan Hovhanessian
and Bart Ehrman translate as "failures."[26] These readings, which go back
to Testuz ("échecs"), portray Paul in a state of (physical?) weakness.[27] His
health and strength might be failing him while in prison (cf. 2.35). "Failures," in particular, commends this notion. While these renderings are
certainly possible, they are ultimately too dependent on the later narrative
context of the *Acts of Paul* (in the Coptic *Heidelberg Papyrus*), which has the
Apostle authoring the letter from a Philippian prison, close to death. In
addition to the difficulties surrounding the Philippi narrative in *P. Heid.*,
there are strong arguments for viewing the letters as originally independent of this larger framing story.[28] If we exclude this later narrative

context, a better translation of the rare word ἀστόχημα in *P. Bodm.* X is "deviant view." This reading is already suggested by Frederick Danker: "since I must deal with numerous errors (in teaching)."²⁹

Plutarch, who provides the first attestation of this nominal form of the verb, ἀστοχέω ("to miss" or "to fail"; literally, "to be off target"), uses it twice in *De curiositate*.³⁰ In speaking of curious "busybodies" (οἱ πολυπράγμονες), he likens them to a grammarian who spends his time collecting "headless lines in Homer and solecisms in the tragedians and the unbecoming and licentious language applied to women by which Archilochus makes a sorry spectacle of himself" (520B).³¹ Such a compilation of the faults (ἁμαρτημάτων) of others is "unbecoming and useless," according to Plutarch. In the same way, "busybodies" are fixated with "gleaning and gathering the blunders and errors and solecisms, not of lines or poems, but of lives" (520B; οὐ στίχων οὐδὲ ποιμάτων, ἀλλὰ βίων ἀστοχήματα καὶ πλημμελήματα καὶ σολοικισμοὺς ἀναλεγόμενοι καὶ συνάγοντες). Ἀστόχημα, then, is semantically related to both ἁμάρτημα and πλημμέλημα, with a sense of "fault," "error," or "missing the norm."

Plutarch also likens the busybody to one who enters Rome in search of a prodigy, bypassing its beautiful statuary and people in favor of the bodily deformed: "those who have no calves, or are weasel-armed, or have three eyes, or ostrich-heads" (520C). From these comparisons with the grammarian and the prodigy-seeker, he concludes: "so let those who are curious about life's failures (τὰ περὶ τὸν βίον ἀστοχήματα), the blots on the scutcheon, the delinquencies and errors in other people's homes (διαστροφάς τινας ἐν οἴκοις ἀλλοτρίοις καὶ πλημμελείας), remind themselves that their former discoveries have brought them no favour or profit." While Hembold translates ἀστοχήματα as "failures" here, it is clear that Plutarch understands τὰ ἀστοχήματα to represent those things that are faulty, erroneous, or otherwise abnormal. Again, they are synonymous with πλημμέλειαι. Our only other known use of the term in a somewhat contemporaneous context comes from Athenaeus (early-third century C.E.). He uses ἀστόχημα in the sense of historical "error" when commenting on the anachronisms in Xenophon (*Deip.* V.216f; τὸ δὲ κατὰ τοὺς χρόνους ἀστόχημα λεκτέον).³²

The verbal form, ἀστοχέω, can be found in several Christian texts either predating or contemporaneous with *3 Corinthians*. Within the New Testament, the verb is found only in the Pastorals, where it implies "wandering" or "deviating" from the faith (1 Tim 1.6; 6.21; 2 Tim 2.18; cf. Tables 5.1 and 5.2), thus "being in error." A similar usage appears in *2 Clement* 17.7:

> But those who are upright, who have acted well, endured torments, and hated the sweet pleasures of the soul, when they observe how those who have deviated from the right path (ἀστοχήσαντας) and denied Jesus through their words or deeds are punished with terrible torments in a fire that cannot be extinguished, they, the upright, will give glory to their God, saying, "there will be hope for the one who has served as God's slave from his whole heart."[33]

This contrast between faithful slavery to God, on the one hand, and being in a state of "deviation" from the faith, on the other, is remarkably similar to *3 Corinthians* 2.1, where Paul is the prisoner who combats his theological opponents on all sides. While lacking the doctrinal context, *Didache* 15.3b also exhorts, "Let no one speak with a person who has committed a sin against his neighbor (παντὶ ἀστοχοῦντι κατὰ τοῦ ἑτέρου), nor let him hear anything from you, until he repents." Like Plutarch, the author of the *Didache* understands ἀστοχέω as semantically equivalent to ἁμαρτάνω.

This evidence, combined with the doctrinal polemic of *3 Corinthians*, supports Danker's reading of ἀστοχήμασι in *3 Corinthians* 2.1 as "errors (in teaching)." Contextually, I render it as "deviant views." Moreover, whether one reads ἐν πολλοῖς ὢν ἀστοχήμασι before or after χαίρειν makes little difference for my understanding of the phrase.[34] Read with 2.1, it is an existential description of Paul's situation. When read with 2.2, as Danker has suggested, it has a causal sense: because Paul finds himself amidst many theological opponents, he is not surprised that the Corinthians are as well. Either way, Paul is pictured as one who is currently surrounded by numerous "errors" or "deviations" from the faith. He is the defender of proto-orthodox theology against every kind of teaching that is "not" (ἀ +) "on target" (στόχος), including those gaining influence at Corinth. His response to Simon and Cleobius is a cure-all for the many (πολλοῖς) heresies that found their origin in the figure of Simon Magus.

Paul and the Apostles

Yet the author of *3 Corinthians* is quick to emphasize that Paul's own teachings came from the other apostles.[35] In a passage that closely parallels 1 Corinthians 11.23 and 15.3, Paul says, "For I entrusted to you in the beginning what I also received *from the apostles* who came before me, and who spent all their time with Jesus Christ" (2.4):

Ἐγὼ γὰρ <u>παρέλαβον</u> <u>ἀπὸ τοῦ κυρίου</u>, ὃ καὶ παρέδωκα ὑμῖν ὅτι (1 Cor 11.23);

παρέδωκα γὰρ ὑμῖν <u>ἐν πρώτοις</u>, ὃ καὶ <u>παρέλαβον</u> ὅτι (1 Cor 15.3);

Ἐγὼ γὰρ <u>ἐν ἀρχῇ</u> παρέδωκα ὑμῖν ἃ καὶ <u>παρέλαβον ὑπὸ τῶν πρὸ ἐμοῦ</u>
<u>ἀποστόλων γενομένων τῶν πάντα χρόνον μετὰ Ἰησοῦ</u> ὅτι (3 Cor. 2.4).

A subtle reconfiguration of these passages has occurred, however. The source of the received traditions (double underline) has changed from Paul's unique relationship to the risen Christ to his dependence upon the previous apostles, who importantly, unlike Paul, spent time with the fleshly Jesus before his crucifixion and resurrection.[36] 1 Corinthians 11.23 stresses that the subsequent Eucharist tradition came *from the Lord*. The source of the traditions underlying 1 Corinthians 15.3b–7 is left unstated.[37] J. Christiaan Beker has argued that these latter traditions come from the Antiochene church.[38] Joseph A. Fitzmyer, following C. H. Dodd and Martin Dibelius, posits its origin in "the primitive proclamation of the Jerusalem community."[39] Others have settled for generalizations like a "Palestinian"/"Semitic" or "Hellenistic" context.[40] Still others emphasize the generality of the tradition, making it suitable for any number of early Christian contexts.[41] The question, for our purposes, is not where the tradition ultimately comes from, but where does the Paul of 1 Corinthians *say* that it comes from. He does not, however, indulge us here. We cannot just assume that because the tradition itself includes references to Cephas, James, and the Twelve that Paul intends for his readers to locate the tradition's origin among them as well. This initial ambiguity about the tradition's origin should be viewed in light of Paul's later claim that his own vision of the resurrected Jesus spurred him to "work harder than all of them [the previously named apostles]" (1 Cor 15.8–10). While 1 Corinthians 15.3b–11 certainly works to establish *continuity* between Paul and other apostolic ministers (cf. also 1 Cor 1.12–13; 3.4–17), he in no way states that his teaching or ministry is *dependent* upon them.[42] His dependence on specific human authorities is left blank, at least from a rhetorical standpoint. The Corinthians might have any number of teachers, but they have only one father, Paul himself (1 Cor 4.14–15).

3 Corinthians 2.4, however, squarely places Paul's message in continuity with *and* dependence upon the original apostles.[43] He does not operate *de novo*, but in line with the "others." The Corinthians say to Paul: "For we have not heard statements such as these from you or from the others"

(*3 Cor.* 1.4). *P. Bodm.* X does not specify here who the "others" are, though later Coptic, Latin, and Armenian manuscripts uniformly have "other apostles."[44] Paul's response in *3 Corinthians* 2.4 suggests that the later manuscripts have correctly interpreted the "others" in *3 Corinthians* 1.4. Hovhanessian, however, understands the "others" as Paul's coworkers who had been in Corinth, potentially Timothy, Apollos, Stephanus, Fortunatus, and/or Achaicus.[45] He argues that "others" cannot refer to the apostles because there is no evidence of apostolic presence in Corinth except Paul. This is wrong on one major count: the particular historical events relating to the original Pauline mission in Corinth are not in view in *3 Corinthians*. The author certainly mimics Pauline language throughout the letter, but there is no attempt to fit the letter within the historical framework of earlier Pauline letters. Rather, Paul's relationship to the apostolic tradition is what is at stake throughout the presentation, so that the "others" seems to be a reference to the apostles, as Paul's response and the tradition's later translators make clear. Furthermore, the verbs παραλαμβάνω (1.5; 2.4; 2.36), παραδίδωμι (2.4), and παραδέχομαι (2.34), strategically placed at the beginning and end of the pseudepigraphical letters, act as a frame, creating a portrait in which the theological assertions of Paul are displayed as falling within the boundaries of the transmitted apostolic tradition.[46]

This second-century construction of Paul as the quintessential defender of the gospel has its roots in the earliest Pauline tradition, where a number of texts portray the Apostle defending his gospel against community disturbers (Rom 3.8; 2 Cor 11; Gal 1.6–9; Phil 3.2; Col 2.16–23; 1 Thess 1.15–16; and the Pastoral Epistles). In fact, the more one looks at the language and polemic of the last of these, the Pastoral Epistles, the more one notices the numerous connections between the Paul of *3 Corinthians* and the Paul of 1 and 2 Timothy and Titus. It is to those connections that we now turn.

3 Corinthians *and the Pastoral Epistles*

The pseudepigraphical techniques of the author of *3 Corinthians* include, as many have noted, the use of language and concepts found in the letters circulating under Paul's name.[47] We have just mentioned the transformation of 1 Corinthians 11.23 and 15.3. Of the numerous correspondences in language, there is a disproportionate dependence upon the polemical language of the Pastoral Epistles—so much so that the Paul of the Pastorals has become the hermeneutical lens through which the author of *3 Corinthians* envisions his own Paul.

Of course, the author of *3 Corinthians* knew nothing of the modern scholarly trend that groups these texts together under this name. Each would have simply been a Pauline letter belonging to the Apostle's larger corpus. These three texts, however, were already being viewed together for thematic purposes by the turn of the third century. Both Tertullian (*Marc.* 5.21) and the Muratorian Canon (*ll.* 60–63) group them together not only because they were written to individuals, but also for their emphasis on "ecclesiastical discipline" (Muratorian Canon: *ecclesiasticae disciplinae*; Tertullian: *ecclesiastico statu*; cf. also Clement of Alexandria, *Strom.* 2.11). These texts also suggest that 1 and 2 Timothy and Titus first circulated separately from a group of Paul's letters to (seven) churches, which would have caused their thematic unity to be easily recognized.[48] Aside from this ancient evidence, their common, unflagging concern for "healthy teaching" (1 Tim 1.10; 2 Tim 4.3; Titus 1.9; 2.1: ὑγιαινούσῃ διδασκαλία), just one of numerous unique phrases and words shared among the Pastoral Epistles, gives further reason for viewing these texts together, even if recent sensitivity to some of the stark differences among the three (particularly between 2 Tim and 1 Tim/Titus) has partially deflated the heuristic value of the designation "Pastoral Epistles."[49] Despite a range of differences, however, these three texts present a unified picture of Paul as heresy-fighter.

The overarching concern of both the Pastorals and *3 Corinthians* is the transmission of and adherence to correct teaching.[50] Of the 19 uses of διδασκαλία in the canonical Pauline letter corpus, 15 come from the Pastorals.[51] As was just mentioned, within the Pastorals διδασκαλία is sometimes modified by the adjectival participle ὑγιαινούσῃ ("sound" or "healthy"), so that the Paul of 2 Timothy 4.3 can predict, "For there will be a time when they will not uphold sound teaching (τῆς ὑγιαινούσης διδασκαλίας)."[52] The battle over fitting διδασκαλία is readily apparent both in the various other adjectives that modify this noun, including "demonic" (1 Tim 4.1: δαιμόνιον), "good" (1 Tim 4.6: κάλος), "pious" (1 Tim 6.6: εὐσέβεια), and "incorruptible" (Titus 2.7: ἀφθορία), as well as in the ostensible creation of the verb ἑτεροδιδασκαλέω, "to teach something different," found in 1 Timothy 1.3 and 6.3.[53]

The same could be said about the use of the term λόγος in the Pastorals, which is variously modified as "trustworthy" (1 Tim 1.15; 3.1; 4.9; 2 Tim 2.11; Titus 1.9; 3.8: πιστός), "sound" (1 Tim 6.3; 2 Tim 1.13; Titus 2.8: ὑγιαινούσῃ/ὑγιής), "of truth" (2 Tim 2.15: ἀληθεία); "of God" (1 Tim 4.5; 2 Tim 2.9; Titus 1.3; 2.5: θεός); and "of faith" (1 Tim 4.6: πίστις). In one case it is made absolute, where Paul says, "Preach *the* word" (2 Tim 4.2:

κήρυξον τὸν λόγον). Negatively, one finds "frivolous speech" (1 Tim 1.6: ματαιολογία) and "going to battle over words" (2 Tim 2.14: λογομαχέω). In 2 Timothy there is a further contrast of "their words" (2.17: ὁ λόγος αὐτῶν) and "our words" (4.15: τοῖς ἡμετέροις λόγοις), a move that forces a boundary between two different sets of teaching.

The Paul of *3 Corinthians*, so concerned with proper διδασκαλία (2.21), λόγοι/ια (1.2, 4; 2.3), δόγματα (2.2), and κανών (2.36), is the Paul of the Pastorals: the Apostle who stands against teaching that is "Other."[54] Yet the similarities between *3 Corinthians* and the Pastorals are not confined to this conceptual level alone. One also finds that *3 Corinthians* is charged by specific phrases from 1 and 2 Timothy and Titus. I lay out here in tabular form the similarities in language, arranged according to certainty of dependence:[55]

Table 5.1 Probable Dependence of *3 Corinthians* on the Pastoral Epistles

3 Corinthians (P. Bodm. X)	Pastoral Epistles (NA[27])
οἵτινες τήν τινων πίστιν ἀνατρέπουσιν (1.2)	ἀνατρέπουσιν τήν τινων πίστιν (2 Tim 2.18)
"who are upsetting the faith of some"	"they are upsetting the faith of some"
· Of Simon and Cleobius	· Of Hymenaeus and Philetus
	οἵτινες ὅλους οἴκους ἀνατρέπουσιν (Titus 1.11)
	"who are upsetting whole houses"
	· Of rebellious men, especially from the circumcision party, who should be silenced
καὶ τούτων ἡ ἄνοια ἔκδηλος γένηται (1.16)	ἡ γὰρ ἄνοια αὐτῶν ἔκδηλος ἔσται πᾶσιν (2 Tim 3.9)
"and their foolishness might become evident"	"For their foolishness will be evident to all"
· Of Simon and Cleobius	· Of unnamed "seducers"
οὕστινας ἀποτρέπεσθε (2.21)	καὶ τούτους ἀποτρέπου (2 Tim 3.5)
"Turn away from these kinds of people"	"Turn away from these people"
· Of those who deny the creation of the world by the Father	· Of those who "hold to a form of godliness, but deny its power"[a]

continued

Table 5.1 (continued)

3 Corinthians (P. Bodm. X)	Pastoral Epistles (NA²⁷)
ἐν πολλοῖς ὤν ἀστοχήμασι (2.1)	ὤν τινες ἀστοχήσαντες ἐξετράπησαν εἰς ματαιολογίαν (1 Tim 1.6)
"in the midst of many deviant views"	"Some, deviating from these things, have turned aside to frivolous speech"
· Of the numerous doctrinal errors that Paul must combat, including those of Simon and Cleobius.	· Of false teachers of the Law with their endless genealogies
	ἥν τινες ἐπαγγελλόμενοι περὶ τὴν πίστιν ἠστόχησαν (1 Tim 6.21)
	"which some professing, have deviated with respect to the faith"
	· Of those who speak empty chatter and profess to have so-called knowledge
	οἵτινες περὶ τὴν ἀλήθειαν ἠστόχησαν (2 Tim 2.18)
	"who have deviated with respect to the truth"
	· Of Hymenaeus and Philetus
ἐκ σπέρματος Δαυίδ (2.5)	ἐκ σπέρματος Δαυίδ (2 Tim 2.8)
"from the seed of David"	"from the seed of David"
· Tradition that Paul has passed on	· One of two parts of Paul's gospel (the other is the resurrection of Jesus from the dead)[b]
Παῦλος ὁ δέσμιος Χριστοῦ Ἰησοῦ (2.1)	ἐμὲ τὸν δέσμιον αὐτοῦ (2 Tim 1.8)
"Paul, the prisoner of Christ Jesus"	"me, his prisoner"
Ἐγὼ γὰρ τὰ δεσμὰ εἰς τὰς χεῖρας ἔχω (2.35)	ἐν ᾧ κακοπαθῶ μέχρι δεσμῶν ὡς κακοῦργος (2 Tim 2.9)
"For I have the bonds on my hands"	"on account of which I suffer evil, to the point of receiving bonds, as if I was a criminal"[c]

[a]This is the only use of ἀποτρέπω in the NT and it is rarely found in second-century Christian texts. In addition to ἀνατρέπω and ἀποτρέπω, the Pastorals also use ἐκτρέπω (1 Tim 1.6; 5.15; 6.20; 2 Tim 4.4).
[b]Also found in the confessional fragment in Rom 1.3 and in Ign. (*Eph.* 18.2; *Rom.* 7.3).
[c]While the prison setting is not unique to 2 Tim, it does play a large role in both this letter and 3 Cor.

Table 5.2 Possible Dependence of *3 Corinthians* on the Pastoral Epistles

3 Corinthians (P. Bodm. X)	Pastoral Epistles (NA[27])
καὶ τὴν πᾶσαν σάρκα ἀνθρώπων πρὸς ἡδονὴν ἐδέσμευεν (2.11) "And he [the unjust ruler] imprisoned all human flesh to lust"	Ἦμεν γάρ ποτε καὶ ἡμεῖς ἀνόητοι, ἀπειθεῖς, πλανώμενοι, δουλεύοντες ἐπιθυμίαις καὶ ἡδοναῖς ποικίλαις (Titus 3.3) "For we ourselves were also at one time foolish, disobedient, led astray, slaves to various desires and lusts" φιλήδονοι μᾶλλον ἢ φιλόθεοι (2 Tim 3.4) "lovers of lust rather than lovers of God" · Of some at the last day
καὶ ὅτι ὁ ἄνθρωπος ὑπὸ τοῦ πατρὸς αὐτοῦ ἐπλάσθη (2.7) "and that humanity was formed by his Father"	Ἀδὰμ γὰρ πρῶτος ἐπλάσθη, εἶτα Εὔα (1 Tim 2.13) "For Adam was formed first, then Eve"[a]

καὶ ἀπὸ τῆς διδασκαλίαις αὐτῶν ἀποφεύγετε (2.21)
"and flee from their teaching"
  · A reaffirmation of the call to "turn away from these kinds of people"
	ταῦτα φεῦγε (1 Tim 6.11)
	
	"flee from these things"
	  · Of "the love of money"
	
	Τὰς δὲ νεωτερικὰς ἐπιθυμίας φεῦγε (2 Tim 2.22)
	"flee from youthful lusts"[b]

οἵτινες τὴν ἀπλάνη θεοσέβειαν ἐκήρυσσον χρόνοις πολλοῖς (2.10)
"who proclaimed the true piety for a long time"
  · Of the prophets
	ὃ πρέπει γυναιξὶν ἐπαγγελλομέναις θεοσέβειαν (1 Tim 2.10)
	"which is fitting for women who profess piety"
	
	  · Of the proper adornment of women[c]

[a] This linguistic connection is a bit tenuous, given that πλάσσω is used by several Christian writers of the second century to describe God's creation of humanity (Just., *Dial.* 19.3; *1 Clem.* 33.4; 38.3; *Barn.* 2.10; 19.2; *Diogn.* 10.2).

[b] Paul tells the Corinthians in other places to flee from "immorality" (1 Cor 6.18) and "idolatry" (1 Cor 10.14).

[c] Again, θεοσέβεια is a frequent second-century Christian attribution, so the potential connection here is noted in light of the more certain borrowings.

Of these parallels, I consider those in Table 5.1 to have certainly come from the Pastorals, whether through direct literary dependence or secondary orality.[56] Those in Table 5.2 are less likely, but have been included to show further potential correspondences in language and concept, if not dependence.[57]

The Pastorals, then, provide the author of *3 Corinthians* not only with a fixed image of Paul as defender of sound teaching, but also a language set for constructing his own work. A third connection might also be present. The author of 2 Timothy summarizes Paul's gospel as twofold: "Remember Jesus Christ, who has been raised from the dead and who is from the seed of David, according to my gospel" (2 Tim 2.8).[58] It contains an affirmation of the resurrection of the dead (Jesus') and a declaration of the continuity of the God of Israel with the God of Jesus. Appropriately, these are the two overarching theological concerns of *3 Corinthians*, whose author has mimicked the Paul found in the Pastorals in an attempt to fend off various teachings that he believes threatened the Church.[59]

3 Corinthians *versus 1 Corinthians 15*

Yet in fending off perceived threats to the Church in the name of apostolic tradition, we find the Paul of *3 Corinthians* espousing views that are in some degree of tension with the very Pauline texts that he invokes. Nowhere is this more apparent than in the pseudepigrapher's use of 1 Corinthians 15 to defend the resurrection of the flesh. In *P. Bodm. X*, his rebuttal to Simon and Cleobius is prefaced with the title, "Paul, to the Corinthians, concerning the flesh (περὶ σαρκὸς)." Whether or not this title accompanied the letters at composition, by the third century c.e. they were recognized chiefly as a rejoinder to false teachings on the flesh, which were the root and cause of all sorts of "deviant views."[60] We must briefly push aside this polemical context, though, in order to see the contrast between 1 Corinthians 15 and *3 Corinthians* with respect to σάρξ. 1 Corinthians makes anthropological distinctions between the body (σῶμα) and the flesh (σάρξ) that the author of *3 Corinthians* cannot.

It would be tempting here to dive headlong into the chaotic sea of Pauline anthropology. For the purposes of this chapter we will focus primarily on 1 Corinthians 15, the passage from which *3 Corinthians* actually draws. The next chapter will discuss more of the canonical data, since Irenaeus draws from various places within the Pauline corpus to defend his reading of 1 Corinthians 15.50. As a way of prefacing our discussion of

1 Corinthians 15, however, a few things should be said about modern studies of Pauline anthropology, inasmuch at 1 Corinthians 15 factors heavily in these discussions.

On the one hand, some have understood Paul's anthropology, or at least his anthropological terminology, to have been unstable. Robert Jewett, for instance, has argued that Paul's terminology was shaped by the particular polemical settings in which he found himself.[61] Jewett worked meticulously through Paul's terms (σῶμα, σάρξ, πνεῦμα, ψυχή, νοῦς, ἔσω/ἔξω ἄνθρωπος, etc.), showing how they were used, circumstantially, in each of his letters. If he is right, then the prospects of identifying a *single* "Pauline anthropology" are quite grim.

More than a few, on the other hand, have attempted to bring coherence to the anthropology of the "undisputed" Pauline letters. Bultmann famously argued, for instance, that Paul had a consistently neutral view of the body (σῶμα).[62] The body signifies personhood and is the arena in which flesh (σάρξ) and Spirit (πνεῦμα) do battle, where σάρξ represents the limitations of life without God (particularly self-righteous boasting) and πνεῦμα indicates the assistance of divine power leading to freedom from σάρξ. One could live either κατὰ σάρκα or κατὰ πνεῦμα (Rom 8.4–5) and the resultant fruit of either life would be evident (Gal 5.19–26).[63]

While Bultmann's views were dominant for several decades in the mid-twentieth century, his primarily moral and existential characterization of the σῶμα eventually came under scrutiny. Daniel Boyarin, for instance, has questioned Bultmann's consistently pejorative interpretation of κατὰ σάρκα in Paul. He notes passages like Romans 1.4 ("[Christ] who was born of the seed of David κατὰ σάρκα") and 9.5 ("The Messiah κατὰ σάρκα"), which certainly do not mean "The Christ who lives without reference to God" or "The Christ who seeks justification by works." Rather, κατὰ σάρκα is "morally neutral, although always subordinated to κατὰ πνεῦμα."[64] Boyarin emphasizes that the phrase becomes pejorative only when living "according to the flesh" has "the negative social effects in Paul's eyes of interrupting the new creation of the universal Israel of God."[65] Before Boyarin, Robert Gundry had already argued that σῶμα always signifies only the "physical body," whether in classical Greek thought, the Old Testament, early Judaism or early Christianity.[66] Bultmann was wrong to suggest that it signified the whole person. Moreover, Gundry found little distinction between σῶμα and σάρξ in Paul. Both represent "the whole body, substance-cum-form without differentiation."[67] Gundry's work was positioned not only against Bultmann, but also against late nineteenth-century "idealist" scholarship (cf. C. Holsten and H. Lüdemann), which understood the distinction between σῶμα and σάρξ in 1 Corinthians 15 in light of Aristotle's distinction between form (μορφή) and substance (ὕλη).[68] While the present σῶμα is stamped on σάρξ, the resurrection body will be stamped on πνεῦμα.

Gundry was too quick to declare this latter position "passé."[69] In fact, an increasing chorus of recent scholars has returned to the basic position of Holsten and Lüdemann: the subordination of flesh to spirit in Paul ultimately stems from Greek philosophical anthropology. Even Bultmann had conceded that Paul employed Greek categories in 1 Corinthians 15, but that he was "misled" into adopting his opponents' way of talking about the body. Paul's normally existential characterization of the σῶμα gave way to metaphysical distinctions that he would not otherwise normally make.[70] For some of these more recent scholars, including Boyarin, Paul's anthropology is ultimately indebted to Plato.[71] The self—or to use a Pauline term, "the inner person" (2 Cor 4.16; Rom 7.22: ὁ ἔσω ἄνθρωπος)—is housed within a body of σάρξ. This fleshly body is "the outer person" (2 Cor 4.16: ὁ ἔξω ἡμῶν ἄνθρωπος) or "earthly tent" (2 Cor 5.1: ἡ ἐπίγειος ἡμῶν οἰκία) that will perish. It is characterized by "mortality" (2 Cor 4.11: θνητός) and "weakness" (Rom 6.19; 8.3; Gal 4.13: ἀσθενεία) and will face "destruction" (1 Cor 15.50; Gal 6.8: φθορά).[72] This is not to say that the flesh, as a creation of God (1 Cor 15.39), is inherently evil. Paul was no Gnostic.[73] Rather, through its mortality and weakness the flesh becomes the house of Sin (cf. Rom 7.17, 18; 8.3), viewed as a hostile power ruling over humanity.

The Paul of the *Hauptbriefe* holds these Platonic categories together, according to Boyarin and others, with his Jewish eschatological hope in the resurrection, looking forward to a New Creation in the "age to come."[74] The apocalyptic nature of Paul's eschatology only serves to heighten whatever anthropological dualism he had received from popular Greek philosophy. The "age to come" is the age of the Spirit and is in a strange way already present among those who are "in Christ" (2 Cor 5.17).[75] Those who "walk in the Spirit" will no longer find themselves being controlled by the Sin in their flesh (Gal 5.16). Σάρξ, which typifies the age that is passing away, has no place in the New Age, the Kingdom of God. Paul firmly states, "Flesh and blood (σὰρξ καὶ αἷμα) cannot inherit the kingdom of God" (1 Cor 15.50).

Others have argued that a popularized Stoicism (rather than a dualist Platonism) provides the best lens for understanding the language and argument of 1 Corinthians 15, regardless of how successful it is for explaining other Pauline passages.[76] Maybe Jewett was right. The Pauline letters do

not employ anthropological terms consistently. But we are only interested
here in how *3 Corinthians* reads 1 Corinthians 15, the text that the former
invokes within its pseudepigraphic guise. The firm statement in the latter,
that "[f]lesh and blood (σὰρξ καὶ αἷμα) cannot inherit the kingdom of God" (1
Cor 15.50), must be read within the broader context of the argument in 1
Corinthians 15, where a distinction is drawn between σάρξ and σῶμα, contra
Gundry and, as we will see in the next chapter, contra Irenaeus. While σάρξ
might not inherit the kingdom of God, the σῶμα certainly will: "It is sown
as a physical body (σῶμα ψυχικόν), but it is raised as a spiritual body (σῶμα
πνευματικόν)" (1 Cor 15.44). Paul, at least here, is no classical Platonist. Very
few in the first century c.e. were.[77] He denigrates σάρξ while at the same
time valuing σῶμα. Pharisaic belief in the resurrection from the dead and/
or the influence of Stoicism must account for this distinction.[78] Dale
Martin, in his important study on concepts of the body in Greco-Roman
antiquity, characterizes the basic Stoic position, which was also the position of most ancient medical philosophers, as follows:

> Flesh, blood, and pneuma are all parts of the body—or rather, dif-
> ferent forms of substance that together make up a body. When Paul
> says that the resurrected body will be a pneumatic body rather than
> simply a psychic body or a flesh-and-blood body, he is saying that
> the immortal and incorruptible part of the human body will be res-
> urrected—or, to put it more accurately, that the body will be raised,
> constituted (due to divine transformation) only by its immortal and
> incorruptible aspects, without its corruptible and corrupting as-
> pects such as sarx. No physical/spiritual dichotomy is involved
> here, much less a material/immaterial one. . . . Paul would have
> thought of *all* of it as "material"—if, that is, he had been able to
> think in such a category without a material/immaterial dichotomy.
> At any rate, all the "stuff" here talked about is indeed stuff.[79]

For Paul, then, who was also an eschatological thinker, future ideal corpore-
ality would be characterized only by πνεῦμα, not the more corruptible σάρξ.[80]
    Gundry disagreed with this tradition of reading 1 Corinthians 15, as has
been mentioned. The σῶμα πνευματικόν "is not a bodily form with spirit as
its substance" since the σῶμα ψυχικόν "is not a bodily form with soul as its
substance."[81] Paul would have posed a σῶμα σαρκικόν to the σῶμα πνευματικόν
if he had meant what Martin and others have argued. Paul also seems to
alternate between σῶμα and σάρξ in 1 Corinthians 15.35–40.[82] Gundry,

however, seems to be talking past his opponents at this point. He argues that "Paul avoids 'flesh' in writing about the resurrection of human beings simply because the term would connote weakness, not because he wants to avoid a physical resurrection."[83] By "physical," Gundry means "material." Martin and others who argue for a σῶμα πνευματικόν at the resurrection do not deny, though, that the σῶμα πνευματικόν is material/physical, as problematic as these terms are. The σῶμα πνευματικόν takes up space and is composed of what we would call "stuff." Furthermore, there is no real alternation between σῶμα and σάρξ in 1 Corinthians 15.35–40. The primary distinction within these verses is between heavenly (ἐπουράνιος) and earthly (ἐπίγειος). Just as there is a variety of earthly bodies, each composed of a different kind of flesh, there is also a variety of heavenly bodies, each having its own glory (δόξα). But the heavenly bodies are distinct from earthly bodies for this precise reason. They are not said to possess flesh. The resurrection body, by implication, will be a heavenly body, possessing its own kind of glory, but stripped of its flesh.

These same kinds of problems are found more recently in an article by Andy Johnson, who tackles Martin head-on, arguing that "flesh and blood" in 1 Corinthians 15.50 does not refer to a particular kind of materiality (or "stuff"), but rather to "living people who are capable of dying."[84] He contends that "flesh and blood" in the few known uses of the phrase predating 1 Corinthians means nothing more than "living people" and is normally used to distinguish that which is only human from that which is divine.[85] The most relevant of these data is found in Galatians 1.16. Johnson begins to get in trouble by disassociating "flesh and blood" in Galatians 1.16 from "those who were apostles before me" in Galatians 1.17 in order to make "flesh and blood" cohere with the ψυχικὸς ἄνθρωπος in 1 Corinthians 2.14, which has an epistemological thrust. The Jerusalem apostles of Galatians 1, for Johnson, are not *mere* "flesh and blood" because they "did make sense of the world in terms of a crucified Messiah."[86] Johnson, however, ignores the "immediately" (εὐθέως) of Galatians 1.16 in relationship to Paul's subsequent narration of trips to Jerusalem. I find it more probable that "flesh and blood" in this passage is a general statement about consultation with humans, whereas Galatians 1.17 is a specific statement about the apostles in Jerusalem. If so, "flesh and blood" includes the apostles and most certainly describes even those who have the Spirit. As with Gundry, it does not seem as if Johnson really understands the tradition within which Martin interprets Paul, stating that "[t]he net effect of this [his study] is to remove 1 Cor 15:50 as a 'trump card' from the hands of those who use it to argue that Paul holds to a more 'spiritual' concept of resurrection as opposed to what they might term a more 'physical/material' one."[87] Again, Martin's whole point is that for Paul, as with the Stoics, everything is what we would call "material." The key question is What kind of material?

Despite a growing movement that sees Paul's anthropology as heavily influenced by Greek philosophy—and I think that Martin and now Troels Engberg-Pedersen offer the most satisfying reading of 1 Corinthians 15— we should remember that the Apostle might not have had a consistent, highly crystallized anthropology. The exact measure of continuity and discontinuity between life in this age and the next is remarkably unclear from letter to letter. Terms could be flexed and stretched in a variety of directions, either by himself, or by his later interpreters.[88] This also means that it might be a bit naïve to ask whether or not a second-century author "got Paul right." If the "historical" Paul was not a static target on this issue, then it would be more advisable to ask about how individual second-century writers interpreted particular Pauline letters and passages. In 1 Corinthians 15.35–58, for instance, Paul seems to posit a significant discontinuity between the present and future bodies in an attempt to answer the nervous question of his opponents: How are corpses raised? With what sort of body (ποίῳ σώματι) do they come? Paul's answer in 1 Corinthians 15.50 suggests that σάρξ was the sticking point.

Given the rather negative appraisal of σάρξ in 1 Corinthians, the reader of 3 Corinthians, ostensibly addressed to the same community, should be surprised to find its Paul saying quite positive things about σάρξ. Vestiges of the earlier Pauline tradition remain, such as the imprisonment of the flesh to "lust" (2.11: ἡδονή) and its "perishing" state (2.15: σαρκός ἀπολλυμένης). Yet through his fleshly birth to Mary (2.5, 6, 13, 15) and subsequent resurrection in the flesh, Jesus acted to "set all flesh free by his own flesh" (2.6: ἐλευθερώσῃ πᾶσαν σάρκα διὰ τῆς ἰδίας σάρκος).[89] His resurrection in the flesh serves as a model for the future fleshly resurrection of believers (2.6; τύπος).[90] Because Christ has saved the flesh, σάρξ becomes an integral part of the resurrection body. Mankind is raised from the dead "as those with flesh (σαρκικούς)" (2.6), a point that is presented as being so deeply entrenched in the apostolic tradition that Paul says, "Now those who say to you 'There is no resurrection of the flesh,' for them there is no resurrection" (2.24).[91]

The pseudepigrapher bolsters his argument for the resurrection of the flesh by weaving together several Scriptural illustrations, each of which emphasizes the continuity of the flesh, pre- and post-resurrection.[92] The first and most important for our inquiry (2.26–28), concerning the sowing and rising of the seed, comes from the discussion of the resurrection body in 1 Corinthians 15.36–38.[93] A number of specific terms (σπέρμα; σῶμα; and γυμνός), as Hovhanessian has noted, connect these passages.[94] The logic of *3 Corinthians*, however, runs counter to what we find in 1 Corinthians. The Paul of 1 Corinthians 15 uses the image of the seed because the transformation that it undergoes while in the ground approximates his own conception of the resurrection body. As he argues, "that which you sow, *you do not sow* the future body (σῶμα), but a bare grain (γυμνὸν κόκκον)" (1 Cor 15.37). At the resurrection God endows what was formerly a bare grain with a "body" (σῶμα) of his own choosing (1 Cor 15.38). This new body stands in distinction from the former body.[95] Paul offers a series of contrasts (1 Cor 15.42–44). No longer being characterized by "perishability" (φθορά), "dishonor" (ἀτιμία), "weakness" (ἀσθενία) and "soulishness" (ψυχικός), the resurrection body will be characterized by "imperishability" (ἀφθαρσία), "glory" (δόξα), "power" (δύναμις), and "spirituality" (πνευματικός), because Christ has "given life" to the mortal body (1 Cor 15.45).[96] There is an unstated connection here between the flesh and the pre-resurrection body. The pre-resurrection body is characterized by terms that have been applied to flesh elsewhere in Pauline letters precisely because it continues to be limited by the qualities of the flesh.

There is also no distinction here between the bodies of believers and non-believers, as well as no suggestion that the flesh has been redeemed from slavery to sin, as is stated in *3 Corinthians*. In order for the body to "inherit the kingdom of God," it must be rid of the flesh (1 Cor 15.50). This ridding of the flesh occurs through the spiritual transformation of the body in the future. Paul continues: "The dead will be raised incorruptible and we will be changed (ἀλλαγησόμεθα)" (1 Cor 15.52). This transformation is described similarly in Philippians 3.21: "[He] will transform (μετασχηματίσει) the body of our humiliation into conformity with the body of his glory."

It is this necessary transformation of the body that the author of *3 Corinthians* misses in taking this illustration from 1 Corinthians 15. He begins:

For they [Simon and Cleobius] do not know, O Corinthian men, about the sowing of wheat or of the other seeds, that they are cast naked onto the earth, and after altogether perishing below are raised by the will of God, and have also been clothed with a body (2.26).

This is essentially the argument of 1 Corinthians. Yet the parable serves only as a window into the conversation of that text, and the author quickly diverges from its line of thought, reconfiguring it along the way. He continues, "So that not only is the body that has been thrown down raised, but it has been blessed with abundant prosperity" (2.27). This is a rather different interpretation of the image of the seed, for the pseudepigrapher suggests that the body that is raised is nothing more than a now-vindicated version of the body that has died. That the body has not undergone any significant transformation is evident from the pseudepigrapher's subsequent example of Jonah, who escapes from Hades with his hair and eyelashes intact (2.30). The argument is similar to that of Tertullian, who uses the wandering children of Israel in the wilderness and the salvation of Jonah as *topoi* for bodily resurrection:

> That the raiment and shoes of the children of Israel remained unworn and fresh from the space of forty years; that in their very persons the exact point of convenience and propriety checked the rank growth of the nails and hair, so that any excess herein might not be attributed to indecency . . . that Jonah was swallowed by the monster of the deep, in whose belly whole ships were devoured, and after three days was vomited out again safe and sound . . . to what faith do these notable facts bear witness, if not to that which ought to inspire in us the belief that they are proofs and documents of our own future integrity and perfect resurrection? (*Res.* 58; cf. *Res.* 35)[97]

Tertullian then legitimates these comparisons by referring to 1 Corinthians 10.6.

The complete continuity, and thus permanence, of the flesh is ultimately driven home by the author of *3 Corinthians* through a reference to 2 Kings 13.20–21, where Elisha's bones give life to a dead Israelite corpse. Paul follows the allusion with a question: "then what about you, upon whom the body and the bones and the Spirit of Christ have been cast, will you not be raised in that day having healthy flesh (ἔχοντες ὑγιῆ τὴν σάρκα)?" (2.32). The cryptic quality of the question should not cause us to miss the pseudepigrapher's final statement regarding σάρξ: it is to be raised "healthy."

We have, then, two different "Pauls." The first is the Paul of 1 Corinthians 15, whose estimation of the flesh is decidedly negative. Σάρξ is an anthropologically and eschatologically inferior quality of "this age," and thus "cannot inherit the kingdom of God." The σῶμα is in need of transformation, which means the stripping off of the flesh and the final putting on of the Spirit. The second is the Paul of *3 Corinthians*, who invokes a key image from 1 Corinthians 15 but has reconfigured it (knowingly or unknowingly) so as to attribute language and thought to the Paul of 1 Corinthians that is quite foreign.[98] The distinction between σῶμα and σάρξ is clearly absent, leaving us with a stunning twist of fate.[99] The Paul of *3 Corinthians* has denied the resurrection of the Paul of 1 Corinthians! As noted above, the Paul of *3 Corinthians* vehemently states, "Now those who say to you 'There is no resurrection of the flesh,' for them there is no resurrection" (2.24). The first half of this statement closely parallels 1 Corinthians:

πῶς λέγουσιν ἐν ὑμῖν τινες ὅτι ἀνάστασις νεκρῶν οὐκ ἔστιν; (1 Cor. 15.2);

δὲ οἱ ὑμῖν λέγουσιν ἀνάστασις οὐκ ἔστιν σάρκος (3 Cor. 2.24).

In each passage the phrase "those who are saying" refers to a group that has caused trouble within the Corinthian church because of aberrant views of the resurrection. Paul's interlocutors in 1 Corinthians are those who deny a resuscitation of corpses. He clarifies his position, coming quite close to his opponents and the modified Platonism of his day by *affirming* the pneumatic (not sarkic) nature of the resurrection body.[100] His adversaries in *3 Corinthians* likewise deny a "fleshly" resurrection. In this case, he not only directly *refutes* their position but also denies their participation in the resurrection. One problem: Paul of 1 Corinthians appears to have agreed with Simon and Cleobius:

σὰρξ καὶ αἷμα βασιλείαν θεοῦ κληρονομῆσαι **οὐ** δύναται (1 Cor 15.50);

οὐδὲ ἀνάστασιν εἶναι **σαρκός** (3 Cor. 1.12).

Excursus: The Resurrection of the Flesh in Early Proto-Orthodox Christianity

Belief in the resurrection of the flesh among the proto-orthodox had its origins in several intertwined factors.[101] Most important was the debate over the nature of Jesus' own body, already visible in the Johannine (John 1.14; 1 John 1.1–3; 4.2–3; 2 John 7) and Ignatian (*Eph.* 7.2; 18.2; 20.2; *Magn.* 1.2; 11.1; *Trall.* 8.1; 9.1–2; *Rom.* 7.3; *Philad.* 4.1; 5.1; *Smyrn.* 1.1–2; 3.1–3; 7.1;

12.2) literature. This debate, of course, included not only the nature of Jesus' pre-crucifixion body, but also the nature of his post-resurrection body. The use of σάρξ to describe Jesus' resurrected state is found as early as the Gospel of Luke: "Look at my hands and feet to see that it is I, myself. Touch me and see. For a spirit does not have flesh (σάρκα) and bones, as you see that I have" (24.39). The *general* resurrection of the *flesh* is found as early as *1 Clement*, where Job functions as proof for the resurrection: "And again, Job says, 'And you will raise up this flesh (σάρκα) of mine, which has suffered all these things.'" (26.3).[102]

Except for these two passages, the "resurrection from the dead (νεκρῶν)" is the overwhelming default language of our earliest texts.[103] But "resurrection from" says nothing about "resurrection to." The resurrection *from* the dead could result in resurrection *to* angelic-like status according to one layer of the triple tradition (Matt 22.30; Mark 12.25; Luke 20.36). Because this latter tradition approaches the notion of astral immortality, it is hard to imagine that it conceives of the post-resurrection existence as fleshly. Procreation, certainly, is out.[104] A. H. C. van Eijk has shown how flexible the verbs ἐγείρω and ἀνίστημι were within early Christian post-mortem hope. The object with which they are paired makes all the difference. "You must qualify them," and neither the "ecclesiastical" nor the "Gnostic" qualifications were distortions of some natural use of these verbs.[105] Dale Martin, contrasting the post-resurrection accounts in the canonical gospels and the *Gospel of Peter*, suggests that there was "no fixed tradition" about the nature of Jesus' resurrection body in the first century C.E.[106] Moreover, as we will see in the following chapter, anthropological ambiguity exists in the Pauline letter corpus as well.[107] The seemingly anti-material and docetic beliefs of some late first-century Christians likely provoked the counter-emphasis on Jesus' *fleshly* resurrection that we see beginning in Ignatius (ἐν σαρκὶ: *Smyrn.* 3.1).[108] Since, according to proto-orthodox logic, Jesus' resurrection was in the flesh and he was the "first-fruits" (1 Cor 15.20; cf. 1 Cor 6.14; 2 Cor 4.14) and the "first-born" (Col 1.18; Rev 1.5), then his followers, too, will be raised with flesh (*1 Clem.* 24.1; Ign., *Trall.* 9.2).[109]

Summary and Conclusion: Constructing the "Paul" of 3 Corinthians

In order to reclaim the Paul of 1 Corinthians from opposing readings like the one we find in the *Gospel of Philip* 56.26–57.1 (cf. Chapter 2), the pseudepigrapher of *3 Corinthians* paints a complex textual image of the Apostle.

He does not merely offer a competing interpretation of 1 Corinthians. Rather, through the use of a variety of techniques, the pseudepigrapher goes several steps further in order to present a Paul who is more than prepared (2.2: "I am not astonished") to confront teaching that stands outside the perceived apostolic norm. Even more, the Paul of *3 Corinthians* not only defends, but is dependent on the traditions of the apostles. This particular portrayal of Paul develops in a number of ways. First, it positions Paul against Simon, the "father of all heretics" (Iren., *Haer.* 3.pref.1) and his sometime right-hand man, Cleobius. For Paul to defeat Simon was to overthrow the "many deviant views" (2.1) of the author's own day.

Second, the Paul of *3 Corinthians* describes his own relationship to the apostolic tradition, the "canon" of the prophets, and the Gospel (2.36), as one of dependence: "For I entrusted to you in the beginning what I also received from the apostles who came before me, and who spent all their time with Jesus Christ" (2.4). The use of language from 1 Corinthians works to establish continuity with this earlier Pauline tradition, while at the same time adding to and altering the tradition in order to clarify the legitimizing source of Paul's teaching. This is similar to another second-century text, the *Epistula Apostolorum*, where the risen Jesus predicts the conversion of Paul, invoking the language of both 1 Corinthians 15.8 and Galatians 1:16 ("The last of the last will become a preacher to the Gentiles"). But it is the eleven who will heal Paul's blindness, not Ananias, as in Acts 9. Furthermore, Jesus exhorts the eleven to "[t]each and remind (him) what has been said in the scriptures and fulfilled concerning me, and then he will be for the salvation of the Gentiles" (31).[110] The original apostles provide the legitimizing force for and doctrinal content of Paul's ministry.

The earlier layer of Pauline material (1 Corinthians and Galatians) itself exhibits a certain tension with respect to Paul's relationship with the other Apostles. Though 1 Corinthians 15 uses technical terminology (15:1, 3–παραλαμβάνω and παραδίδωμι) to place Paul within the context of a larger framework of early Christian experience (15:8) and apostolic calling (15:10–11), it is strangely, if not purposefully, silent on the origin of Paul's gospel. On the other hand, Galatians 1, which has been combined with 1 Corinthians 15 in the *Epistula Apostolorum*, uses the same technical terminology to differentiate Paul's gospel from human authorities, particularly those who "appear to be pillars" (2.9) in Jerusalem:

οὐδὲ γὰρ ἐγὼ παρὰ ἀνθρώπου παρέλαβον αὐτὸ οὔτε ἐδιδάχθην ἀλλὰ δι᾽ ἀποκαλύψεως Ἰησοῦ Χριστοῦ (Gal 1.12);

> For *neither did I receive* it from a human source, nor was I taught it,
> but I received it through a revelation of Jesus Christ (Gal 1.12).

This ambiguity allows the early Pauline tradition to be stretched in either direction, depending on which text is allowed to be the interpretive filter for the other. It is not a matter of, Who gets Paul right? The tradition resists systematization here. Rather, it is a matter of, which Paul? Which Pauline texts are employed to construct a particular image of Paul that is helpful for any particular reputational entrepreneur? How are the texts used, and what place do they have in the entrepreneur's ideological program? The author of *3 Corinthians* finds 1 Corinthians most helpful, but, in deploying its language, he has pushed beyond what the text actually says. In *3 Corinthians*, Pauline teaching is not only consistent with the other apostles, but has been "received from" them (2.4). This is an example of what Shils calls an "endogenous" change in the tradition (cf. Chapter 4). The *traditum* possesses some element of mystery that must be resolved. "Imagining, reasoning, observing, expressing are the activities which go beyond the tradition as it has been presented. . . . There is something in the tradition which calls forth a desire to change it by making improvements in it."[111] The endogenous change, as is often the case, is likely the result of an exogenous change: the rise of competing Pauline traditions that read the same texts within a different framework.

Third, in constructing an image of a Paul who is concerned for dogmatic and apostolic tradition and who can be most helpful in the reclamation of 1 Corinthians 15, the author of *3 Corinthians* programmatically employs the language of the Pastoral Epistles. The Pastoral Paul functions as a *lieu de mémoire* in *3 Corinthians*. Pierre Nora describes a site of memory as "any significant entity, whether material or nonmaterial in nature, which by dint of human will or the work of time has become a symbolic element of the memorial heritage of any community."[112] Communal sites of memory organize and frame the recollection of the past and provide commemorative symbols for constraining the tradition into the future. Memories are nothing but theoretical abstractions, devoid of meaning, unless they have a location, or what Halbwachs called a "landmark."[113] The material landmark (inclusive of texts) fixes the collective memory for the future, as long as it is still accessible.[114]

Barry Schwartz, as we have seen, describes this active attempt to remember one thing in light of another as the process of "keying" and "framing." Keying "transforms the meaning of activities understood in terms of one event by comparing them with activities understood in terms of another. . . . Keying arranges cultural symbols into a publicly visible discourse that flows through the organizations and institutions of the social world."[115] Schwartz is dependent here on Geertz, who also concludes that "Every conscious perception is . . . an act of recognition, a pairing in which an object (or an event, an act, an emotion) is identified by placing it against the background of an appropriate symbol."[116] The author of *3 Corinthians* has keyed Paul to the other Apostles, asking his readers to view the Apostle in light of wider apostolic contributions. He has also framed his own portrayal of Paul within the bounds of a particular material/textual site (the Pastorals), programming his readers to envision the polemical Paul of the Pastorals as the primary reference point for their memory of the Apostle. Marcion did the same with Galatians (Tertullian, *Marc.* 3.4.2; Epiphanius, *Pan.* 42.9.4; 11.8). The Valentinians preferred 1 Corinthians (Irenaeus, *Haer.* 3.2.1; 5.9.1; Tertullian, *Res.* 48.1). Origen found the heart of Pauline theology in Ephesians (*Hom. Ezech.* 7.10; *Princ.* 3.2.4; *Cels.* 3.20), as Luther would later elevate Romans.[117] Each of Paul's entrepreneurs works to frame their image of Paul by keying him to particular sites in the earliest layer of the Pauline tradition.

The keying of *3 Corinthians* to the Pastoral Epistles is the ultimate means of providing an authoritative image of Paul as the defender of the apostolic tradition, "the deposit" (1 Tim 6.20; 2 Tim 1.12, 14). His opponents in Corinth are "upsetting the faith of some" (*3 Cor.* 1.2; cf. 2 Tim 2.18; Titus 1.11). Paul must intervene so that "their foolishness might become evident." (*3 Cor.* 1.16; cf. 2 Tim 3.9). He finally asks the Corinthians to "[t]urn away from these kinds of people" (*3 Cor.* 2.21; cf. 2 Tim 3.5). As we will see in the next chapter, by the end of the second century, the proto-orthodox *regula veritatis* had come to include a definitive statement about the resurrection of the *flesh*. This communal confession was one of the primary constraining forces in how the proto-orthodox read and remembered Paul's texts. For Paul to defend the deposit, then, was for him to speak in favor of the fleshly resurrection.

The reading of 1 Corinthians 15 that *3 Corinthians* offers, then, does not stand on its own, but is part of a larger web of signification whereby a Paul is being constructed whose biography and texts can bear the burden of second-century proto-orthodox theology. James Aageson is quite correct when he states:

If the image of Paul and the theology of his letters were thoroughly interwoven in the early church, as they undoubtedly were, the adaptation of Paul and his words by the early Christians was more than an issue of simple textual reinterpretation. It was also a matter of an evolving Pauline image merging with the developing concerns of the day.[118]

The similarities between *3 Corinthians* and Irenaeus's *Adversus haereses* in their independent constructions of the Pauline tradition, as we will see, suggest that their authors were living in the same generation and that they did not operate *de novo*, but participated in a common stream of Pauline reception.[119] These second-century texts, then, are just as much mirrors of this tradition of Pauline memory as they are attempts to further illumine the Apostle for their readers/hearers. Reputational entrepreneurs, as Schwartz reminds, offer "collective representations—images that existed in the mind of the entrepreneur because they first existed in certain segments of the society."[120] This wider tradition, represented by *3 Corinthians* and *Adversus haereses*, finds anthropological continuity between this age and the next in 1 Corinthians 15 (at least in the case of believers), whereas 1 Corinthians itself posits discontinuity: "flesh and blood cannot inherit the kingdom of God" (15.50). Since the early Pauline texts, as a group, however, do not display a consistent anthropological terminology, Irenaeus, as we will see, was able to gain some traction for his defense of 1 Corinthians 15.50 by surrounding it with a complex interpretive web, constructed mainly of other Pauline texts. To his work we now turn.

6

Expounding Paul: The Image of Paul in Irenaeus's Adversus haereses

> *But is such transcendence possible? We are, whether we acknowledge it or not, what the past has made us and we cannot eradicate from ourselves, even in America, those parts of ourselves which are formed by our relationship to each formative stage in our history.*
>
> ALASDAIR MACINTYRE, After Virtue[1]

IRENAEUS OF LYONS concludes Book Four of his *Adversus haereses* with the following anticipatory statement:

> But it is necessary to subjoin to this composition, in what follows, also the doctrine of Paul after the words of the Lord, to examine the opinion of this man, and expound the apostle, and to explain whatsoever [passages] have received *other interpretations* from the heretics, who have altogether *misunderstood* what Paul has spoken, and to point out *the folly of their mad opinions*; and to demonstrate from that same Paul, from whose [writings] they press questions upon us, that they are indeed *utterers of falsehood*, but that the apostle was a *preacher of the truth*, and that he taught all things agreeable to *the preaching of the truth.* (4.41.4)[2]

As we saw in Chapter 1, this passage is one of several windows into the polemical discourse of the second century over the proper interpretation of Pauline texts specifically, and the Pauline legacy in general.[3] This discourse was necessitated by the rich variety of "Pauline" texts and traditions that were available by the late second century and the concomitant diversity of Christian authors who wrote about Paul or interpreted his texts for their communities. Tertullian would shortly thereafter lament that the followers of Marcion had "adopted" Paul as their own Apostle (*Marc.* 3.5.4: *haereticorum apostolus*). In order to defend a particular image of Paul as a "preacher of the truth," Irenaeus, as we will see, feels compelled to "expound the apostle" in ways that are consonant with his own *regula veritatis*. Image construction and textual interpretation are closely related here, as they were in *3 Corinthians*. And while the proper memory of Paul is what is ultimately at stake, it must be formed and transmitted within the given ideological (social) constraints.

Since the 1990s, the use and interpretation of Paul in Irenaeus has been ably studied at length by Rolf Noormann and in brief by a number of others.[4] This chapter quickly summarizes the state of Irenaean Studies as it relates to the Pauline tradition and then explores several aspects of the portrait of Paul found in *Adversus haereses* that have important affinities with the Pauline tradition in *3 Corinthians*.[5] These similarities allow us to understand both texts as participants in a wider trajectory of Pauline reception (a particular stream of proto-orthodox memory) at the end of the second century. The size of Irenaeus's project will also help us understand the larger ideological boundaries within which his Paul fits. As such, we will observe the social forces that shape his memory of Paul and that drive his own claims about the "real" Paul.

Paul in Irenaeus: A Brief Modern History

Johannes Werner's *Der Paulinismus des Irenaeus*, published in 1889, was the first modern scholarly attempt at a comprehensive statement about the reception of Paul in Irenaeus.[6] Werner identified 206 Pauline citations in *Adversus haereses*, excluding 18 instances where Irenaeus relayed information about his opponents' use of Paul.[7] All of the now canonical Pauline letters were cited except Philemon, resulting in Paul being the most frequently quoted biblical author in Irenaeus.[8] Werner concluded that since Irenaeus never referred to a Pauline text as Scripture (γραφή), his letters had less authority for the heresiologist than did the Jewish Scriptures.[9] Irenaeus even appears to differentiate between Scripture and Paul's letters: *quoniam enim sunt in caelis spiritales conditiones, uniuersae clamant Scripturae, et Paulus autem testimonium perhibet quoniam sunt spiritalia* (*Haer.* 2.30.7; 140–142).[10] Despite this distinction, it was clear to Werner on the basis of Irenaeus's actual argumentative use of Pauline texts that they held serious theological authority for the heresiologist.[11] Yet he concluded that Irenaeus's use of Paul was entirely incongruous with

Paul's own meaning on most occasions and served merely as proof-texts for his own theological polemic (e.g., Irenaeus's use of 2 Cor 4.4 in *Haer.* 3.7.1–2).[12] Werner held the "theology of the cross" to be Paul's central doctrine, and inasmuch as Irenaeus took little notice of this aspect of Pauline teaching, he had neglected (for Werner) the heart of the Apostle.[13] He also charged Irenaeus with incipient Pelagianism and with deviating from Paul's teaching on salvation through faith and grace.[14] Similarly, Irenaeus's view of faith as assent to the "rule of truth" seemed too distant from Paul's emphasis on faith as trust in God's unconditional means of salvation.[15] Finally, Werner held that Irenaeus was compelled to make such heavy use of Paul only in light of the Apostle's authority among his theological opponents.[16]

Werner's work was done in the era, as we have seen, when many Protestant scholars posited a second-century Pauline captivity to the "heretics." When Irenaeus finally took up Paul for the proto-orthodox, a large interpretive gulf of some 125 years lay between Paul and the earliest serious proto-orthodox reflection on his letters. Naturally, for these scholars, Irenaeus got the "historical" Paul all wrong.[17] Harnack and Campenhausen, among others, viewed Irenaeus's Paul as being an elaborate commingling of the "historical" Paul with the non-Pauline Acts and Pastoral Epistles. Their "historical" Paul was the Paul interpreted through developing Lutheranism.[18] As Ernst Dassmann said:

> Werner compares Irenaeus to a constricted Paulinism corresponding to the understanding of Paul *of his own* time, without allowing for a legitimate further development and the translation of Pauline thought in view of new theological questions.[19]

Aside from the simple fact that Irenaeus *does* refer to Pauline texts as γραφή (cf. the use of Gal 5.21 in *Haer.* 1.6.3) and places the testimony of the Apostle (*Haer.* 3.6.5–7.2) between the Prophets (3.6.1–4) and the Savior (3.8.1–3) in his defense of the unity of God, signs of a shift in the narrative undergirding Werner's broader conclusions could already be seen in the early-twentieth century and finally came to full fruition in the 1970s on two fronts.[20] The first was described in Chapter 3. Lindemann, Dassmann, and Rensberger argued that the proto-orthodox never ceded Paul to the "heretics" and that the phenomenon of Pauline pseudepigraphy, the collection and distribution of Pauline letters, and the use of Paul in the Apostolic Fathers was indicative of Paul's authority among their ranks.

The second line of attack came from scholars who saw greater continuity between the "historical" Paul and Irenaeus's use of Paul than had previous generations.[21] This happened across a range of topics, but was most important in the areas of anthropological redemption from Sin "in Christ"[22] and the salvation-historical unity and recapitulation of all things wrought in the Second Adam.[23] Differences in emphasis between Paul and Irenaeus were chalked up to "der Verschiedenheit der jeweiligen Situation."[24] This is the case particularly for Irenaeus's emphasis on the Incarnation rather than the cross.

Rolf Noormann's *Irenäus als Paulusinterpret* (1994) was particularly important, 100 years after Werner, in redrawing how we view Irenaeus's Paulinism. Noormann reminded that Paul is ὁ ἀπόστολος for Irenaeus, who cites him more than any other New Testament writer.[25] More important, he argued that Irenaeus's use of Paul stood within a burgeoning interpretive tradition. Irenaeus may have been the first to author a text in which Paul's letters were so extensively used, but his views about Paul and his interpretation of Pauline texts were largely traditioned to him.[26] Noormann noted Irenaeus's connection to Polycarp, who had previously made wide use of Pauline letters in his *Epistle to the Philippians*.[27] Irenaeus's reception of Paul may have also been partially mediated through "the certain presbyter" mentioned in *Haer.* 4.27.1.[28] Harnack had posited that this presbyter was the source for much of Irenaeus's anti-Marcionite polemic in *Adversus haereses* 4.27–32, including the bevy of references to Pauline letters in this section, one of which (Rom 11.17, 21) is said to have come directly from "the presbyter" (*Haer.* 4.27.2).[29] Some have pushed beyond Noormann here, arguing that Polycarp was Irenaeus's unnamed presbyter.[30]

Noormann's project, like the earlier work of Lindemann, Dassmann, and Rensberger, ultimately challenged the Pauline Captivity narrative.[31] He determined that the sheer breadth of Pauline texts invoked by Irenaeus and the variety of ways in which Irenaeus made use of Pauline literature mitigates any claims that he dealt with Paul only because of his opponents' affinity for the Apostle.[32] The reception of Paul in Irenaeus is "ein vielfältiges Phänomen."[33] As such, Irenaeus was the inheritor of a proto-orthodox theology that had fully assimilated Paul, even if Paul was not foundational within this inheritance.[34] Morever, the Deutero-Paulines and Acts were not the hermeneutical lenses or gate-keepers of Irenaeus's Pauline tradition.[35] 1 Corinthians, Romans, and Galatians are much more frequently cited.[36]

Noormann scrupulously worked through every instance of a Pauline citation/allusion in Irenaeus, often invoking modern scholarship on Paul to measure how close or far Irenaeus's invocation of the Apostle was from the Apostle's "true" meaning.[37] Noormann conceded that in many places Irenaeus did not have Paul "right." Rather than reading Paul in light of the Jew/Gentile issue, or the eschatological tension and apocalyptic dualism so prevalent throughout Paul's letters, Irenaeus invoked Pauline literature to undergird three central themes: salvation history (unity of the Creator with the God of Jesus Christ); Christology (Christ's divine incarnation as Second Adam who restores humanity to immortality); and anthropology (the resurrection of the flesh).[38] On the whole, however, while noting differences, Noormann saw much greater continuity between Paul and Irenaeus's use of Pauline texts than did Werner.[39]

Richard Norris and David Balás, writing at the same time as Noormann (early 1990s), offered corroborating findings, each with important additional angles. Norris argued that Irenaeus normally used Paul constructively, showing how Paul's texts were frequently invoked by Irenaeus as evidence against heretical teaching, *in general*, or to support his own broad theological agenda. They were not cited solely for the purpose of ironing out false readings of particular Pauline texts (though this did happen on occasion; cf. discussion later in this chapter on 1 Cor 15.50).[40] Balás showed that when Irenaeus describes in Book One the texts adduced by his opponents, there is no excessive dependence on Paul by any of them, excepting Marcion.[41] "The fullness of time" in Galatians 4.4–6, according to Norris, provided a particularly fruitful place for Irenaeus to turn in his defense of the unity of God, Christ, and salvation-history (cf. *Haer.* 3.16.3, 7; 3.22.1).[42] He argued that the language of this one text subtly appears in Irenaeus's work at least 13 times (mainly in Books Three and Four), making it hard to distinguish whether or not one is reading a citation of/allusion to Paul or whether the Pauline text had so saturated Irenaeus's theological vocabulary that he was unconsciously returning to it time and again.[43]

Paul and the Apostles

I stand in broad agreement with Noormann, Norris, and Balás about the place of Paul in Irenaeus's thought and polemic. They have succeeded in prying Irenaeus from the clutches of the Pauline Captivity narrative. The remainder of this chapter pushes the conversation further, asking, in particular, about how Irenaeus envisioned the Apostle. What image of Paul does he construct in *Adversus haereses*? What is at stake in this image? How are Pauline texts used and interpreted to aid in its production? There are, of course, numerous aspects of the Pauline tradition in Irenaeus that could be addressed. I have isolated here Irenaeus's portrayal of Paul's relationship to the other apostles, his programmatic use of the Pastoral Epistles in crafting his heresiological tome, and the hermeneutical moves he makes in reading 1 Corinthians 15 as a defense of the resurrection of the flesh—aspects of the Pauline tradition that also appear in *3 Corinthians*. By bringing their shared image of Paul together in successive chapters, we can peer into one stage of one particular trajectory of Pauline reception from two different angles. We should also note that each of these aspects of Irenaeus's use of earlier Pauline materials is different in kind. The portrayal of Paul's relationship with the apostles attempts to provide a particular narrative of Paul. The programmatic use of the Pastorals envisions Paul through the lens of a particular set of Pauline texts. And the extended reading of 1 Corinthians 15.50 offered in Book Five shows how the canon of Pauline literature, as well as Irenaeus's own *regula veritatis*, shapes his reading of any one Pauline text. Each of these elements works together to provide a complex image of the Apostle. By taking them together, we can offer a thick description of the Pauline tradition in Irenaeus.

Like *3 Corinthians*, Irenaeus attempts to bind Paul to the other Apostles, and thus the wider "apostolic tradition."[44] The results of the so-called Jerusalem Council in Acts 15 and Galatians 2 are particularly important for him. From Luke's version, Irenaeus recounts the theological harmony between Paul, James, and Peter (3.12.14). Approval from the Jerusalem apostles, however, was not enough. Irenaeus reminds his readers, citing Galatians 2.5, that from Paul's side there was a willing subjection to them: "For an hour we *did* give place to subjection" (3.13.3; 49: *ad horam cessimus subiectioni*).[45] Although this reading of Galatians is paralleled in certain "Western" witnesses of Paul (D* b d; cf. Tert; MVict[ms]; Ambst; Hier[ms]; Pel; Aug; Prim), it stands at odds with the reading preserved in the rest of the tradition: "to whom we *did not* yield in subjection for even an hour!" (οἷς οὐδὲ πρὸς ὥραν εἴξαμεν τῇ ὑποταγῇ).[46] This latter reading, preferred by the editors of the Nestle-Aland and the United Bible Society and by major commentators, was supported by Marcion, whom Tertullian (in support of Irenaeus's reading) accused of doctoring the text:

> For let us pay attention to the meaning of his [Paul's] words, and the purpose of them, and [your] falsification of scripture will become evident . . . *they did give place* because there were people on whose account concession was advisable. For this was in keeping with

faith unripe and still in doubt regarding the observance of the law, when even the apostle himself suspected he might have run, or might still be running, in vain. . . . Of necessity therefore *he gave place*, for a time. (*Marc.* 5.3.3)[47]

Irenaeus's Pauline text of Galatians, then, portrays an Apostle who is more than ready to subject his own ministry to the Jerusalem church. Not even Paul's boast to have "worked harder than all of them [the other apostles]" (1 Cor 15.10) is allowed to stand as a potential wedge between Paul and the others. Irenaeus explains this claim in light of the special difficulties Paul had in ministering to Gentiles, who lacked both the prophetic oracles about Christ in the Jewish Scriptures as well as any notion of the resurrection of the dead (4.24.1).[48] In another place, citing Galatians 2.8, Irenaeus reminds his readers that "one and the same God" (*unum et ipsum Deum*) worked in Peter and Paul for their apostleships (*Haer.* 3.13.1; 3–4). These stand together not only in Jerusalem, but also in Rome, where they are described as cofounders of that eminent church (3.3.2).[49]

Irenaeus's argument is directed against opponents who claim that "Paul alone knew the truth, and that to him the mystery was manifested by revelation" (3.13.1; 1–3: *solum Paulum vertitatem cognovisse, cui per revelationem manifestatum est mysterium*).[50] Julius Wagenmann correctly concluded, nearly a century ago, that "Dies zu unternehmen sah sich auch Irenäus deshalb genötigt, weil die Gegner von allen Seiten gegen die Katholizität und Apostolizität des Paulus Sturm liefen."[51] In refutation, Irenaeus points to Pauline texts where the Apostle sees his own ministry as part of the larger apostolic movement (3.13.1):

For the One who worked in Peter for apostleship to the Circumcised also worked in me for apostleship to the Gentiles (Gal 2.8);

And how will *they* preach if *they* are not sent? As it is written, "How beautiful are the feet of those who bring good news" (Rom 10.15; emphasis mine);

Whether, then, it was I or they, so we preach and so you have believed (1 Cor 15.11).[52]

Paul's relationship to Luke, discussed first in *Haer.* 3.1.1 ("Luke also, the companion of Paul, recorded in a book the Gospel preached by him

[Paul]"), functions similarly. Irenaeus emphasizes it, on the one hand, in order to attack the selective use of Luke by Marcion and the Valentinians, claiming that Luke was privy to Paul's common teaching and thus knew the truth of the gospel (3.14.1–4).[53] Those who reject the Lukan post-resurrection accounts are, by default, rejecting their own Apostle.[54] On the other side of the theological equation, Irenaeus uses the reverse argument against the Ebionites. If the Ebionites accept the Lukan writings, then they must also accept Paul as a Christ-ordained Apostle (3.15.1). Luke, for instance, narrates Paul's apostolic call on three occasions (Acts 9, 22, 26). In a variety of ways, then, "Luc justifie Paul et Paul justifie Luc."[55]

As in *3 Corinthians*, the relationship between Paul and the apostles in *Adversus haereses* is one of subordination and dependence. The author of *3 Corinthians* uses the language of an earlier Pauline text (1 Cor 11.23; 15.3) to say something quite different from that text. Irenaeus also employs Pauline texts to substantiate the narrative of Acts 15. His version of Galatians 2.5 was particularly helpful for muting any tension between Paul and the "pillars." In both cases we can see how Pauline language and texts were interpreted and employed by his reputational entrepreneurs to preserve and produce a preferred image of the Apostle.

Irenaeus and the Pastoral Epistles

A second similarity exists between the construals of Paul in Irenaeus and *3 Corinthians*. The author of *3 Corinthians* constructs a Paul whose linguistic and theological world is bathed in the Pastoral Epistles. The polemical Paul of the Pastorals has become the hermeneutical lens through which the entire Pauline tradition is framed in *3 Corinthians*. The same is true for Irenaeus. I give extended attention here to this aspect of the Pauline tradition in Irenaeus because recent studies have misjudged the importance of the Pastorals for Irenaeus.

Eusebius of Caesarea provides the original Greek title of what we now call Irenaeus's *Adversus haereses*. If we did not have Eusebius, we could intuit it from the prefaces to Books Two, Four, and Five of Irenaeus's tome. The title contains a clear invocation of 1 Timothy:

Ἔλεγχος καὶ ἀνατροπή τῆς ψευδωνύμου γνώσεως (*Hist. eccl.* 5.7.1);

Ὦ Τιμόθεε, τὴν παραθήκην φύλαξον ἐκτρεπόμενος τὰς βεβήλους κενοφωνίας καὶ ἀντιθέσεις τῆς ψευδωνύμου γνώσεως (1 Tim 6.20).[56]

There is little to suggest that the phrase "falsely named knowledge" had become generalized polemical language by the late-second century. In fact, Clement of Alexandria is the only other second-century Christian writer to use this phrase (*Strom.* 2.11; 3.18; cf. 7.7) and the related ψευδωνύμοι γνωστικοί (*Strom.* 3.4).[57] His first use of the phrase in the *Stromateis* (2.11) is a direct citation of 1 Timothy 6.20, signaling the specific location from where he is drawing this language.

Aside from the exact verbal correspondence between 1 Timothy 6.20 and Irenaeus's title, the connection with 1 Timothy is further signaled by the later, explicit citation of this verse in *Adversus haereses* 2.14.7, as well as by the reinforcing, explicit citation of 1 Timothy in the opening lines of the preface to Book One:

> Certain people are discarding the Truth and introducing deceitful myths and *endless genealogies*, which **as the Apostle says,** *promote speculations rather than the divine training that is in faith* (1 Tim 1.4). By specious argumentation, craftily patched together, they mislead the minds of the more ignorant and ensnare them by falsifying the Lord's words. Thus they become wicked interpreters of genuine words (*Haer.* 1.pref.1);

> γενεαλογίας ἀπεράντους, αἵτινες ζητήσεις μᾶλλον παρέχουσι, **καθὼς ὁ ἀπόστολός φησιν**, ἢ οἰκοδομὴν θεοῦ τὴν ἐν πίστει (fr. gr. 1, 3–5);

> γενεαλογίαις ἀπεράντοις, αἵτινες ἐκζητήσεις παρέχουσιν μᾶλλον ἢ οἰκονομίαν θεοῦ τὴν ἐν πίστει (1 Tim 1.4).[58]

With these clear uses of 1 Timothy in mind, Carston Looks has pointed out other resonances of the language of the Pastoral Epistles in Irenaeus's title. Ἐλέγχω (cf. ἔλεγχος) occurs five times in the Pastoral Epistles (1 Tim 5.20; 2 Tim 4.2; Titus 1.9, 13; 2.15) and two of the three New Testament uses of ἀνατρέπω (cf. ἀνατροπή) are from the Pastoral Epistles (2 Tim 2.18; Titus 1.11).[59]

The prominent position that 1 Timothy (and, if Looks is correct, the other Pastoral Epistles) takes at the opening of Irenaeus's tome once garnered significant attention from scholars. As we have recounted in numerous places already, Harnack, Bauer, and Campenhausen, among a broad swath of scholars, sustained the Pauline Captivity narrative by arguing that it was only with the late-developing pseudonymous Pastoral

Epistles that a Paul emerged who could be useful for the proto-orthodox church in its fight against the "heretics." Irenaeus, in particular, was only able to reclaim Paul through his invocation of the Pastorals.

The dissolution of the Pauline Captivity narrative in the late 1980s brought with it an increased tendency to downplay the role of 1 Timothy and the other Pastorals in Irenaeus, beginning first with Rensberger and following through the work of Noormann and now Aageson.[60] While in basic agreement with the larger theses of these works, particularly as they relate to the Pauline Captivity narrative, I want to argue, building on the work of the literary theorist Gérard Genette, that, in fact, this double use of 1 Timothy at the beginning of Irenaeus's tome suggests a programmatic, intertextual relationship between *Adversus haereses* and the Pastoral Epistles.[61] The bishop of Lyons then returns over and over again to all three of these letters in a way that is uniquely consonant with the initial invocations of 1 Timothy. As is the case with *3 Corinthians*, the polemical Paul of the Pastorals provides a vocational analogue through which Irenaeus can view and construct his work. He has taken up the literary mantle of the Apostle, as particularly portrayed in the Pastorals, and sets out to overturn any theological speculation that falsely represents itself as privy to divine γνῶσις.[62]

The Extent, Nature, and Origin of Irenaeus's Use of the Pastorals

At the end of his "As the Apostle Teaches," Rensberger concluded that "The Pastoral Epistles are an utterly negligible factor in Irenaeus' use of Paul."[63] The paucity of direct references to and the lack of any sustained treatment of particular passages from the Pastoral Epistles were likewise key in Noormann's rejection of the position proffered by Harnack and others.[64] For Noormann, Irenaeus merely laces his polemic with the occasional tip of the hat to the Pastorals. In discussing Irenaeus's use of 1 Timothy 6.20 in *Adversus haereses* 2.14.7, for instance, he says that the heresiologist has taken from this text "nicht mehr als den polemischen Ausdruck."[65] Most recently, James Aageson, while conceding that Irenaeus opens *Adversus haereses* with a citation from 1 Timothy 1.4, concludes that "the Pastorals play only a small exegetical role in Irenaeus' attempt to interpret Paul. On the surface they appear to serve as little more than a source for the author's polemical statements."[66] Irenaeus was only indirectly indebted to the Pastorals for several of its images, which had become part of the theological *lingua franca* of the proto-orthodox by the end of the second century. The "deposit" (παραθήκη) of the Pastorals (1 Tim 6.20; 2 Tim 1.14), for instance, can be compared with Irenaeus's description of apostolic truth being deposited in a bank called the Church, from which all could withdraw (*Haer.* 3.4.1).[67]

Because the Irenaean use of the Pastorals factored so heavily in the older scholarly narrative of a Pauline Captivity to the "heretics" and because Rensberger and others in his wake have not been convinced that Paul had been enslaved to Marcion and the "Gnostics" in the second century, one senses a certain reticence in these authors to give other parts of the narrative, in particular the importance of the Pastorals to Irenaeus, their full due. It is as if ceding the programmatic nature of Irenaeus's use of the Pastorals reanimates the Pauline Captivity narrative *in toto*. This does not, however, have to be the case. The well-worn story of a Pauline Captivity to the "heretics" in the second century can and has been dealt with, as we have seen. But we should not throw out the proverbial baby with the bathwater. Irenaeus does make widespread, variegated, and programmatic use of the Pastoral Epistles in *Adversus haereses*.

Scholars differ on the number of identifiable Irenaean references to the Pastoral Epistles. Since Werner, there is widespread agreement on the six explicit uses of the Pastoral Epistles in *Adversus haereses* (two from each of the three letters).[68] These are introduced by "The Apostle says," "Paul says," or some similar formula:

καθὼς ὁ Ἀπόστολος φησιν (1.pref.1; fr. gr. 1, 4; citing 1 Tim 1.4);

Οὓς ὁ Παῦλος ἐγκελεύται (1.16.3; fr. gr. 10, 579; citing Titus 3.10);

bene Paulus ait (2.14.7; 135; citing 1 Tim 6.20);

Παῦλος ἐν ταῖς πρὸς Τιμόθεον ἐπιστολαῖς (3.3.3; fr. gr. 3, 4; citing 2 Tim 4.21);

ὡς καὶ Παῦλος ἔφησεν (3.3.4; fr. gr. 5, 30; citing Titus 3.10–11);

Paulus manifestavit in epistolis dicens (3.14.1; 36–37; citing 2 Tim 4.9–11).

The number of indirect, or implicit, uses of the Pastorals is less certain. J. Hoh counted an additional 13 "indirect" uses of the Pastorals, resulting in 19 total uses.[69] Noormann's total, including the direct (6), indirect (6) and other likely uses of the Pastorals (12), was 24.[70] Carsten Looks, in his comprehensive analysis of the use of the Pastorals in the second century, settled

on 6 "secure" and 24 "very probable" uses in *Adversus haereses*.[71] The difficulty in calculating the exact number of textual references to the Pastorals
is directly related, I will argue, to how natural their language and contents
have become for Irenaeus (as Norris argued for Gal 4.4–6). The opening
uses of 1 Timothy are enough to show us that he definitely had the Pastorals "on the brain," so to speak, as he sat down to pen the opening book of
his tome. The language of these letters pops up explicitly at times, implic-
itly and allusively at others. Each of the data marshaled forth below is, in
my view, a probable use of the Pastorals. By "probable use" I mean that the
language probably comes directly from Irenaeus's knowledge of and affinity for the Pastoral Epistles. This amounts, in my count, to 37 probable uses
of the Pastorals, divided quite evenly throughout *Adversus haereses*.[72] In the
end, the probability of any given "use" is in the eye of the beholder and develops more or less likelihood in light of a larger network of usage.

While some have pigeonholed Irenaeus's use of the Pastorals as nothing more than a simple borrowing of its polemical language at points, Irenaeus actually makes use of these letters in several other ways.[73] First, he
cites 2 Timothy to establish key biographical elements of Paul's ministry,
particularly as they are concerned with his relationship to the wider apostolic tradition. The connection between Paul and Luke, as we saw above,
was important for Irenaeus's argument. 2 Timothy 4.11, "only Luke is with
me," along with Colossians 4.14, "Luke, the beloved physician, greets you,"
are explicitly cited in making this connection (3.14.1; 36–37: *Paulus manifestavit in epistolis dicens*). In addition to the connection with Luke, 2 Timothy also provides the foundation for the episcopal line in Rome. Irenaeus
reminds his readers that Paul knows and mentions Linus in 2 Timothy
4.21 (*Haer.* 3.3.3; fr. gr. 3, 4: Παῦλος ἐν ταῖς πρὸς Τιμόθεον ἐπιστολαῖς).

Second, Irenaeus uses the language of the Pastorals for *constructive*
arguments of his own. In Book Four, Irenaeus cites 1 Timothy 1.9 to
answer why the Law was not given to the forefathers of Moses:

Quoniam lex non est posita justis (*Haer.* 4.16.3; 50);

ὅτι δικαίῳ νόμος οὐ κεῖται (1 Tim 1.9).[74]

He then explains that by "righteous" Paul meant that "the righteous fathers had the meaning of the Decalogue written in their hearts and souls,
that is, they loved the God who made them, and did no injury to their
neighbour."[75]

In Books Three and Five, Irenaeus uses the language of 1 Timothy 2.5 to explain the restoration of humanity to God:

Ἔδει γὰρ τὸν <u>μεσίτην Θεοῦ</u> τε <u>καὶ ἀνθρώπων</u> διὰ τῆς ἰδίας πρὸς ἑκατέρους οἰκειότητος εἰς φιλίαν καὶ ὁμόνοιαν τοὺς ἀμφοτέρους συναγαγεῖν (*Haer.* 3.18.7; fr. gr. 26, 8–11);

<u>μεσίτης θεοῦ</u> τε <u>καὶ ἀνθρώπων</u> γενόμενος (*Haer.* 5.17.1; fr. gr. 15, 32–33);

εἷς γὰρ θεός, εἷς καὶ <u>μεσίτης θεοῦ καὶ ἀνθρώπων</u>, ἄνθρωπος Χριστὸς Ἰησοῦς (1 Tim 2.5).[76]

In both Irenaean texts, the mediation language of 1 Timothy 2.5 is connected to the restoration of friendship between God and man through Christ. In Book Three the mediation comes through Christ's "kindred relationship" (fr. gr. 26, 10: οἰκειότητος) to both parties. While this is different from the "ransom" (ἀντίλυτρον) language of 1 Timothy 2.6, Irenaeus comes closer in *Adversus haereses* 5.17.1 when he explains this mediation with the language of "propitiation" (*l.* 8: *propitians*), "forgiveness" (*ll.* 12, 21–29: *remitto*), and the "cancelling of our disobedience" (*ll.* 9–10: *nostram inobaudientiam . . . consolatus*).[77] The closest that Irenaeus comes to 1 Timothy 2.6 is in *Adversus haereses* 5.1.1:

<u>*redemptionem semetipsum dedit pro*</u> *his qui in captivitatem ducti sunt* (*Haer.* 5.1.1; 20–22);

<u>ὁ δοὺς ἑαυτὸν ἀντίλυτρον ὑπὲρ</u> πάντων (1 Tim 2.6).[78]

From this same passage, Irenaeus uses the language of 1 Timothy 2.4 in defense of both the universality of God's salvation (*Haer* 1.10.2), as well as his own desire to speak truth in light of Valentinian speculation on the Ogdoad (*Haer.* 2.17.1):

καὶ φωτίζει <u>πάντας ἀνθρώπους</u> τοὺς βουλομένους <u>εἰς ἐπίγνωσιν ἀληθείας ἐλθεῖν</u> (*Haer.* 1.10.2; fr. gr. 1, 1143–1144);

qui velimus <u>*omnes homines ad agnitionem veritatis venire*</u> (*Haer.* 2.17.1; 7–8);

ὃς <u>πάντας ἀνθρώπους</u> θέλει σωθῆναι καὶ <u>εἰς ἐπίγνωσιν ἀληθείας ἐλθεῖν</u> (1 Tim 2.4).[79]

While Irenaeus is the first Christian writer to cite the Pastorals with introductory formulae, the variety of more subtle ways in which he deploys these texts suggests that they already fit comfortably within the Pauline tradition he inherited.[80] We have already noted the use of the Pastorals in the *Acts of Paul and Thecla* and *3 Corinthians*, although the exact nature of their relationship with the former has been debated. Following Looks, I think that there are also some "very probable" uses of the Pastorals in Polycarp and Justin, two important direct influences within Irenaeus's tradition.[81] In Justin there are short correspondences in language (three to four words) on several occasions. For example:

Ἡ γὰρ χρηστότης καὶ ἡ φιλανθρωπία τοῦ θεοῦ καὶ τὸ ἄμετρον τοῦ πλούτου αὐτοῦ (*Dial.* 47.6);

ὅτε δὲ ἡ χρηστότης καὶ ἡ φιλανθρωπία ἐπεφάνη τοῦ σωτῆρος ἡμῶν θεοῦ (Titus 3.4).[82]

Polycarp provides a more significant portion of 1 Timothy 6.7, working in language from surrounding verses (1 Tim 6.10):

Ἀρχὴ δὲ πάντων χαλεπῶν φιλαργυρία εἰδότες οὖν ὅτι οὐδὲν εἰσηνέγκαμεν εἰς τὸν κόσμον ἀλλ᾽ οὐδὲ ἐξενεγκεῖν τι ἔχομεν ὁπλισώμεθα τοῖς ὅπλοις τῆς δικαιοσύνης καὶ διδάξωμεν ἑαυτοὺς πρῶτον πορεύεσθαι ἐν τῇ ἐντολῇ τοῦ κυρίου (*Phil.* 4.1);

οὐδὲν γὰρ εἰσηνέγκαμεν εἰς τὸν κόσμον, ὅτι οὐδὲ ἐξενεγκεῖν τι δυνάμεθα (1 Tim 6.7);

ῥίζα γὰρ πάντων τῶν κακῶν ἐστιν ἡ φιλαργυρία (1 Tim 6.10).

The Pastorals were also being read outside Anatolia and Rome. In the *Acts of the Scillitan Martyrs*, Speratus defies the request of Saturninus (Roman proconsul at Carthage) to swear by the genius of Caesar by borrowing language from 1 Timothy:

Ego imperium huius seculi non cognosco; sed magis illi Deo servio quem nemo hominum vidit nec videre his oculis potest. Furtum non feci, sed siquid emero teloneum redo quia cognosco dominum meum, imperatorem regum et omnium gentium (Act. Scil. 6);

Quem suis temporibus ostendet beatus et solus potens rex regum et Dominus dominantium qui solus habet inmotalitatem lucem habitans *inaccessibiliem <u>quem vidit nullus hominum</u> sed <u>nec videre potest</u> cui honor et imperium sempiternum amen* (1 Tim 6.15–16).[83]

Speratus later confesses to having *libri et epistulae Pauli viri justi* (12).[84] We can surmise, given his knowledge of 1 Timothy, that the Pastorals were included among these Pauline works. Theophilus of Antioch, in his *Ad Autolycum*, conscripted the Pastorals in at least two ways.[85] Like Irenaeus, he opens his apology with the polemical language of the Pastorals. He immediately applies the "depraved mind" of 2 Timothy 3.8 (ἄνθρωποι <u>κατεφθαρμένοι τὸν νοῦν</u>) to his opponent (*Autol.* 1.1.1: ἀθλίοις <u>ἀνθρώποις</u> ἔχουσιν <u>τὸν νοῦν κατεφθαρμένον</u>). In a different context, Theophilus invokes ὁ θεῖος λόγος, stringing together language from 1 Timothy 2.1–2 and Titus 3.1 to ensure that his accuser knows that Christians are subject to the authorities (3.14.4).

Each of the three Pastoral Epistles, then, was used in multiple ways by different authors leading up to and including the era in which Irenaeus wrote. Irenaeus receives them as firmly planted within a broad stream of proto-orthodox tradition.[86] He, in turn, puts these texts to use in equally variegated ways. But more than for others before him, Irenaeus finds in these three texts a bountiful supply of polemical phrases that can sustain his attempts to marginalize the views of his opponents. The use of the polemical language of the Pastorals in *3 Corinthians* is a witness to this specific, later developing use. Before laying out this sustained connection between the polemical language of the Pastoral Epistles and *Adversus haereses*, however, we must ask about how the initial uses of 1 Timothy in the title and preface of Book One function in relationship to later polemical invocations of the Pastorals.

The Pastoral Epistles as Paratext and Hypotext in *Adversus haereses*

Titles and prefaces, according to the literary theorist Gérard Genette, function as paratextual signifiers.[87] By "paratext" Genette means those aspects of a text that "surround it and extend it, precisely in order to *present* it."[88] Paratexts include both "peritexts" (those proximate, printed signifiers surrounding the main text) and "epitexts" (elements distant from the publication, including public and private communications by the author about the text). Paratexts act as a "threshold," inviting readers to enter into the text, but also offering them the opportunity to withdraw.[89] More important, they not only invite, but they also attempt to condition:

Indeed, this fringe, always the conveyor of a commentary that is authorial or more or less legitimated by the author, constitutes a zone between text and off-text, a zone not only of transition but also of *transaction*: a privileged place of a pragmatics and a strategy, of an influence on the public, an influence that—whether well or poorly understood and achieved—is at the service of a better reception for the text and a more pertinent reading of it (more pertinent, of course, in the eyes of the author and his allies).[90]

Paratexts attempt to "ensure for the text a destiny consistent with the author's purpose."[91] Not even the post-structuralist Roland Barthes could avoid efforts to condition (as author) the reading of his texts. As Genette reminds, *Roland Barthes par Roland Barthes* contains the following admonition within its front cover: "It must all be considered as if spoken by a character in a novel."[92]

Literary titles and prefaces are among the various paratexts that Genette explores, in addition to dedications, inscriptions, epigraphs, intertitles, and notes. Formally, literary titles can possess up to three parts: title, subtitle, and genre indication.[93] Not all titles display all three features. Functionally, titles serve either "thematic" (e.g., *War and Peace* by Tolstoy) or "rhematic"/"generic" (e.g., *Unfashionable Observations* by Nietzsche) roles, or both (e.g., *Treatise of Human Nature* by Hume).[94] Irenaeus's title, Ἔλεγχος καὶ ἀνατροπὴ τῆς ψευδωνύμου γνώσεως, serves both functions: its theme, "falsely named knowledge"; its genre, "a refutation and overthrow."[95] References to this title in subsequent prefatory material (*Haer.* 2.pref.1; 4.pref.1; 5.pref.1) and at various points in Books One (1.22.2; 1.31.3) and Two (2.24.4) secure it for the initial publication of Book One, as well as the later installments.[96] Based on a papyrus roll fragment of *Adversus haereses* (P.Oxy. 405) dated to around 200 C.E., it is likely that Irenaeus published his work as a set of rolls.[97] The title would have appeared at any number of locations at publication: at the end of the text in a colophon and/or on the outside of the roll (either written directly on the roll or on a papyrus or parchment tag, a *syllabos*, affixed to the roll at a right angle).[98] Regardless of its physical location, whether attached to a *syllabos*, or reiterated in prefaces throughout the five-volume work, Irenaeus's title is an attempt to influence the reading of *Adversus haereses*.[99] Does this influence, though, go beyond mere significations of genre and subject matter? Before turning to this question in particular, we must briefly explain the paratextual role of prefatory material, particularly in relation to titles.

According to Genette, like other paratextual materials, the *"original preface,* has as its chief function *to ensure that the text is read properly."*[100] It answers the questions of "why" and "how." The preface puts "the (definitely assumed) reader in possession of information the author considers necessary for this proper reading."[101] In relation to the title, the preface acts as an explanation, a commentary.[102] The explicit citation of 1 Timothy 1.4 in the preface to Book One serves as a commentary on what Irenaeus means by "falsely named knowledge": it is nothing but "endless genealogies, which as the Apostle says, promote speculations rather than the divine training that is in faith."[103] These two proximate uses of 1 Timothy in the most important paratextual sites surrounding *Adversus haereses* have a reinforcing effect.

Paratextual materials can serve functions beyond the "thematic" and "rhematic." In particular, they can sometimes signify an important interpretive "hypotext" for the author.[104] In his *Palimpsests: Literature in the Second Degree,* Genette describes the relationship between hypertext (text B) and hypotext (text A) as a "graft[ing]" of two texts "in a manner that is not that of commentary."[105] Intertextual signification in the most privileged of literary positions, the title, often indicates an extended hypertextual relationship with the source-text, a relationship that has "contractual force."[106] While all texts are, by their participation in "literarity," hypertextual, evoking a variety of earlier texts, Genette is particularly concerned with the "sunnier side" of hypertextuality, where the "shift from hypotext to hypertext is both massive . . . and more or less officially stated."[107] Homer's *Odyssey,* for instance, is the programmatic hypotext for Joyce's *Ulysses.* Invoking Umberto Eco ("A title, unfortunately, is in itself a key to interpretation"), Genette asks how we would read Joyce's *Ulysses* if it had a different title.[108] As a title, *Ulysses* has a "symbolic value."[109] Leopold Bloom's movements are to be read in light of the travels of Odysseus. Joseph Conrad's *Heart of Darkness* is a hypotext for T. S. Eliot's "The Hollow Men," as its epigraph invokes this earlier text: "Mistah Kurtz—he dead."[110] Conrad's shadowy Kurtz serves as a robust literary depiction of the kind of men Eliot intends in his poem. While *Palimpsests* deals solely with fiction, Genette readily asserts that "the hypertext can be nonfictional, especially when it derives from a work that is itself nonfictional."[111]

Like a palimpsest, where one text has been written over by another, a hypertext is writing in the "second degree." Its existence is a covering over of a previous text. The hypertext can be related to the hypotext in a number of ways: pastiche, parody, or travesty, to name a few.[112] The reader comes closest to realizing the intended meaning of the hypertext only when he or she recognizes the hypotext and then intuits the relationship between the two (either transformation or imitation, broadly).[113]

Intertextual signifiers in a title are often more implicit and allusive than the example from Joyce suggests. According to Jörg Helbig, the "privileged position" of titular intertextual "traces," however, shows that these connections are purposefully "marked" by the author.[114] He or she relies on the "collective knowledge" of the recipients, particularly their "competence for allusions." Occasionally, the author will help clarify the intertextual echo, often through a later, more direct citation of a larger portion of the intended source-text, including a reference to its author (cf. Irenaeus's explicit citation of 1 Tim 6.20 in *Haer.* 2.14.7).

The paratextual invocations of 1 Timothy at the outset of *Adversus haereses* function as an invitation for the reader to view Irenaeus's project in light of this earlier text. Yet not just this text alone. Each of the "Pastoral Epistles" contributes to the polemical characterizations of Irenaeus's opponents in ways that are both consonant with these initial invocations as well as unique within his use of the broader Pauline tradition. The "Pastoral Epistles," of course, is an etic designation, a modern heuristic construction. In light of this latter fact, one might argue that Irenaeus only intended 1 Timothy as a programmatic hypotext for his own work. As we saw in the previous chapter, however, there is evidence that by the turn of the third century these three texts were already viewed as a thematic group.[115] This same evidence suggests that 1–2 Timothy and Titus first circulated separately from a group of Paul's letters to (seven) churches, likely causing their thematic unity to be easily recognizable. Most important, because they present a unified picture of Paul as heresy-fighter, Irenaeus returns over and over again to their polemical language in his own battle against "falsely named knowledge." The Paul of the Pastorals seems to have programmatic and symbolic value for Irenaeus. He understands his own heresiological task in light of the Paul that he finds in these texts.

Hypotextual Resonances of the Polemical Paul of the Pastorals in *Adversus haereses*

The initial uses of 1 Timothy in the paratexts of *Adversus haereses* serve to indicate Irenaeus's literary program. They are his attempt to control the

Table 6.1 "Falsely Named Knowledge" in *Adversus haereses*

Polemical Language from 1 Timothy	Usage in *Adversus haereses*
"falsely named knowledge" (1 Tim 6.20) τῆς ψευδωνύμου γνώσεως	Applied to specific opponents: · Simon Magus (*Haer.* 1.23.4) · Valentinians (*Haer.* 2.pref.1; 2.14.7) · Cerinthus and the Nicolaitans (*Haer.* 3.11.1) · Marcion (*Haer.* 3.12.12)

reading of his book. These opening forays into the polemical language of the Pastoral Epistles are sustained throughout, suggesting that these para-texts also indicate an important hypotext for Irenaeus. Of first importance is the extension of the appellation "falsely named knowledge," generally applied in the title, to a range of specific opponents throughout *Adversus haereses* (see Table 6.1.).[116]

The related designation, "falsely named Gnostics" (ψευδωνύμοι γνωστικοί), is used similarly (see Table 6.2.).[117]

The constant tagging of his opponents with this moniker from the Pastoral Paul is a way of challenging aberrant knowledge claims with the

Table 6.2 "Falsely Named Gnostics" in *Adversus haereses*

Polemical Language from 1 Timothy	Usage in *Adversus haereses*
"falsely named Gnostics" (cf. 1 Tim 6.20) Ψευδωνύμοι γνωστικοί	Applied to specific opponents: · Followers of Carpocrates (*Haer.* 1.11.1, anticipating *Haer.* 1.25.6) · Followers of Basilides and others (*Haer.* 2.13.10; 2.35.2) · Followers of Saturninus, Basilides, Carpocrates, and others (*Haer.* 2.31.1) · Marcion, Valentinus, Basilides, Carpocrates, Simon, and others (*Haer.* 4.35.4) · Valentinus, followers of Marcion, and others (*Haer.* 5.26.2)

apostolic tradition. Frequent use, of course, is also one of the many ways that an author "marks" his or her key intertexts.[118]

The polemical use of 1 Timothy is not limited to 1 Timothy 6.20. We have already seen how Irenaeus directly cites 1 Timothy 1.4 in the initial preface to *Adversus haereses*. A variety of other expressions from 1 Timothy can also be added (see Table 6.3.).[119]

Inasmuch as 2 Timothy and Titus contain similar kinds of heresy-hunting language, Irenaeus also finds these texts congenial to his literary task. He employs them in a similar fashion to his use of 1 Timothy (see Table 6.4.).[120]

The polemical language of all three of the "Pastoral Epistles" has become such an ingrained part of Irenaeus's lexical stock that it is his default setting for the characterization of his opponents and their "falsely named knowledge." In most instances he does not formally cite these texts. The language merely bubbles to the surface of all five books, though the programmatic use of 1 Timothy at the beginning of *Adversus haereses* (in its paratexts) suggests that there is a conscious deployment of this language throughout. The Pastorals serve as a programmatic intertext that constantly lurks under (hypo) the surface of Irenaeus's tome.

Table 6.3 Other Polemical Language from 1 Timothy in *Adversus haereses*

Polemical Language from 1 Timothy	Usage in *Adversus haereses*
"unhealthy desiring for speculations" (1 Tim 6:4) νοσῶν περὶ ζητήσεις	Of allegorizing opponents (*Haer.* 3.12.11; 393) aegrotans circa quaestiones
"seared conscience" (1 Tim 4.2) κεκαυστηριασμένων τὴν ἰδίαν συνείδησιν	Of the Marcosians (*Haer.* 1.13.7; fr. gr. 10, 123) αἵτινες κεκαυτηριασμέναι τὴν συνείδησιν
"old wives' tales" (1 Tim 4.7) γραώδεις μύθους	Of the Marcosians (*Haer.* 1.16.3; fr. gr. 10, 578) γραώδεσι μύθοις
	Of the Valentinians (*Haer.* 1.8.1; fr. gr. 1, 797) γραῶν μύθους

Table 6.4 Polemical Language from 2 Timothy and Titus in *Adversus haereses*

Polemical Language from 2 Timothy and Titus	Usage in *Adversus haereses*
"who have deviated from the truth" (2 Tim 2.18) οἵτινες περὶ τὴν ἀλήθειαν ἠστόχησαν	Of descendents of Basilides and Carpocrates (*Haer* 1.28.2; 31–33) *non est numerum dicere eorum qui secundum alterum et alterum modum exciderunt a veritate* Of those who do not understand the importance of the flesh (*Haer.* 5.3.1; fr. gr. 4, 49–51) παρεδόθη τῇ ἑαυτοῦ ἀσθενείᾳ ὁ ἄνθρωπος ἵνα μὴ ἐπαρθείς ποτε ἀστοχήσῃ τῆς ἀληθείας
"itching ears" (2 Tim 4.3) κνηθόμενοι τὴν ἀκοήν	Of Valentinian speculation (*Haer.* 2.21.2; 47–48) *prurientibus aures*
"always learn but can never come to the knowledge of the truth" (2 Tim 3.7) πάντοτε μανθάνοντα καὶ μηδέποτε εἰς ἐπίγνωσιν ἀληθείας ἐλθεῖν δυνάμενα	Of those who "desert the preaching of the Church" (*Haer.* 5.20.2; 36–37) *semper quaerentes et numquam verum invenientes* Of "Gentile philosophers" (*Haer.* 2.27.2; 21) *semper inquiret, numquam autem inveniet* Of heretics in general · *et quaerere quidem semper in excusatione habent, . . . , invenire vero numquam possunt* (*Haer.* 3.24.2; 42–44) · *quaeret quidem semper, inveniet autem numquam Deum* (*Haer.* 4.9.3; 91–92)
"Decline a heretic after the first and second warning" (Titus 3.10) αἱρετικὸν ἄνθρωπον μετὰ μίαν καὶ δευτέραν νουθεσίαν παραιτοῦ	Of the Marcosians (*Haer.* 1.16.3; fr. gr. 10, 579–580) μετὰ μίαν καὶ δευτέρον νουθεσίαν παραιτεῖσθαι Of Marcion (*Haer.* 3.3.4; fr. gr. 5, 30–31) Αἱρετικὸν ἄνθρωπον μετὰ μίαν καὶ δευτέρον νουθεσίαν παραιτοῦ

Keying and Framing the Apostolic Tradition
to the Pastoral Paul

It should be admitted that at 37 instances the Pastorals are not the most frequently used Pauline texts in Irenaeus. 1 Corinthians and Romans are cited much more often.[121] They are also not the contested sites of Pauline interpretation that so plagued Irenaeus (cf. his defenses of 2 Cor 4.4 in *Haer.* 3.7.1–2 and of 1 Cor 15.50 in *Haer.* 5.9.1–3). Romans 5.12–21, Galatians 4.4–7 and Ephesians 1.10 appear to have had the greatest constructive influence on his own theology, particularly his views on the economy of salvation and the recapitulation of all things in Christ, the Second Adam. From among the Pauline materials, however, the Pastorals were Irenaeus's favored sites for borrowing stigmatizing language. The importance of the polemical language of these texts, in particular, for Irenaeus's task can be seen when compared with his use of other Pauline letters. The polemical language of the highly combative Galatians, for instance, is never used in this fashion. In fact, as we have seen, Irenaeus reads Galatians in ways that mitigate the combativeness of its Paul (because his opponents in that text are other apostles). Irenaeus is well aware of 2 Thessalonians, citing it more often than 1 Thessalonians; it is also full of combative language, but, as with his use of Galatians, he does not turn to this text for polemical characterizations of his opponents. This is also true for his treatment of Romans, 1 Corinthians, Ephesians, Philippians, Colossians, and 1 Thessalonians. The closest we come to Irenaeus's deployment of the polemical vocabulary of the Pastoral Epistles is his use of 2 Corinthians 11.3 in the preface to Book Four of *Adversus haereses*:

> *Quemadmodum* enim *serpens Evam seduxit*, promittens ei quod non habebat ipse, sic et hi praetendentes majorem agnitionem et mysteria inenarrabilia (*Haer.* 4.pref.4; 44–46);

> φοβοῦμαι δὲ μή πως, ὡς ὁ ὄφις ἐξηπάτησεν Εὕαν ἐν τῇ πανουργίᾳ αὐτοῦ, φθαρῇ τὰ νοήματα ὑμῶν ἀπὸ τῆς ἁπλότητος [καὶ τῆς ἁγνότητος] τῆς εἰς τὸν Χριστόν (2 Cor 11.3).

Irenaeus takes "the serpent deceived Eve" language from 2 Corinthians, which was originally directed at the "super apostles" (2 Cor 11.5), and transfers it to his own opponents. This, however, is an isolated incident.

From among a broad set of Pauline materials, 1 and 2 Timothy and Titus functioned in this *unique* way for Irenaeus. The invocation of 1 Timothy in the paratextual material of *Adversus haereses* (its first two intertexts) is, as I have already indicated, significant and reinforcing. The unique and sustained use of the polemical language of the Pastoral Epistles throughout all five of Irenaeus's books suggests that they offer a particularly useful set of language for Irenaeus's own heresiological tome. The breadth of use to which Irenaeus puts the Pastorals, as well as the ways in which the Pastorals were being used by other authors in the second century, suggests that they already fit comfortably within the proto-orthodox tradition by the time that Irenaeus writes. Because of this, Irenaeus knew that his use of their disparaging characterizations of theological opponents would have traction among his own readers.

Even more important, the Paul that Irenaeus finds in these texts— Paul, the Defender of the Faith and the Protector of the Deposit—provides a vocational analogue through which he can envision his task. I argued in the previous chapter that the author of *3 Corinthians* "keyed" his own version of Paul to a particular *lieu d'mémoire*, the Pastoral Epistles, in an attempt to memorialize a certain image of Paul as heresy-fighter. Something related appears to be going on in *Adversus haereses*. Hypertexts and their corresponding hypotexts can be related in any number of ways. The key to unlocking an author's preferred reading of their hypertext is to locate this relationship. Broadly, there are imitative and transformational relationships between an original text and its palimpsest.[122] Irenaeus establishes an imitative hypertextual relationship to the Pastorals through his paratextual signifiers. Irenaeus, like the Paul of the Pastorals, and like the Pastoral Paul of *3 Corinthians*, is the "protector of the faith."[123] He takes up the mantel of the Apostle as he is pictured in 1–2 Timothy and Titus and writes a *Refutation and Overthrow of Falsely Named Gnosis* from within the world of these texts. As a title, *Against Heresies* shields the reader from the depth of Irenaeus's intertextual program.

Of course, a hypertext *can* be read on its own, possessing "a meaning that is autonomous and thus in some manner sufficient."[124] Ultimately, however, it "invites us to engage in a relational reading."[125] The hypertext "stands to *gain*" through the recognition of its relationship to a hypotext, particularly when this union is forged in paratextual material.[126] When we read the *Refutation and Overthrow of Falsely Named Gnosis* in relationship to the Pastoral Epistles, we not only understand how important the Paul of these texts was for Irenaeus's own polemical task, but we also begin to perceive the extent to which Irenaeus sees himself as waging an Apostolic battle. The synecdochic function of Irenaeus's use of 1 Timothy 6.20 in his title draws us into the world of that text's Paul, who in the same passage encourages Timothy to "guard the deposit" (2 Tim 1.14: τὴν παραθήκην φύλαξον). Irenaeus, as protector of the "rule of truth" (*Haer.* 1.9.4; 1.22.1; 3.2.1; 3.4.2: ὁ κανὼν τῆς ἀληθείας/*regula veritatis*), viewing himself in the line of authorized defenders through his relationship to Polycarp (*Haer.* 3.3.1–4; Eus., *Hist. eccl.* 5.20), inveighs against his own opponents with the force of the Apostolic polemics of the Pastoral Paul. The Pastorals provide an important image of Paul from which he can construct his own work. This frontloading of particular Pauline texts over others creates a hermeneutical frame within which the rest are read, including 1 Corinthians, to which we now turn.

Irenaeus and 1 Corinthians 15.50: "Flesh and Blood Cannot Inherit the Kingdom of God"

Leading directly out of the confident *braggadocio* of the end of Book Four, where Irenaeus states that he will "expound the Apostle" in light of the "other interpretations" of his enemies, much of Book Five of *Adversus haereses*, like *3 Corinthians*, is concerned with Paul's teaching on the flesh. As such, it serves as an extended apology for 1 Corinthians 15.50, which, according to Irenaeus, was a particularly contested site in the Pauline corpus. As we have seen (cf. Chapter 2), he laments: "This is the passage which is adduced by all the heretics (π[άντων αἱρε]τικῶν/*omnibus haereticis*) in support of their folly, with an attempt to annoy us, and to point out that the handiwork of God (πλ[άσμα τοῦ θεοῦ]/*plasmationem Dei*) is not saved" (*Haer.* 5.9.1; 3–5; Jena papyrus).[127] Irenaeus alludes to or quotes this passage on at least 12 occasions throughout *Adversus haereses*, beginning as early as Book One (*Haer.* 1.30.13).[128]

We should say something brief about Irenaeus's anthropology, in general, before turning to his defensive interpretation of 1 Corinthians 15.50.[129] Irenaeus opens Book Four by declaring: "Now man is a mixed organization of soul and flesh, who was formed after the likeness of God, and moulded by His hands, that is, by the Son and Holy Spirit, to whom also He said, 'Let Us make man.'" (*Haer.* 4.pref.4). In other places he equates this mixture of soul and flesh with Paul's ψυχικός ἄνθρωπος (1 Cor 2.14; 15.44, 46), ὁ πρῶτος ἄνθρωπος (1 Cor 15.45, 47) and ὁ παλαιὸς ἄνθρωπος (Rom

6.6; Eph 4.22; Col 3.9).¹³⁰ The ψυχικός ἄνθρωπος possesses the πνοὴ ζωῆς, the "breath of life," but not the πνεῦμα ζωοποιοῦν, the "vivifying Spirit" (*Haer.* 5.12.2; fr. gr. 11.1–3).

Salvation comes to the ψυχικός ἄνθρωπος through the bestowal of God's Spirit, which is available through the incarnation and bloody death of the divine Son of God:

> Since the Lord thus has redeemed us through His own blood, giving His soul for our souls, and His flesh for our flesh, and has also poured out the Spirit of the Father for the union and communion of God and man, imparting indeed God to men by means of the Spirit, and, on the other hand, attaching man to God by His own incarnation, and bestowing upon us at His coming immortality durably and truly, by means of communion with God, - all the doctrines of the heretics fall to ruin. (*Haer.* 5.1.1)

Or again:

> But when the spirit here blended with the soul is united to [God's] handiwork, the man is rendered spiritual and perfect because of the outpouring of the Spirit, and this is he who was made in the image and likeness of God. But if the Spirit be wanting to the soul, he who is such is indeed of an animal nature, and being left carnal, shall be an imperfect being, possessing indeed the image [of God] in his formation, but not receiving the similitude through the Spirit; and thus is this being imperfect. (*Haer.* 5.6.1)

The one who is bestowed with God's Spirit is being transformed into Paul's ὁ πνευματικός (1 Cor 2.15; 3.1; 15.44, 46), being conformed to ὁ ἔσχατος Ἀδὰμ (1 Cor 15.45) and taking on the identity of a καινός ἄνθρωπος/καινὴ κτίσις (2 Cor 5.17; Gal 6.15; Eph 2.15; 4.24). The flesh is perfected by the Spirit, but is in no way abolished since it is the handiwork of God (πλάσμα/πλάσις τοῦ θεοῦ). This is the most important aspect of Irenaeus's understanding of the flesh.¹³¹ Its equation with πλάσμα/πλάσις can be found throughout *Adversus haereses*.¹³² In Book Five, his defense of σάρξ is a defense of the Creator God and the value of His entire creation. Moreover, all humans are capable of receiving the Spirit and becoming ὁ πνευματικός. Irenaeus opposes the fatalistic distinctions between the πνευματικός and the ψυχικός ἄνθρωπος of his Valentinian opponents.¹³³

Irenaeus defends the resurrection of God's "handiwork" from a number of angles in Book Five, most of which, as Maurice Wiles has shown, involve appeals to Pauline texts:

1. Paul (1 Thess 5.23) prays for the body (τὸ σῶμα) to be preserved along with the spirit (τὸ πνεῦμα) and the soul (ἡ ψυχὴ) at the Parousia (*Haer.* 5.6.1);
2. Paul cannot be talking about either the spirit or the soul when he says that God "will give life to your mortal bodies" (Rom 8.11: ζῳοποιήσει καὶ τὰ θνητὰ σώματα ὑμῶν). In Irenaeus's tripartite anthropology, that only leaves the σάρξ (*Haer.* 5.7.1–2; 5.13.3);
3. Since Paul speaks of the Christian, who in the present possesses flesh, as being "in the spirit" (Rom 8:9) and as having "received a spirit of adoption" (Rom 8:15), then the flesh must be capable of inheriting the kingdom of God (i.e., capable of resurrection) (*Haer.* 5.8.1; 5.13.4); and
4. Christ's redemptive work on the cross involved his own flesh and blood (Eph 2.13, 15), which must mean that it is our own flesh and blood that will be redeemed (*Haer.* 5.14.3).[134]

These arguments surround Irenaeus's comments on 1 Corinthians 15.50 itself and provide what D. Jeffrey Bingham describes as the proper "interpretive network" or "canonical connection" for understanding its apparent denigration of flesh and blood.[135] Rather than starting with 1 Corinthians 15.50 and interpreting it within the context of 1 Corinthians 15 itself, Irenaeus builds toward it from other Pauline materials. As Mark Olson notes, "he interprets Paul by Paul."[136] Irenaeus accuses his opponents of "keeping fast hold of the mere expressions *by themselves*, . . . , overturning as far as in them lies the entire dispensation of God" (5.13.2).[137] Tertullian describes this strategy when he states that "although our opponents place it [1 Cor 15.50] in the front of the battle, we have intentionally reserved the objection until now, in order that we may in our last assault overthrow it, after we have removed out of the way all the questions which are auxiliary to it" (*Res.* 48.1).

For Irenaeus, the intertextual connection with Romans 8 is the most important link in his defense of 1 Corinthians 15.50.[138] Romans 8, with its emphasis on the present possession of the Spirit by those who are still in the flesh, is an indication of the kinds of continuities that could be expected in the final consummation of the kingdom. Irenaeus says, "If, therefore, in the present time, fleshly hearts are made partakers of the

Spirit, what is there astonishing if, in the resurrection, they receive that life which is granted by the Spirit?" (*Haer.* 5.13.4). The anthropological differences between present and future ages for the believer are only in "degree *not* substance."[139] The "mortal bodies" (τὰ θνητὰ σώματα) of Romans 8.11, already being "made alive" (ζῳοποιήσει) through the Spirit, are equated with the "flesh" (σάρξ) of 1 Corinthians 15.50 through texts like 2 Corinthians 4.10–11 (*Haer.* 5.13.4–5):

in order that that life of Jesus might also be manifest *in our bodies*

ἵνα καὶ ἡ ζωὴ τοῦ Ἰησοῦ <u>ἐν τῷ σώματι ἡμῶν</u> φανερωθῇ (4.10b);

in order that the life of Jesus might also be manifest *in our mortal flesh*

ἵνα καὶ ἡ ζωὴ τοῦ Ἰησοῦ φανερωθῇ <u>ἐν τῇ θνητῇ σαρκὶ</u> ἡμῶν (4.11b).[140]

The process of immortality, whereby the "perishable" (τὸ φθαρτὸν) and "mortal" (τὸ θνητὸν) put on the "imperishable" (ἀφθαρσίαν) and "immortal" (ἀθανασίαν) (1 Cor 15.53) is already afoot in those whose flesh is being perfected by the Spirit (*Haer.* 5.13.3–4). Those who are "in the Spirit" (Rom 8.9) and have "received the Spirit of adoption" (Rom 8.15; "Spirit of God" in Irenaeus), are rendered "spiritual even *now*, and the mortal *is* swallowed up by immortality" (*Haer.* 5.8.1: *jam spiritales efficit et absorbetur mortale ab immortalitate*; cf. 2 Cor 5.4).[141]

The "canonical connection" between Romans 8 and 1 Corinthians 15 is made not merely at the anthropological level, but extends even to cosmology (Rom 8.19–22), as Bingham notes.[142] Both of these texts find their way into the closing section of Irenaeus's tome (*Haer.* 5.36.2–3), in which he reminds his readers for one last time that death is the final victim of Christ's rule (1 Cor 15.25–28) and that even the creation will be set free from the bondage of corruption (Rom 8.21). In this way, the entire *plasmatio* of God is preserved and transformed in the end.

Having established the appropriate interpretive frame, Irenaeus can quite confidently circumvent the seemingly plain meaning of "flesh and blood" in 1 Corinthians 15.50. Throughout *Adversus haereses* 5.9, Irenaeus reads 1 Corinthians 15.50 with "mere" (καθ'ἑαυτὴν/*solam*/*tantum*) before "flesh and blood." He implies this at first: "those then, as many as they be, who have not that which saves and forms us into life eternal, shall be, and shall be called, flesh and blood (*erunt et vocabuntur caro et sanguis*); for these are they who have not the Spirit of God in themselves" (5.9.1; 14–15).[143] He later explicitly states: "he [Paul] exclaims, that flesh in itself (*carnem solam*/τὴν σάρκα καθ'ἑαυτὴν), and blood, cannot possess the kingdom of God" (5.9.3; 59; fr. gr. 9.6). There is no manuscript evidence for this reading of 1 Corinthians. Through this *interpretive* strategy we find a reading of 1 Corinthians 15 similar to that of *3 Corinthians* 2.32, where the flesh can be saved and enter into the Kingdom of God through the work of the Spirit (5.9.3). Irenaeus continues, "If, however, we must speak strictly we would say that the flesh does not inherit, but is inherited" (5.9.4; fr. gr. 9.8–9: οὐ κληρονομεῖ ἀλλὰ κληρονομεῖται ἡ σάρξ). In the end, he contends that 1 Corinthians 15.50 is actually a warning against heresy and the dissipated lifestyle that results from such errors in thought. In Targumic fashion, he re-reads the passage to say: "Do not err; for unless the Word of God dwell in you, and if ye shall live frivolously and carelessly as if ye were this only, viz., mere flesh and blood (*tantum caro et sanguis*), ye cannot inherit the kingdom of God" (5.9.4; 96).

In some ways, Irenaeus and Bultmann would have made strange but congenial bedfellows on this issue. This final reading of "flesh and blood" as a primarily moral and existential and not a metaphysical category allows Irenaeus to skirt the rather direct language of 1 Corinthians 15.50, which appears to make no distinctions between the "flesh and blood" or "perishability" of believers and non-believers.[144] Through intertextual alliances he links a text with a metaphysical focus (cf. 1 Cor 15:35–"But someone will say, 'How are corpses raised? With what sort of body do they come?'") to texts with moral *foci* (Rom 8.8–13; 1 Cor 6.9–10; Gal 5.19–21), reading the former in light of the latter and answering "all the heretics" in one fell swoop (*Haer.* 5.10.2–5.11.1).[145] The "kingdom of God" language that 1 Corinthians 15, 1 Corinthians 6 and Galatians 5 share provides a further linguistic and conceptual link for Irenaeus.[146] That there are two distinct ways of reading 1 Corinthians 15.50—one metaphysical, the other moral—is clear to him: "For thus they will allege that this passage refers to the flesh strictly so called, and not to fleshly works, as I have pointed out, so representing the apostle as contradicting himself" (*Haer.* 5.13.3).

Bultmann, at least, recognized the tension in Paul's anthropological language; 1 Corinthians 15.50 does appear incompatible with some of Paul's other statements, like 2 Corinthians 4.10–11. In the former, σάρξ and σῶμα are distinct, representing substance and form, whereas in the latter they are synonymous. For Bultmann, Paul had been surreptitiously duped into adopting the metaphysical language of his Platonic opponents. For Irenaeus, however, Paul could have never been so careless nor his arguments so contingent. The Pauline Epistles were a unified testament to the salvation of the σάρξ, which is normally read in place of σῶμα.

What caused Irenaeus, though, to read 1 Corinthians 15 in light of 2 Corinthians 4 and a modified version of Romans 8, substituting σάρξ for σῶμα (cf. his reading of Rom 8.11 above), and not the other way around, giving priority to 1 Corinthians 15.50, as apparently did his opponents? For Irenaeus, the apostolic "rule of truth" (ὁ κανὼν τῆς ἀληθείας/*regula veritatis*: *Haer.* 1.9.4; 1.22.1; 3.2.1; 3.4.2) was the final filter through which Scripture should be interpreted.[147] Together, Scripture and rule provide a coherent, unified tradition for the church:

> Since, therefore, the tradition from the apostles does thus exist in the Church, and is permanent among us, let us revert to the Scriptural proof furnished by those apostles who did also write the Gospel, in which they recorded the doctrine regarding God, pointing out that our Lord Jesus Christ is the truth, and that no lie is in Him. (*Haer.* 3.5.1)

This tradition was passed down through apostolic succession at important sees (*Haer.* 3.3.3–3.4.1). Inasmuch as the apostolic rule looked backward to the "ascension into heaven in the *flesh* of the beloved Christ Jesus" and forward to the return of the same "to raise up anew all *flesh* of the whole human race" (*Haer.* 1.10.1), the Pauline Epistles must have taught similarly.[148] After all, Paul "taught all things agreeable to the preaching of the truth" (*Haer.* 4.41.4). J. Bentivegna summarizes, "By means of this intelligent investigation, done under the guidance of the Canon of Truth, Irenaeus is sure that he will be able to discover an organic body of doctrine about man [in Paul]."[149]

Tradition, or what we might call collective apostolic memory, caused Irenaeus to read 1 Corinthians 15.50 in the way that he does, dispensing (consciously or not) with the actual metaphysical concerns of 1 Corinthians 15 itself.[150] We find here the same sort of textual maneuvers that were needed by the author of *3 Corinthians* to transform 1 Corinthians' hope for "the resurrection from the dead" in a "spiritual body" into an endorsement of the "resurrection of the flesh." Irenaeus's attempt to systematize Pauline anthropology, accusing his opponents of "representing the apostle as contradicting himself" (*Haer.* 5.13.3), only uncovers the ambivalence of the language in the Pauline tradition, as Jewett and others have shown. But where 1 Corinthians 15 clearly posits discontinuity, Irenaeus wants to read as much continuity as possible. He harmonizes the Pauline language to fit his community's rule. Moreover, the intertextual web of signification needed to make such a move appears quite similar to the practices of which Irenaeus accuses his opponents. They are those who "do violence to the good words [of Scripture] in adapting them to their wicked fabrications" (*Haer.* 1.3.6), who pervert the "natural" (*naturam*/κατὰ φύσιν) sense of the Scriptures (*Haer.* 1.9.4; 78; fr. gr. 1.1051), and who "disregard the order and the connection of the Scriptures . . . transfer passages and rearrange them; and, making one thing out of another, they deceive many" (*Haer.* 1.8.1).

Irenaeus's reading of 1 Corinthians 15 raises important questions about what we mean as modern scholars when we ask, Who got Paul right in the second century?[151] Mark Olson has concluded, for instance, that there is only a "slight difference" between Paul and Irenaeus's reading of 1 Corinthians 15.50: "Paul emphasizes that the transformed bodies will no longer be composed of corruptible elements of flesh and blood, whereas Irenaeus stresses that the bodies will still be composed of flesh and blood even though they are in some way transformed and rendered incorruptible."[152] For Noormann, similarly, the differences between Irenaeus and Paul are merely "terminologische."[153] He sees Irenaeus using σάρξ in ways that are germane to his own situation, but which are not in fundamental disagreement with the Apostle.[154] The Irenaean concept of the flesh "paulinischen Konzeption ungleich näher steht als die gnostiche Vorstellung eines inneren pneumatischen Kerns des Menschen."[155]

To ask and answer Who got Paul right? on any number of issues, however, as we have seen, is a complicated matter. It presupposes a certain modern understanding of the "historical" Paul, which often imagines the Apostle as a static entity. It passes over the tensions that exist in the earliest layer of Pauline material and pretends to be able to measure the Pauline "tradition" against the "real" Paul. In reality, each side of this polemical battle over 1 Corinthians 15 has taken a diverse tradition and, as is always necessary when "true" or "real" inheritance is at stake, has fronted some pieces while consigning others to the back, making the tradition appear unified and frozen. Each is in danger of having "oversimplified" Paul.[156] Furthermore, given the nature of tradition and collective memory, both sides of this second-century debate display a mixture of continuity with and change from the earlier layer of the Pauline tradition. Each individual portrayal of Paul and/or his texts is shaped within a mnemonic community that exerts its own social pressures on how individual pieces of tradition should and should not be remembered. Irenaeus's *regula veritatis*, reflective of his own social location, constrains what he sees in 1 Corinthians 15.50. The same is true for the author of the *Gospel of Philip* (cf. Chapter 2). The markedly Platonic language that leads into that text's citation of 1 Corinthians 15.50 frames how the text is read:

> No one would hide a precious expensive object within an expensive thing, yet often someone has kept vast sums in something worth a penny. Such is the case with the soul; it is a precious thing, and it has come to reside in a lowly body. Certain persons are afraid that they may arise (from the dead) naked. . . . (*Gos. Phil.* 56.20–28)

And despite the different ideological starting points and the attendant polemical rhetoric of Irenaeus and the author of the *Gospel of Philip*, one might wonder whether or not they have, in the end, offered such different readings of 1 Corinthians 15.50. The *Gospel of Philip* does retain hope for the salvation of a certain kind of flesh and blood: Jesus', which those destined for salvation share. After denying the resurrection of human flesh and blood, the author goes on to affirm a qualified salvation of flesh and blood in the future:

> What is this flesh that will not inherit it? The one that *we* are wearing. And what, too, is this flesh that will inherit it? It is *Jesus'* flesh, along with his blood. Therefore he said, "He who does not eat my flesh and drink my blood does not have life within him." What is meant by that? His "flesh" means the Word, and his "blood" means the holy spirit: whoever has received these has food, and has drink and clothing. For my part I condemn those others who say that the flesh will not arise. Accordingly, both positions are deficient. You say that the flesh will not arise? Come now, tell me what element is going to arise, so I can congratulate you! You say it is the spirit that resides within the flesh, and also the light that is within the flesh? This thing "that also is within the flesh" is the Word; for what you are talking about is none other than flesh! It is necessary to arise in this kind of flesh, since everything exists in it. In this world those who wear garments are superior to the garments; in the kingdom of heaven the garments are superior to those who put them on. (*Gos. Phil.* 56.34–57.22)[157]

Modern interpreters have, with difficulty, tried to explain the internal tensions of this text.[158] Though cryptic, we find here more continuity between this life and the next than in classic Platonic anthropology.[159] This is a continuity in his opponents' reading of the text that Irenaeus would certainly not want to admit, for to do so would lead to the kind of "embarrassment" that Shils describes when competing traditions come to recognize that they possess a number of similarities at the edges.

As we saw with *3 Corinthians'* use of Pauline traditions, another set of questions seems to be fundamental. Which Paul? Which Pauline texts are employed to construct a particular image of Paul that is helpful for any particular reputational entrepreneur? How are the texts used, and what place do they have in the entrepreneur's ideological program? Tertullian was right. It was and is a matter of ordering. His and Irenaeus's opponents put 1 Corinthians 15.50 "in the front of the battle," where it became the *sine qua non* of Pauline anthropology. The heresiologists, on the other hand, left it for their "last assault . . . after [they] have removed out of the way all the questions which are auxiliary to it" (*Res.* 48.1). Trying to answer these more fundamental questions helps us begin to offer a thick description of Paul's legacy in the second century—a legacy where Pauline texts were the contested sites for preserving a community's image of the Apostle and where each community saw their own memory of Paul as being "natural."[160]

Conclusion: 3 Corinthians, Adversus haereses, *and Proto-Orthodox Memory of Paul*

The Paul of *Adversus haereses* is a complex web of earlier Pauline traditions. By invoking, specifically, the Pastoral Paul in the opening paratexts of Book One, Irenaeus shows his hand: he views Paul through the lens of heresy-hunting. His Paul is ultimately concerned with rooting out "falsely named knowledge" (1 Tim 6.20), which itself leads to nothing but "speculations rather than the divine training that is in faith" (1 Tim 1.4). Irenaeus further sharpens this image in Book Three through narratives of Paul's ministry that show his dependence on the Jerusalem apostles (both in Acts and in his Western version of Galatians). His Pastoral Paul, then, is waging an apostolic war. Since Irenaeus's apostolic *regula veritatis*, a proto-orthodox *traditum* shaped in the context of early Christian disagreements over the nature of Jesus' incarnation and resurrection (cf. Chapter 5), confesses a *fleshly* resurrection of both Jesus and all the rest of humanity, he offers in Book Five what he believes to be a "natural" reading of 1 Corinthians 15.50.

This Paul is substantially similar to the Paul of *3 Corinthians*.[161] Although we consciously avoided a comprehensive, descriptive theological analysis of *3 Corinthians* in the previous chapter, Peter Dunn has drawn attention to the fact that *3 Corinthians* shares the following "commonalities" with Irenaeus's own rule of faith (*Haer.* 1.10.1):

1. God, the *Pantocrator*, as maker of heaven and earth;
2. Salvation through the incarnation of Jesus, born of Mary (*3 Cor.*) or of the virgin (Iren.);
3. The apostasy of the prince, who thinks he is God (*3 Cor.*), or of the fallen angels (Iren.);
4. Eternal judgment of the wicked in fire;
5. The resurrection of the flesh, for which Jesus is the model; and
6. The inspiration of the prophets of Israel by the Holy Spirit.[162]

These near identical portrayals of Paul and rules of faith suggest that the two works were products of the same developing trajectory of the Pauline tradition. It is possible, if not likely, that the "Paulinism" of these two texts reflects a developing constellation of authorized memories of the Apostle among proto-orthodox communities in western Asia Minor in the second half of the second century—communities that, as Paul Trebilco has shown, were familiar with numerous Pauline letters, including the Pastoral Epistles and Acts by the early-second century, and that continued to honor the Apostle's work in their region (cf. Ignatius; Polycarp).[163] Trebilco also notes that early receptions of Paul in western Asia Minor display "a strong element of drawing what we might call 'exclusionary lines' of belief and practice, and of drawing these lines in such a way that they are *in continuity with* later orthodoxy."[164] Irenaeus grew up in western Asia Minor and was influenced heavily by Polycarp of Smyrna (*Haer.* 3.3.1–4; Eus., *Hist. eccl.* 5.20), who makes widespread use of a variety of Pauline texts and traditions, including 1 Timothy, in his *Epistle to the Philippians*. Polycarp may have also been Irenaeus's unnamed "presbyter" (*Haer.* 4.27.1), from whom he draws much of his anti-Marcionite polemic and who certainly knew and used Pauline materials.[165] Asia Minor is also the likely provenance of *3 Corinthians*, which displays a number of resemblances in language, theology, and argument to Ignatius and Polycarp.[166] This provenance would also explain how *3 Corinthians* was quickly assumed into the broader *Acts of Paul* literature (part of whose authorship Tertullian places in "Asia" at the end of the second century) and was transmitted in a variety of directions within a century or two, both as an individual text and as part of the *Acts of Paul* (eastward into Syria and Armenia, southward into Egypt, westward into Italy and North Africa). Furthermore, given its *general* polemic against a number of "Gnostic" heresies, its familiarity with the Simon and Cleobius tradition, and its polemical use of the Pastorals, the latter of which appears to be a development of the late-second century, *3 Corinthians*, like *Adversus haereses*, should be dated to the latter half of the second century.[167]

The fact that both texts portray the same Paul, yet differ in the exact way that they get there, suggests that they are independent witnesses to this one broad stream of proto-orthodox memory of the Apostle in Asia Minor in the latter half of the second century. Reputational entrepreneurs do not invent traditions whole cloth, despite what some extreme versions of the politics of memory school assert.[168] They are members of communities and experience the force of tradition. In a canon as variegated as was the earliest layer of the Pauline tradition, however, entrepreneurs can easily shift pieces of the tradition forward and backward, bringing into conscious view particular elements, eliminating others from public memory, and introducing new bits that must cohere with those that already have currency. The Paul standing behind *3 Corinthians* and *Adversus haereses* developed with a view to the needs of proto-orthodox communities and their *regula veritatis*, exhibiting a mixture of continuity with and changes from earlier layers of Pauline tradition. Through its hermeneutical arrangement of the earlier layer of Pauline texts, in addition to its rationalization of mysterious and potentially problematic Pauline language, the Pauline tradition in Irenaeus and *3 Corinthians* has developed beyond what was received. Of course, this rarely was and continues rarely to be visible to those who stand within a particular developing tradition. As Shils notes, "Such modifications of the received occur even when the tradition is regarded as sacrosanct and the innovator might in good conscience insist that he is adhering to the traditions as received."[169] Irenaeus conceives of his exposition of the Apostle as "sacrosanct," to use the language of Shils, or "natural," to use his own, unable to recognize (except for in his opponents) that "[e]very major tradition is a product of the confluence of contributory traditions, not only at its origin but in the course of its history."[170] Irenaeus fronts and combines Pauline materials of varying age (e.g., 1 Cor and 1 Tim, regardless of the authorship of the latter) and reads them in light of a still later and developing second-century rule of faith that includes statements about the resurrection of the *flesh*. As Jan and Alieda Assmann have argued (see Chapter 4), tradition and memory are constantly evolving and possess at any given time layers from various periods of time.

We can now better narrate the particular trajectory of Pauline tradition (*traditio*) that led from Acts to Irenaeus and *3 Corinthians*. Luke's depiction of the Jerusalem Council (Acts 15) is an endorsement of Paul's circumcision-free gospel. Writing from a pro-Gentile perspective, the author of Acts has cast the story of the earliest church as a preparatory scene for the arrival of the Pauline gospel and has turned Peter into a transitional figure, who was already pushing for Paul's circumcision-free gospel before the council ever met (Acts 10.1–11.17), but only after the narration of Paul's calling (Acts 9.1–30), at least according to Luke's narrative.[171] By the early-second century, whether through the influence of Acts, the circulation of Pauline letters (cf. Gal 1.18; 2.7–9; 1 Cor 3.22; 9.5; 15.5), oral traditions about the apostles, or some combination of all three, Peter and Paul were widely viewed as apostolic brothers in the proto-orthodox tradition (cf. *1 Clem.* 5.1–7; Ign. *Rom.* 4.3; 2 Pet 3.15–16). One could argue that Paul still stood taller, however, than Peter.[172] But as 2 Peter attests, Paul's letters eventually became contested sites of interpretation, and it was he who needed to be pulled toward Peter, the prized disciple of the earthly Jesus and father of the Roman church, not the other way around. The *Epistula Apostolorum*, originating from Asia Minor in the early to mid-second century and clearly concerned with combating theologies that deny the salvation of the flesh (*Ep. Apos.* 12, 21, 24, 26, 39), was the first to portray emphatically Paul's dependence on the teaching of the other apostles.[173]

This stream of Pauline tradition eventually merged with the others found in *3 Corinthians* and *Adversus haereses* as the Pastoral Epistles gained wider circulation and 1 Corinthians 15.50 became a highly contested Pauline text.[174] The Pastorals were particularly useful for portraying a Paul who was concerned for "the deposit" and "healthy teaching." The image of Paul reflected in these texts would then find its way, particularly due to the influence of Irenaeus's *Adversus haereses*, into later Pauline memorials, including the earliest proto-orthodox commentaries on his letters (cf. Origen, Chrysostom, and Theodore on the Greek side and Marius Victorinus, Ambrosiaster, Jerome, Augustine, and Pelagius on the Latin side).[175]

7

Practicing Paul

TWO SETS OF data from the second century, described in Chapter 1, have driven this inquiry into Paul's reception in the second century, in particular, and into Pauline historiography, in general. On the one hand, a wide-ranging set of Christian texts in the second century provide honorific titles to Paul of Tarsus: Paul, "the apostle of the resurrection" (Theodotus); Paul, "the divine apostle" (Clement of Alexandria); Paul, "the great apostle" (*Reality of the Rulers*); Paul, "the sanctified, the martyred, the most worthy of blessing" (Ignatius); and so on. Along with these more specific appellations, Paul also attained in that century the highest of all tributes; he was *"the* Apostle" (Heracleon; *Treatise on the Resurrection*; *A Prayer of Paul the Apostle*; Athenagoras; Irenaeus; Tertullian; Clement of Alexandria). On the other hand, and developing at the same time as Paul's charisma, discourses on the "real" Paul were beginning to play out in early Christian rhetoric—discourses that often centered around the proper interpretation of Pauline texts. Tertullian accused Marcion of "falsifying" and "mutilating" Paul's epistles. Marcion had made similar allegations against his proto-orthodox opponents decades earlier. The lawyer from Carthage also indicted a presbyter from Asia for "thinking to add of his own to Paul's reputation" by putting forth a fabricated *Acts of Paul*. Likewise, the author of 2 Peter blamed "the ignorant and unstable" for "distorting" Pauline texts. The *Gospel of Philip* rebuked "certain persons" for misreading 1 Corinthians 15.50. The "certain persons" here included those who, like Irenaeus, were at the same time rebuffing "heretics" for "misunderstanding" the same passage.

From the outset of our study, we paired this ancient discourse on the "real" Paul with its modern counterpart: the post-Baurian division of the "historical" Paul from the Paul of "tradition." This pairing was necessary because Baur's historical sight was trained not just on Paul, but on the reception of Paul's theology in the early church. Baur, aided by a Rankean-style positivist historiography, whittled Paul down to four letters. Once the "real" Paul of the *Hauptbriefe* became visible from behind his canonical cover, narratives about his reception (read: his distortion and dismemberment) in the second century took hold in the historical imagination. Some mutation of the Pauline Captivity narrative, based ultimately on Baur's "free" and "radical" Protestant theological preference for the *Hauptbriefe*, papered over by the rhetoric of positivist historiography, became the dominant portrayal of the Apostle's second-century fate for over a century.

Its reign came to an end in the 1980s after the appearance of the extended re-treatments of the material by Lindemann, Dassmann, Rensberger, and Penny. Together, these four reset the entire field of study on the early reception of Paul (as indicated by the "Paul and the Legacies of Paul" conference at Southern Methodist University in the late 1980s). With one voice they set the framework for a new account of "Pauline Fragmentation" in the second century, to use Penny's language, in which Paul's image (through narrative, ekphrastic, and other descriptive characterizations) as well as the use of Pauline letters evolved in different directions among a variety of often competing Christian communities, none of which had a monopoly on Paul.

Serious challenges in the twentieth century to the philosophical assumptions of Ranke's historiographical program (to reconstruct the past "wie es eigentlich gewesen") also began to erode confidence in narrations of the past that were built on a clear distinction between subject (historian) and object (traces of the past). The past always bears the stamp of the present. The historian, situated in a specific time and place, cannot help but shape his or her inquiry along ideological lines from the outset. "Reality" does not exist in the past, ready to be uncovered and described with complete immediacy, as proponents of the "real" Paul (whether ancient of modern) would have it. Rather, history-telling is framed within the social location of its narrator. In the wake of these philosophical shifts in historiography, a discernible move toward exploring the "image" of Paul constructed in various second-century texts can be seen over the past thirty years in scholarship on "Paul in the second century." In several very recent of these studies, "memory" is invoked as a historiographical category in speaking about the rise of "Paul." This study has attempted to do finally for Paul what studies of Jesus have been highlighting for almost a decade now: to place the reception of Paul within the context of early Christian memory-making.

Tertullian, cited at the outset of our inquiry, provides the key language for tying the two sets of data under discussion together within the context of memory: the exposed author of the *Acts of Paul [and Thecla]* was "thinking to add of his own to Paul's *reputation*" (*Bapt.* 17.5: *quasi titulo Pauli de suo cumulans*).[2] By the second century Paul had become a widely traditioned *figure*, a charismatic totem through which any number of early Christian communities could understand their own apostolic foundation. The diversity of Pauline images (or reputations) and textual interpretations displayed in the literary evidence from the second century is a result of the broad range of Christian theologies available in the second century, combined with the sheer variety of Pauline material (oral and written) coming from the first. Paul's reputation was pliable and thus could be shaped and formed through the invocation of different pieces of the highly diverse canon of early Pauline traditions, assimilated to prior ideological networks, to produce meaningful images and symbols. What was at stake in the competitive second century was remembering Paul *rightly*.

At this nascent stage of Christianity, because there were very few mechanisms that could prevent the kind of diversity that makes today's varieties of Christianity look quite tame, the early Christian culture-making process was bound to be a contested matter. To a significant degree, the rhetoric of this process was directed at the apostolic age. Apostolic legends, writings, and figures became the grammar by which Christian communities made their existence meaningful. They were part of the "enabling aspect" of early Christian cultural memory, to use the language of Jan Assmann. But because ideologically and socially distinct communities shared some of the same apostolic traditions (e.g., the Pauline letters), the "proper" understanding of these traditions was always at stake. Elizabeth Castelli reminds us:

> Since Christianity in its formative stages (and beyond) engaged in a series of contests over how the past should be understood and who should possess the legitimate claim to tradition (and the authority that accompanied it), it should not be surprising to discover that Christian memory work also participated in the process of contestation.[3]

Tertullian was worried that some Christians were claiming the right for women to teach and baptize based on the *Acts of Paul and Thecla*. In an attempt to ward off such a claim and ensure that both the proper image of Paul and the proper power dynamics within early Christianity remained intact, he tells his readers that this text was a fabrication, a fanciful attempt by an Asian presbyter to "add of his own to Paul's reputation." Tertullian then pits the *Acts of Paul and Thecla* against 1 Corinthians 14.34–35, claiming that the "real" Paul, represented by the latter, would have never allowed such a thing.

Paul, more than any other apostolic authority, had to find a proper home within the matrix of early Christian memory. The Pauline texts and traditions coming from the first century provide the widespread impression that his far-flung mission to the Gentiles was the single most disruptive yet formative social force in the nascent decades of Christianity. This very early characterization guaranteed him commemorative significance in subsequent Christian memory. Canonical and non-canonical pseudepigrapha, various Acts of Paul traditions, Pauline apocalypses, martyrdom legends, theologically redacted Pauline letter collections, and a wide variety of exegetical traditions attest to this.

The work of reputational entrepreneurs was important for ensuring that Paul remained both intelligible and manageable within the cultural memory of their communities. The authors of *1 Clement, 2* Peter, the *Acts of Paul, 3 Corinthians,* the Coptic *Apocalypse of Paul,* and the *Prayer of Paul the Apostle,* along with Ignatius, Polycarp, Marcion, Irenaeus, Tertullian, and many others, had something to gain or lose in their attempts to provide and defend meaningful images of the Apostle for their communities, from which they had received much of their understanding of his significance in the first place. Individual memory is socially constrained. The Pauline image traditions that they received, shaped, constructed, and to some degree altered were models *of* (acting as mirrors) as well as models *for* (acting as lamps) their communities. In their work, the vital task of preserving apostolic authority was at stake. Power relations within a competitive Christian world were involved. Hard positions had to be taken, as the accusations of "misunderstanding," "distortion," and "falsification" suggest.

When we measure, however, the shared image of Paul that appears in *3 Corinthians* and Irenaeus's *Adversus haereses* against such rhetoric, we find that something else was happening on the ground. In trying to provide a thick description of the Pauline tradition in these two texts, we discovered that they display elements of continuity with and change from the earlier layers of the Pauline tradition that they invoke. It is naïve, despite Irenaeus's claims to the contrary, to ask whether or not these texts provide an "accurate" or "correct" reading of the "real" Paul. As Margaret Mitchell has asserted with respect to the later John Chrysostom:

> When one observes, as we shall repeatedly have occasion to do in this book, Chrysostom's penchant for painting portraits of Paul by selecting elements from out of the existing plethora of data within the letters and the Acts of the Apostles and recombining them in novel ways, the criterion of the *right portrait* or *the accurate portrait* of Paul is utterly elusive and ultimately useless. How could we judge such a thing?[4]

What we can say, as Mitchell reminds, is that the authors of *3 Corinthians* and *Adversus haereses* have constructed complex images of the Apostle that capture his significance for one strain of proto-orthodoxy by elevating, fronting, and combining some elements of the diverse earlier Pauline tradition, while obscuring others. In particular, both texts work to construct and preserve a Paul who is the defender of the proto-orthodox rule of faith (cf. *Haer.* 1.10.1).

The problems endemic to answering a question like Who got Paul right in the second century? are the result of the way that communities actually remember and pass down these traditions to successive generations. Once the subject of "Paul in the second century" becomes thoroughly embedded in the language of tradition and memory, rather than those handed on to us by the historiographers of the nineteenth and early-twentieth centuries, a different set of questions from those normally asked takes center stage. The question Who got Paul right in the second century?, loaded with the freight of modern ideology in the guise of positivist historiography, is replaced by a more fruitful and honest kind of question: Which Paul?

The question Which Paul? cuts two ways. First, we should ask about continuities with the past. Which Pauline (written) texts and (oral) traditions have been invoked to provide a particular portrayal of the Apostle? How have they been ordered and interpreted? Second, we should ask about the role of the present in shaping the past. What is the social location of a given author? What communal rules of faith have shaped an individual author's (conscious or unconscious) selection of individual pieces from within the broad and diverse early layer of Pauline traditions? Is the relationship between particular Pauline traditions and their tradents' social location completely homeostatic?

Finally, and from a methodological standpoint, the question Which authors knew and used which Pauline texts in the second century? does not
go nearly far enough in providing a thick description of Paul's influence in
the second century. Not only were Pauline texts coming into wide circulation during this period, but oral traditions, some of which may have been
rooted in communities that Paul founded, other times possibly stemming
from Paul's opponents, were also making their way into the stream of
early Christian memory. In fact, the use and interpretation of Pauline texts
were often in the service of the defense of particular Pauline images that
functioned synecdochically, where "Paul" was signified by the piece of the
tradition that a particular writer wanted to fix in the memory of his or her
community as particularly "Pauline": Paul, "the Apostle of the Resurrection" (Theodotus); Paul, "the sanctified, the martyred, the most worthy of
blessing" (Ignatius); Paul, the Apostle to the Gentiles (Acts; 2 Timothy;
1 Clement; Martyrdom of Paul); Paul, the Orthodox Teacher (Irenaeus;
3 Corinthians); Paul, the Apocalyptic Visionary (Coptic *Apocalypse of Paul;*
Marcion); and so on. As images, these portrayals of the Apostle should not
be viewed as completely transparent, as though any one of them gives us
access to the "real" Paul. Already bearing an interpretive framework, they
obscure and frustrate access to the "real" Paul, if by that rhetoric one
means a Paul denuded of tradition and frozen in time. Just as important,
if not more, however, each Pauline image in the second century provided
meaningful handles for grasping the Apostle's importance for individual
communities in the midst of a sea of diverse apostolic material.

Many other second-century texts will need to be explored from this
vantage point in the future in order to help clarify and fill out the present
Pauline Fragmentation narrative. Michael Kaler's work, for example, on
the Apocalyptic Paul of both the Coptic *Apocalypse of Paul* and Marcion is
exemplary in this regard.[5] Areas of particular need are studies on the
"Paul" of the Montanists and of Clement of Alexandria. I know of no work
on the former, while studies on the latter have been limited to the use of
individual Pauline texts and themes.[6] Particularly fruitful would be attempts to locate constellations of Pauline traditions that develop region-
ally, as I have tried to suggest in locating the particular Pauline tradition of
3 Corinthians and *Adversus haereses* in Asia. Are there commonalities that
exist, for instance, between the Pauline traditions in Marcion and the
Montanists, both of whom represent apocalyptic theologies in central and
northern Anatolia in the mid- to late-second century? Also useful would
be attempts to trace diachronic receptions of Pauline traditions, as I have

done with the relationship between Paul and the Apostles among the proto-orthodox, particularly where personal or textual connections can be made. To what degree, for instance, is Origen's interpretation of Paul derived from Clement? Outside these kinds of studies, early Pauline manuscript traditions should be explored more intentionally, not just for tendentious readings, but for ways in which their organization and overall contents might say something about how their copyists understood Paul.[7]

The Paul of History and the Apostle of Faith: Eight Considerations for Practicing Pauline Studies

In subtle and not so subtle ways, I have tried to make the case for a paradigm shift in Pauline Studies along the lines of what is happening in Historical Jesus Studies. At the heart of the shift in contemporary Historical Jesus Studies lies a deep suspicion of the epistemic certainty with which the field has often proceeded.[8] The personal about-face described in Dale Allison's *Constructing Jesus* is exemplary of the kinds of theoretical and methodological shifts that are occurring in scholarship on Christian origins. Allison turns his back on the whole attempt to secure discrete, unconnected data about the "historical" Jesus from early Christian gospels through the application of abstract criteria and rather grounds his new explorations in memory theory, looking to establish "broad impressions" about the life of Jesus based on "recurrent attestations."[9] Like traditional "Questers" for the Historical Jesus, however, many modern scholars of the "historical" Paul still continue to try to peel away layers of tradition (whether whole texts or interpolations within authentic texts) in order to expose the authentic Pauline core, the "real" Paul. This is done without any regard for the fact that the philosophy, language, and practice of "scientific history" were challenged in the twentieth century as often nothing more than wishful thinking, driven by socially conditioned "self-evident" truths.

As intimated throughout this study, I suggest that before talking about the "real" or "historical" Paul, we should begin to think of ourselves as scholars of Pauline traditions, including (1) the tradition within which the "historical" Paul language of the nineteenth century developed and (2) the second-century Pauline traditions within which our earliest manuscripts of Pauline literature are situated. It remains to be seen, however, whether or not Pauline Studies will be able to embrace such a position. Until we can fully admit that the prevailing modern discourse on the "real" Paul comes from a long-standing tradition that elevates the *Hauptbriefe* to the front and center of the Pauline canon, not just materially (they stand at the front of ancient manuscripts merely because of their length), but theologically and hermeneutically, we will never approach the kind of deconstructive position necessary for developing more transparent methodologies for reconstructing the "real" or the "historical" Paul. If we were serious about this task, and not merely interested in using Paul as a pawn for modern rhetorics, we would begin to view all the Pauline Epistles, for instance, as Pauline "tradition": diverse images of Paul mediated to us through historically and socially conditioned texts and manuscripts. A full embrace of Shils's "substantive traditionality," Gadamer's "historically effected consciousness," Jan Assmann's "cultural memory," and Schwartz's "collective memory" would be helpful in getting there. Each of these argues, as we have seen, for the ubiquity of tradition and explores tradition and memory as complex phenomena that exhibit strong connections with the past as well as innovation for the present, thereby neutralizing and marginalizing discourses that speak of the complete "invention" of tradition or, in our case, of the total "misrepresentation" of Paul.

Once we have historicized later discourses on the "real" Paul and have described the practices of his reception at given times and places, will we be able, though, to pierce through the diversity of first-century Pauline materials and narrate his life, mission, and theology in ways that are devoid of ideological preference and that also allow us to separate some of the material as "non-Pauline," so that it can fill the void between Paul's death and his reception in the second century? I want to offer here, with the aid of the historiographical musings of Michel de Certeau, a few suggestions and cautions for a way forward.

First, historically situating discourses on the "real" should not be viewed as a threat to, but rather a crucial part of, the historiographical process. Certeau urged:

> But taking the place seriously is the condition that allows something to be stated that is neither legendary (or "edifying") nor atopical (lacking relevance). Denial of the specificity of the place being the very principle of ideology, all theory is excluded. Even more, by moving discourse into a non-place, ideology forbids history from speaking of society and of death—in other words, from being history.[10]

Particularly helpful in this regard would be fuller disclosures by historians of early Christianity of their own temporo-spatial (and thus ideological) situatedness. I have tried to signal some of my own history in the preface to this book. Certeau criticized Foucault, who placed numerous discourses about reality, except his own, within their historical and ideological contexts, on this very point.[11] More generally, Certeau argued:

> By a professional reflex, the historian refers any discourse to the socioeconomic or mental conditions that produced it. He needs to apply this kind of analysis to his own discourse in a manner that will make it pertinent to the elucidation of those forces that presently organize representations of the past.[12]

Second, we must therefore become more fully aware of the institutional frameworks of our knowledge. In Chapter 1 I tried to expose the structural and institutional biases toward the Paul of the *Hauptbriefe* in our field. Until we fully describe this bias and its ability to portray a world, we will not be able to come to grips with its formative powers. Certeau, again, reminded:

> Expressed bluntly, the problem is as follows: a *mise en scène* of a (past) actuality, that is, the historiographical discourse itself, occults the social and technical apparatus of the professional institution that produces it. The operation in question is rather sly: the discourse gives itself credibility in the name of the reality which it is supposed to represent, but this authorized appearance of the "real" serves precisely to camouflage the practice which in fact determines it.[13]

Third, institutional structures not only constrain what we know, but *can* also provide a context for the sharpening of our historical vision. Historiography is a properly social and public enterprise where the contestation of methods, assumptions, and interpretations *should* happen. Margaret Mitchell, toward the conclusion of *The Heavenly Trumpet*, reminds us:

> As students of antiquity have long known, the best historical writing is done by scholars whose imaginations allow them to move from the collection and interpretation of sources to form in their minds realistic and vivid pictures of a world gone by. But that is not the last step of the process, for the portrait gained through that process must, by means of creative adaptation of some existing literary conventions, be displayed in the public arena for delectation and ongoing, living revision.[14]

Fourth, robust critical engagements with our methodologies must always remain front and center in Pauline Studies. We must never obscure the mechanisms whereby certain discourses about the "real" Paul come to seem natural. Because of this, a full-scale appraisal of the use of stylometrics and linguistic measures and the discourse surrounding their use in Pauline Studies for the purposes of determining authorship is needed. We must try to locate ways in which the specter of scientific history still haunts Pauline Studies through attempts to over-argue the results of today's computer-based inquiries. The increasingly precise measurement of difference between individual Pauline letters is just that: the measurement of difference. A separate argument then needs to be made about the significance of the difference. Most often these arguments still proceed on certain assumptions, rooted in a tradition of theological preference. The *Hauptbriefe* are the baseline for determining the authenticity of all the other letters. Stylometric studies have often been wielded to obscure choice with "scientificity," as Certeau has sardonically argued:

> The computer opens up the possibility of quantitative, serial analysis of variable relationships among stable units over an extended period of time. For the historian, it is tantamount to discovering the Island of the Blessed. At last he will be able to sever historiography from its compromising relations with rhetoric, with all of its metonymic and metaphorical uses of details that are supposed to be the signifying elements of the ensemble and with all its cunning devices of oratory and persuasion. At last he is going to be able to disengage historiography from its dependence on the surrounding culture, out of which prejudgments and expectancies determine in advance certain postulates, units of study, and interpretations.[15]

Fifth, claims about the "real" Paul must be accompanied by descriptions about how they might also be falsified. Marc Bloch opined:

> On that day when, having first taken care not to discourage it with useless pedantry, we shall succeed in persuading the public to measure the value of a science in proportion to its willingness to make refutation easy, the forces of reason will achieve one of their most smashing victories.[16]

Rather than being swept under the rug and suppressed, stubborn data must be readily confessed, like the reference to ἐπισκόποις καὶ διακόνοις in Philippians 1.1 and the numerous appeals to authoritative tradition and to wider church practice in 1 Corinthians (1 Cor 1.2; 4.17; 7.17; 11.2, 16, 23; 14.33b, 36; 15.1–3, 11; 16.1), two supposedly "genuine" Pauline epistles.

Sixth, inasmuch as there is a high probability that at least some of the canonical Pauline letters go back to Paul's apostolic team (whether Paul himself, his secretaries, or ministry associates), appeals to specific Pauline letters and passages within letters as primary evidence for Saul of Tarsus are appropriate and will always provide the "prime language" for Pauline Studies.[17] As Certeau reminds, the reference, or citation, is the defining feature of historical discourse:

> The role of quoted language is thus one of accrediting discourse. With its referential function, it introduces into the text an effect of reality; and through its crumbling it discreetly refers to a locus of authority. From this angle, the split structure of discourse functions like a machinery that extracts from the citation a verisimilitude of narrative and a validation of knowledge. It produces a sense of reliability.[18]

But until some other ground for exempting some of these texts from critical scrutiny, besides theological preference, can be established, each must be subject to the same degree of skepticism.

Seventh, the establishment of several letters that share a family resemblance (*Hauptbriefe*, Pastorals, Ephesians/Colossians, 1/2 Thessalonians) and that likely stem from close to the same time (say, two or three years, or less) as certainly of "Pauline" origin is probably not enough to establish a "real" Paul. Even authentic Pauline letters would have been rhetorically constructed for specific polemical situations. Self-construction is still construction. And if Paul conducted a nearly three-decade ministry within a new religious movement, we must be open to the possibility that he changed his mind on a few things, big and small, along the way. Lincoln's history is illustrative here. As John Lewis Gaddis has reminded us, biographers "rerun whole lives, not single moments in them."[19]

Eighth, once memory and its operations have become sufficiently established in the historiographical imagination of Pauline Studies, we may need to be prepared to talk about the "historical" Paul in the manner that Allison and others are beginning to talk about Jesus. Rather than working to establish certain letters or smaller portions of letters as authentically Pauline (like the so-called authentic sayings of Jesus), we *may* be on firmer ground to speak of "broad impressions" across the entire early Pauline literature (cf. the end of Chapter 4). As Marc Bloch warned about the manuscript transmission of Aeschylus's *Oresteia*—"There is more certainty in the whole than in its parts"—the transmission of Paul to the church and academy might ultimately fall along lines quite typical of memory: with a gist.[20]

By giving sufficient attention to these suggestions, the modern practice of Pauline Studies can be shaken out of its entrenched discourse on the "real" Paul, rooted in nineteenth-century historical positivism, in favor of a more sophisticated historiography that gives fuller consideration, in line with Certeau, to the interplay of the historian's "social *place*, 'scientific' *practices*, and *writing*."[21] The "real" Paul, once dead, will then be transformed and raised as the Apostle of tradition/memory/time/space/history/faith. As we have shown for the second century, the *imago Pauli* always challenges fundamentalist rhetorics about the past "wie es eigentlich gewesen."

Marking "Paul" in the Society of Biblical Literature (2009–2013)

Several program units within the Society of Biblical Literature (SBL) are dedicated to research on "Paul" and the letters bearing his name in early Christianity (particularly canonical texts). While the Apostle's life, theology, and letters often come up in any number of sections at the annual meeting of the SBL, Tables A.1 through A.6 track the number of papers delivered on individual "Pauline" epistles over the past five years in those several sections whose names bear the words "Paul" or "Pauline," or are devoted to a particular epistle (e.g., Romans Through History and Cultures). This cluster of sections, in particular, has been invested in Paul as an object of knowledge, and their steering committees are the gatekeepers of what counts for "Paul" at the annual meeting. This investigation, of course, could be taken back all the way to the inception of the SBL, and we could look for diachronic trends. That is not my goal here. I am only looking for a synchronic snapshot of our present institutionalized knowledge of "Paul" and which texts characteristically speak for him now, regardless of how they might be interpreted. Five years of data seem long enough to establish that picture without allowing the peculiarities of one particular year to distort the picture.

Only papers whose titles or abstracts mark out a particular epistle for discussion have been included in the following tables. Papers have only been registered once. In the case of broadly construed papers dealing with particular Pauline themes (apocalypticism, law, Israel, power, etc.) across a number of texts, I have counted them only if one particular text seems to stand above the rest in their abstracts. If no Pauline texts are specifically mentioned or alluded to in the title or abstract, then the paper has not been recorded in the tables. Panel discussions of a book about a particular "Pauline" epistle have also been counted once. While this endeavor is imprecise (sometimes the paper title or abstract changes between their acceptance and the actual delivery of the paper, other times the abstracts are woefully vague, etc.), I do believe that it provides a fairly accurate sense of the present state of affairs in our guild.

Table A.1 2009 Annual Meeting (New Orleans, LA)

Section\Text	Rom	1 Cor	2 Cor	Gal	Phil	1 Thess	Phile	Eph	Col	2 Thess	Pastoral Epistles[a]
Pauline Epistles	6	5		1	1	1					
2 Corinthians: Pauline Theology in the Making			11								
Romans Through History and Cultures	4										
Paul and Politics	2			1	1	1			1[b]		
Pauline Soteriology	2					1					
Paul and Scripture[c]											
– Beyond the *Hauptbriefe*					1	1					
– Disputed Paulines									1		1
Disputed Paulines							0	3	1	0	4
Total Papers/Text	14	5	11	2	3	4	0	3	3	0	5

[a]The "Pastoral Epistles" is a problematic category, as many recent studies have shown, but since we still have papers treating the three texts together, I have not differentiated them here.

[b]Jason Myers's paper entitled "Paul's Triumph in Colossians 2:15" is the lone example from 2009 of a "Disputed" Pauline text making its way, unproblematically, into one of the "Undisputed" Pauline Sections.

[c]The Paul and Scripture Section held two sessions, one of which was designated "Disputed Paulines," thereby suggesting that the other session, "Beyond the *Hauptbriefe*" was for "Undisputed" Pauline texts.

Table A.2 2010 Annual Meeting (Atlanta, GA)

Section\Text	Rom	1 Cor	2 Cor	Gal	Phil	1 Thess	Phile	Eph	Col	2 Thess	Pastoral Epistles
Pauline Epistles	2	3	1	2	2	1		1[a]			
2 Corinthians: Pauline Theology in the Making			8								
Romans Through History and Cultures	5										
Paul and Politics	2									1[b]	
Pauline Soteriology	1			1							
Paul and Scripture[c]											
Paul and Judaism[d]											
Disputed Paulines								2	2		4
Total Papers/Text	10	3	9	3	2	1	0	3	2	1	4

[a]The title of Jin Young Choi's paper, "A Formation of *Post*-Pauline Christian Identity in the Roman Empire: The Metaphor of Body and the Language of Unity, Maturity, and Fullness in Ephesians," clearly indicates that he did not consider Ephesians to be a "Pauline" text (emphasis in title mine).

[b]Douglas Farrow's paper entitled "On the Maturation of Evil" is the only other example of a "Disputed" Pauline text making its way into one of the "Undisputed" Pauline Sections in 2010. The abstract of the paper, however, states that 2 Thessalonians represents a "broadly Pauline" position, suggesting some doubt about the latter's authorship.

[c]All five papers in the Paul and Scripture seminar this year were broadly conceived methodological and theoretical proposals. Their titles and abstracts lacked references to particular Pauline texts.

[d]This was a new unit in 2010 and featured invited papers on larger questions.

Table A.3 2011 Annual Meeting (San Francisco, CA)

Section\Text	Rom	1 Cor	2 Cor	Gal	Phil	1 Thess	Phile	Eph	Col	2 Thess	Pastoral Epistles
Pauline Epistles	6	8	1								
2 Corinthians: Pauline Theology in the Making			8		4						
Romans Through History and Cultures	6										
Paul and Politics[a]	3	1		1	1						
Pauline Soteriology		1									
Disputed Paulines								5	1		5
Total Papers/Text	15	10	9	1	5	0	0	5	1	0	5

[a]The "Paul and Politics" and "Pauline Soteriology" groups held a joint session on "Utopian Visions and Salvation in Paul." The data for that session are counted here and not in the "Pauline Soteriology" row.

Table A.4 2012 Annual Meeting (Chicago, IL)

Section\Text	Rom	1 Cor	2 Cor	Gal	Phil	1 Thess	Phile	Eph	Col	2 Thess	Pastoral Epistles
Pauline Epistles	4	3									
1 Corinthians[a]		5		5							
2 Corinthians: Pauline Theology in the Making			9								
Paul and Politics		2	1								
Pauline Soteriology		1									
Paul and Judaism[b]											
Paul and Heritage of Israel[c]											
Disputed Paulines								1	1	1	2
Total Papers/Text	4	11	10	5	0	0	0	1	1	1	2

[a]The full title of this new 2012 seminar is "Systematic Transformation and Interweaving of Scripture in 1 Corinthians."
[b]This section considered a more broadly defined topic in 2012: "What Does Torah Observance Mean in a First Century Diaspora Context, and Thus for Interpreting Paul?"
[c]A one-time joint session of the Book of Acts, Pauline Epistles, and Disputed Paulines sections to discuss the essays in the volume *Paul and the Heritage of Israel*.

Table A.5 2013 Annual Meeting (Baltimore, MD)

Section\Text	Rom	1 Cor	2 Cor	Gal	Phil	1 Thess	Phile	Eph	Col	2 Thess	Pastoral Epistles
Pauline Epistles	3	4	1	3	1	1					
1 Corinthians		4									
2 Corinthians: Pauline Theology in the Making			9								
Paul and Politics	1						2				
Pauline Soteriology		1	1								
Paul and Judaism			1		1						
Disputed Paulines								4			6
Total Papers/Text	4	9	12	3	2	1	2	4	0	0	6

Table A.6 Totals from 2009 to 2013

Section\Text	Rom	1 Cor	2 Cor	Gal	Phil	1 Thess	Phile	Eph	Col	2 Thess	Pastoral Epistles
Pauline Epistles	21	23	3	11	8	3		1			
1 Corinthians[a]		9									
2 Corinthians[a]			45								
Romans Through History and Cultures[b]	15										
Paul and Politics	8	3	1	2	2	1	2		1	1	
Pauline Soteriology	3	3	1	1	1						
Paul and Scripture					1	1					
– Beyond the *Hauptbriefe*									1		
– Disputed Paulines											
Paul and Judaism			1		1						1
Disputed Paulines[c]								15	5	1	21
Total Papers/Text	47	38	51	14	13	5	2	16	7	2	22

[a] 21/45 papers in the "Second Corinthians: Pauline Theology in the Making" Seminar had "Paul," "Pauline," or "Paul's" in the title of the paper, indicating that 2 Corinthians is a text that speaks for "Paul."

[b] 8/14 papers in the "Romans Through History and Cultures" Section had "Paul," "Pauline," or "Paul's" in the title of the paper, indicating that, like 2 Corinthians, Romans is a naturally "Pauline" text.

[c] Only 6/38 papers in the "Disputed Paulines" section had the words "Paul," "Pauline," or "Paul's" in their titles. But in each case the author of the paper, either in the title or in the abstract, modified this language with "effective-history" (Marlatte, 2011), "recasting" (Smith, 2012), "transformation" (Herzer, 2013), or the like. These disputed texts, then, are not genuinely Pauline according to these presenters, but are later reconfigurations of the Apostle.

APPENDIX 2

Marking "Paul" in Selected Major Commentary Series

Table A.7 lists the number of pages that discuss the authenticity of Romans, Colossians, and the Pastoral Epistles (often treated by commentators as a group) in five different major commentary series. The former are representative of the three classes of Pauline Epistles that our guild differentiates: authentic, deutero-Pauline, and pseudepigraphal, in turn. The latter are representative of critical, English-language scholarship. In all cases, Romans is given pride of place as marking the "real" Paul. Very little discussion is given to its authenticity in the commentaries.

Table A.7 Number of Pages Devoted to Authorial Authenticity in Five Major Commentary Series

Series/Text	Romans (Author, Date)	Colossians (Author, Date)	Pastoral Epistles (Author, Date)
Hermeneia	0 (Jewett, 2006)	13 (Lohse, 1972)	5 (Dibelius/ Conzelmann, 1972)
International Critical Commentary	<1 (Cranfield, 1975)	11 (Wilson, 2005)	36 (Marshall, 1999)
Anchor Bible	<1 (Fitzmyer, 1993)	13 (Barth/ Blanke, 1995)	36 (Johnson–1–2 Tim, 2001) 20 (Quinn–Titus, 1990)
Word Biblical Commentary	<1 (Dunn, 1988)	8 (O'Brien, 1982)	84 (Mounce, 2000)
Sacra Pagina	0 (Byrne, 1996)	3 (MacDonald, 2008)	3 (Fiore, 2003)
Totals	1	48	184

English Translation of P. Bodm. X
(3 Corinthians)

The Corinthians, to Paul,

[1]Stephanus and the presbyters with him, Daphnos and Euboulos and Theophilos and Zenon, to Paul, who is in the Lord, greetings. [2]Two men, a certain Simon and Cleobius, have arrived in Corinth, who are upsetting the faith of some with destructive statements, [3]which you must test for yourself. [4]For we have not heard statements such as these from you or from the others. [5]But we keep what we received from you and from them. [6]Therefore, because the Lord has shown mercy to us, you are still in the flesh in order that we might hear from you again. [7]Either come yourself, [8]for we believe as it was revealed to Theonoe, that the Lord saved you from the hand of the Lawless One, or write back to us. [9]For what they are saying and teaching is this:

[10]they say that we ought not use the prophets;
[11]and that God is not Almighty;
[12]and that there is no resurrection of the flesh;
[13]and that the formation of mankind is not from God;
[14]and that the Lord did not arrive in flesh nor was he born from Mary;
[15]and that the world is not from God, but from the angels.

[16]Therefore, brother, display all earnestness to come here in order that the assembly of the Corinthians might remain without a cause of stumbling and their foolishness might become evident.

Farewell in the Lord.

Paul, to the Corinthians, concerning the flesh,

[1]Paul, the prisoner of Christ Jesus, in the midst of many deviant views, to the brethren in Corinth, greetings. [2]I, myself, am not astonished at how quickly the doctrines of the Evil One are advancing, [3]because the Lord Christ, who is rejected by those who are counterfeiting his words, will make his noble appearance quickly. [4]For I entrusted to you in the beginning what I also received from the apostles who came before me, and who spent all their time with Jesus Christ:

[5]that our Lord Christ Jesus was born from Mary, from the offspring of David, when the Holy Spirit was sent from heaven by the Father into her, [6]in order that he might advance into the world and set all flesh free by his own flesh and in order that he might raise us from the dead as those with flesh, in the same way he showed himself as an example; [7]and that mankind was formed by his Father. [8]Therefore, while also perishing, he was sought after in order that he might be made alive through adoption. [9]For then God, who is over all things, the Almighty, who made the heavens and the earth, sent prophets to the Jews first in order that they might be torn away from their sins, [10]for he determined to save the house of Israel. Therefore dividing from the Spirit of Christ, he sent it into the prophets, who proclaimed the true piety for a long time. [11][But the unjust ruler,] who was seeking to be [God], laid hands on them, and imprisoned all human flesh to lust. [12]God, the Almighty One, being righteous and not wanting to invalidate his own creation, [13]sent down the Spirit through fire into Mary the Galilean, [15]in order that the Evil One might be defeated through the same perishing flesh over which he had rights, and might be shown not to be God. [16]For by his own body Christ Jesus saved all flesh, [17]in order that he might display in his own body a temple of righteousness, [18]by which we have been set free.

[19]Therefore, they are not children of righteousness, but children of wrath, who push back the providence of God by saying that the heavens and the earth and everything in them are not the works of the Father. [20]For they have the cursed faith of the Serpent. [21]Turn away from these kinds of people and flee from their teaching.

[24]Now those who say to you "There is no resurrection of the flesh," for them there is no resurrection— [25]those who thus also do not believe in the one who was raised. [26]For they do not know, O Corinthian men, about the sowing of wheat or of the other seeds, that they are cast naked onto the earth, and after altogether perishing below are raised by the will of God, and have also been clothed with a body. [27]So that not only is the body which has been thrown down raised, but it has been blessed with abundant prosperity. [28]Now if we are prohibited from constructing the parable from the seeds, [29]you know that Jonah, the son of Amathias,

because he would not preach in Nineveh, was thrown to a sea monster, ³⁰and after three days and three nights God heard the prayer of Jonah from the lowest part of Hades and no part of him was destroyed, neither a hair nor an eyelash. ³¹O you of little faith, how much more will he raise you, who believe in Christ Jesus, in the same way that he himself was raised. ³²And if, when a corpse was thrown from the sons of Israel onto the bones of the prophet Elisha, the body of the man was raised, then what about you, upon whom the body and the bones and the Spirit of Christ have been cast, will you not be raised in that day having healthy flesh?

³⁴Now if you accept something else, do not cause me troubles. ³⁵For I have the bonds on my hands in order that I might gain Christ and the brands on my body in order that I might come to the resurrection of the dead. ³⁶And if anyone remains in the standard that he received through the blessed prophets and the holy Gospel, he will receive a reward. ³⁷If anyone oversteps these things, then the fire is with him, as was also with the rejecters of God who walked before them, ³⁸who are the children of vipers. ³⁹Turn away from them by the power of the Lord.

⁴⁰And may peace be with you.

Notes

CHAPTER I

1. Epigraph: Marc Bloch, *The Historian's Craft* (trans. P. Putnam; New York: Alfred A. Knopf, 1953), 71.

2. Text and translation of *De baptismo* from Ernest Evans, *Tertullian's Homily on Baptism* (London: SPCK, 1964). For a recent defense of the *Acts of Paul and Thecla* as Pauline hagiography, cf. Glenn E. Snyder, *Acts of Paul: The Formation of a Pauline Corpus* (WUNT 2.352; Tübingen: Mohr Siebeck, 2013), 120–137.

3. The language of "reputational entrepreneurs" comes from Barry Schwartz's work on the commemoration of Abraham Lincoln and other important figures of American history. We will explore Schwartz's work in Chapter 4.

4. I use scare quotes around several terms in this introductory chapter to signify their contested nature in modern scholarship. These terms, including "real," "historical," "tradition," "ecclesiastical," "Gnostic," and "proto-orthodox," are normally deployed in the midst of ideological discourses, and thus are often not transparent. Several of these terms and the discourses behind them are the subject of this book and, as such, will retain the scare quotes throughout. Others, however, are less central to my concerns. For these, such as "Gnostic" and "proto-orthodox," a simple footnote to the ongoing scholarly discussion will suffice and then the scare quotes will drop out for the benefit of the reader. On the "Gnostics" and "Gnosticism," for instance, cf. "Paul and the Heretics: Marcion" in Chapter 2. On the use of "proto-orthodox" as an etic designation for the theological forerunners of what would become "orthodoxy," cf. Bart D. Ehrman, *The New Testament: a Historical Introduction to the Early Christian Writings* (3rd ed.; New York: Oxford University Press, 2004), 7.

5. On the connection between authorship and authority in antiquity, cf. Wolfgang Speyer, *Die literarische Fälschung im hiednischen und christlichen Altertum: Ein Versuch ihrer Deutung* (Handbuch der Altertumswissenschaft 1/2; München: Beck,

1971) and now Bart D. Ehrman, *Forgery and Counterforgery: The Use of Literary Deceit in Early Christian Polemics* (New York: Oxford University Press, 2012).

6. Cf., for instance, Gordon D. Fee, *The First Epistle to the Corinthians* (NICNT; Grand Rapids: Eerdmans, 1987), 699–708; William O. Walker, "Interpolations in the Pauline Letters," in *The Pauline Canon* (ed. S. Porter; Pauline Studies 1; Leiden: Brill, 2004), 189–235; and Philip B. Payne, "Fuldensis, Sigla for Variants in Vaticanus, and 1 Cor 14.34–5," *NTS* 41 (1995): 240–262; "Ms. 88 as Evidence for a Text without 1 Cor 14:34–35," *NTS* 44 (1998): 152–158; and "The Text–Critical Function of the Umlauts in Vaticanus, with Special Attention to 1 Corinthians 14.34–35: a Response to J Edward Miller," *JSNT* 27 (2004): 105–112.

7. Ernst Käsemann, "Paul and Early Catholicism," in *New Testament Questions of Today* (trans. W. J. Montague; Philadelphia: Fortress Press, 1969), 249. Emphasis mine in each of the following quotes.

8. Ernst Haenchen, *The Acts of the Apostles: a Commentary* (trans. B. Noble and G. Shinn; Oxford: Basil Blackwell, 1971), 114. Cf. also 116. Brackets mine.

9. Robert Morgan, "Paul's Enduring Legacy," in *The Cambridge Companion to St. Paul* (ed. J. D. G. Dunn; Cambridge Companions to Religion; Cambridge: Cambridge University Press, 2003), 252.

10. Douglas Campbell, *The Deliverance of God: an Apocalyptic Rereading of Justification in Paul* (Grand Rapids, MI: Eerdmans, 2009), 936.

11. The "domestication" language is particularly popular in this schema. Cf. Marcus J. Borg and John Dominic Crossan, *The First Paul: Reclaiming the Radical Visionary Behind the Church's Conservative Icon* (New York: HarperCollins, 2009), 15; James D. G. Dunn, "Introduction," *The Cambridge Companion to St. Paul*, 2; Anthony T. Hanson, "The Domestication of Paul: a Study in the Development of Early Christian Theology," *BJRL* 63 (1981): 402–418; and Robert Morgan, "Paul's Enduring Legacy," in *Cambridge Companion to St. Paul*, 243.

12. These include the following sections: Pauline Epistles, 2 Corinthians, Romans through History and Culture, Paul and Politics, Pauline Soteriology, Paul and Scripture, Paul and Judaism and the Disputed Paulines.

13. James D. G. Dunn, *Romans* (2 vols.; WBC; Waco: Word Books, 1988), 1: xxxix.

14. C. E. B. Cranfield, *Critical and Exegetical Commentary on the Epistle to the Romans* (2 vols.; ICC; London: T&T Clark, 1979), 2.

15. Jacob Taubes, Alain Badiou, Giorgio Agamben, and Slavoj Žižek, among others, have found Paul's messianism and apocalypticism helpful in providing a critique of current socio-political systems. The relevant works are Jacob Taubes, *The Political Theology of Paul* (ed. A. Assmann w/J. Assmann; trans. D. Hollander; Cultural Memory in the Present; Stanford, CA: Stanford University Press, 2004 [1993]); Alain Badiou, *Saint Paul: The Foundation of Universalism* (trans. R. Brassier; Cultural Memory in the Present; Stanford, CA: Stanford University Press, 2003 [1997]); Giorgio Agamben, *The Time That Remains: A Commentary on the Letter to the Romans* (trans. P. Dailey; Meridian: Crossing Aesthet-

ics; Stanford, CA: Stanford University Press, 2005 [2000]); and Slavoj Žižek, *The Ticklish Subject: The Absent Center of Political Ontology* (Woe es War; London: Verso, 1999); *The Fragile Absolute: Or, Why is the Christian Legacy Worth Fighting For?* (Wo es War; London: Verso, 2000); *The Puppet and the Dwarf: The Perverse Core of Christianity* (Short Circuits; Cambridge, MA: MIT Press, 2003). Agamben and Taubes have mainly provided readings of Romans. Romans (41 references) is also the primary Pauline text in Alain Badiou's *St. Paul*, although the other *Hauptbriefe* also feature prominently in his argument (1 Cor: 31x; 2 Cor: 16x; Gal: 13x). Philippians (1x) and 1 Thessalonians (2x) make brief appearances as well. Žižek's use of specific Pauline texts is little different from Badiou's. In *The Puppet and the Dwarf*, for instance, he refers to Romans 9 times, 1 Corinthians 10 times, 2 Corinthians 3 times, and Galatians 2 times. No other Pauline texts are mentioned here. Nor are they employed in *The Fragile Absolute*, where Romans (3x), 1 Corinthians (4x), and 2 Corinthians (1x) carry the full Pauline load. The trickle-down effect of largely Protestant scholarship on Paul since F. C. Baur into the wider cultural imagination of secularist philosophy is most clearly seen, beyond the data collected above, in passages from Badiou and Žižek. Badiou, *St. Paul*, 18: "Moreover, one must be suspicious even of "Paul's epistles," canonically gathered together in the New Testament at least a century after the apostle's death. Scholarly exegesis has demonstrated the apocryphal nature of many of them, to the extent that the corpus of this fundamental author must, in the final analysis, be reduced to six rather brief texts: Romans, Corinthians I and II, Galatians, Philippians, and Thessalonians I. This is nonetheless enough to establish certain major subjective traits and guarantee certain decisive episodes." Or, Žižek, *Puppet and the Dwarf*, 117–118: "Paul's negative appreciation of law is clear and unambiguous: 'For no human being will be justified in his sight by deeds prescribed by the law, for through the law comes the knowledge of sin' (Romans 3:20). 'The sting of death is sin, and the power of sin is the law' (1 Corinthians 15:56), and consequently, 'Christ redeemed us from the curse of the law' (Galatians 3:13). So when Paul says that 'the letter kills, but the spirit gives life' (2 Corinthians 3:6), this letter is precisely the letter of the Law. The strongest proponents of this radical opposition between the law and the divine love moving him to grace are Lutheran theologians like Bultmann."

16. Evans, *Tertullian's Homily on Baptism*, xi, dates the text to the turn of the third century, before Tertullian's interest in Montanism.

17. Texts and translations of *Against Marcion* come from Ernest Evans, *Tertullian: Adversus Marcionem* (Oxford: Oxford University Press, 1972), unless otherwise noted. *Against Marcion* is usually dated from 207 to 208 C.E., but is actually the third edition of a piece against Marcion that Tertullian had been working on for some time (*Marc.* 1.1.1–2). The first edition may have been published as early as 197 C.E. (Evans, *Tertullian*, xviii). Emphasis mine in each of the following quotes.

18. All translations of ancient Greek sources, including the New Testament, are my own unless noted otherwise. Translations of the New Testament are based on the Nestle-Aland 27th revised edition. Many, if not most, New Testament scholars date 2 Peter to the early-second century. Cf, for instance, J. N. D. Kelly, *The Epistles of Peter and of Jude* (HNTC; New York: Harper & Row, 1969), 231, who places it between 100 and 110 C.E.

19. All translations of the Nag Hammadi library come from Bentley Layton, *The Gnostic Scriptures* (ABRL; New York: Doubleday, 1987), unless noted otherwise. The *Gospel of Philip*, like the rest of the Nag Hammadi literature, is notoriously difficult to date. The reference to interpretive differences over 1 Corinthians 15, however, seems to reflect the kinds of debate on this text that we find in Irenaeus's *Adversus haereses* (cf. Chapters 2 and 6 in this volume). For this reason, this particular saying from the *Gospel of Philip* likely dates back to the second century, regardless of the entire text's final composition.

20. All English translations from Book One of *Adversus haereses* come from Dominic J. Unger, *St. Irenaeus of Lyons: Against the Heresies* (ACW 55; New York: Paulist Press, 1992), while translations from Books Two–Five come from *The Ante-Nicene Fathers* (ed. A. Roberts and J. Donaldson; Grand Rapids, MI: Eerdmans, 1985 [1885–1887]), unless noted otherwise.

21. I use the term "Pauline" throughout to indicate texts bearing Paul's name as author as well as texts about Paul, in addition to the stories, images, and other forms of tradition about Paul that were mediated to and through a variety of communities.

22. The subtitle, "Reclaiming the Radical Visionary Behind the Church's Conservative Icon," of Borg and Crossan's recent book, *The First Paul*, is typical of this kind of archaizing argument.

23. Stanley K. Stowers, "What Does *Unpauline* Mean?," in *Paul and the Legacies of Paul* (ed. W. S. Babcock; Dallas: Southern Methodist University Press, 1990), 77.

24. Andreas Lindemann, *Paulus im ältesten Christentum: Das Bild des Apostels und die Rezeption der paulinischen Theologie in der frühchristlichen Literatur bis Marcion* (BHT 58; Tübingen: J. C. B. Mohr (Paul Siebeck), 1979); Ernst Dassmann, *Der Stachel im Fleisch: Paulus in der frühchristlichen Literatur bis Irenäus* (Münster: Aschendorff, 1979); and David Rensberger, "As the Apostle Teaches: The Development of the Use of Paul's Letters in Second-Century Christianity" (Ph.D. diss., Yale University, 1981).

25. Richard I. Pervo, *The Making of Paul: Constructions of the Apostle in Early Christianity* (Minneapolis: Fortress Press, 2010); and Michael F. Bird and Joseph R. Dodson, eds., *Paul in the Second Century* (LNTS 412; New York: T&T Clark, 2011). Cf. also Kenneth Liljeström, ed., *The Early Reception of Paul* (Publications of the Finnish Exegetical Society 99; Helsinki: Finnish Exegetical Society, 2011), which focuses on the first 30 to 40 years after the death of Paul. Two relatively recent dissertations have explored various aspects of the use of Paul

in the second century, but each is problematic, either in terms of methodology, argument, and/or substance, as described in subsequent chapters: David H. Warren, "The Text of the Apostle in the Second Century: A Contribution to the History of its Reception" (Th.D. diss., Harvard University, 2001); and Jason M. Scarborough, "The Making of an Apostle: Second and Third Century Interpretations of the Writings of Paul" (Ph.D. diss., Union Theological Seminary, 2007). A series of volumes being published by T&T Clark under the title "Paul and Patristics Scholars in Debate" address Paul in relation to individual writers. The first volume, edited by Todd D. Still and David E. Wilhite, has recently appeared: *Tertullian & Paul* (New York: Bloomsbury T&T Clark, 2013).

26. Cf. Michel Foucault, *The Order of Things: An Archaeology of the Human Sciences* (New York: Vintage Books, 1994 [1966]); *The Archaeology of Knowledge and The Discourse on Language* (trans. A. M. Sheridan Smith; New York: Pantheon Books, 1972 [1969]); and Elizabeth A. Clark, *History, Theory, Text: Historians and the Linguistic Turn* (Cambridge, MA: Harvard University Press, 2004), 113–119.

27. Hans-Georg Gadamer, *Truth and Method* (trans. J. Weinsheimer and D. G. Marshall; 2nd rev. ed.; New York: Crossroad, 1989 [1960]), 388.

28. On these matters, cf. Paul Ricoeur, *Memory, History, Forgetting* (trans. K. Blamey and D. Pellauer; Chicago: University of Chicago Press, 2004) and Chapter 4 of this volume.

29. Cf. Edward Shils, *Tradition* (Chicago: University of Chicago Press, 1981), 17: "The physical artifacts—manuscripts—are traditions. . . . The manuscripts and printed books in which the text is recorded, the text and the interpretations of it are all *tradita*." Emphasis his.

30. Cf. Charles H. Cosgrove, "A Response to Ruth Clements and Sze-kar Wan: Will the Real Paul Please Stand Up!," in *Early Patristic Readings of Romans* (ed. K. L. Gaca and L. L. Welborn; Romans Through History and Cultures: Receptions and Critical Interpretations 1; New York: T&T Clark, 2005), 203: "it is almost impossible today to speak about the way premodern interpreters read Paul without assuming that the real Paul is the historical Paul (in the modern sense of the term), and that 'we' have a pretty sure grasp on that historical Paul." Cf. also Maurice Wiles, *The Divine Apostle: The Interpretation of St. Paul's Epistles in the Early Church* (Cambridge: Cambridge University Press, 1967), 132: "'How far then did the early commentators give a true interpretation of Paul's meaning?' Yet the very form in which the question arises is not without danger. It implies the assumption that we have a true interpretation of Paul's meaning—or at least a truer one than that of those whom we have studied—in the light of which theirs may be tested and judged."

31. For recent criticisms not only of the conclusions of historical Jesus research, but on the historiographical methods and theories behind it, cf. Wayne Meeks, *Christ is the Question* (Louisville, KY: Westminster John Knox, 2006), and Dale

Allison, Jr., *The Historical Christ and the Theological Jesus* (Grand Rapids, MI: Eerdmans, 2009).

32. Wayne A. Meeks, "The Christian Proteus," in *The Writings of St. Paul: Annotated Texts, Reception and Criticism* (ed. W. A. Meeks and J. T. Fitzgerald; Norton Critical Editions in the History of Ideas; New York: W. W. Norton & Company, 2007 [1972]), 690–691. Emphasis mine.

33. Meeks, "Christian Proteus," 691–692.

34. Cf. Stowers, "What Does *Unpauline* Mean?," 76–77; and Robert Seesengood, *Paul: A Brief History* (Blackwell Brief Histories of Religion; Chichester, UK: Wiley-Blackwell, 2010), 5–8.

35. Calvin J. Roetzel, *Paul: the Man and the Myth* (Minneapolis: Fortress Press, 1999 [1997]), 176. Emphasis mine.

36. On "the earliest layer of the Pauline tradition," cf. above. For comments on the early reception-history of the Pastoral Epistles, cf. Chapters 5 and 6.

37. On pseudepigraphy in early Christianity, cf. Speyer, *Die literarische Fälschung*, and Ehrman, *Forgery and Counterforgery*. On the "Pauline School," cf. Hans Conzelmann, "Paulus und die Weisheit," *NTS* 12 (1966): 231–244; "Die Schule des Paulus," in *Theologia Crucis—Signum Crucis: Festschrift für Erich Dinkler zum 70. Geburtstag* (ed. C. Andreson and G. Klein: Tübingen: J.C.B. Mohr (Paul Siebeck), 1979), 85–96; Hans-Martin Schenke, "Das Weiterwirken des Paulus und die Pflege seines Erbes durch die paulus–Schule," *NTS* 21 (1974–1975): 505–518; Robert Jewett, "The Redaction of 1 Corinthians and the Trajectory of the Pauline School," *JAARSup* 44 (1978): 389–344; Wolf-Henning Ollrog, *Paulus und seine Mitarbeiter: Untersuchungen zu Theorie und Praxis der paulinischen Mission* (WMANT 50; Neukirchen-Vluyn: Neukirchener, 1979); Peter Müller, *Anfänge der Paulusschule: Dargestellt am zweiten Thessalonicherbrief und am Kolosserbrief* (ATANT 74; Zürich: Theologischer Verlag, 1988); Knut Backhaus, "'Mitteilhaber des Evangeliums' (1 Kor 9,23): Zur christologischen Grundlegung einer 'Paulus–Schule' bei Paulus," in *Christologie in der Paulus-Schule: zur Rezeptionsgeschichte des paulinischen Evangeliums* (ed. K. Scholtissek; SBS 181; Stuttgart: Verlag Katholisches Bibelwerk, 2000), 44–71; Thomas Schmeller, *Schulen im Neuen Testament? Zur Stellung des Urchristentums in der Bildungswelt seiner Zeit* (Herders biblische Studien 30; Freiburg: Herder, 2001); George H. Van Kooten, *Cosmic Christology in Paul and the Pauline School: Colossians and Ephesians in the Context of Graeco-Roman Cosmology, with a New Synopsis of the Greek Texts* (WUNT 2.171; Tübingen: Mohr Siebeck, 2003); and Angela Standhartinger, "Colossians and the Pauline School," *NTS* 50 (2004): 572–593.

38. Karl Mannheim, *Ideology and Utopia: an Introduction to the Sociology of Knowledge* (Routledge Sociology Classics; London: Routledge, 1991 [1929]), 238. Emphasis his.

39. Michel Foucault, "Truth and Power," in *Power/Knowledge: Selected Interviews & Other Writings - 1972–1977* (ed. C. Gordon; trans. C. Gordon, L. Marshall,

J. Mepham, K. Soper; New York: Pantheon Books, 1980), 118. Cf. also Alasdair MacIntyre, *After Virtue: a Study in Moral Theory* (Notre Dame, IN: Notre Dame University Press, 1981), 104.

40. Cf. Foucault, *Archaeology of Knowledge*, 49, where he describes discourses as "practices that systematically form the objects of which they speak." Ideology, accompanied by its rhetorical discourses, is just as much production as it is conservation.

41. Cf. Werner Kelber, "The Case of the Gospels: Memory's Desire and the Limits of Historical Criticism," *Oral Tradition* 17 (2002): 55–86; Alan Kirk, "The Memory of Violence and the Death of Jesus in Q," in *Memory, Tradition, and Text: Uses of the Past in Early Christianity* (ed. A. Kirk and T. Thatcher; SemeiaSt 52; Atlanta: Society of Biblical Literature, 2005), 191–206; Barry Schwartz, "Christian Origins: Historical Truth and Social Memory," in *Memory, Tradition, and Text*, 43–56; Tom Thatcher, *Why John Wrote a Gospel: Jesus—Memory—History* (Louisville, KY: Westminster John Knox, 2006); Samuel Byrskog, "A New Quest for the *Sitz im Leben*: Social Memory, the Jesus Tradition and the Gospel of Matthew," *NTS* 52 (2006): 319–336; Jan Assmann, "Form as a Mnemonic Device: Cultural Texts and Cultural Memory," in *Performing the Gospel: Orality, Memory and Mark* (ed. R. A. Horsley, J. A. Draper, and J. M. Foley; Minneapolis: Fortress Press, 2006); Holly E. Hearon, "The Construction of Social Memory in Biblical Interpretation," *Enc* 67 (2006): 343–359; Alan Kirk, "Tradition and Memory in the *Gospel of Peter*," in *Evangelium nach Petrus: Text, Kontexte, Intertexte* (ed. T. Nicklas and T. Kraus; Berlin: Walter de Gruyter, 2007), 135–158; Tom Thatcher, "John's Memory Theater: the Fourth Gospel and Ancient Mnemo–Rhetoric," *CBQ* 69 (2007): 487–505; James D. G. Dunn, "Social Memory and the Oral Jesus Tradition," in *Memory in the Bible and Antiquity: the Fifth Durham-Tübingen Research Symposium (Durham, September 2004)* (ed. L. T. Stuckenbruck, S. C. Barton, and B. G. Wold; WUNT 212; Tübingen: Mohr Siebeck, 2007), 179–194; Anthony Le Donne, "Theological Memory Distortion in the Jesus Tradition: a Study in Social Memory Theory," in *Memory in the Bible and Antiquity*, 163–177; Jens Schröter, "The Gospels of Eyewitness Testimony?: A Critical Examination of Richard Bauckham's *Jesus and the Eyewitnesses*," *JSNT* 31 (2008): 195–209; Anthony Le Donne, *The Historiographical Jesus: Memory, Typology, and the Son of David* (Waco, TX: Baylor University Press, 2009); Werner Kelber and Samuel Byrskog, eds., *Jesus in Memory: Traditions in Oral and Scribal Perspectives* (Waco, TX: Baylor University Press, 2009); Dale C. Allison, Jr., *Constructing Jesus: Memory, Imagination, and History* (Grand Rapids, MI: Baker Academic, 2010); and Rafael Rodriguez, *Structuring Early Christian Memory: Jesus in Tradition, Performance and Text* (LNTS 407; London T&T Clark, 2010).

42. Cf. Pervo, *The Making of Paul*, 19.

43. Elizabeth A. Castelli, *Martyrdom and Memory: Early Christian Culture Making* (Gender, Theory, and Religion; New York: Columbia University Press, 2004), 4.

44. Lindemann, *Paulus im ältesten Christentum*.

45. Rensberger, "As the Apostle Teaches," 56.

46. Clifford Geertz, *The Interpretation of Cultures: Selected Essays* (New York: Basic Books, 1973), 3–30. Geertz's largely textual approach to doing social anthropology has come under critique by many and I do not intend to wade into those waters here. Cf. Clark, *History, Theory, Text*, 145–155. I do, however, want to reinforce that the language originated in Gilbert Ryle's philosophical work on the nature of thought and reflection, as Geertz himself notes (*Interpretation of Cultures*, 5–9), and was then applied by Geertz to anthropological theory. Its utility for describing the process of "sorting out the structures of signification," regardless of the object of hermeneutical attention, can be seen in the number of disciplines that have deployed it. Cf. Geertz, *Interpretation of Cultures*, 9.

CHAPTER 2

1. Epigraph: Paul Ricoeur, *Memory, History, Forgetting*, 178.

2. Cf. John Lewis Gaddis, *The Landscape of History: How Historians Map the Past* (Oxford: Oxford University Press, 2002); and Hayden White, *Metahistory: The Historical Imagination in Nineteenth-Century Europe* (Baltimore, MD: Johns Hopkins University Press, 1973).

3. "The objectivity of history" is Baur's language in his *Die Epochen der kirchliche Geschichtsschreibung*, the English translation of which can be found in *Ferdinand Christian Baur on the Writing of Church History* (ed. and trans. P. C. Hodgson; Library of Protestant Thought; Oxford: Oxford University Press, 1968 [1852]), 189.

4. For a full account of the "Tübingen School," cf. Horton Harris, *The Tübingen School: a Historical and Theological Investigation of the School of F. C. Baur* (Leicester: Apollos, 1990 [1975]). Major monographs on the life and thought of Baur include Wolfgang Geiger, *Spekulation und Kritik: Die Geschichtstheologie Ferdinand Christian Baurs* (Forschungen zur Geschichte und Lehre des Protestantismus 10.28; Munich: Chr. Kaiser Verlag, 1964); and Peter C. Hodgson, *The Formation of Historical Theology: A Study of Ferdinand Christian Baur* (Makers of Modern Theology; New York: Harper & Row, 1966). There are also several good summary essays: Robert Morgan, "Ferdinand Christian Baur," in *Nineteenth Century Religious Thought in the West* (vol. 1; ed. N. Smart, J. Clayton, S. Katz, and P. Sherry; Cambridge: Cambridge University Press, 1985), 261–289; and Heinz Liebing, "Historical-Critical Theology: In Commemoration of the One Hundredth Anniversary of the Death of Ferdinand Christian Baur, December 2, 1960," in *Distinctive Protestant and Catholic Themes Reconsidered* (ed. E. Käsemann, et al.; Journal for Theology and the Church 3; Tübingen: J. C. B. Mohr (Paul Siebeck), 1967), 55–69.

5. *The Church History of the First Three Centuries* (trans. A. Menzies; 3rd ed.; 2 vols.; London: Williams and Norgate, 1878–1879 [1853–1860]).

6. Cf. Hans Rollmann, "From Baur to Wrede: The quest for a historical method," *SR* 17 (1988): 447–450; and Liebing, "Historical-Critical Theology," 62–64.

7. Cf. "Die Christuspartie in der Corinthischen Gemeinde," *Zeitschrift für Theologie* 4 (1831): 61–206.

8. *Paul the Apostle of Jesus Christ: His Life and Works, His Epistles and Teachings* (2 vols.; trans. A. Menzies; Peabody, MA: Hendrickson, 2003 [1845]), I.3.

9. *Paul the Apostle of Jesus Christ*, I.255–381.

10. *Paul the Apostle of Jesus Christ*, 2.1–111.

11. *Über den sogenannten ersten Brief des Paulus an den Timotheos: Ein kritisches Sendschreibung an J. C. Gass* (Berlin: Realschulbuch, 1807).

12. Cf. Hermann Patsch, "The Fear of Deutero-Paulinism: The Reception of Friedrich Schleiermacher's 'Critical Open Letter' Concerning 1 Timothy," trans. D. J. Doughty, *Journal of Higher Criticism* 6 (1993): 3–31.

13. *Jenaische Allgemeine Literaturzeitung* 4/255 + 256 (1807): 220.

14. Klaus Penzel, "Will the Real Ferdinand Christian Baur Please Stand Up?," *JR* 48 (1968): 314.

15. Penzel, "Will the Real Ferdinand Christian Baur Please Stand Up?," 312.

16. Cited from Harris, *The Tübingen School*, 147–148.

17. For the depth of Hegelian influence on Baur's language and thought, cf. e.g. this line from a speech given for the commemoration of the 25th term of King Wilhelm: "That the finite spirit is also the infinite Spirit which raises itself out of the finitude of its nature to the infinitude of its nature; that the essence of the spirit generally is nothing other than the infinite self-mediation of thinking—this is the standpoint of a philosophy which has won such an important significance for our ages." Cited from Harris, *The Tübingen School*, 39.

18. *Paul the Apostle of Jesus Christ*, 2.106–107.

19. Cf. the critique of Baur in Robert Morgan, "The Significance of 'Paulinism'," in *Paul and Paulinism: Essays in Honor of C. K. Barrett* (ed. M. D. Hooker and S. G. Wilson; London: SPCK, 1982), 325. Cf. also Hans Christian Knuth, "Ferdinand Christian Baurs 'Paulus' und sein Verhältnis zu Hegel in der Spätzeit," in *Paulus, Apostel Jeus Christi: Festschrift für Günter Klein zum 70. Geburtstag* (Tübingen: Mohr Siebeck, 1998), 227–244.

20. On the historical-critical side, cf. his "Die Christuspartie in der Corinthischen Gemeinde" (1831) and *Die sogenannten Pastoralbriefe des Apostles Paulus aufs neue kritisch untersucht* (Stuttgart and Tübingen, 1835). On the theological side, cf. *Der Gegensatz des Katholicismus und Protestantismus nach den Principien und Hauptdogmen der beiden Lehrbegriffe. Mit besonderer Rücksicht auf Herrn Dr. Möhler's Symbolik* (Tübingen, 1834). On the latter, cf. Joseph Fitzer, *Moehler and Baur in Controversy, 1832–38: Romantic-Idealist Assessment of the Reformation and Counter-Reformation* (AARSR 7; Tallahassee, FL: American Academy of Religion, 1974); and Notger Slenczka, "Die Einheit der Kirche und die Wahrheit

der Reformation: Theologiegeschichtliche Errinnerungen an die Kontroverse zwischen J. A. Möhler und F. C. Baur angesichts der aktuellen Situation der Ökumene," *KD* 48 (2002): 172–196.

21. Cf. Bruno Bauer, *Kritik der paulinischen Briefe* (3 vols.; Berlin: Hempel, 1850–1852), and the small Dutch tradition that followed him: Hermann Detering, "The Dutch Radical Approach to the Pauline Epistles," *Journal of Higher Criticism* 3 (1996): 163–193.

22. Harold Hoehner, "Did Paul Write Galatians?," in *History and Exegesis: New Testament Essays in Honor of E. Earle Ellis for his 80th Birthday* (ed. S. W. Son; New York: T&T Clark, 2006), 158.

23. Cf. Hans-Georg Gadamer, *Truth and Method*, 275: "Nineteenth-century historiography is its [Romanticism's] finest fruit and sees itself precisely as the fulfillment of the Enlightenment, as the last step in the liberation of the mind from the trammels of dogma, the step to objective knowledge of the historical world, which stands on a par with the knowledge of nature achieved by modern science."

24. Gaddis, *The Landscape of History*, 89.

25. Richard J. Evans, *In Defence of History* (London: Granta Books, 1997), 17–20. Ranke's famous dictum comes from the preface of his *Geschichte der romanischen und germanischen Völker von 1494 bis 1514* (Leipzig: Weimer, 1824).

26. Eric Hobsbawm, *On History* (London: Weidenfeld & Nicolson, 1997), 271.

27. Evans, *In Defence of History*, 20. Cf. also R. G. Collingwood, *The Idea of History* (ed. J van der Dussen; rev. ed.; Oxford: Clarendon Press, 1993 [1946]), 126–133.

28. Cf. Georg Iggers and James Powell, eds., *Leopold von Ranke and the Shaping of the Historical Discipline* (Syracuse, NY: Syracuse University Press, 1990).

29. Clark, *History, Theory, Text*, 10.

30. Frederick C. Beiser, "Hegel and Ranke: A Re-examination," in *A Companion to Hegel* (ed. S. Houlgate and M. Baur; Blackwell Companions to Philosophy; West Sussex: Wiley-Blackwell, 2011), 335.

31. Beiser, "Hegel and Ranke," 336–339.

32. Cited from his *Aus Werk und Nachlass* IV, 77, 79 in Beiser, "Hegel and Ranke," 338.

33. *Die Epochen der kirchlichen Geschichtsschreibung* (Tübingen: L. F. Fues, 1852), 268ff. Cf. also Robert Morgan, "Ferdinand Christian Baur," 262, 273; and Hodgson, *Formation of Historical Theology*, 148.

34. Morgan, "Ferdinand Christian Baur," 262; Liebing, "Historical-Critical Theology," 59; and Hodgson, *The Formation of Historical Theology*, 9, 169.

35. Cf. Hodgson, *Formation of Historical Theology*, 161–174, for an expanded account of Baur's historiographical philosophy and procedure. Cf. also Klaus Scholder, "Ferdinand Christian Baur als Historiker," *EvT* 21 (1961): 435–458; and Carl Hester, "Gedanken zu Ferdinand Christian Baurs Entwicklung als Historiker anhand zweier unbekannter Briefe," *ZKG* 84 (1973): 249–269.

36. *Ferdinand Christian Baur on the Writing of Church History*, 186–187.

37. *Ferdinand Christian Baur on the Writing of Church History*, 189.

38. White, "Rhetoric and History," in Hayden White and Frank E. Manuel, *Theories of History: Papers read at a Clark Library Seminar, March 6, 1976* (Los Angeles: William Andrews Clark Memorial Library, 1978), 5.
39. White, "Rhetoric and History," 6, 8.
40. Beiser, "Hegel and Ranke," 335.
41. Shils, *Tradition.* Cf. also David Gross, *The Past in Ruins: Tradition and the Critique of Modernity* (Critical Perspectives on Modern Culture; Amherst: University of Massachusetts Press, 1992); and Samuel N. Eisenstadt, *Tradition, Change and Modernity* (New York: Wiley, 1973). On the differences between "modern" and "traditional" societies, cf. Max Weber, *Economy and Society: an Outline of Interpretive Sociology* (2 vols.; ed. G. Roth and C. Wittich; Berkeley: University of California Press, 1978), 1:212–301.
42. Josef Pieper, *Tradition: Concept and Claim* (trans. E. C. Kopff; Crosscurrents; Wilmington, DE: ISI Books, 2008 [1970]), 22, 23, 38–39.
43. Karl Marx, *The 18th Brumaire of Louis Bonaparte* (New York: International Publishers, 1963 [1852]), 15; and Friedrich Nietzsche, "On Truth and Lies in a Nonmoral Sense," in *Philosophy and Truth: Selections from Nietzsche's Notebooks of the Early 1870's* (trans. and ed. D. Breazeale; Atlantic Highlands, NJ: Humanities Press, 1979), 83–84. On the contributions of earlier movements to the Enlightenment, cf. Gadamer, *Truth and Method*, 174–177, 275; Gross, *Past in Ruins*, 23–24; and Jaroslav Pelikan, *Obedient Rebels: Catholic Substance and Protestant Principle in Luther's Reformation* (New York: Harper and Row, 1964), 27–53. Alasdair MacIntyre, *After Virtue*, 78, has described the shift into the Enlightenment as a decisive break with the Aristotelian tradition: "What they agreed in denying and excluding was in large part all those aspects of the classical view of the world which were Aristotelian. From the seventeenth century onwards it was a commonplace that whereas the scholastics had allowed themselves to be deceived about the character of the facts of the natural and social world by interposing an Aristotelian interpretation between themselves and experienced reality, we moderns—that is, we seventeenth-century and eighteenth-century moderns—had stripped away interpretation and theory and confronted fact and experience just as they are. It was precisely in virtue of this that those moderns proclaimed and named themselves the Enlightenment, and understood the medieval past by contrast as the Dark Ages. What Aristotle obscured, they see. This conceit of course was, as such conceits always are, the sign of an unacknowledged and unrecognized transition from one stance of theoretical interpretation to another. The Enlightenment is consequently the period par excellence in which most intellectuals lack self-knowledge."
44. Karl Marx, "Contribution to the Critique of Hegel's Philosophy of Right," in *On Religion* (New York: Schocken Books, 1964), 51.
45. Marx, "Contribution to the Critique of Hegel's Philosophy of Right," 41–42. Cf. Marx, "*Capital*, Book 1 (Extracts)," in *On Religion*, 135: "The religious world is but the reflex of the real world."

46. Morgan, "Ferdinand Christian Baur," 264.

47. Samuel N. Eisenstadt, "Some Comparative Reflections on the Continual Reconstruction of Tradition," in *Tradition and Tradition Theories*, 9. Cf. Gadamer, *Truth and Method*, 278.

48. Gadamer, *Truth and Method*, 276. Cf. also MacIntyre, *After Virtue*, 58, who characterized the Enlightenment, in disapproval, as "the achievement by the self of its proper autonomy."

49. Rollmann, "From Baur to Wrede," 449.

50. *Paulinism: A Contribution to the History of Primitive Christian Theology* (trans. E. Peters; 2 vols.; London: Williams & Norgate, 1877 [1873]).

51. *Saint Paul and the Ante-Nicene Church* (London: Black, 1903), 64.

52. *The Formation of the Christian Bible* (trans. J. A. Baker; Philadelphia: Fortress Press, 1972 [1968]), 144, cited in Rensberger, "As the Apostle Teaches," 1.

53. *Formation of the Christian Bible*, 181. Campenhausen, "Polykarp von Smyrna und die Pastoralbriefe," in *Aus der Frühzeit des Christentums: Studien zur Kirchengeschichte des ersten und zweiten Jahrhunderts* (Tübingen: Mohr Siebeck, 1963), 197–251, famously argued that Polycarp wrote the Pastorals in response to Marcion.

54. *Beiträge zur Einleitung in die biblischen Schriften* (2 vols.; Halle: Buchhandlung des Waisenhauses, 1832–1838), 1.94–99. I am indebted to David Rensberger's "As the Apostle Teaches" for some portions of this section, particularly with respect to nineteenth-century German scholarship on Justin.

55. *Justin der Märtyrer: Eine kirchen- und dogmengeschichtliche Monographie* (2 vols.; Breslau: Schulz, 1842), 2.233–246.

56. Baur, *The Church History of the First Three Centuries*, 1.146–147.

57. Cf. Rensberger, "As the Apostle Teaches," 8–9.

58. Albrecht Ritschl, *Die Entstehung der altkatholischen Kirche* (2nd ed.; Bonn: Marcus, 1857), 271–344; J. B. Lightfoot, *St Paul's Epistle to the Galatians* (3rd ed.; London: Macmillan, 1869 [1865]), 318–320; and Theodor Zahn, *Geschichte des Neutestamentlichen Kanons* (2 vols.; Hildesheim: Georg Olms Verlag, 1975 [1888–1892]), 1.559–575.

59. On "Jewish Christian" opposition to Paul in the second century, cf. the recent essay by Joel Willitts, "Paul and Jewish Christians in the Second Century," in *Paul and the Second Century*, 140–168. Willitts tempers the argument that anti-Paulinism characterized the entirety of Jewish Christianity in the second century. Rather, it was a more localized phenomenon. Markus Bockmuehl, *The Remembered Peter: in Ancient Reception and Modern Debate* (WUNT 262; Tübingen: Mohr Siebeck, 2010), 94–113, argues similarly, calling into question the traditional interpretation of the *Pseudo-Clementines* that equated Simon Magus with Paul. More traditionally, in the line of Baur, cf. A. Salles, "La diatribe anti-paulinienne dans le 'Roman Pseudo-Clémentin' et l'origine des 'Kérygmes de Pierre,'" *RB* 64 (1957): 516–551; Georg Strecker, *Das Judenchristentum in den*

Pseudoklementinen (TUGAL 70; Berlin: Akadamie-Verlag, 1958); A. F. J. Klijn and G. J. Reinink, eds., *Patristic Evidence for Jewish-Christian Sects* (NovTSup 36; Leiden: Brill, 1973); David Flusser, "Paul's Jewish-Christian Opponents in the *Didache*," in *Gilgul: Essays on Transformation, Revolution and Permanence in the History of Religions* (ed. S. Shaked, D. Shulman, and G. Stroumsa; Leiden: Brill, 1987), 71–90; Martin Hengel, "Der Jakobusbrief als antipaulinische Polemik," in *Tradition and Interpretation in the New Testament* (ed. G. F. Hawthorne and O. Betz; Grand Rapids, MI: Eerdmans, 1987), 248–278; Gerd Lüdemann, *Opposition to Paul in Jewish Christianity* (trans. M. E. Boring; Minneapolis: Fortress Press, 1989); F. Stanley Jones, *An Ancient Jewish Christian Source on the History of Christianity: Pseudo-Clementine Recognitions 1.21–71* (SBLTT 37; Atlanta: Scholars Press, 1995); L. Padovese, "L'antipaulinisme chrétien au IIᵉ siècle," *RSR* 90 (2002): 390–422; and Margaret Mitchell, "The Letter of James as a Document of Paulinism?," in *Reading James with New Eyes: Methodological Reassessments of the Letter of James* (ed. R. L. Webb and J. S. Kloppenborg; New York: T&T Clark, 2007), 75–98.

60. Further proponents of Justin's Jewish-Christian affinities include Ernest Renan, *Histoire des origins du christianisme* (7 vols.; Paris: Lévy, 1861–1893), 3:324–325, 366–370; and Adolf Hilgenfeld, *Der Kanon und die Kritik des Neuen Testaments in ihrer geschichtlichen Ausbildung und Gestaltung* (Halle: Pfeffer, 1863), 26–27; and "Zur Geschichte des Unions-Paulinismus," *ZWT* 15 (1872): 497–499, 505–508.

61. "Bezeihungen auf Paulinische Briefe bei Justin dem Märtyrer und dem Verfasser des Briefes an Diognet," *ZHT* 12 (1842): 51–54; and "Nachträglisches über den Gebrauch Neutestamentlicher Schriften bei Justin dem Märtyrer und dem Verfasser des Briefes an Diognet," *ZHT* 13 (1843): 36–38.

62. Zahn, *Geschichte des Neutestamentlichen Kanons*, 1.559–566. Cf. Mortiz von Engelhardt, *Das Christenthum Justins des Märtyrers* (Erlangen: Deichert, 1878), 364–369. Zahn, *Geschichte des Neutestamentlichen Kanons*, 1.565–566, did argue for direct Pauline citations (of 1 Cor 15.50) in Justin's *On the Resurrection* (found in Methodius's text of the same name)—a much more likely context for a Pauline reference. Cf. also Günther Zuntz, *The Text of the Epistles: A Disquisition upon the Corpus Paulinum* (Oxford: Oxford University Press, 1953), 224. Most, however, have not followed Zahn in attributing this text to Justin. Cf. Martin Heimgartner, *Pseudojustin–Über die Auferstehung: Text und Studie* (PTS 54; Berlin: Walter de Gruyter, 2001), 193–232.

63. Cf. Franz Overbeck, "Über das Verhältniss Justins des Märtyrers zur Apostelgeschichte," *ZWT* 15 (1872): 305–349; and Albrecht Thoma, "Justins literarishes Verhältnis zu Paulus und zum Johannes-Evangelium," *ZWT* 18 (1875): 385–412.

64. Adolf von Harnack, *Lehrbuch der Dogmengeschichte* (4th ed.; 3 vols.; Darmstadt: Wissenschaftliche Buchgesellschaft, 1964 [1909]), 1:382–386; and Walter Bauer,

Orthodoxy and Heresy in Earliest Christianity (Philadelphia: Fortress Press, 1971 [1934]), 213–228. Cf. also Franz Overbeck, *Über die Auffassung des Streits des Paulus mit Petrus in Antiochien (Gal. 2, 11 ff.) bei den Kirchenvätern* (Libelli 183; Darmstadt: Wissenschaftliche Buchgesellschaft, 1968 [1877]), 8; Johannes Werner, *Der Paulinismus des Irenaeus: Eine kirchen- und dogmengeschichtliche Untersuchung über das Verhältnis des Irenaeus zu der paulinischen Briefsammlung und Theologie* (TUGAL 6.2; Leipzig: J. C. Hinrichs, 1889), 46–58; Wilhelm Bousset, *Kyrios Christos* (trans. J. E. Steely; Nashville, TN: Abingdon Press, 1970 [1913]), 254–255, 446; E. J. Goodspeed, *The Formation of the New Testament* (Chicago: University of Chicago Press, 1926), 56; Julius Wagenmann, *Die Stellung des Apostels Paulus neben den Zwölf in den ersten zwei Jahrhunderten* (BZNW 3; Gießen: Töpelmann, 1926), 151–155; and Albert E. Barnett, *Paul Becomes a Literary Influence* (Chicago: University of Chicago Press, 1941), 186–221.

65. *Lehrbuch*, 1.379–386; and *Marcion: The Gospel of the Alien God* (trans. J.E. Steely and L.D. Bierma; Durham, NC: Labyrinth Press, 1990 [1921]), 131–132. Cf. also John Knox, *Marcion and the New Testament: an Essay in the Early History of the Canon* (Chicago: University of Chicago Press, 1942), 31, 70; and Campenhausen, *Formation of the Christian Bible*, 148, 153, 163.

66. Bauer, *Orthodoxy and Heresy*, 213–228.

67. Bauer, *Orthodoxy and Heresy*, 233. Cf. more recently Ernst Käsemann, "Paul and Early Catholicism," 238–239, 249.

68. Aleith, *Das Paulusverständnis in der alten Kirche* (BZNW 18; Berlin: Töpelmann, 1937), 119. Cf. also Means, *Saint Paul*, 100–122, 179–203.

69. Schneemelcher, "Paulus in der griechischen Kirche des zweite Jahrhunderts," *ZKG* 75 (1964): 1–20. Cf. also Campenhausen, *Formation of the Christian Bible*, 177–182, 193–194; Käsemann, "Paul and Early Catholicism," 239; Georg Strecker, "Paulus in Nachpaulinischer Zeit," *Kairos* 12 (1970): 208–216; and Elaine Pagels, *The Gnostic Paul* (Minneapolis: Fortress Press, 1975), 161.

70. Schneemelcher, "Paulus in der griechischen Kirche," 6, 8, 16.

71. Schneemelcher, "Paulus in der griechischen Kirche," 9.

72. Schneemelcher, "Paulus in der griechischen Kirche," 11.

73. Schneemelcher, "Paulus in der griechischen Kirche," 7, 9, 19.

74. Kurt Aland, "Methodische Bemerkungen zum Corpus Paulinum bei den Kirchenvätern des zweiten Jahrhunderts," in *Kerygma und Logos: Beiträge zu den geistesgeschichtlichen Beziehungen zwischen Antike und Christentum* (Festschrift für Carl Andresen zum 70. Geburtstag) (ed. A. M. Ritter; Göttingen: Vandenhoeck & Ruprecht, 1979), 30–40.

75. Aland, "Methodische Bemerkungen," 47.

76. Aland, "Methodische Bemerkungen," 46.

77. Aside from Harnack (cf. below), summaries of Marcion's life and thought can be found in Peter Lampe, *From Paul to Valentinus: Christians at Rome in the First Two Centuries* (trans. M. Steinhauser; Minneapolis: Fortress Press, 2003

[1989]), 241–256; and Heikki Räisänen, "Marcion," in *A Companion to Second-Century Christian 'Heretics'* (ed. A. Marjanen and P. Luomanen; Leiden: Brill, 2008), 100–124.

78. *Marcion: Der moderne Gläubige des 2. Jahrhunderts, der erste Reformator; die Dorpater Preisschrift (1870); kritische Edition des handschriftlichen Exemplars mit einem Anhang* (ed. F. Steck; TUGAL 149; Berlin: Walter de Gruyter, 2003 [1870]).

79. Cf., for instance, the influence of Harnack on Knox, *Marcion and the New Testament*, and R. Joseph Hoffmann, *On the Restitution of Christianity: An Essay on the Development of Radical Paulinist Theology in the Second Century* (AARAS 46; Chico, CA: Scholars Press, 1984).

80. *Marcion*, 134–139. This and all further references to *Marcion* are references to Harnack's later work of that name.

81. *History of Dogma* (7 vols.; trans. N. Buchanan; Boston: Little, Brown, and Co., 1901 [1885]), 1:89–90.

82. *Marcion*, 134.

83. The order of the Marcionite *Apostolikon* is given in Epiphanius, *Pan.* 42.9.4; 11.8: Gal, 1–2 Cor, Rom, 1–2 Thess, Eph, Col, Phile, Phil, Laod. Cf. also Tertullian, *Marc.* 3.4.2, where he claims that Marcion has "got hold of" (*nactus*) Galatians.

84. *Marcion*, 21–24.

85. *Marcion*, 5.

86. We have access to Marcion's work only through Tertullian's *Adversus Marcionem*, Epiphanius's *Panarion*, and the *Dialogue of Adamantius*. On the text of Marcion's *Apostolikon*, cf. Knox, *Marcion and the New Testament*, 46–47, 51–53; Lindemann, *Paulus in altesten Christentum*, 381–383; John J. Clabeaux, *A Lost Edition of the Letters of Paul: A Reassessment of the Text of the Pauline Corpus Attested by Marcion* (CBQMS 21; Washington, DC: Catholic Biblical Association of America, 1989); Ulrich Schmid, *Marcion und sein Apostolos: Rekonstruktion und historische Einordnung der marcionitischen Paulusbriefausgabe* (ANT 25; Berlin: Walter de Gruyter, 1995); and Gilles Quispel, "Marcion and the Text of the New Testament," *VC* 52 (1998): 349–360. The same has been proposed for Marcion's treatment of Luke. Cf. David Salter Williams, "Reconsidering Marcion's Gospel," *JBL* 108 (1989): 477–496; and Dieter T. Roth, "Marcion's Gospel and Luke: The History of Research in Current Debate," *JBL* 127 (2008): 513–527.

87. Cf. the series of essays in *Marcion und seine kirchengeschichtliche Wirkung = Marcion and His Impact on Church History: Vortrage der Internationalen Fachkonferenz zu Marcion, gehalten vom 15.–18. August 2001 in Mainz* (ed. G. May and K. Greschat; TUGAL 150; Berlin: Walter de Gruyter, 2002), which is the 150th volume of the Texte und Untersuchungen zur Geschichte der altchristlichen Literatur series, created by Harnack. The volume is a celebration of Harnack's work while also offering major critiques of various elements of it. Harnack's claim, for instance, that Marcion forced the canon-making process upon

the Catholic Church has come under particular scrutiny. Marcion may have made the burgeoning Catholic Church more conscious of the canonical process that was already occurring in the early-second century, but he was not the first to draw up the combination of Gospel and Apostle. Marcion was the recipient of this schema. Cf. David Balás, "Marcion Revisited: A 'Post-Harnack' Perspective," in *Texts and Testaments: Critical Essays on the Bible and Early Church Fathers* (ed. W. E. March; San Antonio, TX: Trinity University Press, 1980), 95–108; Bruce Metzger, *The Canon of the New Testament: Its Origin, Development, and Significance* (Oxford: Clarendon Press, 1987), 99; Barbara Aland, "Die Rezeption des neutestamentlichen Textes in den ersten Jahrhunderten," in *The New Testament in Early Christianity* (ed. J.-M. Sevrin; BETL 86; Louvain: Leuven University Press, 1989), 1–38; John Barton, "Marcion Revisited," in *The Canon Debate* (ed. L. M. McDonald and J. A. Sanders; Peabody, MA: Hendrickson, 2002), 341–354; François Bovon, "The Canonical Structure of Gospel and Apostle," in *The Canon Debate*, 516–527; Harry Gamble, "The New Testament Canon: Recent Research and the Status Quaestionis," in *The Canon Debate*, 292; Ulrich Schmid, "Marcions Evangelium und die neutestamentlichen Evangelien–Rückfragen zur Geschichte und Kanonisierung der Evangelienüberlieferung," in *Marcion und seine kirchengeschichtliche Wirkung*, 67–68; and Lee Martin McDonald, *The Biblical Canon: Its Origin, Transmission, and Authority* (Peabody, MA: Hendrickson, 2007 [1995]), 329, 332. Barton, in particular, presents a very conservative picture of Marcion.

88. Barbara Aland, "Marcion: Versuch einer neuen Interpretation," *ZTK* 70 (1973): 429–435. Cf. also her *Was ist Gnosis?: Studien zum frühen Christentum, zu Marcion und zur kaiserzeitlichen Philosophie* (WUNT 239; Tübingen: Mohr Siebeck, 2009). Before Aland, cf. E. C. Blackman, *Marcion and His Influence* (London: SPCK, 1948); and Hans Jonas, *The Gnostic Religion: The Message of the Alien God and the Beginnings of Christianity* (2nd ed.; Boston: Beacon Press, 1963 [1958]), 137–139. Both Blackman and Jonas, while acknowledging some differences with the Gnostics, lumped Marcion together with their wider thought-world. Blackman, *Marcion and His Influence*, 82–87, 103–110, argued that Marcion was not particularly dependent on Paul and that he shared with the Gnostics a metaphysical dualism, a disdain of the Old Testament, a docetic Christology, and an acute concern for evil. Shortly after Aland, cf. Kurt Rudolf, *Gnosis: the Nature & History of Gnosticism* (trans. R. M. Wilson; San Francisco: Harper, 1984 [1977]), 313, who argued similarly.

89. Williams, *Rethinking "Gnosticism": an Argument for Dismantling a Dubious Category* (Princeton, NJ: Princeton University Press, 1996); and King, *What is Gnosticism?* (Cambridge, MA: Harvard University Press, 2003). Cf. also Bentley Layton, "Prolegomena to the Study of Ancient Gnosticism," in *The Social World of the First Christians: Essays in Honor of Wayne A. Meeks* (ed. L. M. White and O. L. Yarborough; Minneapolis: Fortress Press, 1995), 334–350, for a more

constructive approach. I do not think that Williams's "biblical demiurgical traditions" helps to clarify matters. One could easily include under this term the Gospel of John, Colossians, Philo, much of the Jewish wisdom literature, etc. Further, there is some evidence in both Irenaeus (*Haer.* 1.25.6) and Hippolytus (*Haer.* 5.6) that suggests that several of these groups self-identified as "Gnostics." In the end, I am more drawn to the projects of Layton, Birger Pearson, *Ancient Gnosticism: Traditions and Literature* (Minneapolis: Fortress Press, 2007), and David Brakke, *The Gnostics: Myth, Ritual and Diversity in Early Christianity* (Cambridge, MA: Harvard University Press, 2011), which are good attempts at unity in diversity.

90. May's most important essays in this regard are "Marcion ohne Harnack," in *Marcion und seine kirchengeschichtliche Wirkung*, 1–7, and "Marcion in Contemporary Views: Results and Open Questions," *SecCent* 6 (1988): 129–151. Cf. also his *Markion: Gesammelte Aufsätze* (ed. K. Greschat and M. Meiser; Veröffentlichungen des Instituts für Europäische Geschichte Mainz 68; Mainz: Philipp von Zabern, 2005). Further revisions of the traditional portrayal of Marcion include Markus Vinzent, "Christ's Resurrection: the Pauline Basis for Marcion's Teaching," *StPatr* 31 (1997): 225–233; "Der Schluss des Lukasevangeliums bei Marcion," in *Marcion und seine kirchengeschichtliche Wirkung*, 79–94; Andrew McGowan, "Marcion's Love of Creation," *JECS* 9 (2001): 295–311; Dieter Löhr, "Did Marcion Distinguish Between a Just God and a Good God?," in *Marcion und seine kirchengeschichtliche Wirkung*, 131–146; and Eve-Marie Becker, "Marcion und die Korintherbriefe nach Tertullian, Adversus Marcionem V," in *Marcion und seine kirchengeschichtliche Wirkung*, 95–110.

91. May, "Marcion in Contemporary Views," 141–142, 147. May (133–134, 137–143) also sets out on a more cautious course with the data than did Harnack, noting both the problems in getting to Marcion's text through the Church Fathers as well as the differences among the Church Fathers in their representations of Marcion's primary theological emphases. With regard to Marcion's relationship to philosophy, cf. also Ugo Bianchi, "Marcion: theologien biblique ou docteur gnostique?," *VC* 21 (1967): 141–149; John Gager, "Marcion and Philosophy," *VC* 26 (1972): 53–59; Ekkehard Mühlenberg, "Marcion's Jealous God," in *Disciplina Nostra: Essays in Honor of Robert F. Evans* (ed. D. F. Winslow; PMS 6; Philadelphia: Catholic University of America Press, 1979), 93–113; David L. Balás, "Marcion Revisited," 95–108; and Enrico Norelli, "Marcion: ein christlicher Philosoph oder ein Christ gegen die Philosophie?," in *Marcion und seine kirchengeschichtliche Wirkung*, 113–130. In continued support of Harnack's thesis that Marcion was primarily a Paulinist, cf. R. Joseph Hoffmann, *Marcion: On the Restitution of Christianity*; and "How Then Know this Troublous Teacher? Further Reflections on Marcion and His Church," *SecCent* 6 (1987–1988): 173–191.

92. Sebastian Moll, *The Arch-Heretic Marcion* (WUNT 250; Tübingen: Mohr Siebeck, 2010).

93. Moll, *The Arch-Heretic Marcion*, 159. Largely following Moll is Todd D. Still, "Shadow and Light: Marcion's (Mis)Construal of the Apostle Paul," in *Paul and the Second Century*, 91–107.

94. Moll, *The Arch-Heretic Marcion*, 160.

95. May, "Marcion ohne Harnack"; "Marcion in Contemporary Views"; Wolfram Kinzig, "Ein Ketzer und sein Konstrukteur: Harnacks Marcion," in *Marcion und seine kirchengeschichtliche Wirkung*, 253–274; and Achim Detmers, "Die Interpretation der Israel-Lehre Marcions im ersten Drittel des 20. Jahrhunderts: theologischen Voraussetzungen und zeitgeschichtlicher Kontext," in *Marcion und seine kirchengeschichtliche Wirkung*, 275–292.

96. Cf., most recently, Todd D. Still, "Shadow and Light," in *Paul and the Second Century*, 91–107.

97. May, "Marcion in Contemporary Views," 147.

98. May, "Marcion in Contemporary Views," 147.

99. Judith M. Lieu, "'As much my apostle as Christ is mine': The dispute over Paul between Tertullian and Marcion," *Early Christianity* 1 (2010): 58.

100. On Valentinus's life, thought, and influence, cf. Lampe, *From Paul to Valentinus*, 292–318; Christoph Markschies, *Valentinus Gnosticus?* (WUNT 65; Tübingen: J. C. B. Mohr (Paul Siebeck), 1992); Ismo Dunderberg, "The School of Valentinus," in *A Companion to Second-Century Christian 'Heretics'*, 64–99; *Beyond Gnosticism: Myth, Lifestyle, and Society in the School of Valentinus* (New York: Columbia University Press, 2008); Einar Thomassen, "Orthodoxy and Heresy in Second-Century Rome," *HTR* 97 (2004): 241–256; and *The Spiritual Seed: The Church of the 'Valentinians'* (Leiden: Brill, 2008 [2006]).

101. English translation from Robert Pierce Casey, *The Excerpta ex Theodoto of Clement of Alexandria*. (SD 1; London: Christophers, 1934).

102. This is not to say that the Valentinians were in agreement on all matters of philosophy and theology. This was manifestly not the case. Cf. Thomassen, *Spiritual Seed*, 492–494, on the two major schools of Valentinian thought. On the relationship between Valentinianism and middle-Platonism, cf. John M. Dillon, *The Middle Platonists: A Study of Platonism, 80 B.C. to A.D. 220* (Ithaca, NY: Cornell University Press, 1977), 384–389; and Christoph Marschies' commentary on the fragments of Valentinus: *Valentinus Gnosticus?*

103. The major studies dedicated, specifically, to the Valentinian use of Paul are Geoffrey L. Story, "The Valentinian (Gnostic) Use of the Letters of Paul" (Ph.D. diss., Northwestern University, 1968); Hans-Friedrich Weiss, "Paulus und die Häretiker: Zum Paulusverständnis in der Gnosis," in *Christentum und Gnosis* (ed. W. Eltester; BZNW 37; Berlin: Töpelmann, 1969), 116–128; Elaine Pagels, *The Gnostic Paul*; Klaus Koschorke, "Paulus in den Nag-Hammadi-Texten: ein Beitrag zur Geschichte der Paulusrezeption im frühen Christentum," *ZTK* 78 (1981): 177–205; J. P. H. John, "The Importance of St. Paul and the Pauline Epistles in Second Century Gnosticism (apart from Marcion)"

(Ph.D. diss., Oxford University, 1984); and Nicholas Perrin, "Paul and Valentinian Interpretation," in *Paul and the Second Century*, 126–139. Cf. also the pertinent sections in Lindemann, *Paulus im ältesten Christentum*, 298–306, 313–343, and Rensberger, "As the Apostle Teaches," 141–149, 221–251. Pheme Perkins, "Gnosticism and the Christian Bible," in *The Canon Debate*, 368–369, provides a helpful chart of which Pauline letters are referred to (and how many times) in each of the Nag Hammadi texts, including the Valentinians texts. These charts are collations of the information found in Craig A. Evans, Robert L. Webb, and Richard A. Wiebe, eds., *Nag Hammadi Texts and the New Testament: a Synopsis and Index* (NTTS 18; Leiden: Brill, 1993). Valentinian texts from Nag Hammadi that make use of Pauline material include *A Prayer of Paul the Apostle* (NHC I, 1): Jean-Daniel Dubois, "L'utilisation gnostique du centon biblique cité en 1 Corinthiens 2,9," in κατὰ τούς ο: *Selon les Septante: Trente études sur la Bible grecque des Septante: En Hommage à Marguerite Harl* (ed. G. Dorival and O. Munnich; Paris: Cerf, 1995), 371–379; and Michael Kaler, "The Prayer of the Apostle Paul in the Context of Nag Hammadi Codex I," *JECS* 16 (2008): 319–339; *The Gospel of Truth* (NHC I, 3; XII, 2): W.C. van Unnik "The 'Gospel of Truth' and the New Testament," in *The Jung Codex: A Newly Recovered Gnostic Papyrus* (ed. by F. L. Cross; London: A. R. Mowbray, 1955), 81–129; Harold W. Attridge, "The Gospel of Truth as an Exoteric Text," in *Nag Hammadi, Gnosticism, & Early Christianity* (ed. C. W. Hedrick and R. Hodgson, Jr.; Peabody, MA: Hendrickson, 1986), 239–255; and Jacqueline A. Williams, *Biblical Interpretation in the Gnostic Gospel of Truth from Nag Hammadi* (SBLDS 79; Atlanta: Scholars Press, 1988); *Treatise on the Resurrection* (NHC I, 4): Bentley Layton, "Vision and Revision: a Gnostic View of Resurrection," in *Colloque International sur les textes de Nag Hammadi* (ed. B. Barc; Bibliothèque copte de Nag Hammadi 1; Québec: Presses de L'Université Laval, 1981), 190–217; and Hugo Lundhaug, "'These are the Symbols and Likenesses of the Resurrection': Conceptualizations of Death and Transformation in the *Treatise on the Resurrection* (NHC I, 4)," in *Metamorphoses: Resurrection, Body and Transformative Practices in Early Christianity* (ed. T. K. Seim and J. Økland; Ekstasis 1; Berlin: Walter de Gruyter, 2009), 187–205; *Tripartite Tractate* (NHC I, 5); *Gospel of Philip* (NHC II, 3): Robert McL. Wilson, "The New Testament in the Nag Hammadi *Gospel of Philip*," *NTS* 9 (1963): 291–294; William J. Stroud, "New Testament Quotations in the Nag Hammadi Gospel of Philip," in *SBLSP* 29 (1990): 68–81; *Apocalypse of Paul* (NHC V, 2): Hans-Josef Klauck, "Die Himmelfahrt des Paulus (2 Kor. 12.2–4) in der koptischen Paulusapokalypse aus Nag Hammadi (NHC V/2)," *Studien zum Neuen Testament und seiner Umwelt* 10 (1985): 151–190; J.R. Harrison, "In Quest of the Third Heaven: Paul and His Apocalyptic Imitators," *VC* 58 (2004): 24–55; Pierluigi Piovanelli, "*La Prière et apocalypse de Paul* au sein de la littérature apocryphe d'attribution Paulinienne," *Apocrypha* 15 (2004): 31–40; Michael Kaler, Louis Painchaud, and Marie-Pierre Bussières, "The Coptic *Apocalypse of Paul*, Irenaeus' *Adversus haereses* 2.30.7, and the Second-Century Battle for Paul's Legacy," *JECS* 12 (2004): 173–193; Michael Kaler, "Towards an Expanded Understanding of Nag Hammadi Paulinism," *SR* 33 (2004): 301–317; and *Flora Tells a Story: the Apocalypse of Paul and its Contexts* (Studies in Christianity and Judaism; Waterloo: Wilfrid Laurier University Press, 2008); and *The Interpretation of Knowledge* (NHC IX, 1): Stephen Emmel, "Exploring the Pathway that Leads from Paul to Gnosticism: What is the Genre of The Interpretation of Knowledge (NHC XI,1)?," in *Weisheit—Ursprünge und Rezeption: Festschrift für Karl Löning zum 65. Geburtstag* (ed. K. Lönig, M. Fassnacht, A. Leinhäupl-Wilke, and S Lücking; NTAbh 44; Münster: Aschendorff, 2003), 257–276.

104. Ptolemy's cosmogony, according to Irenaeus, was supported by references to Rom, 1 Cor, Gal, Eph, and Col. Ptolemy's *Epistle to Flora* contains direct citations of "the Apostle Paul" (Rom 7.12; 1 Cor 5.7; Eph 2.15). Heracleon cites Rom 12.1 from "the Apostle" and alludes to several other Pauline texts, including Rom 13.1–4 and 1 Cor 15.53–54. In Clement's *Excerpta ex Theodoto*, Paul is "the Apostle" (22.1; 67.1; 85.3) as well as "the Apostle of the resurrection" (23.2). Pauline texts are cited and alluded to throughout Theodotus (Rensberger, "As the Apostle Teaches," 236–241). There might also be a few echoes of Pauline language in the fragments of Valentinus: cf. Rensberger, "As the Apostle Teaches," 144–146.

105. Story, "The Valentinian (Gnostic) Use of the Letters of Paul," 295.

106. This kind of analysis can be found in the works listed in n. 103 above.

107. Cf., for example, allusions to 1 Cor 15.53–54 in *Treat. Res.* 45.14–18; 45.39–46.2 and *Gos. Truth* 20.30–32; 25.15–19. Cf. also Heracleon, fr. 40, and Theodotus, *Exc.* 80.3. The latter uses language from 1 Cor 15.49. A full analysis of 1 Cor 15.50 in "Gnostic" literature can be found in Mark J. Olson, *Irenaeus, the Valentinian Gnostics, and the Kingdom of God: The Debate about 1 Corinthians 15:50* (Lewiston, NY: Mellen Biblical Press, 1995). Cf. also Ysabel de Andia, "La Résurrection de la Chair Selon les Valentiniens et Irénée de Lyon," *Quatres Fleuves* 15/16 (1982): 59–70.

108. Robert McL. Wilson, "The New Testament in the Nag Hammadi *Gospel of Philip*," 294. Cf. also his *The Gospel of Philip* (New York: Harper, 1962), 12: "It is all the more remarkable, therefore, that his discussion of the resurrection of the flesh (23), if the interpretation suggested in the notes is correct, reflects so accurately the Pauline doctrine."

109. Jacques É. Ménard, *L'Evangile de Vérité* (Leiden: Brill, 1972), 8. My translation of the French original: "Ce tableau laisse voir combien profonde est l'influence paulinienne sur l'*Evangile de Vérité*. La réciprocité de la connaissance de Dieu et des élus . . . est une doctrine typiquement paulinienne."

110. Malcolm L. Peel, "Gnostic Eschatology and the New Testament," *NovT* 12 (1970): 160.

111. Theodor Zahn, *Geschichte des neutestamentlichen Kanons*, 1:756; Georg Heinrici, *Die Valentinianische Gnosis und die heilige Schrift: eine Studie* (Berlin: Wiegandt und Grieben, 1871), 46; Carola Barth, *Die Interpretation des NT in der Valentinianischen Gnosis* (TUGAL 37, 3; Leipzig: Hinrichs, 1911), 44; and Story, "The Valentinian (Gnostic) Use of the Letters of Paul," 294, 316–325.

112. Pagels, *Gnostic Paul*, 3, is representative of this rhetorical move.

113. Cf. David Dawson, *Allegorical Readers and Cultural Revision in Ancient Alexandria* (Berkeley: University of California Press, 1992), 127–182; Robert M. Grant, *The Letter and the Spirit* (London: SPCK, 1957), 72; Story, "Valentinian (Gnostic) Use of the Letters of Paul," 309–311; Williams, *Biblical Interpretation*, 199–204; and Layton, *Gnostic Scriptures*, 272–273. For a somewhat imaginative Valentinian allegorical reading of Romans 1–4, cf. Elaine Pagels, "Valentinian Claim to Esoteric Exegesis of Romans as Basis for Anthropological Theory," *VC* 26 (1972): 241–258.

114. On Valentinianism as a response to Marcionism, cf. Christoph Markschies, "Die valentinische Gnosis und Marcion–einige neue Perspektiven," in *Marcion und seine kirchengeschichtliche Wirkung*, 159–176. Tertullian, *Praescr.* 38, comments on the differences between Marcionite and Valentinian approaches to Scripture: "One man perverts the Scriptures with his hand, another their meaning by his exposition. For although Valentinus seems to use the entire volume, he has none the less laid violent hands on the truth only with a more cunning mind and skill than Marcion. Marcion expressly and openly used the knife, not the pen, since he made such an excision of the Scriptures as suited his own subject-matter. Valentinus, however, abstained from such excision, because he did not invent Scriptures to square with his own subject-matter, but adapted his matter to the Scriptures; and yet he took away more, and added more, by removing the proper meaning of every particular word, and adding fantastic arrangements of things which have no real existence" (*ANF* 3:262).

115. Translation from Layton, *Gnostic Scriptures*, 312.

CHAPTER 3

1. Epigraph: Hayden White, "Rhetoric and History," 24.

2. Barrett, "Pauline Controversies in the Post-Pauline Period," *NTS* 20 (1974): 229–245.

3. Barrett, "Pauline Controversies," 244.

4. For a condensed version of Lindemann's tome, cf. his "Der Apostel Paulus im 2 Jahrhundert," in *The New Testament in Early Christianity*, 39–67. Cf. also his *Paulus, Apostel und Lehrer der Kirche: Studien zu Paulus und zum frühen Paulusverständnis* (Tübingen: Mohr Siebeck, 1999).

5. Lindemann, *Paulus im ältesten Christentum*, 10, builds on the suggestions of Walter Schmithals, *Das kirchliche Apostelamt: Eine historische Untersuchung*

(FRLANT 19; Göttingen: Vandehoeck and Ruprecht, 1961), 244ff., and Otto
Kuss, *Paulus: Die Rolle des Apostels in der theologischen Entwicklung der Urkirche*
(2nd ed.; Regensberg: Pustet, 1976 [1971]), 229–235.

6. Dassmann, *Der Stachel im Fleisch*, 1–21, 316–320.
7. Lindemann, *Paulus im ältesten Christentum*, 17–18.
8. *Paulus im ältesten Christentum*, 20–35. Cf. also now the essays in Kenneth
   Liljeström, ed., *The Early Reception of Paul* (2011), which argue for an early and
   sustained reception of Paul's letters in the late-first and early-second centuries.
   Lindemann thinks that the process of redaction and collection was complex,
   rejecting suggestions that there was a single collector/redactor (contra
   Schmithals) in a single locale (Ephesus = Goodspeed; Corinth = Zahn and
   Harnack). He also argues that the collection process was accompanied by an
   elevation of the letters as religiously authoritative texts. The bibliography on
   the collection of the Pauline letter corpus is voluminous. For the past 35 years,
   cf. Harry Y. Gamble, "The Redaction of the Pauline Letters and the Formation
   of the Pauline Corpus," *JBL* 94 (1975): 403–418; Kurt Aland, "Die Entstehung
   der Corpus Paulinum," in *Die neutestamentliche Entwurfe* (ed. K. Aland;
   Munich: Kaiser, 1979), 302–350; Alexander Sand, "Überlieferung und Sammlung der Paulusbriefe," in *Paulus in den neutestamentlichen Spätschriften* (ed.
   K. Kertelge; QD 89; Freiburg: Herder, 1981), 11–24; E. H. Lovering, Jr., "The
   Collection, Redaction, and Early Circulation of the Corpus Paulinum," (Ph.D.
   diss., Southern Methodist University, 1988); David Trobisch, *Die Entstehung
   der Paulusbriefsammlung: Studien zu den Anfängen christlicher Publizistik* (Fri-
   bourg: Universitätsverlag, 1989); *Paul's Letter Collection: Tracing the Origins*
   (Minneapolis: Augsburg Fortress Press, 1994); Harry Y. Gamble, "The New
   Testament Canon: Recent Research and the Status Quaestionis," in *The Canon
   Debate*, 267–294; Robert M. Price, "The Evolution of the Pauline Canon,"
   HvTSt 53 (1997): 36–67; Andreas Lindemann, "Die Sammlung der Paulus-
   briefe im 1. und 2. Jahrhundert," in *The Biblical Canons* (ed. J.-M. Auwers and
   H. J. DeJonge; Leuven: Leuven University Press, 2003), 321–351; and Stanley E.
   Porter, "When and How Was the Pauline Canon Compiled? An Assessment of
   Theories," in *The Pauline Canon*, 95–127; and "Paul and the Pauline Letter Col-
   lection," in *Paul and the Second Century*, 19–36.
9. On the use of Paul in the Apostolic Fathers, in general, cf. J. B. Lightfoot, *The
   Apostolic Fathers: Clement, Ignatius, and Polycarp* (2nd ed.; 5 vols.; Peabody, MA:
   Hendrickson, 1989 [1889–1890]); Oxford Society of Historical Theology, *The
   New Testament in the Apostolic Fathers* (Oxford: Clarendon Press, 1905); J. Al-
   lenbach, ed., *Biblia patristica: index des citations et allusions bibliques dans la lit-
   térature Patristique* (6 vols.; Paris: Éditions du Centre National de la Recherche
   Scientifique, 1975); Kurt Aland, "Methodische Bemerkungen zum Corpus
   Paulinum bei den Kirchenvätern des zweiten Jahrhunderts"; Otto Knoch,
   "Petrus und Paulus in den Schriften der Apostolischen Väter," in *Kontinuität*

und Einheit: für Franz Mussner (ed. P.-G. Müller and W. Stenger; Freiburg: Herder, 1981), 240–260; Andreas Lindemann, "Paul in the Writings of the Apostolic Fathers," in *Paul and the Legacies of Paul*, 25–45; and Andrew F. Gregory and Christopher M. Tuckett, *The Reception of the New Testament in the Apostolic Fathers* (The New Testament and the Apostolic Fathers 1; Oxford: Oxford University Press, 2005); *Trajectories through the New Testament and the Apostolic Fathers* (The New Testament and the Apostolic Fathers 2; Oxford: Oxford University Press, 2005). On *1 Clement*, cf. Ernst Dubowy, *Klemens von Rom über die Reise Pauli nach Spanien* (Freiburg: Herder, 1914); Donald A. Hagner, *The Use of the Old and New Testaments in Clement of Rome* (NovTSup 34; Leiden: Brill, 1973); Jerome D. Quinn, "'Seven Times He Wore Chains' (1 Clem 5.6)," *JBL* 97 (1978): 574–576; Hermut Löhr, "Zur Paulus-Notiz in 1 Clem 5,5–7," in *Das Ende des Paulus: Historische, theologische und literaturgeschichtliche Aspekte* (ed. F.W. Horn; BZNW 106; Berlin: Walter de Gruyter, 2001), 197–213; Andrew F. Gregory, "*1 Clement* and the Writings that later formed the New Testament," in *The Reception of the New Testament in the Apostolic Fathers*, 129–158; and Andreas Lindemann, "Paul's Influence on 'Clement' and Ignatius," in *Trajectories through the New Testament and the Apostolic Fathers*, 9–14. On **Ignatius**, cf. Graydon F. Snyder, "The Continuity of Early Christianity: A Study of Ignatius in Relation to Paul" (Ph.D. diss., Princeton Theological Seminary, 1961); Robert M. Grant, "Scripture and Tradition in St Ignatius of Antioch," *CBQ* 25 (1963): 322–335; Rudolf Bultmann, "Ignatius und Paulus," in *Exegetica: Aufsätze zur Erforschung des Neuen Testaments* (ed. E. Dinkler; Tübingen: J. C. B. Mohr (Paul Siebeck), 1967), 400–411; Heinrich Rathke, *Ignatius von Antiochien und die Paulusbriefe* (TUGAL 99; Berlin: Akademie-Verlag, 1967); Walter Rebell, "Das Leidensverständnis bei Paulus und Ignatius von Antiochien," *NTS* 32 (1986): 457–465; Robert F. Stoops, "If I Suffer . . . Epistolary Authority in Ignatius of Antioch," *HTR* 80 (1987): 161–178; Osger Mellink, "Ignatius' Road to Rome: From Failure to Success or In the Footsteps of Paul?," in *Recycling Biblical Figures: Papers Read at a NOSTER Colloquium in Amsterdam, 12–13 May 1997* (ed. A. Brenner and J. W. van Henten; Studies in Theology and Religion 1; Leiden: Deo, 1999), 127–165; Harry O. Maier, "The Politics and Rhetoric of Discord and Concord in Paul and Ignatius," in *Trajectories through the New Testament and the Apostolic Fathers*, 307–324; David M. Reis, "Following in Paul's Footsteps: *Mimesis* and Power in Ignatius," in *Trajectories through the New Testament and the Apostolic Fathers*, 287–305; Paul Foster, "The Epistles of Ignatius of Antioch and the Writings that later formed the New Testament," in *The Reception of the New Testament in the Apostolic Fathers*, 159–186; Matthew W. Mitchell, "In the Footsteps of Paul: Scriptural and Apostolic Authority in Ignatius of Antioch," *JECS* 14 (2006): 27–45; Boudewijn Dehandschutter, "Ignatius, *Letter to the Magnesians* 8:2 Once Again," in *Jesus, Paul, and Early Christianity: Studies in Honour of Henk Jan de Jonge* (ed. R. Buitenwerf,

H. W. Hollander, and J. Tromp; NovTSup 130; Leiden: Brill, 2008), 89–99; and Carl B. Smith, "Ministry, Martyrdom, and Other Mysteries: Pauline Influence on Ignatius of Antioch," in *Paul and the Second Century*, 37–56. On **Polycarp**, cf. Hans von Campenhausen, "Polykarp von Smyrna und die Pastoralbriefe"; Charles Merritt Nielsen, "Polycarp, Paul and the Scriptures," *AThR* 47 (1965): 199–216; Boudewijn Dehandschutter, "Polycarp's Epistle to the Philippians: an Early Example of 'Reception,'" in *The New Testament in Early Christianity*, 275–291; D. Richard Stuckwisch, "Saint Polycarp of Smyrna: Johannine or Pauline Figure?," *CTQ* 61 (1997): 113–125; Kenneth Berding, *Polycarp and Paul: an Analysis of Their Literary and Theological Relationship in Light of Polycarp's Use of Biblical and Extra-Biblical Literature* (Supplements to Vigiliae christianae 62; Leiden: Brill, 2002); Paul Hartog, *Polycarp and the New Testament: the Occasion, Rhetoric, Theme, and Unity of the Epistle to the Philippians and its Allusions to New Testament Literature* (WUNT 2.134; Tübingen: Mohr Siebeck, 2002); Peter Oakes, "Leadership and Suffering in the Letters of Polycarp and Paul to the Philippians," *Trajectories through the New Testament and the Apostolic Fathers*, 353–374; Michael W. Holmes, "Polycarp's *Letter to the Philippians* and the Writings that later formed the New Testament," in *The Reception of the New Testament in the Apostolic Fathers*, 187–228; Kenneth Berding, "John or Paul? Who was Polycarp's Mentor?," *TynBul* 59 (2008): 135–143; Paul Hartog, "Polycarp, Ephesians, and 'Scripture,'" *WTJ* 70 (2008): 255–275; and Michael W. Holmes, "Paul and Polycarp," in *Paul and the Second Century*, 57–69. On the ***Epistle of Barnabas***, cf. James Carleton Paget, "Paul and the Epistle of Barnabas," *NovT* 38 (1996): 359–381; and "The *Epistle of Barnabas* and the Writings that later formed the New Testament," in *The Reception of the New Testament in the Apostolic Fathers*, 229–250. On the ***Epistle to Diognetus***, cf. Andreas Lindemann, "Paulinische Theologie im Brief an Diognet," in *Kerygma und Logos*, 337–350; Rolf Noormann, "Himmelsbürger auf Erden: Anmerkungen zum Weltverhältnis und zum 'Paulinismus' des Auctor ad Diognetum," in *Die Weltlichkeit des Glaubens in der Alten Kirche: Festschrift für Ulrich Wickert zum siebzigsten Gerburtstag* (ed. D. Wyrwa, et. al.; BZNW 85; Berlin: Walter de Gruyter, 1997), 199–229; and Michael F. Bird, "The Reception of Paul in the *Epistle to Diognetus*," in *Paul and the Second Century*, 70–90.

10. Dassmann, *Der Stachel im Fleisch*, 316, notes the importance of both Paul's person and work in the second century.

11. *Paulus im ältesten Christentum*, 177–199. This was also the conclusion of A. J. Carlyle, *The New Testament in the Apostolic Fathers*, 37–55, as well as most other commentators, including more recently Andrew F. Gregory, "*1 Clement* and the Writings that later formed the New Testament," 154.

12. Lindemann, *Paulus im ältesten Christentum*, 199–221.

13. Lindemann, *Paulus im ältesten Christentum*, 87–91, 221–232. Cf. also Lindemann, "Paul's Influence on 'Clement' and Ignatius," 24.

14. Dassmann, *Der Stachel im Fleisch*, 149–58; 286–292.

15. Lindemann, *Paulus im ältesten Christentum*, 400.

16. Lindemann, *Paulus im ältesten Christentum*, 401–402.

17. Lindemann, *Paulus im ältesten Christentum*, 112, 401; Dassmann, *Der Stachel im Fleisch*, 316–317.

18. Lindemann, *Paulus im ältesten Christentum*, 402.

19. *Paulus im ältesten Christentum*, 101–109, 367–371. Dassmann, *Der Stachel im Fleisch*, 108–125, concurred. The Epistle of James was not written against Paul, but against a libertine misunderstanding of him. Additionally, neither the *Pseudo-Clementines* nor the Ebionites represent groups that were still part of the mainstream Church.

20. Lindemann, *Paulus im ältesten Christentum*, 300.

21. Lindemann, *Paulus im ältesten Christentum*, 304–305.

22. Dassmann, *Der Stachel im Fleisch*, 176–244, esp. 199.

23. Cf. also at this time the essays in Karl Kertelge, ed., *Paulus in den neutestamentlichen Spätschriften: zur Paulusrezeption im Neuen Testament* (1981), which trace the reception of Paul in the canonical pseudo-Pauline literature as well as Acts, self-consciously deconstructing the priority of justification by faith in the evaluation of the early Pauline tradition.

24. Rensberger's data comes from the *Biblia patristica*, though he has "carefully sifted" out potential allusions that are not the "most certain," including general "Christological formulae, metaphors (the church as body; the believer as temple), bits of liturgy and song, and the like, which occur in Paul but may not have been his creations, or could have been created again independently of him, or even if original only with him could have passed readily into common tradition, as so in any case can have been learned by later writers through channels other than direct acquaintance with his letters." ("As the Apostle Teaches," 59–60).

25. Rensberger, "As the Apostle Teaches," 57.

26. Rensberger, "As the Apostle Teaches," 56.

27. Rensberger, "As the Apostle Teaches," 350, 363.

28. Rensberger, "As the Apostle Teaches," 331–332, 362.

29. Rensberger, "As the Apostle Teaches," 344.

30. Rensberger, "As the Apostle Teaches," 333, 338.

31. Rensberger, "As the Apostle Teaches," 332–336. The absence of Christ's name in Tatian and Theophilus does not constitute antagonism toward Christ, as Rensberger notes.

32. Rensberger, "As the Apostle Teaches," 358.

33. Rensberger, "As the Apostle Teaches," 331, 361.

34. Rensberger, "As the Apostle Teaches," 359–375. Cf. also Lindemann, *Paulus im ältesten Christentum*, 341–343.

35. Williams, *Biblical Interpretation*, 186–187.

36. Rensberger, "As the Apostle Teaches," 332.

37. Rensberger, "As the Apostle Teaches," 337, 349.

38. Rensberger, "As the Apostle Teaches," 250. Cf. his negative conclusions on the relationship between Paul and the *Gospel of Truth* (146–148), Ptolemy (225–231), and the *Treatise on the Resurrection* (245–246). After Rensberger, cf. Bentley Layton, "Vision and Revision," 210–212, 217, Olson, *Irenaeus, the Valentinian Gnostics, and the Kingdom of God*, 26, and more recently Einar Thomassen, "Valentinian Ideas About Salvation as Transformation," in *Metamorphoses*, 169, and Hans-Friedrich Weiss, *Frühes Christentum und Gnosis: eine rezeptionsgeschichtliche Studie* (WUNT 225; Tübingen: Mohr Siebeck, 2008), 399–479.

39. Donald N. Penny, "The Pseudo-Pauline Letters of the First Two Centuries" (Ph.D. diss., Emory University, 1979).

40. Cf. Wolfgang Speyer, *Die literarische Fälschung*; Norbert Brox, *Falsche Verfasserangaben: Zur Erklärung der frühchristlichen Pseudepigraphie* (Stuttgart: KBW Verlag, 1975); "Zum Problemstand in der Erforschung der altchristlichen Pseudepigraphie," *Kairos* 15 (1973): 10–23. The most recent work on pseudepigraphy in early Christianity has only strengthened the basic conclusions of Speyer and Brox: Jeremy Duff, "A Reconsideration of Pseudepigraphy in Early Christianity" (Ph.D. diss., Oxford University, 1998); Armin D. Baum, *Pseudepigraphie und literarische Fälschung im frühen Christentum* (WUNT 2.138; Tübingen: Mohr Siebeck, 2001); Martina Janßen, *Unter falschem Namen: Eine kritische Forschungsbilanz früchristlicher Pseudepigraphie* (ARGU 14; Frankfurt: Peter Lang, 2003); Terry L. Wilder, *Pseudonymity, the New Testament, and Deception: An Inquiry Into Intention and Reception* (Lanham, MD: University Press of America, 2004); Jörg Frey, Jens Herzer, Martina Janßen, and Clare K. Rothschild, eds., *Pseudepigraphie und Verfasserfiktion in frühchristlichen Briefen*; and Bart D. Ehrman, *Forgery and Counterforgery*.

41. Colossians is relegated to a short appendix because Penny believes it was authored by Paul. In the appendix he explores how the letter would be read if pseudepigraphical.

42. Penny, "Pseudo-Pauline Letters," 2.

43. Penny, "Pseudo-Pauline Letters," 30–31. Contra Arnold Meyer, "Religiöse Pseudepigraphie als ethisch-psychologisches Problem," *ZNW* 35 (1936): 262–279.

44. Penny, "Pseudo-Pauline Letters," 34–46.

45. Penny, "Pseudo-Pauline Letters," 5.

46. Penny, "Pseudo-Pauline Letters," 8–16.

47. Cf. also Hans-Martin Schenke, "Das Weiterwirken des Paulus und die Pflege seines Erbes durch die paulus-Schule," 505–518, who argued that the image and legends of Paul that we find in Acts predated the collection of Paul's letters (in fact, they might have spurred the collection). The legendary Paul is then taken up again in the *Acts of Paul*. Schenke also argued that in the second century the Pauline school divided into Gnostic (Ephesians and Colossians) and anti-Gnostic (Pastorals) camps, each with different images of the Apostle.

48. Revised conference papers were published in *Paul and the Legacies of Paul* (1990). Both Lindemann and Dassmann contributed to this conference and its published volume.

49. Babcock, ed., *Paul and the Legacies of Paul*, xiii.

50. Babcock, ed., *Paul and the Legacies of Paul*, xiv.

51. For example, Calvin Roetzel, in a short essay entitled "Paul in the Second Century" for the *Cambridge Companion to St. Paul* (2003), finds a certain "avoidance of Paul" among some second-century Christians, while Marcion and Valentinus "rescue Paul from obscurity" (p. 228). But even Roetzel confesses in an endnote that "Admittedly, our knowledge about Papias is scanty" (240 n.7). Unfortunately, the poor state of the data does not seem to deter his rather confident historical reconstruction. Cf. also Roetzel's *Paul: The Man and the Myth*, 152–157; Helmut Koester, *Introduction to the New Testament* (2 vols.; 2nd ed.; Berlin: Walter de Gruyter, 1995–2000 [1982]), 2.9–10; and the essay by Alain Le Boulluec, "The Bible in Use among the Marginally Orthodox in the Second and Third Centuries," in *The Bible in Greek Christian Antiquity* (ed. P.M. Blowers; The Bible Through the Ages 1; Notre Dame: University of Notre Dame Press, 1997 [1984]), 197–216. Roetzel served as a reader for a 2007 dissertation at Union Theological Seminary by Jason M. Scarborough entitled "The Making of an Apostle: Second and Third Century Interpretations of the Writings of Paul," which likewise preserves much of the Pauline Captivity narrative. For Scarborough, Marcionite and Gnostic appropriations of Paul forced Irenaeus to "bring[s] the Pauline Epistles back into the mainstream of Christian thought" (i). Before Irenaeus, "Paul's theology was all but absent from the writings of the apostolic period" (277) and the threat of Marcion cast a "crisis of apostolic authority that dominated the latter half of the second century, and complicated Paul's inclusion in the canon" (71). Ptolemy was "distinctly influenced by Paul" (131) while "Pauline theology forms much of the substructure of Heracleon's thought" (136). Scarborough traces the use of Paul from Marcion, through the Valentinians, on to Justin, Irenaeus, and Origen. He completely ignores the use of Paul in the Apostolic Fathers, 2 Peter, and the *Acts of Paul*, making his aforementioned statements about the absence of Paul among the proto-orthodox in the early second century foregone conclusions. Equally problematic, but for other reasons, is the 2001 Harvard dissertation of David H. Warren ("The Text of the Apostle in the Second Century: A Contribution to the History of Its Reception"), who explores the use of Pauline texts in seven second-century writers: *1 Clement*, Ignatius, Polycarp, Aristides, Marcion, Justin, and Irenaeus. Warren compares the rather elaborate concern in Irenaeus for citing Paul's letters, including numerous citation formulae and arguments over the exact wording of Pauline texts, with the allusiveness with which these same texts are employed in the earlier authors. Ironically, Warren sees Marcion as a precursor to Irenaeus's concern. The commonality between these two opponents is their lack of experience of the gift of prophecy (321–329).

While the other authors reviewed by Warren each claim divine inspiration and do not need to cite Paul directly as an authority for their position, the Apostle's texts came to serve as the authority base for both Marcion and Irenaeus. Warren discounts several other explanations of the data: (1) that Pauline allusions are the result of citing texts from memory; (2) the Pauline letters were not yet viewed as Scripture by these authors; and (3) increasing sophistication in the citation of Scripture, spurred on by Ptolemy and the Valentinians, who used the exact words of texts as jumping-off points for allegorical exegesis (3–11). Warren's dissertation is useful for its collection of Pauline allusions and citations in the seven texts that he explores. He does convincingly argue that Justin knew the Pauline Epistles and that his use of the letters is comparable to Aristides' prior use of Romans. This is important because it allows him to deny that the lack of references to Paul in Justin has anything to do with a reaction to Marcion (286–287). On the other hand, one wonders whether Warren has undersold the data leading up to Irenaeus. He concedes that Polycarp directly cites from Pauline letters four times (107). He confesses that both Ptolemy and Marcion are concerned for the exact wording of specific Pauline texts. Rensberger's data reveal a number of other second-century authors either predating or contemporaneous with Irenaeus who make explicit citation of Paul and are concerned for the interpretation of his texts: Basilides; Isidore; Epiphanes; Theodotus; Tatian; Julius Cassianus; several Irenaean sources, including the unnamed Presbyter; and Theophilus ("As the Apostle Teaches," 345–354). These Pauline citations occur in a variety of contexts, including the substantiation of doctrine, and in a variety of kinds of Christian thinkers. It would seem, then, that Irenaeus follows a practice that had been in use for quite some time. I doubt, moreover, that any of the "Gnostic" thinkers listed above would have shied away from claiming divine inspiration for their work.

52. Evans, *In Defence of History*, 28–29.
53. Evans, *In Defence of History*, 30.
54. Thomas Kuhn, *The Structure of Scientific Revolutions* (Chicago: University of Chicago Press, 1962).
55. Cf. Michael Polanyi, *Science, Faith, and Society* (Chicago: University of Chicago Press, 1964).
56. Polanyi, *Science, Faith, and Society*, 15. Cf. 82.
57. Bloch, *The Historian's Craft*, 14, 17.
58. E. H. Carr, *What is History?: The George Macaulay Trevelyan Lectures Delivered in the University of Cambridge, January–March 1961* (New York: Alfred A. Knopf, 1962), 24.
59. R. G. Collingwood, *The Idea of History* (Oxford: Oxford University Press, 1946), V: 4–5.
60. Hutton, *History as an Art of Memory*, 157.
61. Clark, *History, Theory, Text*, 63–75.

62. Clark, *History, Theory, Text*, 70.

63. Bloch, *The Historian's Craft*, 65.

64. Bloch, *The Historian's Craft*, 44.

65. Evans, *In Defence of History*, 228.

66. Hobsbawm, *On History* (London: Weidenfeld & Nicolson, 1997), 273–274.

67. Hobsbawm, *On History*, 271–272.

68. Paul Veyne, "Foucault Revolutionizes History," in *Foucault and His Interlocutors* (ed. A. I. Davidson; Chicago: University of Chicago Press, 1998), 147, cited in Clark, *History, Theory, Text*, 73.

69. Clark, *History, Theory, Text*, 115, citing Foucault, *The Archaeology of Knowledge*, 139–140.

70. Foucault, *Order of Things*, xiv.

71. Clark, *History, Theory, Text*, 115–116.

72. Evans, *In Defence of History*, 3. For a good discussion of the linguistic turn from the perspective of a prominent scholar of early Christianity and late ancient studies, cf. Elizabeth A. Clark, *History, Theory, Text*.

73. White, "Rhetoric and History," 14. His influential works include *Metahistory: The Historical Imagination in Nineteenth-Century Europe* (Baltimore, MD: Johns Hopkins University Press, 1973); *Tropics of Discourse: Essays in Cultural Criticism* (Baltimore, MD: Johns Hopkins University Press, 1978); *The Content of the Form: Narrative Discourse and Historical Representation* (Baltimore, MD: Johns Hopkins University Press, 1987); and *Figural Realism: Studies in the Mimesis Effect* (Baltimore, MD: Johns Hopkins University Press, 1999).

74. White, *Metahistory*, 1–42.

75. White, *Metahistory*, 43–425.

76. White, *Metahistory*, 434. Cf. Evans, *In Defence of History*, 101.

77. White, "The Politics of Historical Interpretation: Discipline and De-Sublimation," in *The Politics of Interpretation* (ed. W. J. T. Mitchell; Chicago: University of Chicago Press, 1983), 136–137. Cf. also "Rhetoric and History," 16, and *Content of the Form*, 1–25.

78. Cf. White, "Rhetoric and History," where he claims that "all historical discourse . . . can be shown on analysis to be a set of figurative statements" (7) and "all such professions of antirhetoricity are always themselves a rhetorical ploy, the substitution of the rhetoric of antirhetoric for the rhetoric of rhetoric" (16).

79. White, "Rhetoric and History," 15.

80. White, *Content of the Form*, 26–57.

81. White, *Content of the Form*, 42–44.

82. Evans, *In Defence of History*, 78.

83. White, *Tropics of Discourse*, 78 n. 27. Cf. also "Rhetoric and History," 3: "My thesis is that the principal source of a historical work's strength as an *interpretation* of the *events* which it treats as the *data to be explained* is rhetorical in nature. So too the rhetoric of a historical work is, in my view, the principal

source of its *appeal* to those of its readers who accept it as a 'realistic' or 'objective' account of 'what really happened' in the past." Emphasis his.

84. On Acts and "disputed" Pauline texts of the New Testament, cf. Raymond F. Collins, "The Image of Paul in the Pastorals," *LTP* 31 (1975): 147–173; Stephen G. Wilson, "The Portrait of Paul in Acts and the Pastorals," in *SBLSP* 15 (1976): 397–411; Gottfried Schille, *Das älteste Paulus-Bild: Beobachtungen zur lukanischen und zur deuteropaulinischen Paulus-Darstellung* (Berlin: Evangelische Verlagsanstalt, 1979); C. J. A. Hickling, "The Portrait of Paul in Acts 26," in *Les Actes des Apôtres: traditions, rédaction, théologie* (ed. J. Kremer; BETL 48; Gembloux: J Duculot, 1979), 499–503; Joachim Gnilka, "Das Paulusbild im Kolosser– und Epheserbrief," in *Kontinuität und Einheit*, 179–193; William R. Long, "The *Paulusbild* in the Trial of Paul in Acts," in *SBLSP* 22 (1983): 87–105; Robert A. Wild, "The Image of Paul in the Pastoral Letters," *TBT* 23 (1985): 239–245; F. F. Bruce, "St. Luke's Portrait of St. Paul," 181–191; Beverly R. Gaventa, "The Overthrown Enemy: Luke's Portrait of Paul," in *SBLSP* 24 (1985): 439–449; Leander E. Keck, "Images of Paul in New Testament," *Int* 43 (1989): 341–351; John C. Lentz, Jr., *Luke's Portrait of Paul* (SNTSMS 77; Cambridge: Cambridge University Press, 1993); Marie Eloise Rosenblatt, *Paul the Accused: His Portrait in the Acts of the Apostles* (Zacchaeus Studies-New Testament; Collegeville, MN: Liturgical Press, 1995); Philip Towner, "The Portrait of Paul and the Theology of 2 Timothy: the Closing Chapter of the Pauline Story," *HBT* 21 (1999): 151–170; Steve Walton, *Leadership and Lifestyle: The Portrait of Paul in the Miletus Speech and I Thessalonians* (SNTSMS 108; Cambridge: Cambridge University Press, 2000); Michael Labahn, "Paulus—ein homo honestus et iustus: das lukanische Paulusportrait von Act 27–28 im Lichte ausgewählter antiker Parallelen," in *Ende des Paulus*, 75–106; and Daniel Marguerat, "L'Image de Paul dans les Actes des Apôtres," in *Les Actes des Apôtres: histoire, récit, théologie. XXe congrès de l'Association catholique française pour l'étude de la Bible (Angers, 2003)* (ed. M. Berder; LD 199; Paris: Cerf, 2005), 121–154.

85. Martinus C. de Boer, "Images of Paul in the Post-Apostolic Period," *CBQ* 42 (1980): 359–380. On Schenke, cf. n. 47.

86. De Boer, "Images of Paul," 363, argues that Paul's own "the Apostle to the Gentiles" becomes "the Apostle" in the second century when the church had become predominantly Gentile. The characterization of Paul as "*the* Apostle," however, went against both Paul's own understanding of his relationship to other apostles (Gal 1.17; 1 Cor 15.7, 9) as well as the understanding of the author of Acts.

87. As a corollary to the first two aspects of this image, de Boer (366–368) argues that the field of Paul's achievements moves from "the Gentiles" (a Jewish perspective) to "the whole world" (1 *Clem.* 5.6–7), "the end of the earth" (Acts 13.47, quoting Isaiah 49.6), and "all nations" (2 Tim 4.17).

88. His suffering was necessary as a means of propelling the gospel into the *oik-oumene* ("Images of Paul," 368–369).

89. De Boer argues from 1 Tim 1.13 and Acts (370–378). His evidence from Colossians and Ephesians is less convincing. He discusses no non-canonical texts here.

90. De Boer explores the Pastorals and Acts 20 (378–379).

91. De Boer, "Images of Paul," 380.

92. De Boer, "Images of Paul," 380.

93. Martinus de Boer, "Which Paul?," in *Paul and the Legacies of Paul*, 49, 51.

94. De Boer, "Which Paul?" 51–2.

95. De Boer overstates his case in this particular instance. It seems to me that the author of *1 Clement* gets right to the heart of 1 Corinthians, echoing the language of Paul's thesis statement (1 Cor 1.10) throughout (cf. esp. *1 Clem.* 42–49).

96. Theoretically, de Boer is correct. It is hard to say, practically, thogh, which epistolary Paul any given writer in the second century knew. The lack of use of a particular Pauline text does not mean lack of knowledge of and/or influence by a particular Pauline text.

97. François Bovon, for instance, makes the distinction between Paul as "document" and Paul as "monument": "Paul comme Document et Paul comme Monument," in *Chrétiens en conflit. L'Épître de Paul aux Galates* (ed. J. Allaz; Essais bibliques 13; Genève: Labor et Fides, 1987), 54–65. Christian Grappe, "De quelques images de Paul et de la manière dont elles se déploient au cours des deux premiers siècles," *FoiVie* 94 (1995): 49–59, traces the development of Paul as: (1) Apostle; (2) Missionary; (3) Converted Persecutor; (4) Persecuted Witness of Christ; (5) Writer; (6) Defender of the Gospel; and (7) Founder and Organizer of Communities.

98. Karlfried Froehlich, "Which Paul?: Observations on the Image of the Apostle in the History of Biblical Exegesis," in *New Perspectives on Historical Theology: Essays in Memory of John Meyendorff* (ed. B. Nassif; Grand Rapids, MI: Eerdmans, 1996), 289.

99. Froehlich, "Which Paul?," 290.

100. Michael Kaler, "Towards an Expanded Understanding of Nag Hammadi Paulinism," 309.

101. Kaler, "Towards an Expanded Understanding," 312.

102. Kaler, *Flora Tells a Story*, 94–117.

103. Cf. Calvin Roetzel, *Paul: The Man and the Myth*, 157–170. On Paul as wonderworker, cf. also Ernst Käsemann, "Paul and Early Catholicism," 242.

104. Margaret Y. MacDonald, "Rereading Paul: Early Interpreters of Paul on Women and Gender," in *Women & Christian Origins* (ed. R. S. Kraemer and M. R. D'Angelo; New York: Oxford University Press, 1999), 236–253. Cf. also her earlier *The Pauline Churches: A Socio-Historical Study of Institutionalization in the Pauline and Deutero-Pauline Writings* (SNTSMS 60; Cambridge: Cambridge University Press, 1988).

105. Margaret MacDonald, "Rereading Paul," 238.
106. Dennis R. MacDonald, *The Legend and the Apostle: The Battle for Paul in Story and Canon* (Philadelphia: Westminster Press, 1983).
107. D. R. MacDonald, *The Legend and the Apostle*, 17–33.
108. D. R. MacDonald, *The Legend and the Apostle*, 26–33. Cf. Axel Olrik, "Epic Laws of Folk Narrative," in *The Study of Folklore* (ed. A. Dundes; Englewood Cliffs, NJ: Prentice-Hall, 1965), 131–141. MacDonald consistently misspells this author's first name as "Alex."
109. D. R. MacDonald, *The Legend and the Apostle*, 34–53.
110. D. R. MacDonald, *The Legend and the Apostle*, 34, 21. For similar views of the origin of these legends, cf. Stevan L. Davies, *The Revolt of the Widows: The Social World of the Apocryphal Acts* (Carbondale: Southern Illinois University Press, 1980); "Women, Tertullian and the *Acts of Paul*," *Semeia* 38 (1986): 139–143; Virginia Burrus, *Chastity as Autonomy: Women in the Stories of Apocryphal Acts* (Lewiston, NY: Edwin Mellen Press, 1987); Stephen J. Davis, *The Cult of Saint Thecla: A Tradition of Women's Piety in Late Antiquity* (Oxford Early Christian Studies; Oxford: Oxford University Press, 2001); Shelly Matthews, "Thinking of Thecla: Issues in Feminist Historiography," *JFSR* 17 (2002): 39–65; Gail P. C. Streete, "Authority and Authorship: the *Acts of Paul and Thecla* as a Disputed Pauline Text," *LTQ* 40 (2005): 265–276; Johannes N. Vorster, "Construction of Culture Through the Construction of Person: The Construction of Thecla in the *Acts of Thecla*," in *A Feminist Companion to the New Testament Apocrypha* (ed. by A.-J. Levine and M. M. Robbins; Feminist Companion to the New Testament and Early Christian Writings 11; London: T&T Clark, 2006), 98–117.
111. D. R. MacDonald, *The Legend and the Apostle*, 54–77.
112. D. R. MacDonald, *The Legend and the Apostle*, 98–99.
113. D. R. MacDonald, *The Legend and the Apostle*, 102.
114. He manages to salvage a single constructive element from the Pastorals: "The most important contribution of the Pastorals to Christian theology may be their reminder that Christ can be seen not only in the Christian community but also in nature and culture" (*The Legend and the Apostle*, 101).
115. Cf., in particular, Peter Dunn, "The *Acts of Paul* and the Pauline Legacy in the Second Century" (Ph.D. diss, Cambridge, 1996). Dunn (41) admits that there is, on the surface, a rather stark difference between 1 Timothy 2.12—"I do not permit a woman to teach or to have authority over a man"—and the *Acts of Paul and Thecla*, where Paul tells Thecla, "Go and teach the word of God" (*Acts Paul* IV, 16). A little digging, however, renders doubt about most of MacDonald's conclusions. Dunn (50) draws attention to MacDonald's selective use of Axel Olrik's work on oral tradition and exposes places where he outright misuses him (e.g., Olrik did not argue that one could easily decipher the oral traditions behind written texts, though this is how MacDonald tries to use him).

He further argues (51) that the "narrative inconsistencies" in the *Acts of Paul and Thecla* are just as likely to be the result of the poor editorial work of the Presbyter, who was dealing with at least some *written* sources, as they are evidence of early oral traditions behind the *Acts of Paul*. Neither the *Martyrdom of Paul* nor the Ephesian Episode, both of which MacDonald tries to tie to ascetic, liberated women story-tellers, shows specific interest in the authority of women within the church. This leaves only the stories involving Thecla. Their eventual use among women at the time of Tertullian, however, says nothing about their original *Sitz im Leben* (55). The crowds of influential women opposing the state in the *Acts of Paul and Thecla* are not a sign that these stories ultimately came from and supported women *qua* women any more than the men who defend Paul in the *Martyrdom of Paul* reflect a particular community of marginalized Christian men. Rather, the crowds of women are present as a common motif in ancient literature (51, 58). Dunn also counters rather easily MacDonald's assertion that the "young widows" of 1 Timothy 5.3–16 are virgins like Thecla and points out that, in accordance with 1 Timothy 2.12, Thecla only teaches Tryphaena and her female attendants, while (possibly) baptizing only herself (59–64). Technically, then, she and the Pastor are not in disagreement. The fact that the Great Church venerated Thecla seems to suggest that they saw nothing out of order with her behavior. Tertullian is the only indication of problems regarding the influence of Thecla (67). Dunn's larger thesis is that the *Acts of Paul* represents an orthodox narrative expansion of Paul's letters. They carry forward the image of Paul found in 1 Corinthians 6–7. He concludes: "Paul's image in the *ActPl* is not un-Pauline. The Presbyter often drew his inspiration from the Pauline epistles.... What appears the most bizarre to modern scholars, the ascetic and the divine Paul, likewise arise out of a second-century reading of the Pauline epistles, and may indeed be in closer keeping with the Paul of the epistles, dare I say, than some modern caricatures of Paul" (157). The redactor of the *Acts of Paul*, the Presbyter mentioned by Tertullian, built his narrative on oral and written traditions, along with an imaginative reading of 2 Timothy, Galatians, 1 Corinthians and Philippians (194). The supposed opposition between the *Acts of Paul* and the Pastoral Epistles is "superficial" and, in fact, the two sets of literature are quite harmonious with one another (iii). As an early interpreter of Paul, the author of the *Acts of Paul* locates the center of Pauline thought in his "*hope of a physical resurrection for which the Christian embraces the ascetic lifestyle of the future age in the likeness of the heavenly angels, renounces luxuries, beauty, and riches, which will burn in the eschatological fire, and even desires to die unjustly at the hands of wicked men in the perfect imitation of the Lord Jesus*" (iii). Emphasis his. While the Presbyter has located these elements as the heart of Pauline theology based on "the needs of his times," they "appear in the Pauline epistles with no less frequency than the theme of justification by faith which figures so prominently in the crisis of the

228 *Notes to Pages 57–61*

judaizers and in modern Protestantism" (198). Dunn, like MacDonald, is trying to reclaim the *Acts of Paul* as a not-so-tendentious reflection of Pauline tradition in the second century, while, contra MacDonald, minimizing its distance from the Pastorals. Cf. also now Snyder, *Acts of Paul*, 137–147.

116. Cf. E. Margaret Howe, "Interpretations of Paul in *The Acts of Paul and Thecla*," in *Pauline Studies: Essays Presented to F. F. Bruce on his 70th Birthday* (ed. D. A. Hagner and M. J. Harris; Grand Rapids, MI: Eerdmans, 1980), 33–49; Willi Braun, "Physiotherapy of Femininity in the *Acts of Thecla*," in *Text and Artifact in the Religions of Mediterranean Antiquity: Essays in Honor of Peter Richardson* (ed. M. Desjardins and S. G. Wilson; Studies in Christianity and Judaism 9; Waterloo: Wilfrid Laurier University Press, 2000), 209–230; Beate Wehn, "'Blessed are the bodies of those who are virgins': Reflections on the Image of Paul in the *Acts of Thecla*," *JSNT* 79 (2000): 149–164; Elisabeth Esch-Wermeling, *Thekla— Paulusschülerin wider Willen?: Strategien der Leserlenkung in den Theklaakten* (NTAbh 53; Münster: Aschendorff, 2008); Jeremy W. Barrier, *The Acts of Paul and Thecla: A Critical Introduction and Commentary* (WUNT 2.270; Tübingen: Mohr Siebeck, 2009), 57; and Snyder, *Acts of Paul*, 100–120.

117. Pagels, *The Gnostic Paul*, 5.
118. Cf. Rensberger, "As the Apostle Teaches," 141–142.
119. Pagels, *The Gnostic Paul*, 164.
120. Anthony J. Blasi, *Making Charisma: The Social Construction of Paul's Public Image* (New Brunswick, NJ: Transaction Publishers, 1991).
121. Blasi, *Making Charisma*, 4. Cf. also 143.
122. Blasi, *Making Charisma*, 6.
123. Blasi, *Making Charisma*, 12–13.
124. Blasi, *Making Charisma*, 146.
125. Blasi, *Making Charisma*, 135.
126. Bruce Malina and Jerome Neyrey, *Portraits of Paul: An Archaeology of Ancient Personality* (Louisville: Westminster John Knox, 1996), xii.
127. Malina and Neyrey, *Portraits of Paul*, 16.
128. Malina and Neyrey, *Portraits of Paul*, 218.
129. Cf. Oda Wischmeyer, "Paulus als Ich-Erzähler: Ein Beitrag zu seiner Person, seiner Biographie und seiner Theologie"; and Lukas Bormann, "Autobiographische Fiktionalität bei Paulus," in *Biographie und Persönlichkeit des Paulus* (ed. E.-M. Becker and P. Pilhofer; WUNT 187; Tübingen: Mohr Siebeck, 2005), 88–105, 106–124, respectively.
130. Malina and Neyrey, *Portraits of Paul*, 61.
131. Malina and Neyrey, *Portraits of Paul*, 62.
132. Gk.: εἶδεν δὲ τὸν Παῦλον ἐρχόμενον, ἄνδρα μικρὸν τῷ μεγέθει, ψιλὸν τῇ κεφαλῇ, ἀγκύλον ταῖς κνήμαις, εὐεκτικόν, σύνοφρυν, μικρῶς ἐπίρρινον, χάριτος πλήρη· ποτὲ μὲν γὰρ ἐφαίνετο ὡς ἄνθρωπος, ποτὲ δὲ ἀγγέλου πρόσωπον εἶχεν (*Act of Paul and Thecla* 3). Text from Richard A. Lipsius, ed., *Acta Petri-Acta Pauli-Acta Petri et Pauli-Acta Pauli et*

Theclae-Acta Thaddaei (Acta Apostolorum Apocrypha 1; Hildesheim: Georg Olms, 1990 [1891]), 237. On this passage, cf. Robert M. Grant, "The Description of Paul in the Acts of Paul and Thecla," *VC* 36 (1982): 1–4; Abraham J. Malherbe, "A Physical Description of Paul," *HTR* 79 (1986): 170–175; Janos Bollok, "The Description of Paul in the *Acta Pauli*," in *The Apocryphal Acts of Paul and Thecla* (ed. J. N. Bremmer; Studies on the Apocryphal Acts of the Apostles 2; Kampen: Kok Pharos, 1996), 1–15; Monika Betz, "Die betörenden Worte des fremden Mannes: zur Funktion der Paulusbeschreibung in den Theklaakten," *NTS* 53 (2007): 130–145; and Heike Omerzu, "The Portrayal of Paul's Outer Appearance in the *Acts of Paul and Thecla*: Reconsidering the Correspondence between the Body and Personality in Ancient Literature," *R&T* 15 (2008): 252–279.

133. Grant, "Description of Paul," 1–4.

134. Malina and Neyrey, *Portraits of Paul*, 148.

135. In addition to Sterling, cf. also Hanns Christof Brennecke, "Die Anfänge einer Paulusverehrung," in *Biographie und Persönlichkeit des Paulus*, 295–305, and Bernard Meunier, "Paul et les pères grecs," *RSR* 94 (2006): 331–355. Brennecke highlights Paul as Martyr in early Christian texts (*1 Clement* and the *Acts of Paul*), while also giving due space to this image in New Testament texts. Meunier tips his hat early on to the importance of "la personne de Paul" as "croyant," "missionnaire," and "théologien" in the Greek Fathers (331), but winds up addressing only the last of these from Justin to Origen. Based on the data from *Biblia patristica*, Meunier claims that there was a certain "oubli" (omission) of Paul in the first half of the second century (332). If he would have explored the image of Paul in early eastern writers like Ignatius and Polycarp, this conclusion could have been avoided.

136. Gregory E. Sterling, "From Apostle to the Gentiles to Apostle of the Church: Images of Paul at the End of the First Century," *ZNW* 99 (2008): 74–98. Cf. also Jens Schröter, "Kirche im Anschluss an Paulus: Aspekte der Paulusrezeption in der Apostelgeschichte und in den Pastoralbriefen," *ZNW* 98 (2007): 77–104, who comes to a similar conclusion with respect to Acts and the Pastoral Epistles. Paul is remembered as the great martyr-teacher upon whose ministry the Gentile church was founded.

137. Daniel Marguerat, "Paul après Paul: une histoire de réception," *NTS* 54 (2008): 317–337.

138. Marguerat, "Paul après Paul," 321. Cf. also Andrew Gregory and Christopher Tuckett, "Reflections on Method: What constitutes the Use of the Writings that later formed the New Testament in the Apostolic Fathers?," in *The Reception of the New Testament in the Apostolic Fathers*, 80.

139. Marguerat, "Paul après Paul," 321. He is uncommitted as to whether or not the author of Acts knew any of the Pauline letters.

140. Marguerat, "Paul après Paul," 323–324. Cf. Philipp Vielhauer, "On the 'Paulinism' of Acts," in *Studies in Luke-Acts: Essays Presented in Honor of Paul Schubert*

(ed. L. Keck; Nashville, TN: Abingdon, 1966), 33–50. For agreement with Marguerat on this point, cf. Stowers, "What Does *Unpauline* Mean?," 71–72; Dunn, "*Acts of Paul* and the Pauline Legacy," 198 ; and Roetzel, *Paul: The Man and the Myth*, 163–170.

141. Marguerat, "Paul après Paul," 337.

142. Marguerat, "Paul après Paul," 330. Cf. Froehlich, "Which Paul?"

143. Marguerat, "Paul après Paul," 334. The one unfortunate conclusion from this piece is Marguerat's assertion that *1 Clement*, Ignatius of Antioch and Polycarp of Smyrna were not interested in the person of Paul (321). This is odd in light of his thesis and the data from each of these early second-century texts that will be highlighted in Chapter 4.

144. James W. Aageson, *Paul, the Pastoral Epistles, and the Early Church* (Library of Pauline Studies; Peabody: Hendrickson, 2008), 208.

145. Aageson, *Paul, the Pastoral Epistles, and the Early Church*, 1–2.

146. Aageson, *Paul, the Pastoral Epistles, and the Early Church*, 91–93.

147. Aageson, *Paul, the Pastoral Epistles, and the Early Church*, 112.

148. Aageson makes the oft-repeated distinction between Paul being "*the* Apostle" in the Pastorals, whereas in Acts Paul is "not strictly speaking" even *an* apostle (*Paul, the Pastoral Epistles, and the Early Church*, 113). Aageson does not confront the fact that Paul is never called ὁ ἀπόστολος in the Pastorals and yet is called an ἀπόστολος, along with Barnabas, in Acts 14.4, 14.

149. Aageson, *Paul, the Pastoral Epistles, and the Early Church*, 206.

150. Aageson, *Paul, the Pastoral Epistles, and the Early Church*, 154, 206.

151. Aageson, *Paul, the Pastoral Epistles, and the Early Church*, 2.

152. Aageson, *Paul, the Pastoral Epistles, and the Early Church*, 209–210. Cf. James M. Robinson and Helmut Koester, *Trajectories through Early Christianity* (Philadelphia: Fortress Press, 1971).

153. Cf. James D. G. Dunn, *The New Perspective on Paul* (rev. ed.; Grand Rapids, MI: Eerdmans, 2007); and Stephen Westerholm, *Perspectives Old and New on Paul: The "Lutheran" Paul and His Critics* (Grand Rapids, MI: Eerdmans, 2003).

154. Pervo, *Making of Paul*, xiii. Cf. also 4, 237.

155. Pervo, *Making of Paul*, 11. Cf. also Marguerat, "Paul après Paul," 322.

156. Pervo, *Making of Paul*, 185.

157. Pervo, *Making of Paul*, 233.

158. Pervo, *Making of Paul*, 235.

159. Pervo, *Making of Paul*, 235.

160. Pervo, *Making of Paul*, 132.

161. Pervo, *Making of Paul*, 12.

162. Pervo, *Making of Paul*, 4, 205, 224, 229.

163. Pervo, *Making of Paul*, 6, states, "The present consensus is that Paul wrote seven epistles: Romans, 1 and 2 Corinthians, Galatians, Philippians, 1 Thessalonians, and Philemon. These are 'undisputed.' This book regards the others

(Ephesians, Colossians, 2 Thessalonians, 1 and 2 Timothy, and Titus) as post-Pauline compositions. The object is not to strip away this unseemly husk to reveal the 'real Paul,' but to utilize the Deutero-Pauline letters as components of the developing Pauline legacy."

164. Pervo, *Making of Paul*, 9.
165. Pervo, *Making of Paul*, 60.
166. Pervo, *Making of Paul*, xii, 2. Examples of such comparisons between the historical Paul and the Paul of tradition within the canonical literature occur on pp. 13–15, 65–96, and 150–156. He denies, for instance, that Paul is an Apostle in Acts without addressing the problematic data in Acts 14.4, 14. Outside the New Testament canon, this kind of distinction between the historical Paul and his early interpreters occurs on pp. 128, 133, and 142.
167. Pervo, *Making of Paul*, 187. Cf. 192, 198. Emphasis his.
168. Pervo, *Making of Paul*, 227.
169. Pervo, *Making of Paul*, 19. Cf. 210, 228, and his comments on the *Treat. Res.*: "The argument of this treatise is thoroughly Pauline and, for the most part, is no less defensible as valid exegesis than the counter claims that Paul spoke about resurrection of the flesh. . . . Not since Colossians and Ephesians had believers made such insightful use of the Pauline corpus." (217).
170. Pervo, *Making of Paul*, 139.
171. Cf. Morgan, "The Significance of 'Paulinism,'" 320–338.
172. Judith Lieu, "The Battle for Paul in the Second Century," *Irish Theological Quarterly* 75 (2010): 3.
173. Lieu, "The Battle for Paul," 5–7.
174. Snyder, *Acts of Paul*, 137, 145.
175. Dodson, "Introduction," in *Paul and the Second Century*, 10.
176. Berding, *Polycarp and Paul*, 172, cited in Dodson, "Introduction," 10.
177. Dodson, "Introduction," 10 n. 78.
178. Liljeström, "Approaching the Early Reception of Paul," 6 n. 3.
179. Bockmuehl, *The Remembered Peter*; and *Simon Peter in Scripture and Memory: The New Testament Apostle in the Early Church* (Grand Rapids, MI: Baker Academic, 2012).

CHAPTER 4

1. Epigraphs: Shils, *Tradition*, 45; Pieper, *Tradition*, 22 (emphasis his).
2. Shils, *Tradition*, 15. Cf. Gabriel Motzkin, "Tradition, Time, and Memory," in *Tradition and Tradition Theories* (ed. T. Larbig and S. Wiedenhofer; Studies in Tradition Theory; Berlin: LIT Verlag, 2006), 178, 182.
3. *Ideology and Utopia*, 264. Cf. also Peter L. Berger and Thomas Luckmann, *The Social Construction of Reality: a Treatise in the Sociology of Knowledge* (New York: Doubleday, 1966), 18, who cite Emile Durkheim, *The Rules* of

Sociological Method, 14: "The first and fundamental rule is: *Consider social facts as things.*" Emphasis is Berger and Luckmann's, who argue for a dialectical relationship between humans and their social realities: "*Society is a human product. Society is an objective reality. Man is a social product.*" (61; cf. 129). Again, emphasis theirs.

4. White, "Response to Arthur Marwick," *Journal of Contemporary History* 30 (1995): 245–246.

5. "Modernity," as a unified representation, has been recently challenged by increased sensitivity to competing "modernities." Cf. James Clifford, "Traditional Futures," in *Questions of Tradition* (ed. M. S. Phillips and G. Schochet; Toronto: University of Toronto Press, 2004), 153.

6. Donald G. Marshall, "Introduction," in *The Force of Tradition: Response and Resistance in Literature, Religion, and Cultural Studies* (ed. D. G. Marshall; Lanham, MD: Roman & Littlefield, 2005), 4–5.

7. Gadamer, *Truth and Method,* 279–280. Max Horkheimer and Theodor W. Adorno, *Dialectic of Enlightenment* (trans. J. Cumming; New York: Herder and Herder, 1972 [1944]), 3–42, argued that the Enlightenment, while proclaiming "the autonomy of ideas" (i.e., their own), was no less "totalitarian" or dictatorial in the propagation of its own sacred tradition (mythology) than the superstitious ancients whom it was trying to displace.

8. Gadamer, *Truth and Method,* 275–276. Emphasis his. Cf. MacIntyre, *After Virtue,* 205–206.

9. Shils, *Tradition,* 12.

10. Delwin Brown, "Limitation and Ingenuity: Radical Historicism and the Nature of Tradition," in *Tradition and Tradition Theories,* 218. Cf. Josef Pieper, *Tradition,* 9.

11. Cf. Jan Assmann, "Introduction: What is Cultural Memory?," in *Religion and Cultural Memory: Ten Studies* (Cultural Memory in the Present; Stanford, CA: Stanford University Press, 2006), 26–27; Michael McKeon, "Tacit Knowledge: Tradition and Its Aftermath," in *Questions of Tradition,* 173; and Michael Polanyi, *The Tacit Dimension* (London: Routledge, 1966).

12. Polanyi, *The Tacit Dimension,* 4. Emphasis his.

13. Wiedenhofer, "Tradition – History – Memory: Why Do We Need a Comprehensive Theory of Tradition?," in *Tradition and Tradition Theories,* 380. Stephen Turner, *The Social Theory of Practices: Tradition, Tacit Knowledge, and Presuppositions* (Chicago: University of Chicago Press, 1994), has argued that such totalizing concepts as tradition, culture, presuppositions, tacit knowledge, worldview, practices, habitus, and paradigms have functioned as quasi-objects that have a causal relationship to individual habits. He argues that the reification of these concepts in social theory does not explain how individuals, through trial and error and cognition, develop habits. These terms have some descriptive value, but little explanatory power. The conceptual usefulness of "tradition," in particular, is rooted in at least two observations: "the anomalous

persistence of patterns of behaviour . . . and the difficulty of understanding other cultures" (79–80). He concludes, "The picture that I have developed here is one in which practices is a word not for some sort of mysterious hidden collective object, but for the individual formations of habit that are the condition for the performances and emulations that make up life" (123). The reviews of Turner have been quite critical. Cf. Robert Alford, *Contemporary Sociology* 24 (1995): 705–707; James Bohman, *History and Theory* 36 (1997): 93–107; Neil Gross, *Theory and Society* 27 (1998): 117–127; Mikael Hård, *Technology and Culture* 37 (1996): 652–653; and Daniel Little, *Ethics* 106 (1996): 665–666, among others.

14. Wiedenhofer, "Tradition – History – Memory," 376; and Gerald L. Bruns, "Tradition and the Terror of History: Christianity, the Holocaust, and the Jewish Theological Dilemma," in *The Force of Tradition*, 20–21.

15. Shils, *Tradition*, 217.

16. Shils, *Tradition*, 97.

17. Shils, *Tradition*, 13. Cf. Motzkin, "Tradition, Time, and Memory," 178.

18. Gross, *Past in Ruins*, 9. Cf. Jan Vansina, *Oral Tradition as History* (Madison: University of Wisconsin Press, 1985), 3.

19. Joel Weinsheimer and Donald Marshall, "Translator's Preface," in *Truth and Method*, xiii–xiv.

20. Bruns, "Tradition and the Terror of History," 21. Cf. Vansina, *Oral Tradition as History*, xii: "Traditions must always be understood as reflecting both past and present in a single breath."

21. Gross, *Past in Ruins*, 13.

22. Gadamer, *Truth and Method*, 293.

23. On the Gadamer-Habermas "debate," cf. Ingrid Scheibler, *Gadamer: Between Heidegger and Habermas* (Lanham, MD: Rowman & Littlefield, 2000), 1–70; Demetrius Teigas, *Knowledge and Hermeneutic Understanding: A Study of the Habermas-Gadamer Debate* (Lewisburg, PA: Bucknell University Press, 1995); and Richard J. Bernstein, "The Constellation of Hermeneutics, Critical Theory, and Deconstruction," in *The Cambridge Companion to Gadamer* (ed. R. J. Dostal; Cambridge Companions to Philosophy; Cambridge: Cambridge University Press, 2002), 267–282.

24. Gadamer, *Truth and Method*, 355–357.

25. Shils, *Tradition*, 38–40. Cf. Phillips, "What Is Tradition When It Is Not 'Invented'? A Historiographical Introduction," in *Questions of Tradition*, 7.

26. Gadamer, *Truth and Method*, xxiv. Jaroslav Pelikan, in *The Vindication of Tradition* (New Haven, CT: Yale University Press, 1984), 81, argued similarly in relation to ecclesiastical history: "For the dichotomy between tradition and insight breaks down under the weight of history itself. A 'leap of progress' is not a standing broad jump, which begins at the line of where we are now; it is a running broad jump through where we have been to where we go next."

27. Gross, *Past in Ruins*, 63. Emphasis mine. Cf. Gadamer, *Truth and Method*, 282.
28. Shils, *Tradition*, 21.
29. Gadamer, *Truth and Method*, 357–358.
30. Gadamer, *Truth and Method*, 358. Emphasis his. Cf. also 360: "A person who does not admit that he is dominated by prejudices will fail to see what manifests itself by their light." Cf. also in this regard MacIntyre, *After Virtue*, 205–206: "For the story of my life is always embedded in the story of those communities from which I derive my identity. I am born with a past; and to try to cut myself off from that past, in the individualist mode, is to deform my present relationships. . . . What I am, therefore, is in key part what I inherit, a specific past that is present to some degree in my present. I find myself part of a history and that is generally to say, whether I like it or not, whether I recognise it or not, one of the bearers of a tradition."
31. Cf. his *Marcion and the New Testament*.
32. Cf. Michael Fishbane, *Biblical Interpretation in Ancient Israel* (Oxford: Clarendon Press, 1985), 543: "Accordingly, our received traditions are complex blends of traditum and traditio in dynamic interaction, dynamic interpenetration, and dynamic interdependence." He is addressing the tension between continuity and change in the Jewish Scriptural tradition.
33. Shils, *Tradition*, 36. Cf. Kathryn Tanner, "Tradition and Theological Judgment in Light of Postmodern Cultural Criticism," in *Tradition and Tradition Theories*, 233.
34. Shils, *Tradition*, 204.
35. Shils, *Tradition*, 205. Cf. 198: "One of the main reasons why what is given by the past is so widely accepted is that it permits life to move along lines set and anticipated from past experience and thus subtly converts the anticipated into the inevitable and the inevitable into the acceptable."
36. Gadamer, *Truth and Method*, 292.
37. Shils, *Tradition*, 14. Cf. also Gross, *Past in Ruins*, 18; and Turner, *Social Theory of Practices*, 84: "Yet each of these small changes may well have seemed, from the point of view of the participants, to preserve 'sameness' in the sense that was relevant to them. At no point, perhaps, did they have any sense of the 'inaccessibility' of the culture of their parents or teachers. If the past is another country, it did not become so overnight."
38. Cf. Shils, *Tradition*, 45: "Such modifications of the received occur even when the tradition is regarded as sacrosanct and the innovator might in good conscience insist that he is adhering to the traditions as received."
39. Eric Hobsbawm, "Introduction: Inventing Traditions," in *The Invention of Tradition* (ed. E. Hobsbawm and T. Ranger; Past and Present Publications; Cambridge: Cambridge University Press, 1983), 1. Emphasis mine.
40. Hobsbawm, "Introduction: Inventing Traditions," 1. For more on Hobsbawm, cf. Patrick H. Hutton, *History as an Art of Memory* (Hanover, NH: University Press of New England, 1993), 5.

41. Hobsbawm, "Introduction: Inventing Traditions," 2.

42. Hobsbawm, "Introduction: Inventing Traditions," 2–3.

43. Hobsbawm, "Introduction: Inventing Traditions," 4–5.

44. Phillips, "What is Tradition When It is Not 'Invented'?," 5–6.

45. Cf. Phillips, "What is Tradition When It is Not 'Invented'?," 6: "A simple opposition between 'genuine' and 'invented' traditions is unworkable. It corresponds to nothing we know about the transmission of culture, either in the conditions of modern West or elsewhere."

46. Cf. Gadamer, *Truth and Method*, 280; Shils, *Tradition*, 24; Gross, *Past in Ruins*, 10; and Gordon Schochet, "Tradition as Politics and the Politics of Tradition," in *Questions of Tradition*, 305.

47. Gross, *Past in Ruins*, 8. Cf. Schochet, "Tradition as Politics and the Politics of Tradition," 300: "There are few defences of authority that work so well as the invocation of historical continuity."

48. Polanyi, *The Tacit Dimension*, 61–62.

49. Gross, *Past in Ruins*, 12. Cf. Pieper, *Tradition*, 18, 23–35.

50. Brown, "Limitation and Ingenuity," 218. Or, similarly, "A tradition is the process of negotiation—ingenuity—that takes place within, and sometimes with, the boundaries—limitation—of canon." (224).

51. Brown, "Limitation and Ingenuity," 220.

52. Shils, *Tradition*, 213.

53. Shils, *Tradition*, 215.

54. Shils, *Tradition*, 215. Endogenous changes are often predicated on an "epistemological crisis" (Marshall, "Introduction," 9).

55. Brown, "Limitation and Ingenuity," 219. Cf. James Clifford, *The Predicament of Culture: Twentieth-Century Ethnography, Literature, and Art* (Cambridge, MA: Harvard University Press, 1988), 338.

56. Shils, *Tradition*, 240.

57. Shils, *Tradition*, 258–259.

58. Brown, "Limitation and Ingenuity," 216.

59. Brown, "Limitation and Ingenuity," 223.

60. Brown, "Limitation and Ingenuity," 217.

61. Fishbane, *Biblical Interpretation in Ancient Israel*, 18.

62. Shils, *Tradition*, 266, 272.

63. Shils, *Tradition*, 270.

64. Shils, *Tradition*, 270.

65. Cf. Anthony C. Thistleton, *New Horizons in Hermeneutics: The Theory and Practice of Transforming Biblical Reading* (Grand Rapids, MI: Zondervan, 1992), 237: "On the other hand, the exegetical conclusions at which the interpreter arrives cannot be isolated from his or her provisional understanding of the mind of Paul, or of Pauline thought as a whole."

66. Ca. 90–100 c.e. Cf. Bart Ehrman, "The First Letter of Clement to the Corinthians – Introduction," in *The Apostolic Fathers* (2 vols.; LCL 24–25;

Cambridge, MA: Harvard University Press, 2003), 1:23–25; Horacio E. Lona, *Der erste Clemensbrief* (Kommentare zum Apostolischen Väter; Göttingen: Vandenhoeck & Ruprecht, 1998), 75–78; and Andreas Lindemann, *Die Clemensbriefe* (HNT; Tübingen: J. C. B. Mohr (Paul Siebeck), 1992), 12.

67. Ca. 80–90 c.e. in Richard Bauckham, *Jude, 2 Peter* (WBC 50; Waco: Word Books, 1983), 157–158. Ca. 100–110 in J. N. D. Kelly, *The Epistles of Peter and of Jude*, 231.

68. Ca. 98–117 c.e. Cf. Bart Ehrman, "Letters of Ignatius – Introduction," in *The Apostolic Fathers*, 1:205; William R. Schoedel, *Ignatius of Antioch: A Commentary on the Letters of Ignatius of Antioch* (Hermeneia; Minneapolis: Fortress Press, 1985); Christine Trevett, *A Study of Ignatius of Antioch in Syria and Asia* (Studies in the Bible and Early Christianity; Lewiston, NY: Edwin Mellen Press, 1992); and Allen Brent, *Ignatius of Antioch and the Second Sophistic: a Study of an Early Christian Transformation of Pagan Culture* (STAC 36; Tübingen: Mohr Siebeck, 2006).

69. Ca. 110–135 c.e. Cf. Bart Ehrman, "Letter of Polycarp to the Philippians – Introduction," *The Apostolic Fathers*, 1:328–329; and Paul Hartog, *Polycarp and the New Testament*.

70. On the relationship between the *Acts of Paul and Thecla* and the canonical Pauline literature, cf. esp. D.R. MacDonald, *The Legend and the Apostle*; Willy Rordorf, "Tradition and Composition in the *Acts of Thecla*: the State of the Question," *Semeia* 38 (1986): 43–52; "Nochmals: Paulusakten und Pastoralbriefe," in *Tradition and Interpretation in the New Testament: Essays in Honor of E. Earle Ellis for his 60th Birthday* (ed. G. F. Hawthorne and O. Betz; Grand Rapids, MI: Eerdmans, 1987), 319–327; W. Edward Glenny, "1 Corinthians 7:29–31 and the Teaching of Continence in *The Acts of Paul and Thecla*," *Grace Theological Journal* 11 (1990): 53–70; Peter W. Dunn, "The *Acts of Paul* and the Pauline Legacy"; Stephen J. Davis, "A 'Pauline' Defense of Women's Right to Baptize? Intertextuality and Apostolic Authority in the *Acts of Paul*," *JECS* 8 (2000): 453–459; and Glenn Snyder, *Acts of Paul*, 137–145.

71. Cf. Aageson, *Paul, the Pastoral Epistles, and the Early Church*, 8: "it is not just Paul's letters or his theology that are significant for the early church but also his personal legacy and the authority that brings to bear." Again, a "thick description," as opposed to a "thin description," attempts to describe individual performances (in this case, a citation or echo of a Pauline text) within larger networks of meaning (in this case, a total understanding of Paul as a persona).

72. Margaret M. Mitchell, *The Heavenly Trumpet: John Chrysostom and the Art of Pauline Interpretation* (Louisville, KY: Westminster John Knox Press, 2002).

73. Mitchell, *The Heavenly Trumpet*, 384.

74. Mitchell, *The Heavenly Trumpet*, 409.

75. Cf. Chapter 3 (n. 8) on the collection of the Pauline letter corpus.

76. Gadamer, *Truth and Method*, 134–144.

77. Jan Vansina, *Oral Tradition as History*, 27–28, describes oral traditions as "verbal messages which are reported statements from the past beyond the present generation . . . There must be transmission by word of mouth over at least a generation."

78. Cf. Mary Carruthers, *The Book of Memory: a Study of Memory in Medieval Culture* (2nd ed.; Cambridge Studies in Medieval Culture; Cambridge: Cambridge University Press, 2008 [1990]), 13: "True fundamentalism understands words not as signs or clues but takes them as things in themselves. . . . Fundamentalism denies legitimacy to interpretation."

79. Gadamer, *Truth and Method*, 387, citing Droysen, *Historik: Vorlesungen über Enzyklopadie und Methodologie der Geschichte* (ed. R. Hübner; München: R. Oldenbourg, 1937), 63. Cf. Gross, *Past in Ruins*, 102: "If they [texts] come from the past, they capture and crystallize not tradition as such but a certain moment in the tradition. That moment is etched into the text and then passed down exactly as it was, with the same sentences, statements, and meanings that were there at the instant it was written."

80. Gadamer, *Truth and Method*, 388. Emphasis his.

81. Fishbane, *Biblical Interpretation in Ancient Israel*, 2.

82. Vansina, *Oral Tradition as History*, 156.

83. Brian Stock, *Listening for the Text: On the Uses of the Past* (Parallax: Re-visions of Culture and Society; Baltimore, MD: Johns Hopkins University Press, 1990).

84. Earlier studies on literacy include Jack Goody, *The Domestication of the Savage Mind* (Cambridge: Cambridge University Press, 1977); *The Interface between the Written and the Oral* (Cambridge: Cambridge University Press, 1987); and Walter Ong, *Orality and Literacy: The Technologizing of the Word* (London: Routledge, 2002 [1982]).

85. Stock, *Listening for the Text*, 7.

86. Stock, *Listening for the Text*, 10.

87. Carruthers, *Book of Memory*, 9–10.

88. Carruthers, *Book of Memory*, 14.

89. Carruthers, *Book of Memory*, 18: "In none of the evidence is the act of writing itself regarded as a supplanter of memory, not even in Plato's *Phaedrus*. Rather books are themselves memorial cues and aids, and memory is most like a book, a written page or a wax tablet upon which something is written."

90. Translations from Carruthers, *Book of Memory*, 18, 19, 24. Emphases hers.

91. Cf. also Jocelyn Small, *Wax Tablets of the Mind: Cognitive Studies of Memory and Literacy in Classical Antiquity* (London: Routledge, 1997), who shows how classical theories on training memory and the ancient production of books were related.

92. Carruthers, *Book of Memory*, 19.

93. Carruthers, *Book of Memory*, 20, 26.

94. Carruthers, *Book of Memory*, 25–26.

95. Carruthers, *Book of Memory*, 20, 276.

96. Cf. Ruth Webb, *Ekphrasis, Imagination and Persuasion in Ancient Rhetorical Theory and Practice* (Burlington, VT: Ashgate Publishing, 2009), and, more broadly, Peter Wagner, ed., *Icons—Texts—Iconotexts: Essays on Ekphrasis and Intermediality* (European Cultures 6; Berlin: Walter de Gruyter, 1996).

97. Cf. Mitchell, *The Heavenly Trumpet*, 41–42, 61–62.

98. Translation of *Vita Constantini* from Mitchell, *The Heavenly Trumpet*, 41 n. 32. Cf. also Averil Cameron, *Christianity and the Rhetoric of Empire: The Development of Christian Discourse* (Sather Classical Lectures 55; Berkeley: University of California Press, 1991), 54.

99. Carruthers, *Book of Memory*, 277. The modern French of *painture* is *peinture*. I have retained the older spelling of Fournival, through Carruthers.

100. Carruthers, *Book of Memory*, 277, citing *Li Bestiaire d'amours*, 5.

101. Carruthers, *Book of Memory*, 291.

102. D. Reisberg, D. G. Pearson, and S. M. Kosslyn, "Intuitions and Introspections about Imagery: The Role of Imagery Experience in Shaping an Investigator's Theoretical Views," *Applied Cognitive Psychology* 17 (2003): 147–160, find that as of 2003 only 6% of leading psychologists, neuroscientists, and philosophers who had published widely-used work on mental imagery adhered to a strict propositional theory of mental representation. In the early-twentieth century, behaviorist psychologists (e.g., J. B. Watson, followed by B. F. Skinner), on account of the "inherently private nature" of mental images, tried to marginalize theories based on them as unscientific. In the last 50 years a minority of cognitive psychologists (e.g., Zenon Pylyshyn) have further argued that the brain only processes information propositionally/descriptively. In this view, depictive representation is not fundamental to the process of human cognition and internal representation. Mental images are merely epiphenomenal. For a history of claims against mental imagery, cf. Stephen M. Kosslyn, William L. Thompson, and Giorgio Ganis, *The Case for Mental Imagery* (Oxford Psychology Series; Oxford: Oxford University Press, 2006), 3–59. Most of the relevant bibliography for mental imagery from the perspective of cognitive psychology can be found there, but cf. also John T. E. Richardson, *Mental Imagery and Human Memory* (New York: St. Martins, 1980); Robert G. Kunzendorf, ed., *Mental Imagery* (New York: Plenum Press, 1991); Cesare Cornoldi, Robert H. Logie, Maria A. Brandimonte, Geir Kaufmann, and Daniel Reisberg, eds., *Stretching the Imagination: Representation and Transformation in Mental Imagery* (Counterpoints: Cognition, Memory, and Language; Oxford: Oxford University Press, 1996); and Hugh Clapin, Phillip Staines, and Peter Slezak, eds., *Representation in Mind: New Approaches to Mental Representation* (Perspectives on Cognitive Science; Amsterdam: Elsevier, 2004). For a philosophical defense of mental imagery, cf. Mark Rollins, *Mental Imagery: On the Limits of Cognitive Science* (New Haven, CT: Yale University Press, 1989).

103. Kosslyn, Thompson, and Ganis, *Case for Mental Imagery*, 15. Emphasis theirs.
104. Kosslyn, Thompson, and Ganis, *Case for Mental Imagery*, 4.
105. Kosslyn, Thompson, and Ganis, *Case for Mental Imagery*, 38, 41–42.
106. Carruthers, *Book of Memory*, 27. Emphasis hers.
107. Translation from G. R. T. Ross, *Aristotle: De sensu and De memoria* (Cambridge: Cambridge University Press, 1906), 105–107.
108. Like proponents of mental imagery, whether ancient or modern, Ludwig Wittgenstein had to clarify his early "picture–theory" of language found in the *Tractatus Logico-Philosophicus*, wherein he described a proposition as "a picture of reality . . . a model of reality as we imagine it" (*Tractatus* 4.01) and as "a likeness of what is signified" (*Tractatus* 4.012). Verbal imagery, consequently, "like a tableau vivant . . . presents a state of affairs" (*Tractatus* 4.0311). Cited from Mitchell, *Iconology: Image, Text, Ideology* (Chicago: University of Chicago Press, 1987), 20–21. Cf. Ludwig Wittgenstein, *Tractatus Logico-Philosophicus* (trans. D. G. Pears and B. F. McGuinness; London: Routledge & Kegan Paul, 1961 [1921]). As Mitchell, *Iconology*, 15, reminds, Wittgenstein then spent the rest of his career undoing what he believed to be false inferences from his "picture theory" of language. The mental images produced by language obscure reality no less than do graphic (material) images and/or language itself (*Iconology*, 26). This same point is made by Kosslyn, Thompson, and Ganis, *Case for Mental Imagery*, 41–42. Imagery, regardless of the species (graphic, optical, perceptual, mental and linguistic, to use the categories found in Mitchell), is always deceptive.
109. Mitchell, *Iconology*, 8.
110. Carruthers, *Book of Memory*, 26, following John T. E. Richardson, *Mental Imagery and Human Memory*.
111. Mitchell, *Iconology*, 26–27.
112. Mitchell, *Iconology*, 30.
113. Kosslyn, Thompson, and Ganis, *Case for Mental Imagery*, 19. Emphasis theirs.
114. Kosslyn, Thompson, and Ganis, *Case for Mental Imagery*, 12.
115. Kosslyn, Thompson, and Ganis, *Case for Mental Imagery*, 43.
116. Kosslyn, Thompson, and Ganis, *Case for Mental Imagery*, 44.
117. Cf. Vansina, *Oral Tradition as History*, 12–13, on the differences between oral tradition and oral history. Sensitivity to ancient preferences for oral history (firsthand accounts) has shaped recent work on the Jesus tradition in the canonical Gospels. Cf. Samuel Byrskog, *Story as History—History as Story: The Gospel Tradition in the Context of Ancient Oral History* (Leiden: Brill, 2002 [2000]); James D. G. Dunn, *Jesus Remembered* (Christianity in the Making 1; Grand Rapids, MI: Eerdmans, 2003); Richard Bauckham, *Jesus and the Eyewitnesses: The Gospels as Eyewitness Testimony* (Grand Rapids, MI: Eerdmans, 2006); and Markus Bockmuehl, *Seeing the Word: Refocusing New Testament Study* (Studies in Theological Interpretation; Grand Rapids, MI: Baker Academic, 2006), 169–170.

118. Cf. Averil Cameron, *Christianity and the Rhetoric of Empire*, 144–146, on late ancient Christian Lives as "verbal icons" that "are full of meaning, signs by which Christians taught one another how to interpret the present and past and how to live in the future." Cf. Patricia Cox, *Biography in Late Antiquity: A Quest for the Holy Man* (The Transformation of the Classical Heritage 5; Berkeley: University of California Press, 1983), xvi, xii, on these Lives as "imaginal histories" "where the history of a man's life and his biographer's vision of human divinity meet and mingle."

119. Pieper, *Tradition*, 22; Vansina, *Oral Tradition as History*, xi; Hutton, *History as an Art of Memory*, 92; Elizabeth A. Castelli, *Martyrdom and Memory*, 12; J. Assmann, *Religion and Cultural Memory*, 8; Motzkin, "Tradition, Time, and Memory," 181; and Aleida Assmann, "The Religious Roots of Cultural Memory," *Norsk teologisk tidsskrift* 109 (2008): 289.

120. Hutton, *History as an Art of Memory*, xiii. Cf. Barbie Zelizer, "Reading the Past Against the Grain: the Shape of Memory Studies," *Critical Studies in Mass Communication* 12 (1995): 216, 235.

121. Hutton, *History as an Art of Memory*, 1.

122. Cf. Shils, *Tradition*, 263: "The boundaries of a tradition are in one respect the boundaries of adherence of collectivities defined by their community of beliefs; in another respect they are the boundaries of symbolic constructions."

123. Cf. Maurice Halbwachs, *The Collective Memory* (trans. F. J. Ditter, Jr., and V. Y. Ditter; New York: Harper Colophon, 1980 [1950]); *On Collective Memory* (ed. D. N. Levine; trans. L. Coser; The Heritage of Society; Chicago: University of Chicago Press, 1992). These are modern English editions of the original French *Les cadres sociaux de la mémoire* (1925), *La topographie légendaire des Évangiles en Terre Sainte: étude de mémoire collective* (1941) and *La mémoire collective* (1950). Introductions by Mary Douglas and Lewis Coser in each of these volumes are helpful places to start for reckoning with Halbwachs' thought. Writing in this same period was F. C. Bartlett, *Remembering: A Study in Experimental and Social Psychology* (Cambridge: Cambridge University Press, 1932), who showed through experimentation the social makeup of individual memory.

124. Other important figures for the sociology of knowledge, in addition to Marx and Mannheim, include Nietzsche, Max Scheller, who coined the term "sociology of knowledge" in his *Die Wissensformen und die Gesellschaft* (1925), and Wilhelm Dilthey. Cf. Berger and Luckmann, *Social Construction of Reality*, 1–19.

125. Karl Mannheim, *Ideology and Utopia*, 237. Cf. also the collection of Mannheim's influential essays: *Essays on the Sociology of Knowledge* (New York: Oxford University Press, 1952). Writing almost four decades later, though still heavily indebted to Mannheim, Berger and Luckmann, *Social Construction of Reality*, 3, described the sociology of knowledge as being "*concerned with the analysis of the social construction of reality.*" Emphasis theirs.

126. Mannheim, *Ideology and Utopia*, 3.
127. Berger and Luckmann, *Social Construction of Reality*, 51.
128. Mannheim, *Ideology and Utopia*, 238. Emphasis his. Mannheim also pushed past Marx in arguing that other factors beyond social class are responsible for how one perceives the world. He surmises that Marx never made the final step to a total conception of the sociology of knowledge because of a "subconscious reluctance to think out the implications of a concretely formulated insight to a point where the theoretical formulations latent in it would be clear enough to have a disquieting effect on one's own position" (249).
129. Mannheim, *Ideology and Utopia*, 6.
130. Berger and Luckmann, *Social Construction of Reality*, 95–108.
131. Mannheim, *Ideology and Utopia*, 7, 241–242. For Mannheim, the constant tension between ideology and utopia figures the historical and epistemological fields. One sees in this basic tension the influence of Max Weber.
132. Halbwachs, *On Collective Memory*, 53; and *The Collective Memory*, 48. Cf. Jan Assmann, *Religion and Cultural Memory*, 1. There is a rapidly growing set of basic modern introductions to issues involving memory, particularly its social component: Barry Schwartz, "The Social Context of Commemoration: A Study in Collective Memory," *Social Forces* 61 (1982): 374–402; David Lowenthal, *The Past is a Foreign Country* (Cambridge: Cambridge University Press, 1985); Paul Connerton, *How Societies Remember* (Cambridge: Cambridge University Press, 1989); David Middleton and Derek Edwards, eds., *Collective Remembering* (Newbury Park, CA: Sage, 1990); James Fentress and Chris Wickham, *Social Memory* (Oxford: Blackwell, 1992); Jacques Le Goff, *History and Memory* (New York: Columbia University Press, 1992); Gillian Cohen, George Kiss, and Martin E. Le Voi, *Memory: Current Issues* (Open Guides to Psychology; Philadelphia: Open University Press, 1993); Jonathan Boyarin, ed., *Remapping Memory: The Politics of TimeSpace* (Minneapolis: University of Minnesota Press, 1994); Zelizer, "Reading the Past Against the Grain," 214–239; Eviatar Zerubavel, "Social Memories: Steps to a Sociology of the Past," *Qualitative Sociology* 19 (1996): 283–299; Jeffrey K. Olick and Joyce Robbins, "Social Memory Studies: From 'Collective Memory' to the Historical Sociology of Mnemonic Practices," *Annual Review of Sociology* 24 (1998): 105–140; Alan Kirk, "Social and Cultural Memory," in *Memory, Tradition, and Text*, 1–24; Astrid Erll, Ansgar Nünning, and Sara B. Young, eds., *Cultural Memory Studies: an International and Interdisciplinary Handbook* (Media and Cultural Memory 8; Berlin: Walter de Gruyter, 2008).
133. Jan Assmann, *Das kulturelle Gedächtnis: Schrift, Errinnerung und politische Identität in frühen Hochkulturen* (Munich: C. H. Beck, 1997), 20–21, has helpfully categorized the various tools of memory: (1) mimetic memory (memory through repetition); (2) material memory (memory preserved in objects and places); (3) communicative memory (memory preserved in language

and communication); and (4) cultural/bonding memory (memory as connectedness and identity-formation).

134. Cf. Zerubavel, "Social Memories," 290; Schwartz, *Abraham Lincoln and the Forge of National Memory* (Chicago: University of Chicago Press, 2000), 8–9; and Fishbane, *Biblical Interpretation*, 7, where tradition-building is also "Gemeindebildung."

135. Cf. Zelizer, "Reading the Past Against the Grain," 222–223; and Kirk, "Social and Cultural Memory," 2–3. Halbwachs was Durkheim's student in Paris before he joined the editorial board of Durkheim's influential *L'Année Sociologique*. Cf. Mary Douglas, "Introduction: Maurice Halbwachs (1877–1945)," in *The Collective Memory*, 6. On language, cf. *On Collective Memory*, 43–45.

136. Halbwachs, *On Collective Memory*, 200.

137. Cf. Jonathan Boyarin, "Space, Time, and the Politics of Memory," in *Remapping Memory* 26: "What we are faced with—what we are living—is the constitution of both group 'membership' and individual 'identity' out of a dynamically chosen selection of memories, and the constant reshaping, reinvention, and reinforcement of those memories as members contest and create the boundaries and links among themselves."

138. Cf. Halbwachs, *On Collective Memory*, 40, 49: "everything seems to indicate that the past is not preserved but is reconstructed on the basis of the present . . . at the moment of reproducing the past our imagination remains under the influence of the present social milieu." Cf. also Kirk, "Social and Cultural Memory," 11.

139. Halbwachs, *The Collective Memory*, 52. Assmann, *Religion and Cultural Memory*, 2, calls "autobiographical" memory "episodic" memory, to be distinguished from "semantic" memory, which is learned. For a full assessment of autobiographical memory, cf. the essays in David C. Rubin, ed., *Remembering our Past: Studies in Autobiographical Memory* (Cambridge: Cambridge University Press, 1996).

140. Identity-formation is one of the primary functions of memory. Cf. George Herbert Mead, *Mind, Self & Society from the Standpoint of a Social Behaviorist* (ed. C. W. Morris; Chicago: University of Chicago Press, 1934); Yael Zerubavel, *Recovered Roots: Collective Memory and the Making of Israeli National Tradition* (Chicago: University of Chicago Press, 1995); John R. Gillis, "Memory and Identity: the History of a Relationship," in *Commemorations: The Politics of National Identity* (ed. J. R. Gillis; Princeton: Princeton University Press, 1996), 3–24; and Heidrun Friese and Aleida Assmann, eds., *Identities: Time, Difference, and Boundaries* (Making Sense of History 2; New York: Berghahn Books, 2002).

141. Zerubavel, "Social Memories," 286.

142. Cf. Vansina, *Oral Tradition as History*, 8–10, on how personal reminiscences are shaped by the community. Halbwachs, *On Collective Memory*, 41–42, viewed dreams as a sort of anti-memory, inasmuch as they are individually

perceived and lack the organization and coherency that comes from social re-inforcement. They are inaccessible, as experiences, to others.

143. Cf. Roy Rosensweig and David Thelen, *The Presence of the Past: Popular Uses of History in American Life* (New York: Columbia University Press, 1998); and Mary Susan Weldon, "Remembering as a Social Process," *The Psychology of Learning and Motivation: Advances in Research and Theory* 40 (2000): 67–120.

144. Halbwachs, *On Collective Memory*, 216–222.

145. Halbwachs saw a large and untraversable chasm existing between Jesus' fol-lowers and the late first-century church (*On Collective Memory*, 199–200).

146. Halbwachs, *On Collective Memory*, 194–198.

147. Cf. Halbwachs, *On Collective Memory*, 204, 225: "Yet there was the image of the holy city—an image that the universal Christian community had slowly con-strued . . . This outline of holy places is a construction. One clearly wished to make Jerusalem the center of Christian attention since it had been the theater of the Passion."

148. Cf. Halbwachs, *The Collective Memory*, 69: "As I have said many times, a remembrance is in very large measure a reconstruction of the past achieved with data borrowed from the present, a reconstruction prepared, furthermore, by reconstructions of earlier periods wherein past images had already been altered."

149. Zerubavel, "Social Memories," 287.

150. Halbwachs, *On Collective Memory*, 182. Cf. Assmann, *Religion and Cultural Memory*, 94: "he [Halbwachs] insists . . . on the distinction between *reconstruire* and *retrouver*. The past is not 'rediscovered,' but reconstructed."

151. For good interdisciplinary introductions to the issues surrounding memory distortion, cf. Daniel L. Schacter, ed., *Memory Distortion: How Minds, Brains, and Societies Reconstruct the Past* (Cambridge, MA: Harvard University Press, 1997) and Daniel L. Schacter, *The Seven Sins of Memory: How the Mind Forgets and Remembers* (Boston: Houghton Mifflin, 2001).

152. On the vagaries of eyewitness testimony, cf. Hugo Munsterberg, *On the Wit-ness Stand: Essays on Psychology and Crime* (New York: Clark, Boardman, Dou-bleday, 1909); Elizabeth F. Loftus, *Eyewitness Testimony* (Cambridge, MA: Har-vard University Press, 1979); Gary L. Wells and Elizabeth F. Loftus, eds., *Eyewitness Testimony: Psychological Perspectives* (New York: Cambridge Univer-sity Press, 1984); and recently, Judith C. S. Redman, "How Accurate Are Eye-witnesses? Bauckham and the Eyewitnesses in the Light of Psychological Re-search," *JBL* 129 (2010): 177–197, in response to Richard Bauckham's *Jesus and the Eyewitnesses*.

153. Bartlett, *Remembering*, 199–204.

154. Cf. J. Assmann, *Religion and Cultural Memory*, 93–94, on the differences here between Halbwachs and Nietzsche. Some of the more important voices in the field of "the politics of memory" include Maurice Agulhon, *Marianne into Battle:*

Republican Imagery and Symbolism in France, 1789–1880 (trans. J. Lloyd; Cambridge: Cambridge University Press, 1981); Pierre Nora, ed., *Realms of Memory: Rethinking the French Past* (trans. A. Goldhammer; 3 vols.; European Perspectives; New York: Columbia University Press, 1996 [1984–1992]); Hobsbawm and Ranger, eds., *The Invention of Tradition*; David Lowenthal, *The Past is a Foreign Country*; John Bodnar, *Remaking America: Public Memory, Commemoration, and Patriotism in the Twentieth Century* (Princeton, NJ: Princeton University Press, 1992); and the essays found in Gillis, *Commemorations: the Politics of National Identity.* Particularly good in this last volume is Yael Zerubavel, "The Historic, the Legendary, and the Incredible: Invented Tradition and Collective Memory in Israel," 105–123, in which she shows how some periods of Israel's history are elevated in the service of modern Zionist interests, while others (such as living in exile) are forgotten.

155. Cf. James Loewen, *Lies My Teacher Told Me: Everything Your American History Textbook Got Wrong* (New York: New Press, 1995) and Robert Lerner, Althea K. Nagai, and Stanley Rothman, *Molding the Good Citizen: The Politics of High School History Texts* (Westport, CT: Praeger, 1995).

156. Jonathan Boyarin, "Space, Time, and the Politics of Memory," 2.

157. Hutton, *History as an Art of Memory*, xvi.

158. A. Assmann, "Religious Roots of Cultural Memory," 275.

159. Each of the contributors to Hobsbawm and Ranger's *The Invention of Tradition* attempts to show how the political winners of the revolutions in Europe in the eighteenth and nineteenth centuries invented traditions for the purpose of social cohesion in a period when traditional authorities were being overturned. On the American side, John Bodnar's *Remaking America* tracks the "official memory" of our nation's past as preserved in publicly sanctioned *lieux de mémoire*, or "sites of memory." Using the political struggle over the construction of the Vietnam Veterans' Memorial in Washington, D.C., as an *entrée* into "official" and "vernacular" memory, Bodnar details how those in power (normally white Protestants) in the late-nineteenth and twentieth centuries preserved that power through rhetorically shaped commemorations of our nation's past that emphasized national unity and loyalty. This was done in the face of increasingly diverse populations whose own "vernacular memories" were a threat to the preferred version of the past of elites. On the notion of "hidden transcripts," cf. James C. Scott, *Domination and the Arts of Resistance: Hidden Transcripts* (New Haven, CT: Yale University Press, 1990).

160. Hutton, *History as an Art of Memory*, xxiv.

161. Cf. Pierre Nora, ed., *Realms of Memory: Rethinking the French Past*; "Between Memory and History: Les Lieux de Mémoire," *Representations* 26 (1989): 7–25.

162. Hutton, *History as an Art of Memory*, 150.

163. Nora, "Between History and Memory," 7. Similarly, cf. Yosef Hayim Yerushalmi, *Zakhor: Jewish History and Jewish Memory* (The Samuel and Althea

Stroum Lectures in Jewish Studies; Seattle: University of Washington Press,
1996 [1982]), on the supposed shift from memory to history in modern Judaism in the eighteenth and nineteenth centuries.

164. Nora, "Between History and Memory," 8. Cf. Hutton, *History as an Art of
Memory*, 149.
165. Nora, "Between History and Memory," 13.
166. Nora, "Between History and Memory," 19.
167. Nora, "Between History and Memory, 18–19."
168. Cf. J. Assmann, *Religion and Cultural Memory*, 8–9: "Such aides–mémoires are
also the *lieux de mémoire*, memory sites in which the memory of entire national
or religious communities is concentrated, monuments, rituals, feast days and
customs. In short, the entire panoply of things that go to make up what Halbwachs called tradition and which he contrasted with *mémoire vécue* can be understood as a system of memory sites, a system of markers that enables the
individual who lives in this tradition to belong, that is, to realize his potential
as the member of a society in the sense of a community where it is possible to
learn, remember, and to share in a culture."
169. Kirk, "Social and Cultural Memory," 9.
170. Cited in Mitchell, *Heavenly Trumpet*, 45 n. 54.
171. Cf. Hutton, *History as an Art of Memory*; J. Assmann, *Das kulturelle Gedächtnis*;
Religion and Cultural Memory; Barry Schwartz, "The Social Context of Commemoration"; *Abraham Lincoln and the Forge of National Memory*; and *Abraham Lincoln in the Post-Heroic Era: History and Memory in Late Twentieth-
Century America* (Chicago: University of Chicago Press, 2008). Hutton, *History
as an Art of Memory*, xxv, is exemplary: "History draws on both sides of the
memory puzzle. It seeks to reconstruct the past through an act of recollection.
But the past that prompts the historian's consideration is borne in the present
by oft–repeated habits of mind."
172. J. Assmann, *Religion and Cultural Memory*, 6.
173. J. Assmann, *Religion and Cultural Memory*, 11. Cf. also *Schrift und Gedächtnis:
Beitrage zur Archäologie der literarische Kommunikation* (ed. A. Assmann, J.
Assmann, and C. Hardmeier; Munich: Fink, 1983); *Mnemosyne: Formen und
Funktionen der kulturellen Erinnerung* (ed. A. Assmann and F. Harth; Frankfurt
am Main: Fischer Taschenbuch Verlag, 1991); Aleida Assmann, *Erinner-
ungsräume: Formen und Wandlungen des kulturellen Gedächtnisses* (München:
C.H. Beck, 1999); and Aleida Assmann, "The Religious Roots of Cultural
Memory."
174. A. Assmann, "Religious Roots of Cultural Memory," 271. Cf. Kirk, "Social and
Cultural Memory," 20. Schwartz, *Abraham Lincoln and the Forge of National
Memory*, 225, following Geertz, speaks of this as the "framing" aspect of memory.
175. J. Assmann, *Religion and Cultural Memory*, 92. Others concur. Barry Schwartz,
Abraham Lincoln and the Forge of National Memory, xi, argues that "Culture

solves the problem of meaning, I believe, by providing perspectives explaining otherwise enigmatic, stressful, and disorganizing happenings." Likewise, Timothy Hutton, *History as an Art of Memory*, xv, warns, "Postmodern historians were interested in memory as a resource in the mobilization of political power, and they were dismissive of the intrinsic value of tradition itself."

176. It is a "continuous negotiation" of past and present, as James Clifford reminds (cf. n. 55 in this chapter).

177. Cf. Zelizer, "Reading the Past Against the Grain," 227, and Vansina, *Oral Tradition as History*, 94: "as all messages from tradition are uttered in the present, when they are recorded they are strongly influenced by the social present. . . . Some sociologists go further and hold that the total content of oral tradition is only a social product of the present. . . . This is exaggerated. Where would social imagination find the stuff to invent from? How does one explain cultural continuities?"

178. J. Assmann, *Religion and Cultural Memory*, 25.

179. A. Assmann, "Religious Roots of Cultural Memory," 275–282.

180. J. Assmann, *Religion and Cultural Memory*, 27.

181. Cf. Halbwachs, *On Collective Memory*, 224–225: "To be sure, collective memory reconstructs its various recollections to accord with contemporary ideas and preoccupations. But it encounters resistance in the form of material vestiges and written texts as much as in what has become embodied in rites and institutions."

182. Hutton, *History as an Art of Memory*, xx–xxi.

183. Hutton, *History as an Art of Memory*, 20.

184. Schwartz, "The Social Context of Commemoration," 396.

185. Cf. Vansina, *Oral Tradition as History*, 137: "The collective representations of a culture include not only substantive matter, data of cognition, but also of imagery. To the historian it is important to understand not only intended meanings . . . but also what can be called the context of meaning: the imagery and its impact."

186. Schwartz's second and most recent book on Lincoln, *Abraham Lincoln in the Post-Heroic Era* (2008), moves from the Great Depression into the late-twentieth century. I am mainly dependent on his first volume because I see the sort of initial fragmentation of Lincoln's image in the 50 or so years after his death as similar, in many ways, to what we find with the Apostle Paul's image in the 50 or so years after his own death.

187. Schwartz, *Abraham Lincoln and the Forge of National Memory*, 33. He is dependent here on Durkheim's *Elementary Forms of the Religious Life*.

188. Schwartz, *Abraham Lincoln and the Forge of National Memory*, 58.

189. Schwartz, *Abraham Lincoln and the Forge of National Memory*, 226. For a later example, Woodrow Wilson was keyed (through various media) to both Lincoln and Washington during World War I, which is quite suggestive of the way many viewed America's participation in that war (231–232).

190. Schwartz, *Abraham Lincoln and the Forge of National Memory*, 91, 103.

191. Schwartz, *Abraham Lincoln and the Forge of National Memory*, 116–117.

192. On reputation and prestige from a thoroughgoing Weberian perspective, cf. William J. Goode, *The Celebration of Heroes: Prestige as a Social Control System* (Riverside Literature Series; Berkeley: University of California Press, 1978).

193. Schwartz, *Abraham Lincoln and the Forge of National Memory*, 67.

194. Schwartz, *Abraham Lincoln and the Forge of National Memory*, 22 (cf. 255, 295). Cf. Gladys Engel Lang and Kurt Lang, "Recognition and Renown: The Survival of Artistic Reputation," *The American Journal of Sociology* 94 (1988): 84: "A reputation from the sociological point of view is an objective social fact, a prevailing collective definition based on what the relevant public 'knows' about the artist." Lang and Lang address why artists of similar ability are remembered differently in subsequent generations. Differences in artistic reputation are directly related to differences in the abilities and the zeal of the artist's reputational entrepreneurs in making their work publically available.

195. Schwartz, *Abraham Lincoln and the Forge of National Memory*, 297.

196. Schwartz, *Abraham Lincoln and the Forge of National Memory*, 11, calls strict "politics of memory" approaches nothing but "cynical muckraking." Cf. Michael Schudson, "The Present in the Past and the Past in the Present," *Communication* 11 (1989), 113, for a similar appraisal of the cynical nature of the "politics of memory."

197. Schwartz, in an article co-authored with Tong Zhang, came to a similar conclusion for Confucius: "Confucius and the Cultural Revolution: A Study in Collective Memory," *International Journal of Politics, Culture and Society* 11 (1997): 189–212.

198. Schwartz, *Abraham Lincoln and the Forge of National Memory*, 9. Emphasis his. In another place, he defines collective memory as "sense-making through time" (98). Cf. Blasi, *Making Charisma*, 10: "An appropriate scientific stance toward this kind of phenomenon requires our not forgetting either pole of the dialectic. Lincoln would not be Lincoln if he were not revered, but he would not be revered if he were not the individual who became famous."

199. Schwartz, *Abraham Lincoln and the Forge of National Memory*, 7, citing Geertz, "Religion as a Cultural System," in The *Interpretation of Cultures*, 93–94.

200. On the mirroring function of Lincoln, cf. Schwartz, *Abraham Lincoln in the Post-Heroic Era*, xi, 266. The "mirror" vs. "lamp" comparison in cultural and literary studies was made prominent by M. H. Abrams, *The Mirror and the Lamp: Romantic Theory and the Critical Tradition* (New York: Oxford University Press, 1953).

201. Shils, *Tradition*, 36, 38.

202. Cf. Schwartz, *Abraham Lincoln and the Forge of National Memory*, 222: "Different memories result, however, from a common method of making them meaningful: selecting the elements of Lincoln's life to be included in its representation and translating these into a form that will maintain their relevance."

203. Schwartz, *Abraham Lincoln and the Forge of National Memory*, 298: "Some might say that Progressive era entrepreneurs 'constructed' a new Lincoln or 'reconstructed' an old one, but it would be more precise to say that this era accentuated aspects of Lincoln's life no previous or subsequent era could see as vividly."

204. Schwartz, *Abraham Lincoln and the Forge of National Memory*, 211.

205. Schwartz, *Abraham Lincoln and the Forge of National Memory*, 206, citing Lincoln's words as given in the Congressional Record, February 12, 1908, HR 2282.

206. Schwartz, *Abraham Lincoln and the Forge of National Memory*, 210, citing Lincoln as referenced in a 1920 publication of the National Industrial Conference Board.

207. Cf. Mannheim, *Ideology and Utopia*, 251–252: "For each of the participants the 'object' has a more or less different meaning because it grows out of the whole of their respective frames of reference, as a result of which the meaning of the object in the perspective of the other person remains, at least in part, obscure."

208. Schwartz, *Abraham Lincoln and the Forge of National Memory*, 146, 152–155, 168, 256–292.

209. Cf. Schwartz, *Abraham Lincoln in the Post-Heroic Era*, 11: "Lincoln in text and picture is certainly 'constructed' in the sense that writers and artists represent him one way rather than another, but to assert that the episodes of his life are no more than 'representations' presumes knowledge of how reality differs from appearance. Without such knowledge, one can demonstrate that perceptions of Lincoln change, but one cannot determine which of those changes distort reality and which do not. Without knowing the past as it was, one cannot estimate how significantly perception distorts reality or how it affects Lincoln's place in American memory."

210. Schwartz, *Abraham Lincoln and the Forge of National Memory*, 223. Emphases mine. Cf. also 254: "But the exaggeration of Lincoln's virtues does not explain why he had become a model in the first place. Lincoln, in fact, was not a model because he was idealized; he was rather idealized because he was already a model. And he was already a model because of *real*, not imaginary, that is, constructed, accomplishments and traits." Emphasis mine.

211. Schwartz, *Abraham Lincoln and the Forge of National Memory*, 223.

212. Cf. Michael Lind, *What Lincoln Believed: The Values and Convictions of America's Greatest President* (New York: Doubleday, 2004), 191–232. Citation from p. 195. The development of Lincoln's thought on these issues can be traced in speeches found in Michael P. Johnson, ed., *Abraham Lincoln, Slavery, and the Civil War: Selected Writings and Speeches* (Bedford Series in History and Culture; Boston: Bedford Press, 2001) and more recently, Ronald C. White, Jr., *The Eloquent President: A Portrait of Lincoln through His Words* (New York: Random House, 2005).

213. Cf. Lind, *What Lincoln Believed*, 209. On the shifting thoughts of the late Lincoln, cf. Schwartz, *Abraham Lincoln in the Post-Heroic Era*, 13: "Realizing in the last years of his life that blacks would remain permanently in America, he favored their having equal political rights, but the prospect of integrating them into society on the basis of complete social equality was to him, as to most Americans of his time, problematic."

214. Lind, *What Lincoln Believed*, 214.

215. Cf. Gaddis, *The Landscape of History*, 2, 50, 128.

216. Cf. Shils, *Tradition*, 229: "Christianity in the lifetime of Jesus could still be considered by Jews and Gentiles and even by the first Christians as a deviant Jewish sect. Within fifty years of the death of Jesus, it was clear that it was much more than that."

217. On Paul as "Evangelist of the Entire World," cf. Pervo, *Making of Paul*, 12–13, 53, 59, and de Boer, "Images of Paul," 366–368.

218. Allison, Jr., *Constructing Jesus*, 10–20. We will return to Allison's historiographical categories in Chapter 7.

219. Translation from Schneemelcher, *New Testament Apocrypha*, 2.261.

220. Gregory Sterling, "From Apostle to the Gentiles to Apostle to the Church," 74–75, characterizes both Ephesians and Acts as late-first century c.e. memorializations of Paul's singular influence in creating the church as it was known at that time.

221. On the relationship between Paul's mission and martyrdom, cf. de Boer, "Pauline Images," 368–369. On the commemorative importance of martyrs, cf. Kirk, "Social and Cultural Memory," 19: "Martyrs, by definition heroic persons who have displayed steadfast commitment—to the death—to a set of emblematic virtues, attract intense cults of commemoration."

222. Gaddis, *Landscape of History*, 120.

223. The relevant primary sources are Iren., *Haer.* 1.26.2; Origen, *Hom. Jer.* 19.12; *Cels.* 5.66; Eus. *Hist. eccl.* 3.27.1–6; Epiphan., *Pan.* 28, 30; *Clem. Rec.* 1.70–71; *Epitula Petri* 2; and *Clem. Hom.* 17.13–19.

224. Language from Shils, *Tradition*, 266: "Where there are no precise rules and no custodianship which takes to itself, or has assigned to it and is acknowledged to possess, the powers of regulating and stipulating the tradition, as in the telling of fairy tales and legends, a great variety of possibilities of transmission of the tradition exists." Cf. also on Mannheim above.

225. Vansina, *Oral Tradition as History*, 19–21.

226. Vansina, *Oral Tradition as History*, 30.

227. Vansina, *Oral Tradition as History*, 153.

228. Cf., for example, Ernst Benz, "Das Paulusverständnis in der morgenländischen und abendländischen Kirche," *ZRGG* 3 (1951): 291, who characterizes the later Eastern reception of Paul as a reception of the Paul of the Corinthian correspondence, while the reception of Paul in the West was dependent on the Paul of Romans.

229. Benjamin Dunning has recently noted this with respect to Paul's views on human sexuality. Cf. his *Specters of Paul: Sexual Difference in Early Christian Thought* (Divinations: Rereading Late Ancient Religion; Philadelphia: University of Pennsylvania Press, 2011), 8, 23, 24, 168 n. 32.

230. Cf. Froehlich, "Which Paul?," 290: "Pauline pluralism was fed, on the one hand, by an appropriation of his legendary image with regional variations. On the other hand, more importantly, it was fed by the many unreconciled strands and the general versatility of Paul's own theologizing in the surviving remnants of his correspondence. What the historical Paul fervently desired but never accomplished the epistolary Paul finally achieved: It was he who became 'all things to all people' (1 Cor. 9:22)."

231. Cf. Vansina, *Oral Tradition as History*, 124: "Communication of oral tradition is part of the process of establishing collective representations."

232. Cf. Gross, *The Past in Ruins*, 17.

233. Cf. Shils, *Tradition*, 268.

234. Brown, "Limitation and Ingenuity," 219.

235. Brown, "Limitation and Ingenuity," 220.

236. Gaddis, *Landscape of History*, 115.

237. Cf. Halbwachs, *The Collective Memory*, 78, 86; and Zelizer, "Reading the Past Against the Grain," 216–217.

238. Mitchell, *The Heavenly Trumpet*, 428.

CHAPTER 5

1. Epigraph: Mitchell, *Iconology*, 47.

2. Cf. Tertullian, *Res.* 48.1.

3. Portions of this chapter first appeared in Benjamin L. White, "Reclaiming Paul?: Reconfiguration as Reclamation in *3 Corinthians*," *JECS* 17 (2009): 497–523. Permission to reproduce some of that article has been granted by the Johns Hopkins University Press.

4. Cf. Chapter 4 on "keying," "framing," and *"lieux de mémoire."*

5. Shils, *Tradition*, 217.

6. Shils, *Tradition*, 268.

7. Cf. Chapter 4 for Geertz and Schwartz on "models *of*" and "models *for*."

8. Several centuries ago, William Whiston, *A Collection of Authentick Records Belonging to the Old and New Testament, Part II* (London, 1728), and Wilhelm Rinck, *Das Sendschreiben der Korinther an den Apostel Paulus und das dritte Sendschreiben Pauli an die Korinther* (Heidelberg: E. I. Winter, 1823), argued for the authenticity of *3 Cor.* It is found between 2 Cor and Gal in most of the Armenian manuscripts. Zohrapian's edition of the Armenian Bible in 1805 placed the text in an appendix between the *Rest of the Evangelist John* and the *Prayer of Manasseh.*

9. The *editio princeps* of *P. Bodm.* X was published by Michel Testuz, *Papyrus Bodmer X–XII: Manuscrit du IIIe siècle* (Cologny-Geneva: Bibliotheca Bodmeriana, 1959). The contents of this papyrus codex include: I and II Peter, Jude, Psalms 33–34, *Nativity of Mary*, *3 Corinthians*, the eleventh *Ode of Solomon*, a fragment of a liturgical hymn, and the Easter homilies of Melito of Sardis. Snyder, *Acts of Paul*, 152–153, offers several qualifications for accepting *P. Bodmer* X as the base text of *3 Cor.*

10. For early critical editions of the Armenian, Latin, and Coptic manuscripts, cf. Paul Vetter, *Der apokryphe dritte Korintherbrief* (Vienna: Mechitharisten-Buchdruckerei, 1894); and Carl Schmidt, *Acta Pauli aus der Heidelberger Koptischen Papyrushandschrift Nr. 1* (Hildesheim: G. Olms, 1965 [1905]).

11. The shorter text of the letters is also found in the Heidelberg Papyrus (Coptic), the Armenian translation of Ephraim's Syriac commentary on *3 Corinthians*, and in part of the Latin tradition (manuscript "L": *Cod, Laon* 45).

12. For two recent and detailed histories of research on *3 Cor.*, including its textual history, cf. Vahan Hovhanessian, *Third Corinthians: Reclaiming Paul for Christian Orthodoxy* (Studies in Biblical Literature 18; New York: Peter Lang, 2000), 1–79, and Steve Johnston, "La Correspondance apocryphe entre Paul et les Corinthiens: un pseudépigraphe Paulinien au service de la polémique anti–gnostique de la fin du IIE siècle" (M.A. thesis, l'Université Laval, 2004), 1–77.

13. The citations of *3 Cor.* throughout this chapter will follow the traditional enumeration of the verses, but will be preceded by either a 1 (Letter from the Corinthians) or a 2 (Letter from Paul). All English translations are my own unless otherwise noted.

14. The use of the Fathers rather than Nag Hammadi as a starting point is justified inasmuch as *3 Cor.* is a proto-orthodox text that attempts to construct its opponents, as we will show, in typical heresiological fashion.

15. **Marcionites**: Martin Rist, "Pseudepigraphic Refutations of Marcionism," *JR* 22 (1942): 46–50; and "III Corinthians as a Pseudepigraphic Refutation of Marcionism," *The Iliff Review* 26 (1969): 56–58. **Valentinian or Ophite groups**: Hovhanessian, *Third Corinthians*, 129–131. **Saturnilus**: Thomas W. Mackay, "Content and Style in Two Pseudo-Pauline Epistles (3 Corinthians and the Epistle to the Laodiceans)," in *Apocryphal Writings of the Latter-Day Saints* (ed. C. W. Griggs; The Religious Studies Monograph Series 13; Provo, UT: Religious Studies Center, BYU, 1986), 224; Willy Rordorf, "Hérésie et orthodoxie selon la Correspondance apocryphe entre les Corinthiens et l'Apôtre Paul," in *Orthodoxie et hérésie dans l'Eglise ancienne: perspectives nouvelles* (ed. H.-D. Altendorf, et al.; Cahiers de la Revue de théologie et de philosophie 17; Genève: Revue de théologie et de philosophie, 1993), 57; and Peter W. Dunn, "Testing Pauline Pseudonymity: *3 Corinthians* and the Pastoral Epistles Compared," *Proceedings: Eastern Great Lakes and Midwest Biblical Societies* 20 (2000): 64–65. **Simon Magus**: A. F. J. Klijn, "The Apocryphal Correspondence Between Paul and the Corinthians," *VC* 17 (1963): 22.

16. I note recent problems with the terms "Gnostic" and "Gnosticism" in Chapter 2. Cf. Penny, "Pseudo–Pauline Letters," 310; Gerard Luttikhuizen, "The Apocryphal Correspondence with the Corinthians and the Acts of Paul," in *The Apocryphal Acts of Paul and Thecla*, 91; Steve Johnston, "La Correspondance apocryphe entre Paul et les Corinthiens: Problèmes relies à l'identification des adversaires," in *Colloque international. "L'évangile selon Thomas et les textes de Nag Hammadi." Québec, 29–31 mai 2003* (ed. L. Painchaud and P.-H. Poirier; Québec: Presses de l'Université Laval, 2007), 221–225; Pervo, *Making of Paul*, 104; and Snyder, *Acts of Paul*, 161–166.

17. The text of *P. Bodm.* X, corrected by both Testuz (the editor) as well as Thomas W. Mackay, "Observations on P. Bodmer X (Apocryphal Correspondence Between Paul and the Corinthian Saints)," *Papyrologica Bruxellensia* 18 (1979): 119–128, can be found with accentuation in Rordorf, "Hérésie et orthodoxie," 60–62.

18. Hovhanessian, *Third Corinthians*, 137. The other recent major monograph is Alberto D'Anna, *Terza lettera ai Corinzi. La risurrezione* (Letture cristiane del primo millenio 44; Milan: Pauline, 2009).

19. See J. Christiaan Beker, *Heirs of Paul: Their Legacy in the New Testament and the Church Today* (Grand Rapids, MI: Eerdmans, 1996 [1991]), 28.

20. Cf. also the later *Apostolic Constitutions* 6.8, which has taken over much of the *Didascalia*.

21. Gerd Lüdemann, "The Acts of the Apostles and the Beginnings of Simonian Gnosis," *NTS* 33 (1987): 421. On Simon as a constructed figure, cf. Mark Edwards, "Simon Magus, the Bad Samaritan," in *Portraits: Biographical Representation in the Greek and Latin Literature of the Roman Empire* (ed. M. J. Edwards and S. Swain; Oxford: Clarendon, 1997), 69–91; Alberto Ferreiro, *Simon Magus in Patristic, Medieval and Early Modern Traditions* (Studies in the History of Christian Traditions 125; Leiden: Brill, 2005); and Stephen Haar, *Simon Magus: the First Gnostic?* (BZNW 119; Berlin: Walter de Gruyter, 2003).

22. Cf. *Haer.* 3.12.12.

23. Cf. Glenn Snyder, *Acts of Paul*, 162–166.

24. Wilhelm Schneemelcher, *New Testament Apocrypha* (2 vols.; Louisville, KY: Westminster John Knox, 1992 [1989]), 2:255; and Willy Rordorf, "Actes de Paul," in *Écrits apocryphes chrétiens* (ed. F. Bovon and P. Geoltrain, 2 vols.; Paris: Gallimard, 1997), 1:1163.

25. *The Apocryphal New Testament* (Oxford: Clarendon Press, 1993), 380.

26. Hovhanessian, *Third Corinthians*, 77; and Bart D. Ehrman, *Lost Scriptures: Books that Did Not Make it into the New Testament* (Oxford: Oxford University Press, 2003), 158.

27. Testuz, *Papyrus Bodmer X–XII*, 35.

28. Cf. Rordorf, "Hérésie et orthodoxie," 22–35, and Hovhanessian, *Third Corinthians*, 47–56. Hovhanessian marshals together strong manuscript, patristic, con-

textual, theological, and stylistic evidence against the claim that *3 Cor.* was initially authored as a part of the *Acts of Paul.*

29. F. W. Danker, ed., *A Greek-English Lexicon of the New Testament and Other Early Christian Literature* (3rd ed.; Chicago: University of Chicago Press, 2000), 146.

30. H. G. Liddell and R. Scott, eds., *A Greek-English Lexicon* (9th ed.; Oxford: Clarendon, 1996 [1897]), 262.

31. The Greek texts and translations of Plutarch's *De curiositate* are from William Hembold, *Plutarch's Moralia, Vol. 6* (LCL 337; Cambridge, MA: Harvard University Press, 1962). I have given the individual English translations of the Loeb editions for Plutarch, Athenaeus, *2 Clement*, and the *Didache* in this section to show how in other contexts multiple translators have rendered this tricky word (group), none of which approaches the sense given by the modern translators of *3 Cor.*

32. The Greek text of Athenaeus is from S. Douglas Olson, *The Learned Banqueters, 2: Books III.106e–V* (LCL 208; Cambridge, MA: Harvard University Press, 2006), 536.

33. Translations of *2 Clem.* and the *Did.* are from Bart D. Ehrman, *The Apostolic Fathers.*

34. Cf. Testuz, *Papyrus Bodmer X–XII*, 34, for the manuscript evidence.

35. See Hovhanessian, *Third Corinthians*, 101; Rordorf, "Hérésie et orthodoxie," 45 n. 126; and Penny, "Pseudo–Pauline Letters," 303–306.

36. His authority as an Apostle of Christ, unmediated by the Jerusalem apostles, is also the subject of his rhetoric in Galatians 1–2. Note the similarities in language, but differences in rhetorical context, in Gal 1.17 (οὐδὲ ἀνῆλθον εἰς Ἱεροσόλυμα πρὸς **τοὺς πρὸ ἐμοῦ ἀποστόλους**) and *3 Cor.* 2.4. (**τῶν πρὸ ἐμοῦ ἀποστόλων** γενομένων).

37. Cf. David M. Moffitt, "Affirming the 'Creed': The Extent of Paul's Citation of an Early Christian Formula in 1 Cor 15, 3b–7," *ZNW* 99 (2008): 49–73, for a persuasive argument that the full appearance list is part of the pre-Pauline tradition.

38. J. Christiaan Beker, *Paul the Apostle: the Triumph of God in Life and Thought* (Philadelphia: Fortress Press, 1980), 125.

39. Cf. Joseph A. Fitzmyer, *First Corinthians: A New Translation with Introduction and Commentary* (AB 32; New Haven, CT: Yale University Press, 2008), 541. Cf. also Anders Eriksson, *Traditions as Rhetorical Proof: Pauline Argumentation in 1 Corinthians* (ConBNT 29; Stockholm: Almqvist & Wiksell International, 1998), 90–91.

40. Cf. Hans Conzelmann, *1 Corinthians: A Commentary on the First Epistle to the Corinthians* (Hermeneia; trans. J. W. Leitch; Philadelphia: Fortress Press, 1975 [1969]), 252–254; and Raymond F. Collins, *First Corinthians* (SP 7; Collegeville, MN: Liturgical Press, 1999), 531.

41. Cf. Anthony Thistleton, *The First Epistle to the Corinthians* (NIGTC; Grand Rapids, MI: Eerdmans, 2000), 1189.

42. Cf. Collins, *First Corinthians*, 532: "Paul is concerned that his apostolate be considered as similar to that of those who were among the earliest witnesses to the resurrection, the leaders of the Jerusalem community, Cephas and James, and the Twelve of earliest Christian memory." Notice that Collins uses "similar" and not "dependent."

43. Cf. Penny, "Pseudo–Pauline Letters," 304. Cf. the end of this chapter for some comments on Paul and the Apostles in Acts.

44. Rordorf, "Hérésie et orthodoxie," 45; and Hovhanessian, *Third Corinthians*, 140.

45. Hovhanessian, *Third Corinthians*, 63.

46. Paul is never directly referred to as an apostle in these letters, as Penny, "Pseudo-Pauline Letters," 303, has reinforced. However, given that "the others" (1.4) probably means "the other apostles" and that Paul is presented as the defender of apostolic faith, there is no reason to make too much of this point. On the technical language for the transmission of tradition, cf. Eriksson, *Traditions as Rhetorical Proof*, 73–134.

47. Mackay, "Content and Style," 218–220; Rist, "III Corinthians," 53–56; Penny, "Pseudo-Pauline Letters," 292–293; and Hovhanessian, *Third Corinthians*, 96–97.

48. Cf. Gamble, *Books and Readers*, 59–63, and Stanley Porter, "When and How was the Pauline Canon Compiled?," 95–127, on early Pauline letter collections.

49. Cf. William D. Mounce, *Pastoral Epistles* (WBC 46; Nashville, TN: Thomas Nelson Publishers, 2000), civ–cxii, for comprehensive lists of the so-called non–Pauline language of the Pastorals. Some recent studies on the Pastorals have questioned the propriety of viewing the Pastoral Epistles as a literary and theological unity. Cf. Michael Prior, *Paul the Letter-Writer and the Second Letter to Timothy* (JSNTSS 23; Sheffield: JSOT Press, 1989), 61–90; Jerome Murphy-O'Connor, "2 Timothy Contrasted with 1 Timothy and Titus," *RB* 98 (1991): 403–418; Luke Timothy Johnson, *The First and Second Letters to Timothy: a New Translation with Introduction and Commentary* (AB 35A; New York: Doubleday, 2001); *Letters to Paul's Delegates: 1 Timothy, 2 Timothy, Titus* (Valley Forge, PA: Trinity Press International, 1996); James D. Miller, *The Pastorals Letters as Composite Documents* (SNTSMS 93; Cambridge: Cambridge University Press, 1997); William Richards, *Difference and Distance in Post-Pauline Christianity: an Epistolary Analysis of the Pastorals* (Studies in Biblical Literature 44; Bern: Peter Lang, 2002); Rüdiger Fuchs, *Unerwartete Unterschiede: müssen wir unsere Ansichten über "die" Pastoralbriefe revidieren?* (Bibelwissenschaftliche Monographien 12; Wuppertal: R. Brockhaus, 2003); J. Herzer, "Abschied vom Konses?: Die Pseudepigraphie der Pastoralbriefe als Herausforderung an die neutestamentliche Wissenschaft," *TLZ* 129 (2004): 1267–1282; Gerd Häfner, "Das Corpus Pastorale als literarisches Konstrukt," *TQ* 187 (2007): 258–273; and James W. Aageson, *Paul, the Pastoral Epistles, and the Early Church*, 57–89, among others. I am sympathetic to this growing trend, but regardless of where the scholarship leads on this issue, the "Pastoral Epistles" are undeniably ho-

mogeneous in their portrayal of Paul as the defender of "sound teaching." Cf. Aageson, *Paul, the Pastoral Epistles, and the Early Church*, 63–64, 69–70.

50. Cf. Rist, "Pseudepigraphic Refutations of Marcionism," 54; and I. Howard Marshall, *A Critical and Exegetical Commentary on the Pastoral Epistles* (ICC; Edinburgh: T&T Clark, 1999), 41.

51. 1 Tim 1.10; 4.1, 6, 13, 16; 5.17; 6.1, 3; 2 Tim 3.10, 16; 4.3; Titus 1.9; 2.1, 7, 10.

52. Cf. also 1 Tim 1.10; Titus 1.9; 2.1.

53. See *BDAG*, 399.

54. Cf. also Pervo, *Making of Paul*, 104: "In conclusion, this text is an attempt to say what the Pastor would have said had he lived in the second half of the second century."

55. I do not think it is plausible to suggest that the language of the Pastorals might be dependent upon *3 Cor.*

56. By "secondary orality" I follow Risto Uro's use of the term in *"Thomas and the Oral Gospel Tradition," Thomas at the Crossroads: Essays on the Gospel of Thomas* (ed. Risto Uro; Edinburgh: T&T Clark, 1998), 8–32. Secondary orality is ultimately dependent upon a written text made accessible through oral/aural transmission.

57. The authoritative work on the use of the Pastorals in the second century is Carsten Looks's *Das Anvertraute bewahren: Die Rezeption der Pastoralbriefe im 2. Jahrhundert* (Münchner Theologische Beiträge 3; München: Herbert Utz Verlag, 1999). Looks examines the entire range of second-century evidence, dividing potential instances of dependence into the following categories: sicher = safe/secure; sehr wahrscheinlich = very probable; gut möglich bis wahrscheinlich = good possibility to probable; möglich, aber unsicher = possible, but uncertain; unwahrscheinlich = unlikely; ausgeschlossen = impossible. In the case of *3 Cor.*, he labels the first two and last entries in Table 5.1 above as "very probable."

58. On 2 Tim 2.8 as a creedal formulation incorporated by the author, cf. Martin Dibelius and Hans Conzelmann, *The Pastoral Epistles* (trans. P. Buttolph and A. Yarbro; Hermeneia; Philadelphia: Fortress Press, 1972 [1955]), 108; and James D. Miller, *The Pastoral Letters as Composite Documents*, 109.

59. Cf. Penny, "Pseudo–Pauline Letters," 310–311.

60. Hovhanessian, *Third Corinthians*, 66, argues for the originality of the title. He suggests that *P. Bodm.* X represents the pre-canonical *3 Cor.* and that the title was dropped as it entered the canon of the Syriac church and was assimilated to Paul's other letters, which don't have titles.

61. Jewett, *Paul's Anthropological Terms: a Study of Their Use in Conflict Settings* (AGJU 10; Leiden: Brill, 1971), 9–10. Cf. Jorunn Økland, "Genealogies of the Self: Materiality, Personal Identity, and the Body in Paul's Letters to the Corinthians," *Metamorphoses*, 91: "In the heat of argument, Paul can utilize any philosophical model at hand." Cf. also Outi Lehtipuu, "'Flesh and Blood Cannot Inherit the Kingdom

of God': The Transformation of the Flesh in the Early Christian Debates," in *Metamorphoses*, 155: "Paul is not quite consistent in his use of these words."

62. Rudolf Bultmann, *Theology of the New Testament* (trans. K. Grobel; New York: Charles Scribner's Sons, 1951), 194–198.

63. Bultmann, *Theology of the New Testament*, 241–242, 334–336.

64. Daniel Boyarin, *A Radical Jew: Paul and the Politics of Identity* (Berkeley: University of California Press, 1994), 71–72.

65. Boyarin, *A Radical Jew*, 73.

66. Cf. Robert H. Gundry, *Sōma in Biblical Theology: with Emphasis on Pauline Anthropology* (SNTSMS 29; Cambridge: Cambridge University Press, 1976).

67. Gundry, *Sōma in Biblical Theology*, 162.

68. Gundry, *Sōma in Biblical Theology*, 162. Cf. Jorunn Økland, "Genealogies of the Self," in *Metamorphoses*, 91.

69. Gundry, *Sōma in Biblical Theology*, 161.

70. Bultmann, *Theology of the New Testament*, 192.

71. Cf. Boyarin, *A Radical Jew*, 59–64; Paula Fredriksen, "Vile Bodies: Paul and Augustine on the Resurrection of the Flesh," in *Biblical Hermeneutics in Historical Perspective: Studies in Honor of Karlfried Froehlich on His Sixtieth Birthday* (ed. M. S. Burrows and P. Rorem; Grand Rapids, MI: Eerdmans, 1991), 75–82; Walter Burkert, "Towards Plato and Paul: The 'Inner' Human Being," in *Ancient and Modern Perspectives on the Bible and Culture: Essays in Honor of Hans Dieter Betz* (ed. A. Y. Collins; Atlanta, GA: Scholars Press, 1998), 59–82; Emma Wasserman, "The Death of the Soul in Romans 7: Revisiting Paul's Anthropology in Light of Hellenistic Moral Psychology," *JBL* 126 (2007): 793–816; and George H. Van Kooten, *Paul's Anthropology in Context: The Image of God, Assimilation to God, and Tripartite Man in Ancient Judaism, Ancient Philosophy and Early Christianity* (WUNT 232; Tübingen: Mohr Siebeck, 2008), 298–312. Several others contend that Paul is subverting Platonic language. Cf. Gerhard Sellin, *Der Streit um die Auferstehung der Toten: Eine religionsgeschichtliche und exegetische Untersuchung von 1 Kor 15* (FRLANT 138; Göttingen: Vandenhoeck & Ruprecht, 1986), who argues that Paul combats a Platonic/Philonic anthropology in 1 Cor 15 (mediated through Apollos) by starting with an agreed-upon fact, the bodily resurrection of Jesus (1 Cor 15.1–11), and then moving to show the unity between Christ and the believer. Similar, though dealing more with the "inner man" language in Paul, is Theo Heckel, *Der Innere Mensch: Die paulinische Verarbeitung eines platonischen Motivs* (WUNT 2.53; Tübingen: J. C. B. Mohr (Paul Siebeck), 1993); and "Body and Soul in Saint Paul," in *Psyche and Soma: Physicians and Metaphysicians on the Mind-Body Problem from Antiquity to Enlightenment* (ed. J. P. Wright and P. Potter; Oxford: Clarendon Press, 2000), 117–132, who argues that Paul often invokes the Platonic language of his opponents and then subtly stands it on its head. Cf. also, in this regard, Christoph Markschies, "Die platonische Metapher vom 'inneren Menschen':

Eine Brücke zwischen antiker Philosophie und altchristlicher Theologie," *ZKG* 105 (1994): 1–17; and Hans Dieter Betz, "The Concept of the 'Inner Human Being' (ὁ ἔσω ἄνθρωπος) in the Anthropology of Paul," *NTS* 46 (2000): 315–324. Boyarin highlights Philo as a Jewish precedent. Others have pointed to the literature at Qumran as providing a conceptual background for Paul's understanding of flesh and spirit. Cf. K. G. Kuhn, "Πειρασμός – Ἁμαρτία – Σάρξ im Neuen Testament und die damit zusammenhängenden Vorstellungen" *ZTK* 49 (1952): 200–222, and more recently Jörg Frey, "The Notion of 'Flesh' in 4QInstruction and the Background of Pauline Usage," in *Sapiential, Liturgical and Poetical Texts from Qumran* (ed. D. K. Falk, F. G. Martinez and E. M. Schuller; STDJ 35; Leiden: Brill, 2000), 197–226.

72. James Dunn, *The Theology of Paul the Apostle* (Grand Rapids, MI: Eerdmans, 1998), 66, concludes that σάρξ in Paul is essentially "human mortality/frailty."

73. Boyarin, *A Radical Jew*, 77; and Gundry, *Sōma in Biblical Theology*, 137–138.

74. Boyarin, *A Radical Jew*, 63–64; and Fredriksen, "Vile Bodies," 80.

75. Dunn, *Theology of Paul the Apostle*, 463.

76. Cf. Dale B. Martin, *The Corinthian Body* (New Haven, CT: Yale University Press, 1995), 123–129; Troels Engberg-Pedersen, "Complete and Incomplete Transformation in Paul—a Philosophical Reading of Paul on Body and Spirit," in *Metamorphoses*, 123–146; *Cosmology and Self in the Apostle Paul: The Material Spirit* (New York: Oxford University Press, 2011); and Økland, "Genealogies of the Self," 91, 94: "The fact that he does not do so faithfully, or does not always appear as a Stoic philosopher does not prevent him from sometimes doing it. This just means that his texts must be interpreted on a text-to-text basis. . . . Still among the options available, I see Paul as coming closest to an Aristotelian/Stoic line of argument on this topic—which of course does not prevent him from sounding more like a Platonist elsewhere."

77. Martin, *Corinthian Body*, 15.

78. For Stoic primary texts on the embodiment of all things, including the active principle, πνεῦμα, cf. A. A. Long and D. N. Sedley, *The Hellenistic Philosophers* (2 vols.; Cambridge: Cambridge University Press, 1987), 1:272–274. For short descriptions of the Stoic position, cf. R. W. Sharples, *Stoics, Epicureans and Sceptics: an Introduction to Hellenistic Philosophy* (London: Routledge, 1996), 43–55, 67–78; and Heinrich von Staden, "Body, Soul, and Nerves: Epicurus, Herophilus, Erasistratus, the Stoics, and Galen," in *Psyche and Soma*, 96–105.

79. Martin, *Corinthian Body*, 128. Emphasis his.

80. Martin, *Corinthian Body*, 104–136. Cf., more recently, Jorunn Økland, "Genealogies of the Self," 89, 91–92; and Troels Engberg-Pedersen, "Complete and Incomplete Transformation in Paul," 145–146.

81. Gundry, *Sōma in Biblical Theology*, 165.

82. Jewett, *Paul's Anthropological Terms*, 454, calls this the "traditional Judaic use of σάρξ."

83. Gundry, *Sōma in Biblical Theology*, 167.

84. Johnson, "On Removing a Trump Card: Flesh and Blood and the Reign of God," *BBR* 13 (2003): 175–192. Citation from 181.

85. Johnson, "On Removing a Trump Card," 182.

86. Johnson, "On Removing a Trump Card," 183.

87. Johnson, "On Removing a Trump Card," 190.

88. Cf. Lehtipuu, "Transformation of the Flesh," 150: "However, both Paul and other early traditions of resurrection were ambiguous enough to allow for diverging views to develop."

89. Cf. 2.16: "For Christ Jesus saved all flesh by his own body (τῷ γὰρ ἰδίῳ σώματι Χριστὸς Ἰησοῦς πᾶσαν ἔσωσε σάρκα)."

90. Cf. 2.31–32 and 1 Cor 15.20.

91. I take this as meaning that there will be no resurrection of the flesh for those who deny such an event. Their fate is fiery damnation (2.37). Hovhanessian, *Third Corinthians*, 123, disagrees. He takes the phrase to mean that "there is no resurrection according to the teachings of those who reject the resurrection of the flesh."

92. On the continuity/identity between pre-mortem life and post-mortem resurrection in the early Church Fathers, cf. Harry A. Wolfson, "Immortality and Resurrection in the Philosophy of the Church Fathers," *Harvard Divinity School Bulletin* 22 (1957): 5–40.

93. Peter Dunn, "The Influence of 1 Corinthians on the *Acts of Paul*," *SBLSP* 35 (1996): 446–447, has ably defended this allusion to 1 Cor 15 against the arguments for an alternative Jewish, non-Pauline, tradition by Rordorf, "Hérésie et orthodoxie," 53–56.

94. Hovhanessian, *Third Corinthians*, 123.

95. Dale Martin, *Corinthian Body*, 125; Ben Witherington, III, *Conflict & Community in Corinth: a Socio-Rhetorical Commentary on 1 and 2 Corinthians* (Grand Rapids, MI: Eerdmans, 1995), 308; and Anthony Thistleton, *The First Epistle to the Corinthians*, 1271.

96. Dale Martin, *Corinthian Body*, 127, argues that these contrasting qualities should be viewed hierarchically, not ontologically. One set of bodily qualities is superior to the other.

97. Cf. David Satran, "Fingernails and Hair: Anatomy and Exegesis in Tertullian," *JTS* 40 (1989): 116–120.

98. Cf. Penny, "Pseudo–Pauline Letters," 302.

99. Cf. H. B. Swete, "The Resurrection of the Flesh," *JTS* 18 (1917): 135–141.

100. Cf. Martin, *Corinthian Body*, 122–123.

101. J. G. Davies, "Factors Leading to the Emergence of Belief in the Resurrection of the Flesh," *JTS* 23 (1972): 448–455, describes four factors leading to the belief in the resurrection of the flesh: (1) early resurrection appearance stories combined with the concept of Jesus as "first-fruits"; (2) millenarian thought among many

Christian thinkers of the second century; (3) reaction to Gnostic denigration of the flesh; and (4) the acceptance of an increasingly Hellenistic anthropology.

102. The LXX of Job 19.26 reads: ἀναστήσαι τὸ δέρμα μου τὸ ἀνατλῶν ταῦτα παρὰ γὰρ κυρίου ταῦτά μοι συνετελέσθη. Note the switch in *1 Clement* from δέρμα to σάρξ.

103. In the New Testament, cf. Matt 10.8; 11.5/par.; 14.12/par.; 17.9/par.; 22.31/par.; 27.64; 28.7; Luke 16.31; 24.46; John 2.22; 5.21; 12.1, 9, 17; 20.9; 21.14; Acts 3.15; 4.2, 10; 10.41; 13.30, 34; 17.3, 31, 32; 23.6; 24.21; 26.8, 23; Rom 1.4; 4.17, 24; 6.4, 9, 13; 7.4; 8.11; 10.7, 9; 11.15; 1 Cor 15; 2 Cor 1.9; Gal 1.1; Eph 1.20; 5.14; Phil 3.11; Col 1.18; 2.12; 1 Thess 1.10; 4.16; 2 Tim 2.8; Heb 6.2; 11.19, 35; 13.12; 1 Pet 1.3, 21; and Rev 1.5; 20.5.

104. For the relevant comparative texts in early Judaism, cf. W. D. Davies and Dale C. Allison, Jr., *A Critical and Exegetical Commentary on the Gospel According to Saint Matthew* (ICC; 3 vols.; Edinburgh: T&T Clark, 1997), 3:227–230.

105. A. H. C. van Eijk, "Resurrection–Language: Its Various Meanings in Early Christian Literature," *StPatr* 12 (1975): 271–276.

106. Martin, *The Corinthian Body*, 124. For recent monographs on the early Christian belief in the resurrection of Jesus, as well as the development of the doctrine of the resurrection of the flesh, cf. Gunnar af Hällström, *Carnis Resurrectio: The Interpretation of a Credal Formula* (Commentations Humanarum Litterarum 86; Helsinki: Societas Scientiarum Fennica, 1988); Horacio E. Lona, *Über die Auferstehung des Fleisches: Studien zur frühchristlichen Eschatologie* (BZNW 66; Berlin: Walter de Gruyter, 1993); Friedrich Avemarie and Hermann Lichtenberger, eds., *Auferstehung = Resurrection: the Fourth Durham-Tübingen Research Symposium "Resurrection, Transfiguration and Exaltation in Old Testament, Ancient Judaism and Early Christianity" (Tübingen, September, 1999)* (WUNT 135; Tübingen: Mohr Siebeck, 2001); Claudia Setzer, *Resurrection of the Body in Early Judaism and Early Christianity: Doctrine, Community, and Self-Definition* (Leiden: Brill, 2004); Dale Allison, *Resurrecting Jesus: The Earliest Christian Tradition and Its Interpreters* (New York: T&T Clark, 2005); and Jürgen Becker, *Die Auferstehung Jesu Christi nach dem Neuen Testament: Ostererfahrung und Osterverständnis im Urchristentum* (Tübingen: Mohr Siebeck, 2007). Earlier literature is cited in Gundry, *Sōma in Biblical Theology*, 166 n. 2.

107. Cf. Outi Lehtipuu, "The Transformation of the Flesh," 150.

108. Cf. Swete, "The Resurrection of the Flesh," 137; Nielsen, *Adam and Christ*, 80–86; Davies, "Factors," 453–454; Pieter J. Lalleman, "The Resurrection in the Acts of Paul," in *The Apocryphal Acts of Paul and Thecla*, 129, 140; and Dunn, *The Theology of Paul the Apostle*, 73.

109. Davies, "Factors," 448.

110. English translation from J. K. Elliott, *The Apocryphal New Testament: a Collection of Apocryphal Christian Literature in an English Translation based on M. R. James* (Oxford: Clarendon Press, 1999 [1993]). Cf. Rensberger, "As the Apostle Teaches," 88–92, 166.

111. Shils, *Tradition*, 214.
112. Nora, *Realms of Memory*, 1: xvii.
113. Halbwachs, *On Collective Memory*, 222.
114. Halbwachs, *On Collective Memory*, 224–225.
115. Schwartz, *Abraham Lincoln and the Forge of National Memory*, 226.
116. Clifford Geertz, "Ideology as a Cultural System," in *The Interpretation of Cultures*, 215, cited in Schwartz, *Abraham Lincoln and the Forge of National Memory*, 215.
117. On the importance of Ephesians for Origen, cf. Richard A. Layton, "Origen as a Reader of Paul: A Study of the *Commentary on Ephesians*" (Ph.D. diss., University of Virginia, 1996), 305–311, 331–335; "Recovering Origin's Pauline Exegesis: Exegesis and Eschatology in the *Commentary on Ephesians*," *JECS* 8 (2000): 374; and Ronald E. Heine, *The Commentaries of Origen and Jerome on St Paul's Epistle to the Ephesians* (Oxford Early Christian Studies; Oxford: Oxford University Press, 2002), 48. Luther's *Preface to St. Paul's Epistle to the Romans* begins: "This letter is truly the most important piece in the New Testament. It is purest Gospel. It is well worth a Christian's while not only to memorize it word for word but also to occupy himself with it daily, as though it were the daily bread of the soul. It is impossible to read or to meditate on this letter too much or too well. The more one deals with it, the more precious it becomes and the better it tastes."
118. Aageson, *Paul, the Pastorals, and the Early Church*, 1–2.
119. Cf. also Pervo, *Making of Paul*, 102.
120. Schwartz, *Abraham Lincoln and the Forge of National Memory*, 22.

CHAPTER 6

1. Epigraph: MacIntyre, *After Virtue*, 122.
2. Emphases mine. Portions of this chapter first appeared in Benjamin L. White, "How to Read a Book: Irenaeus and the Pastoral Epistles Reconsidered," *VC* 65 (2011): 125–149. Permission to reproduce portions of that article has been granted by E. J. Brill.
3. Cf. D. Jeffrey Bingham, "Irenaeus Reads Romans 8: Resurrection and Renovation," in *Early Patristic Readings of Romans*, 114: "He [Irenaeus] studied Paul's material within the context of an exegetical controversy."
4. Richard A. Norris, Jr., "Irenaeus' Use of Paul in His Polemic Against the Gnostics," in *Paul and the Legacies of Paul*, 79–98; David Balás, "The Use and Interpretation of Paul in Irenaeus' Five Books *Adversus Haereses*," *SecCent* 9 (1992): 27–39; Rolf Noormann, *Irenäus als Paulusinterpret: Zur Rezeption und Wirkung der paulinischen und deuteropaulinischen Briefe im Werk des Irenäus von Lyon* (WUNT 2.66; Tübingen: J. C. B. Mohr (Paul Siebeck), 1994); and Ben Blackwell, "Paul and Irenaeus," in *Paul and the Second Century*, 190–206. Cf. also Elio Peretto, *La Lettera ai Romani, cc 1–8, nell'*

Adversus Haereses d'Ireneo (Vetera christianorum 6; Bari: Università di Bari [Istituto di Letteratura Cristiana Antica], 1971).

5. More general studies of Irenaeus's life, theology, and polemic can be found in F. R. Montgomery Hitchcock, *Irenaeus of Lugdunum: a Study of His Teaching* (Cambridge: Cambridge University Press, 1914); John Lawson, *The Biblical Theology of Saint Irenaeus* (London: Epworth Press, 1948); Gustaf Wingren, *Man and the Incarnation: A Study in the Biblical Theology of Irenaeus* (trans. Ross Mackenzie; Edinburgh: Oliver & Boyd, 1959 [1947]); Alfred Bengsch, *Heilsgeschichte und Heilswissen: Eine Untersuchung zur Struktur und Entfaltung des Theologischen Denkens im Werk "Adversus Haereses" des Hl. Irenäus von Lyon* (ETS 3; Leipzig: St. Benno, 1957); André Benoit, *Saint Irénée: Introduction à l'étude de sa théologie* (Études d'histoire et de philosophie religieuses 52; Paris: Presses Universitaires de France, 1960); Gérard Vallée, *A Study in Anti-Gnostic Polemics: Irenaeus, Hippolytus and Epiphanius* (Studies in Christianity and Judaism 1; Waterloo: Wilfrid Laurier University Press, 1981), 9–40; Jacques Fantino, *La Théologie d'Irénée: Lecture des Écritures en réponse à l'exégèse gnostique— Une approche trinitaire* (Paris: Cerf, 1994); Denis Minns, *Irenaeus* (Outstanding Christian Thinkers; London: Geoffrey Chapman, 1994); *Irenaeus: An Introduction* (London: T&T Clark, 2010); Mary A. Donovan, *One Right Reading?: A Guide to Irenaeus* (Collegeville, MN: Liturgical Press, 1997); Robert M. Grant, *Irenaeus of Lyon* (The Early Church Fathers; London: Routledge, 1997); Eric Osborn, *Irenaeus of Lyons* (Cambridge: Cambridge University Press, 2001); and Paul Foster and Sara Parvis, eds., *Irenaeus: Life, Scripture, Legacy* (Minneapolis: Fortress Press, 2012). Important bibliography from 1970–1984 can be found in Mary A. Donovan, "Irenaeus in Recent Scholarship," *SecCent* 4 (1984): 219–241.

6. Johannes Werner, *Der Paulinismus des Irenaeus: Eine kirchen- und dogmengeschichtliche Untersuchung über das Verhältnis des Irenaeus zu der paulinischen Briefsammlung und Theologie* (TUGAL 6.2; Leipzig: J. C. Hinrichs, 1889).

7. Werner, *Paulinismus*, 8, reduces the number (324 citations) given in the index of W.W. Harvey, *Sancti Irenaei Episcopi Lugdunensis: Libros quinque adversus haereses* (Cambridge: Cambridge University Press, 1857). J. Hoh, *Die Lehre des Hl. Irenäus über das Neue Testament* (NTAbh 7; Münster: Aschendorff, 1919), 198, puts the number of direct citations at 247 and the number of indirect at 95 (although on p. 38 n. 4 he puts the number of direct citations at 248). More recent are Bruce Metzger, *The Canon of the New Testament*, 154, who counted 280, and Mark Olson, *Irenaeus, the Valentinian Gnostics, and the Kingdom of God*, 127–141, who lists 333 references to Pauline texts. The differences, as has been pointed out by D. H. Warren, "The Text of the Apostle," 314, are related to how any individual modern interpreter distinguishes between overt citations and indirect allusions. Warren, "Text of the Apostle," 294–317, explores at length the mechanics of Irenaeus's citations of Paul.

8. Werner, *Paulinismus*, 8: Rom–54 citations; 1 Cor–68; 2 Cor–13; Gal–24; Eph–16; Col–7; 1 Thess–2; 2 Thess–9; 1 Tim–2; 2 Tim–2; Titus–2.

9. Werner, *Paulinismus*, 33, 38.

10. Werner, *Paulinismus*, 44. Greek and Latin citations are given from the critical edition of Adelin Rousseau and Louis Doutreleau, *Irénée de Lyon: Contre les Hérésies* (SC; 5 vols.; Paris: Cerf, 1965–1982).

11. Werner, *Paulinismus*, 46–58, 214. Irenaeus marks, for Werner, a transitional phase in the acceptance of the Pauline letters as Scripture.

12. Werner, *Paulinismus*, 96–103.

13. Werner, *Paulinismus*, 212.

14. Werner, *Paulinismus*, 131, 137.

15. Werner, *Paulinismus*, 148–149. Cf. Wilhelm Schneemelcher, "Paulus in der griechischen Kirche," 19.

16. Werner, *Paulinismus*, 47, 214.

17. Cf. Eva Aleith, *Paulusverständnis in der alten Kirche*, 70–81, where she concludes that "Die Mißverständnisse sind zwar unleugbar" (80) and that Irenaeus answers many theological problems "in nicht paulinischem Sinne" (81). Cf. also the conclusion of Schneemelcher, "Paulus in der griechischen Kirche," 19: "Allerdings darf nicht verschwiegen werden, daß trotzdem der Abstand zwischen Irenäus und Paulus vielfach erstaunlich groß ist."

18. Cf. Lawson, *Biblical Theology*, 186–197, 224–229, 245–251 for summaries of Werner and other Protestant interpreters of Irenaeus in his wake (Ritschl, Loofs, Seeberg, Bousset, and Harnack, among others).

19. Dassmann, *Der Stachel im Fleisch*, 312. My translation from the German: "Werner mißt Irenäus an einem eingeengten Paulinismus entsprechend dem Paulusverständnis *seiner* Zeit, ohne eine legitime Weiterentwicklung und die Übersetzung paulinischer Gedanken im Hinblick auf neue theologische Fragen gelten zu lassen." Emphasis original. Cf. also Hoh, *Die Lehre des Hl. Irenäus*, 114, from an earlier period: "wenn man lutherische Prinzipien mit Paulinismus gleich setzt, kann W[erner] allerdings sagen, daß Ir[enaeus] dem Verständnis Pauli meilenfern geblieben ist."

20. The Greek of *Haer.* 1.6.3 (fr. gr. 1.630–3) reads: Διὸ δὴ καὶ τὰ ἀπειρημένα πάντα ἀδεῶς οἱ τελειότατοι πράττουσιν αὐτῶν, περὶ ὧν αἱ γραφαὶ διαζεξαιοῦνται τοὺς ποιοῦντας αὐτὰ βασιλείαν Θεοῦ μὴ κληρονομήσειν. In the early-twentieth century, cf. Hitchcock, *Irenaeus*, 223–224, and Hoh, *Die Lehre des Hl. Irenäus*, 64–65, 90–91. Hoh, 64, concedes that Werner did make note of *Haer.* 1.6.3, but that "sucht sie daher in die Ecke zu drücken." Cf. now André Benoit, *Saint Irénée*, 136–141; Pierre Nautin, "Irénée et la canonicité des Epîtres pauliniennes," *RHR* 182 (1972): 113–130; Dassmann, *Der Stachel im Fleisch*, 301–305; Rensberger, "As the Apostle Teaches," 317–318, 320; Olson, *Irenaeus*, 62–63; Warren, "The Text of the Apostle," 298–299; and Denis Farkasfalvy, "Theology of Scripture in St. Irenaeus," *RBén* 78 (1968): 331–332, the latter of whom shows how the Spirit is

said to have spoken through Paul in the same ways that it had to the prophets and other Apostles (*Haer.* 3.7.2; 4.8.1). The Pauline Epistles may also be deemed "Scripture" in *Haer.* 1.8.2–3; 1.9.1; 3.12.12; 4.pref.1; and 5.14.4. The debate over whether or not Irenaeus ever calls Paul's letters γραφή is marginalized, to some extent, however, by the variegated ways in which Irenaeus uses this term for a whole range of writings, from his own (*Haer.* 3.6.4; 3.17.4; 5. pref.1) to his opponents' (*Haer.* 1.20.1; 3.3.3). Cf. Hitchcock, *Irenaeus*, 226.

21. Cf. Dassmann, *Der Stachel im Fleisch*, 305–313, for a short review of Werner and the shift occurring in the 1970s. Mark Olson, *Irenaeus*, 2, 81, represents the extreme version of this trend, declaring that Irenaeus "grasp[ed] the essential elements of Paul's thought" and that he normally arrived at the "natural sense of Paul's letters." Olson ends up making too many concessions, however, to take these statements seriously (cf. 84–85 on Irenaeus's readings of 2 Cor 4.4, 1 Cor 3.7 and Eph 5.30). He hedges, importantly, on Irenaeus's reading of 1 Cor 15.50 as well (96).

22. Andrew J. Bandstra, "Paul and an Ancient Interpreter: a Comparison of the Teaching of Redemption in Paul and Irenaeus," *CTJ* 5 (1970): 43–63, argued that Irenaeus's teaching on redemption (particularly his emphases on Christ's victory over sin, death and Satan, as well as the infusion of immortality through the Spirit) closely parallels Paul's, while noting some differences. Cf. the earlier conclusion of Lawson, *Biblical Theology*, 187–188: "In reply we may say that S. Irenaeus was nearer to an understanding of S. Paul's estimate of Christ's death than were many later Latin and Reformation theologians." Ben C. Blackwell, *Christosis: Pauline Soteriology in Light of Deification in Irenaeus and Cyril of Alexandria* (WUNT 2.314; Tübingen: Mohr Siebeck, 2011), has most recently argued in this same vein.

23. John S. Coolidge, "The Pauline Basis of the Concept of Scriptural Form in Irenaeus," in *The Center for Hermeneutical Studies in Hellenistic and Modern Culture* (ed. Wilhelm Wuellner; Berkeley, CA: The Center, 1973), 1, argued that Irenaeus's defense of the unity of Scripture was rooted in Pauline themes and that Irenaeus made "consistent inferences from [Paul's] thought." Irenaeus, for example, defends the unity of the Jewish Scriptures and the canonical Gospels and Paul through an appeal to the Pauline image of the unified body of Christ (*Haer.* 4.20.6; 4.32.1; 4.33.10). Moreover, the unity of Scripture and the history it portrays (pointing to Christ) is described throughout *Adversus haereses* with the language of Ephesians 1.10: ἀνακεφαλαίωσις/recapitulatio (cf. 3.18.1, 7; 3.22.3; 4.6.2; 4.38.1; 5.23.2). The Pauline declaration of cosmic unity wrought in Christ ("the summing up of all things in him"; Eph 1.10) became such a fixed part of Irenaeus's thought that it can be described by Coolidge as "the key to his whole biblical theology" (11). Irenaeus understood Ephesians 1.10, however, in light of Romans 5.12–21. Christ's recapitulation of all things is both a summation of humanity under Adam and "a reversal of its outcome" (13–14).

He interprets it in the context of salvation-history and not the cosmos. Cf. also E. Scharl, *Recapitulatio mundi: Der Rekapitulationsbegriff des Hl. Irenäus und seine Anwendung auf die Körperwelt* (Freiburger theologische Studien 60; Freiburg: Herder, 1941); Paul Potter, "St Irenaeus and 'Recapitulation,'" *Dominican Studies* 4 (1951): 192–200; Maurice Wiles, *The Divine Apostle*, 73–74; Benoit, *Saint Irénée*, 225–229; Farkasfalvy, "Theology of Scripture in St. Irenaeus," 319–333; John McHugh, "A Reconsideration of Ephesians 1.10b in the Light of Irenaeus," in *Paul and Paulinism*, 302–309; Noormann, *Irenäus*, 379–466; and Fantino, *La théologie d'Irénée*, 203–382, who discusses recapitulation in the context of οἰκονομία (240–264), providing an exhaustive list (135 instances) of Irenaeus's use of this language in *Adversus haereses* (410–3). For the fullest treatment of Adam/Christ relationship in Irenaeus, cf. Jan Tjeerd Nielsen, *Adam and Christ in the Theology of Irenaeus of Lyons* (Van Gorcum's Theologische Bibliotheek 40; Assen, Netherlands: Van Gorcum, 1968), who continued to see large differences between Paul and Irenaeus on this issue: "In Rom. 5.12–21 Paul sets the Adam–Christ typology in the context of the redemption of sin. For Paul sin is a deep, intensive crack in creation. . . . Christ, the second Adam, came to conquer and destroy sin. There is tension between 'now already' and 'not yet.' For Irenaeus sin is no more than an intermezzo. Adam was a child, when he was disobedient. There is no arc of tension for Irenaeus between 'now already' and 'not yet'" (92–93). Overcoming guilt and death also appear to be more important to Irenaeus than the deep weight of Sin (cf. Dassmann, *Der Stachel im Fleisch*, 309).

24. Bengsch, *Heilsgeschichte*, 174.
25. Noormann, *Irenäus*, 40–42, 517.
26. Noormann, *Irenäus*, 519–520.
27. Noormann, *Irenäus*, 520.
28. Noormann, *Irenäus*, 40–41, 519 n. 17.
29. Adolf von Harnack, "Der Presbyter–Prediger des Irenäus (IV,27,1 – IV,32,1). Bruchstücke und Nachklänge der ältesten exegetisch–polemischen Homilieen," in *Philotesia: Paul Kleinert zum LXX Geburtstag* (Berlin: Trowitzsch & Sohn, 1907), 1–37. Cf. Lindemann, *Paulus*, 391–392; and Rensberger, "As the Apostle Teaches," 208–213.
30. Cf. Michael Holmes, "Paul and Polycarp," in *Paul and the Second Century*, 58, and the studies cited there: Frank D. Gilliard, "The Apostolicity of Gallic Churches," *HTR* 68 (1975): 29 n. 30; Pier Franco Beatrice, "Der Presbyter des Irenäus, Polycarp von Smyrna und der Brief an Diognet," in *Pléroma Salus Carnis. Homenaje a Antonio Orbe, S.J.* (ed. E. Romero-Pose; Santiago de Compostella, 1990), 179–202; and Charles E. Hill, *From the Lost Teaching of Polycarp: Identifying Irenaeus' Apostolic Presbyter and the Author of Ad Diognetum* (WUNT 186; Tübingen: Mohr Siebeck, 2006), 7–24.
31. Noormann, *Irenäus*, 520.

32. Noormann, *Irenäus*, 520–521.

33. Noormann, *Irenäus*, 517.

34. Cf. also in this regard Benoit, *Saint Irénée*, 135, and Balás, "The Use and Interpretation of Paul," 38, where the latter argues that Irenaeus received a theological tradition where Paul was already "an integral and substantial part of the apostolic witness to Christ."

35. *Irenäus*, 530.

36. Cf. also now Ben Blackwell, "Paul and Irenaeus," 205–206.

37. Noormann, *Irenäus*, 70–375.

38. Noormann, *Irenäus*, 377–516, 523–529.

39. Noormann, *Irenäus*, 518–519.

40. This general point is also noted by Rensberger, "As the Apostle Teaches," 328.

41. Balás, "The Use and Interpretation of Paul," 31.

42. Norris, "Irenaeus' Use of Paul," 89–91.

43. Norris, "Irenaeus' Use of Paul," 89, n. 20.

44. Cf. Wagenmann, *Die Stellung des Apostels Paulus*, 202–217; Schneemelcher, "Paulus in der griechischen Kirche," 12; and Noormann, *Irenäus*, 39–52.

45. Cf. Wagenmann, *Die Stellung des Apostels Paulus*, 217.

46. Cf. UBS (4th rev. ed.) for the evidence in favor of this latter reading. On the Western text-type reflected in Irenaeus, cf. Alexander Souter, "The New Testament Text of Irenaeus," in *Novum Testamentum sancti Irenaei episcopi Lugdunensis* (ed. W. Sanday and C.H. Turner; Old-Latin Biblical Texts 7; Oxford: Clarendon, 1923); August Merk, "Der Text des Neuen Testaments beim hl. Irenaeus," *ZKT* 49 (1925): 302–315; and Karl Schäfer, "Die Zitate in der lateinischen Irenäusübersetzung und ihr Wert für die Textgeschichte des Neuen Testamentes," in *Vom Wort des Lebens: Festschrift für Max Meinertz des 70. Lebensjahres 19. Dezember 1950* (ed. N. Adler; NTAbh 1; Münster: Aschendorff, 1951), 50–59.

47. Cf. Hans Dieter Betz, *Galatians* (Hermeneia; Philadelphia: Fortress Press, 1979), 91; and J.L. Martyn, *Galatians* (AB 33A; New York: Doubleday, 1997), 197–198. Marcion's version, however, left out οἷς, so that Paul yielded to neither the "pillars" nor the "false brethren." According to Victorinus (Rome) and Ambrosiaster, certain Greek and Latin manuscripts also had this reading. Ephraem and the Peshitta also lack οἷς.

48. Cf. Maurice Wiles, *The Divine Apostle*, 18–19.

49. Cf. Markus Bockmuehl, "The Icon of Peter and Paul between History and Reception," in *Seeing the Word*, 121–136, for a critique of Baur's narrative of Pauline/Petrine opposition in earliest Christianity. Bockmuehl points to the overwhelmingly early picture of Pauline/Petrine cooperation/coordination (Acts, *1 Clement*, Ignatius of Antioch, 2 Peter).

50. There is some disagreement over whom Irenaeus has in mind here. Cf. Lindemann, *Paulus*, 97, who posits either Marcion (following Harnack) or the Valentinians (following Pagels).

51. Wagenmann, *Die Stellung des Apostels Paulus*, 217.

52. Wiles, *The Divine Apostle*, 18–19; and Aageson, *Paul, the Pastoral Epistles, and the Early Church*, 163.

53. The "we" passages in Acts are key to Irenaeus's link between Luke and Paul, in combination with 2 Tim 4.10–11 and Col 4.14.

54. Cf. Balas, "The Use and Interpretation of Paul," 33–35.

55. Benoit, *Saint Irénée*, 130.

56. On the intertextual relationship between Irenaeus's title and 1 Timothy, Rolf Noormann, *Irenäus*, 73, concludes, "Die Verwendung des Ausdrucks im Titel des irenäischen Werkes ist als eine dem Leser erkennbare Anspielung zu werten." Carsten Looks, *Das Anvertraute bewahren*, 334–335, concurs.

57. Cf. also *Strom.* 3.4; 4.4; 7.16 and *Protr.* 2.25 for additional uses of the adjective ψευδώνυμος.

58. Cf. Noormann, *Irenäus*, 73 n. 20, for Irenaeus's use of a "Western" text here. Irenaeus's citations of the Pastorals deviate, textually, a bit more from the manuscript tradition than does his use of the other Pauline letters. Cf. Ernst Dassmann, *Der Stachel im Fleisch*, 296–297.

59. Looks, *Das Anvertraute bewahren*, 335.

60. Rensberger, "As the Apostle Teaches"; Noormann, *Irenäus*; and Aageson, *Paul, the Pastoral Epistles and the Early Church*.

61. Gérard Genette, *Palimpsests: Literature in the Second Degree* (trans. C. Newman and C. Doubinsky; Lincoln: University of Nebraska Press, 1997 [1982]); and *Paratexts: Thresholds of Interpretation* (trans J. E. Lewin; Literature, Culture, Theory 20; Cambridge: Cambridge University Press, 1997 [1987]).

62. D.H. Warren, "The Text of the Apostle," 315, comes closest to what I propose when he says, "In his partial quotation of 1 Tim 1:4 above, Irenaeus has in mind not just the twelve words he explicitly quotes from Paul but the entire situation which Paul is addressing." Yet rather than making a case for the importance of the Pastoral Epistles, in particular, in Irenaeus's polemics, Warren concludes that the citation of 1 Tim shows that "Paul is his main authority. Paul is the person he tries to imitate." This may be the case from Irenaeus's standpoint. I am interested, however, in answering the question: "Which Paul?" Or, "Which Pauline texts provide for Irenaeus an image of Paul that he can imitate in his own heresiological efforts?"

63. Rensberger, "As the Apostle Teaches," 321. Neither Norris, "Irenaeus' Use of Paul," nor Balás, "The Use and Interpretation of Paul," took special notice of the Pastorals either. Norris ignored them completely.

64. Noormann, *Irenäus*, 521–522.

65. Noormann, *Irenäus*, 73.

66. Aageson, *Paul, the Pastoral Epistles, and the Early Church*, 159. Cf. Noormann, *Irenäus*, 521–522.

67. Aageson, *Paul, the Pastoral Epistles, and the Early Church*, 159, 167–170.

68. Cf. Werner, *Paulinismus*, 8–9; J. Hoh, *Die Lehre des Hl. Irenäus*, 44; and Noormann, *Irenäus*, 521 n. 34, 571.

69. Hoh, *Die Lehre des Hl. Irenäus*, 198.

70. Noormann, *Irenäus*, 521 n. 34, 571. Mark Olson, *Irenaeus, the Valentinian Gnostics, and the Kingdom of God*, 141, listed 19 references to the Pastorals (undifferentiated between direct and indirect uses). Olson seems to get his data from the footnotes and indices of the *Ante-Nicene Fathers* version of *Adversus haereses*, though he does not state this. In several places he appears to have corrected the indices there. He has also missed one reference given in that volume (*Haer.* 4.9.3, citing 2 Tim 3.7; *ANF* 1:473).

71. Looks, *Das Anvertraute bewahren*, 361. There is one additional use of 1 Tim 1.9 in *Epid.* 35. Looks's *Das Anvertraute bewahren: Die Rezeption der Pastoralbriefe im 2. Jahrhundert* (1999) is a much neglected book which does not fall prey to the aforementioned simplistic conclusions of Rensberger, Noormann, and Aageson. Though published 10 years prior, it is not listed in the bibliography of Aageson's *Paul, the Pastoral Epistles and the Early Church*. Looks finds only nine "safe/secure" uses of the Pastorals in the second century and they all come from Irenaeus and Tertullian. But as the footnotes throughout the remainder of this section reveal, he identifies numerous passages where Irenaean use of the Pastorals is either "very probable" or "good possibility to probable" (cf. Chapter 5, n. 57 in this volume for his classificatory system).

72. Title: once; Book One: eight uses; Book Two: eight uses; Book Three: nine uses; Book Four: five uses; and Book Five: six uses.

73. In addition to the biographical, theological, and polemical uses of the Pastorals, which I will enumerate below, Looks, *Das Anvertraute bewahren*, 364–366, also notes the ethical and missionary aspects of Irenaeus's use of the Pastorals. He calculates that of the 65 "possible" to "safe/secure" uses of the Pastorals in Irenaeus, 60% are dedicated to "polemische oder antihäretische Formulierungen," 20% to "christologische oder systematische–theologische Wendungen," and 10% to the "christlich-ethischen und missionarischen Bereich."

74. Looks, *Das Anvertraute bewahren*, 342–343, rates this use as "very probable," and Noormann, *Irenäus*, 571, registers it as "implicit." Irenaeus also uses this verse in *Epid.* 35.

75. Noormann, *Irenäus*, 199–200, 390–392, uses this clarification of 1 Tim 1.9 as a way of pointing out the stark difference between Irenaeus's use of the Pastorals and the "historical" Paul (cf. Rom 4.13).

76. Looks, *Das Anvertraute bewahren*, 339–341, rates these uses as "very probable," and Noormann, *Irenäus*, 571, registers them as "implicit."

77. Noormann, *Irenäus*, 141, 337–338.

78. Noormann, *Irenäus*, 267–8. Looks, *Das Anvertraute bewahren*, 345–346, deems this a "very probable" use of the 1 Tim 2.6. Cf. also the close relationship between the redemption language of Titus 2.14 and *Haer.* 3.5.3 (cf. Looks, 353).

79. Looks, *Das Anvertraute bewahren*, 336, marks these uses as "very probable," while Noormann, *Irenäus*, 571, registers them as "implicit."

80. Cf. Looks, *Das Anvertraute bewahren*, 335, who also argues that the repeated use of 1 Tim 6.20 in *Adversus haereses* (cf. below) means that the Pastorals had gained substantial authority in the church before their use by Irenaeus.

81. Looks, *Das Anvertraute bewahren*, 156–157; 252–255. All Greek and Latin texts cited in the remainder of this section come from Looks. I acknowledge the problems related to Marcion's knowledge (or lack thereof) of the Pastorals and to the presence or absence of the Pastorals in P[46]. Cf. I. Howard Marshall, *A Critical and Exegetical Commentary on the The Pastoral Epistles*, 2–8, for the dearth of evidence of the use of the Pastoral Epistles in the second century (at least before Irenaeus). On P[46] cf. Jerome D. Quinn, "P[46] – The Pauline Canon?," *CBQ* 36 (1974): 379–385; Jeremy Duff, "P[46] and the Pastorals: a Misleading Consensus?," *NTS* 44 (1998): 578–590; and Eldon Jay Epp, "Issues in the Interrelation of New Testament Textual Criticism and Canon," in *The Canon Debate*, 485–515. On Marcion, Tertullian certainly thought that that he had rejected the Pastorals from his own corpus (*Marc.* 5.21). We will likely never know whether Marcion actually eliminated the Pastorals from his canon or whether their absence shows that they did not circulate with Paul's other letters, and thus were unknown to him.

82. Cf. also *Dial.* 7.3 and 35.2, citing 1 Tim 4.1.

83. Looks, *Das Anvertraute bewahren*, 459–460, deems this a "very probable" use of 1 Tim.

84. On the various interpretations of this phrase, cf. Harry Y. Gamble, *Books and Readers*, 150–151.

85. Looks, *Das Anvertraute bewahren*, 265–267, deems each of these instances as "very probable." He gives several others as "possible to probable" (268–269). F. Loofs, *Theophilus von Antiochien "Adversus Marcionem" und die anderen theologischen Quellen bei Irenaeus* (TUGAL 46.2; Leipzig: J.C. Hinrichs, 1930), 67–75, argued that Theophilus' now lost *Adversus Marcionem* (cf. Eusebius, *Hist. eccl.* 4.24) was a source for Irenaeus's work.

86. Cf. also now Frisius, "Interpretive Method and Theological Controversy," 42–64, on Tertullian's use of the Pastorals.

87. Cf. Genette, *Paratexts: Thresholds of Interpretation*.

88. Genette, *Paratexts*, 1. Emphasis his.

89. Genette, *Paratexts*, 2.

90. Genette, *Paratexts*, 2. Emphasis his.

91. Genette, *Paratexts*, 407.

92. Genette, *Paratexts*, 210.

93. Genette, *Paratexts*, 56.

94. Genette, *Paratexts*, 78–89.

95. Eusebius characterizes several early Christian works as ἔλεγχοι: Agrippa Castor's κατὰ Βασιλείδου ἔλεγχος (*Hist. eccl.* 4.7.6); Justin's ἔλεγχος, directed πρὸς Ἕλληνας (4.18.4); and Dionysius of Alexandria's ἔλεγχος ἀλληγοριστῶν (7.24.2). Cf. also Hippolytus's heresiological tome (κατὰ πασῶν αἱρεσέων ἔλεγχος).

96. Unger, *St. Irenaeus of Lyons: Against the Heresies*, 2.

97. Cf. Gamble, *Books and Readers*, 80–81.

98. Cf. R. P. Oliver, "The First Medicean MS of Tacitus and the Titulature of Ancient Books," *TAPA* 82 (1951): 232–261; W. Luppe, "Rückseitentitel auf Papyrusrollen," *ZPE* 27 (1977): 89–99; and E. G. Turner, *Greek Manuscripts of the Ancient World* (ed. P.J. Parsons; 2nd rev. ed.; London: University of London Institute of Classical Studies, 1987 [1971]), 34.

99. On the significance of the use of 1 Tim 6.20 in the title to Irenaeus's work, cf. Looks, *Das Anvertraute bewahren*, 335: "Dies alles spricht in entschiedenem Maße gegen einem geringen Stellenwert der Pastoralbriefe für Irenäus."

100. Genette, *Paratexts*, 197. Emphasis his.

101. Genette, *Paratexts*, 209. Cf. Pierluigi Piovanelli, "The Miraculous Discovery of the Hidden Manuscript, or the Paratextual Function of the Prologue to the *Apocalypse of Paul*," in *The Visio Pauli and the Gnostic Apocalypse of Paul* (ed. J. Bremmer and I. Czachesz; Studies on Early Christian Apocrypha 9; Leuven: Peeters, 2007), 23–49 (esp. 41–44), who discusses how the opening story of the *Visio Pauli* works to condition the reading of the subsequent text as a genuine work of Paul.

102. Genette, *Paratexts*, 213–215.

103. In antiquity, the preface was not separated spatially from the main text. The first lines of a given text serve this function. Genette, *Paratexts*, 163, speaks of a certain "economy of means" within ancient manuscripts.

104. Genette, *Palimpsests*, 7, argues that the five types of transtextuality (hypertextuality, paratextuality, intertextuality, metatextuality, and architextuality) are not "separate and absolute categories," but rather "their relationships to one another are numerous and often crucial."

105. Genette, *Palimpsests*, 5.

106. Genette, *Palimpsests*, 8.

107. Genette, *Palimpsests*, 9.

108. Genette, *Paratexts*, 93, citing Umberto Eco, *Postscript to "The Name of the Rose"* (trans. W. Weaver; San Diego: Harcourt Brace Jovanovich, 1984), 2. On the question of Joyce's title, *Ulysses*, cf. Genette, *Paratexts*, 2, 83, 409.

109. Genette, *Paratexts*, 83.

110. Graham Allen, *Intertextuality* (The New Critical Idiom; London: Routledge, 2000), 105–106.

111. Genette, *Palimpsests*, 397.

112. Genette, *Palimpsests*, 8.

113. Allen, *Intertextuality*, 106.

114. Jörg Helbig, *Intertextualität und Markierung: Untersuchungen zur Systematik und Funktion der Signalisierung von Intertextualität* (Beiträge zur neueren Literaturgeschichte 3.141; Heidelberg: Universitätsverlag C. Winter, 1996), 108.

115. Cf. Tertullian, *Marc.* 5.21; *Muratorian Canon*, ll. 60–63; and Clement of Alexandria, *Strom.* 2.11.

116. The phrase also appears at 2.pref.1, 4.pref.1, 4.41.4, and 5.pref.1 in summary statements about the work as a whole.

117. Noormann, *Irenäus*, 72 n.13. The interchange between "falsely named knowledge" and "falsely named Gnostics" can also be seen in Clement of Alexandria (*Strom.* 2.11; 3.4; 3.18).

118. Helbig, *Intertextualität und Markierung*, 100–101.

119. Looks, *Das Anvertraute bewahren*, 347–348, gives a "good possibility to probable" rating to the uses of 1 Tim 4.2, 7. He gives a "possible but uncertain" rating to the use of 1 Tim 6.4, while Noormann, *Irenäus*, 571, labels it an "indirect" use.

120. Looks, *Das Anvertraute bewahren*, 349–352, lists each of the following uses of 2 Tim as "good possibility to probable." Cf. Noorman, *Irenäus*, 275 n. 77. The uses of Titus are direct citations from "Paul."

121. Cf. Hoh, *Die Lehr des Hl. Irenäus*, 198, for instance, who counts 95 citations from Romans and 109 from 1 Corinthians.

122. Genette, *Palimpsests*, 24–30.

123. Aageson, *Paul, the Pastoral Epistles, and the Early Church*, 167.

124. Genette, *Palimpsests*, 397.

125. Genette, *Palimpsests*, 399.

126. Genette, *Palimpsests*, 398. Emphasis his.

127. Cf. Tertullian, *Res.* 48.1.

128. *Haer.* 1.30.13; 5.9.1,3,4; 5.10.1–2; 5.11.1; 5.12.3; 5.13.2; 5.13.5; 5.14.4. The data come from Mark Olson's *Irenaeus, the Valentinian Gnostics, and the Kingdom of God*, 138, the only full-length monograph on the interpretation of 1 Cor 15.50 in both Irenaeus and the Valentinians. On the "Gnostic" use of 1 Cor 15.50, cf. Chapter 2 of this volume; Olson, *Irenaeus the Valentinian Gnostics, and the Kingdom of God*, 11–56; and Christoph Markschies, "A Response to Jeffrey Bingham and Susan Graham," in *Early Patristic Readings of Romans*, 152–158.

129. The secondary literature on this topic is voluminous. Cf. Ernst Klebba, *Die Anthropologie des hl. Irenaeus: eine dogmenhistorische Studie* (Kirchengeschichtliche Studien 2.3; Münster: H. Schöningh, 1894); Wingren, *Man and the Incarnation*; Godehard Joppich, *Salus carnis: Eine Untersuchung in der Theologie des hl. Irenäus von Lyon* (Münsterschwarzacher Studien 1; Münsterschwarzach: Vier-Türme, 1965); Wiles, *The Divine Apostle*, 43; J. Bentivegna, "Pauline Elements in the Anthropology of St. Irenaeus," *Studia Evangelica* 5 (1968): 229–233; Dai S. Kim, "The Doctrine of Man in Ireaneus of Lyons" (Ph.D. diss.; Boston University, 1969); Antonio Orbe, "La definición

del hombre en la teología del s IIo," *Greg* 48 (1967): 522–576; *Antropologia de San Ireneo* (BAC 286; Madrid: Ed Católica, 1969); "San Ireneo y la creación de la materia," *Greg* 59 (1978): 71–127; "Adversarios anónimos de la Salus carnis," *Greg* 60 (1979): 9–53; "San Ireneo y la doctrina de la reconciliación," *Greg* 61 (1980): 5–50; François Altermath, *Du corps psychique au corps spiritual: Interprétation de 1 Cor. 15, 35–49 par les auteurs chrétiens des quatre premiers siècles* (BGBE 18; Tübingen: J. C. B. Mohr (Paul Siebeck), 1977), 78–92; Barbara Aland, "Fides und Subiectio: zur Anthropologie des Irenäus," in *Kerygma und Logos*, 9–28; Ysabel de Andia, "La Résurrection de la Chair Selon les Valentiniens et Irénée de Lyon," *Quatres Fleuves* 15/16 (1982): 59–70; *Homo Vivens: Incorruptibilité et divinisation de l'homme selon Irénée de Lyon* (Paris: Augustiniennes, 1986); Jacques Fantino, *L'Homme image de Dieu chez S. Irénée de Lyon* (Paris: Cerf, 1986); *La Théologie d'Irénée*, 332–337; Olson, *Irenaeus, the Valentinian Gnostics, and the Kingdom of God*, 92–97; and Noormann, *Irenäus*, 467–516.

130. The key passages for the following summary of Irenaeus's anthropology are *Haer.* 3.22.1–4; 3.23.7; 5.6.1; 5.8.2; 5.9.3; 5.10.2; 5.12.2–4.

131. Noormann, *Irenäus*, 509–510.

132. For the identification of σάρξ with πλάσμα/πλάσις/πλάσσω cf. 1.9.3 (fr. gk. 1, 1025–1041); 3.21.10–3.22.1 (fr. gk. 33, 4–13); 3.22.2 (fr. gr. 34, 18–20); 4.pref.4; 4.31.2; 5.1.1 (fr. gk. 3, 13–17); 5.3.3 (fr. gk. 5, 47–54); 5.12.3 (fr. gk. 12, 9–15); and 5.12.4 (Jena 12, 74–81).

133. Cf. Aland, "Fides und Subiectio," 20; and Noormann, *Irenäus*, 509.

134. Wiles, *Divine Apostle*, 43–44.

135. D. Jeffrey Bingham, "Irenaeus Reads Romans 8: Resurrection and Renovation," in *Early Patristic Readings of Romans*, 129.

136. Olson, *Irenaeus, the Valentinian Gnostics, and the Kingdom of God*, 80.

137. Emphasis mine.

138. Cf. his use of Rom 8 in *Haer.* 5.7.1; 5.8.1–2; 5.10.2.

139. Bingham, "Irenaeus Reads Romans 8," 119. Emphasis his.

140. Bingham, "Irenaeus Reads Romans 8," 120–121. Cf. Noormann, *Irenäus*, 506–507.

141. Emphasis mine. On the notion of theosis in Paul and Irenaeus, cf. now Ben Blackwell, *Christosis*.

142. Bingham, "Irenaeus Reads Romans 8," 126–128. Cf. Olson, *Irenaeus, the Valentinian Gnostics, and the Kingdom of God*, 98.

143. I have slightly adjusted the translation of *ANF*, which includes "mere" in square brackets. The key language (καθ'ἑαυτὴν/solam/tantum) is absent in this instance. Cf. *Haer.* 5.9.3–4.

144. Wiles, *Divine Apostle*, 28–29.

145. Cf. Lawson, *Biblical Theology*, 231–232; Noormann, *Irenäus*, 504, 510; and Bingham, "Irenaeus Reads Romans 8," 123–124.

146. Noormann, *Irenäus*, 505.

147. Cf. Philip J. Hefner, "Theological Methodology and St. Irenaeus," *JR* 44 (1964): 296, and Fantino, *La théologie d'Irénée*, 16, for the range of synonymns used by Irenaeus for the "rule of truth."

148. Emphasis mine. I give the translation of *ANF* rather than Unger here because Unger obscures Irenaeus's use of σάρξ/carne in *Haer.* 1.10.1; 10; fr. gr. 1, 1111. Unger translates, misleadingly, "the bodily ascension into heaven of the beloved Son." Cf. also *Haer.* 1.22.1; 1, 28, where Irenaeus, in explaining the *regula veritatis*, condemns those denying a resurrection "in the flesh" (in *carne*).

149. Bentivegna, "Pauline Elements," 230. Cf. Philip J. Hefner, "Saint Irenaeus and the Hypothesis of Faith," *Di* 2 (1963): 300–306; "Theological Methodology," 294–309; Olson, *Irenaeus, the Valentinian Gnostics, and the Kingdom of God*, 2, 64, 81; and Fantino, *La théologie d'Irénée*, 15–28.

150. Cf. Olson, *Irenaeus, the Valentinian Gnostics, and the Kingdom of God*, 96.

151. Jouette M. Bassler, "A Response to Jeffrey Bingham and Susan Graham," 138–142.

152. Olson, *Irenaeus, the Valentinian Gnostics, and the Kingdom of God*, 96.

153. Noormann, *Irenäus*, 509.

154. Noormann, *Irenäus*, 510.

155. Noormann, *Irenäus*, 512. Noormann is dependent on Selin, *Der Streit um die Auferstehung der Toten*, 72f., and Joppich, *Salus carnis*, 37, who argue that Paul does not understand σάρξ as "die rein physische Substanz unseres materiellen Leibes." Cf. Chapter 5 for a discussion on σάρξ in 1 Corinthians 15.

156. Cf. Wiles, *Divine Apostle*, 132, who concluded that Irenaeus and the Apostle's later proto-orthodox commentators have themselves "oversimplified the pattern of Paul's thought at the cost of complicating the exegesis of his words."

157. Emphasis mine. Cf. Lehtipuu, "'Flesh and Blood Cannot Inherit the Kingdom of God,'" 163: "The author goes beyond Paul in claiming that actually a *certain kind* of flesh and blood shall inherit the kingdom of God, namely, the flesh and blood of Jesus." Emphasis hers.

158. Cf. Olson, *Irenaeus, the Valentinian Gnostics, and the Kingdom of God*, 28–32.

159. Lehtipuu, "'Flesh and Blood Cannot Inherit the Kingdom of God,'" 165–167, and A. H. C. van Eijk, "The Gospel of Philip and Clement of Alexandria: Gnostic and Ecclesiastical Theology on the Resurrection and the Eucharist," *VC* 25 (1971): 96, argue that there are more similarities between Valentinian and proto-orthodox views of the resurrection than either side would like to admit.

160. Cf. Jouette M. Bassler, "A Response to Jeffrey Bingham and Susan Graham," 142: "Yet the path of Pauline interpretation is littered with the textual debris of this drive toward theological consistency. Thus the mirror Irenaeus holds up reveals an Irenaeus in each of us. We grant interpretive authority to a master narrative or grid; on the basis of this we prioritize certain verses in our interpretation; we strive toward an ideal of consistency. The crucial point is the degree of openness to alternative readings. Irenaeus rejects them, but the text itself pushes us toward openness. There is a resilient level of indeterminacy to

Paul's language, especially his anthropological language. It resists definitive packaging."

161. Cf. Nielsen, *Adam and Christ*, 94: "In the 'apocryphal correspondence between the Corinthians and the apostle Paul' typical Gnostic questions are dealt with, and the answers give to them are more after the manner of Irenaeus than after the manner of Paul."

162. Dunn, "Testing Pauline Pseudepigraphy," 65–66.

163. Paul Trebilco, "Christian Communities in Western Asia Minor into the Early Second Century: Ignatius and Others as Witnesses against Bauer," *JETS* 49 (2006): 35–38.

164. Trebilco, "Christian Communities in Western Asia Minor," 41. Emphasis his.

165. On the early biography of Irenaeus, cf. Grant, *Irenaeus of Lyons*, 2–3. On the use of Pauline materials in Polycarp's Epistle to the Philippians, cf. Chapter 2 of this volume.

166. Cf. Johnston, "La Correspondance apocryphe entre Paul et les Corinthiens," 223–224; Rordorf, "Hérésie et orthodoxie," 58–59; and Klijn, "Apocryphal Correspondance," 22–23.

167. Cf. Johnston, "La Correspondance apocryphe entre Paul et les Corinthiens," 224–226; Hovhanessian, *Third Corinthians*, 126–131; and Testuz, *Papyrus Bodmer X–XII*, 23.

168. Cf. Shils, *Tradition*, 198: "But it should also be pointed out that no situation is made by a single human being."

169. Shils, *Tradition*, 45.

170. Shils, *Tradition*, 97.

171. Cf. J. A. Fitzmyer, *The Acts of the Apostles: a New Translation with Introduction and Commentary* (AB 31; New York: Doubleday, 1998), 544; and Gregory Sterling, "From Apostle to the Gentiles to Apostle of the Church," 90–91.

172. Cf. Andreas Lindemann, "Paul, 'Clement,' and Ignatius," 10; and Pervo, *Making of Paul*, 132. Cf. also Dionysius of Corinth (ca. 170 C.E.) for the co-joining of Peter and Paul as fellow martyrs in Rome (Eus., *Hist. eccl.* 2.25.8).

173. Cf. Charles Hill, "The Epistula Apostolorum: An Asian Tract from the Time of Polycarp," *JECS* 7 (1999): 1–53; and A. Stewart-Sykes, "The Asian Context of the New Prophecy and of the Epistula Apostolorum," *VC* 51 (1997): 416–438.

174. Cf. Shils, *Tradition*, 47: "an individual possesses a culture of which the constituent elements are of different ages." Furthermore, "A society is a 'trans-temporal' phenomenon" (327).

175. Wiles, *The Divine Apostle*, 44.

CHAPTER 7

1. Epigraph: Marc Bloch, *The Historian's Craft*, 29.

2. Translation from Ernest Evans. Cf. Chapter 1, n. 2.

3. Castelli, *Martrydom and Memory*, 24.

4. Mitchell, *The Heavenly Trumpet*, 20. Emphasis hers.

5. Cf. Chapter 3.

6. Cf. Larry L. Welborn, "The Soteriology of Romans in Clement of Alexandria, *Stromateis* 2: Faith, Fear, and Assimilation to God," in *Early Patristic Readings of Romans*, 66–83; Elisa Mascellani, *Prudens dispensator verbi: Romani 5:12–21 nell'esegesi di Clemente Alessandrino e Origene* (Florence: Nuova Italia, 1990); Raoul Mortley, "Mirror and I Cor 13:12 in the Epistemology of Clement of Alexandria," *VC* 30 (1976): 109–120; and Fritz Buri, *Clemens Alexandrinus und der Paulinische Freiheitsbegriff* (Zürich: M. Niehans, 1939).

7. Cf. Eric W. Scherbenske, *Canonizing Paul: Ancient Editorial Practice and the Corpus Paulinum* (New York: Oxford University Press, 2013), on the effect of ancient editorial practices on the interpretation of several important Pauline letter collections. Some have suggested that the presence of Hebrews, right behind Romans in P[46], may say something about the Pauline tradition within which its scribe was situated. On Hebrews in P[46], cf. C. P. Anderson, "The Epistle to the Hebrews and the Pauline Letter Collection," *HTR* 59 (1966): 429–438; "Hebrews among the Letters of Paul," *SR* 5 (1975–1976): 258–266; Elliott J. Mason, "The Position of Hebrews in the Pauline Corpus in the Light of Chester Beatty Papyrus II" (Ph.D. diss, University of Southern California, 1968); Knut Backhaus, "Der Hebräerbrief und die Paulus–Schule," *BZ* 37 (1993): 183–208; Dieter Georgi, "Hebrews and the Heritage of Paul," in *Hebrews: Contemporary Methods—New Insights* (ed. G Gelardini; BibInt 75; Leiden: Brill, 2005), 239–244; and Clare K. Rothschild, *Hebrews as Pseudepigraphon: the History and Significance of the Pauline Attribution of Hebrews* (WUNT 235; Tübingen: Mohr Siebeck, 2009).

8. Cf. Chapter 1.

9. Allison, *Constructing Jesus*, 1–30.

10. Certeau, "The Historiographical Operation," in *The Writing of History* (trans. T. Conley; New York: Columbia University Press, 1988), 69. Cf. Certeau, "History: Science and Fiction," in *Heterologies: Discourse on the Other* (trans. B. Massumi; Theory and History of Literature 17; Minneapolis: University of Minnesota Press, 1986), 214; MacIntyre, *After Virtue*, 69; Evans, *In Defence of History*, 248; Gaddis, *Landscape of History*, 125; and Joyce Appleby, Lynn Hunt, and Margaret Jacob, *Telling the Truth about History* (New York: W. W. Norton, 2004), 271.

11. Cf. Certeau, "The Black Sun of Language: Foucault," in *Heterologies*, 178.

12. Certeau, "History: Science and Fiction," 216.

13. Certeau, "History: Science and Fiction," 203. Cf. Certeau, "The Historiographical Operation," 58–69.

14. Mitchell, *The Heavenly Trumpet*, 430. Cf. Gaddis, *The Landscape of History*, 38; and Appleby, Hunt, and Jacob, *Telling the Truth about History*, 281, 284, 309.

15. Certeau, "History: Science and Fiction," 208.

16. Bloch, *The Historian's Craft*, 88. Cf. Certeau, "History: Science and Fiction," 202; and Karl Popper, *The Logic of Scientific Discovery* (London: Hutchinson, 1959).

17. Certeau, "The Historiographical Operation," 94.

18. Certeau, "The Historiographical Operation," 94.

19. Cf. Chapter 4.

20. Bloch, *The Historian's Craft*, 133. On memory as "gistified," cf. Allison, *Constructing Jesus*, 11.

21. Certeau, "The Historiographical Operation," 57. Emphases his.

Bibliography

Aageson, James W. "The Pastoral Epistles and the *Acts of Paul*: a Multiplex Approach." *Lexington Theological Quarterly* 40(2005): 237–248.

———. "The Pastoral Epistles, Apostolic Authority, and the Development of the Pauline Scriptures." Pages 5–26 in *The Pauline Canon*. Edited by Stanley Porter. Leiden: Brill, 2004.

———. *Paul, the Pastoral Epistles, and the Early Church*. Library of Pauline Studies. Peabody, MA: Hendrickson, 2008.

Abrams, M. H. *The Mirror and the Lamp: Romantic Theory and the Critical Tradition*. New York: Oxford University Press, 1953.

Agamben, Giorgio. *The Time That Remains: A Commentary on the Letter to the Romans*. Translated by Patricia Dailey. Meridian: Crossing Aesthetics. Stanford, CA: Stanford University Press, 2005 [2000].

Agulhon, Maurice. *Marianne into Battle: Republican Imagery and Symbolism in France, 1789–1880*. Translated by Janet Lloyd. Cambridge: Cambridge University Press, 1981.

Aland, Barbara. "Die Rezeption des neutestamentlichen Textes in den ersten Jahrhunderten." Pages 1–38 in *The New Testament in Early Christianity*. Edited by Jean-Marie Sevrin. Louvain: Leuven University Press, 1989.

———. "Fides und Subiectio: zur Anthropologie des Irenäus." Pages 9–28 in *Kerygma und Logos: Beiträge zu den geistesgeschichtlichen Beziehungen zwischen Antike und Christentum (Festschrift für Carl Andresen zum 70. Geburtstag)*. Edited by Adolf Martin Ritter. Göttingen: Vandenhoeck & Ruprecht, 1979.

———. "Marcion: Versuch einer neuen Interpretation." *Zeitschrift für Theologie und Kirche* 70(1973): 420–447.

———. *Was ist Gnosis?: Studien zum frühen Christentum, zu Marcion und zur kaiserzeitlichen Philosophie*. Wissenschaftliche Untersuchungen zum Neuen Testament 239. Tübingen: Mohr Siebeck, 2009.

Aland, Kurt. "Die Entstehung der Corpus Paulinum." Pages 302–350 in *Die neutes-tamentliche Entwürfe*. Edited by Kurt Aland. Theologische Bucherei 63. Munich: Kaiser, 1979.

———. "Methodische Bemerkungen zum Corpus Paulinum bei den Kirchenvätern des zweiten Jahrhunderts." Pages 29–48 in *Kerygma und Logos: Beiträge zu den geistesgeschichtlichen Beziehungen zwischen Antike und Christentum (Festschrift für Carl Andresen zum 70. Geburtstag)*. Edited by Adolf Martin Ritter. Göttingen: Vandenhoeck & Ruprecht, 1979.

Aleith, Eva. *Das Paulusverständnis in der alten Kirche*. Beihefte zur Zeitschrift für die neutestamentliche Wissenschaft und die Kunde der älteren Kirche 18. Berlin: Töpelmann, 1937.

Allen, Graham. *Intertextuality*. The New Critical Idiom. London: Routledge, 2000.

Allenbach, J., ed. *Biblia patristica: index des citations et allusions bibliques dans la littérature Patristique*. 6 vols. Paris: Éditions du Centre national de la recherche scientifique, 1975.

Allison, Dale C., Jr. *Constructing Jesus: Memory, Imagination, and History*. Grand Rapids, MI: Baker Academic, 2010.

———. *The Historical Christ and the Theological Jesus*. Grand Rapids, MI: Eerdmans, 2009.

———. *Resurrecting Jesus: the Earliest Christian Tradition and its Interpreters*. London: T&T Clark, 2005.

Al Sayyad, Nezer, ed. *The End of Tradition?* London: Routledge, 2004.

Altermath, François. *Du corps psychique au corps spirituel: Interprétation de 1 Cor. 15,35–49 par les auteurs chrétiens des quatre premiers siècles*. Beiträge zur Geschichte der biblischen Exegese 18. Tübingen: J. C. B. Mohr (Paul Siebeck), 1977.

Anderson, C. P. "The Epistle to the Hebrews and the Pauline Letter Collection." *Harvard Theological Review* 59(1966): 429–438.

———. "Hebrews among the Letters of Paul." *Studies in Religion* 5 (1975–1976): 258–266.

Andia, Ysabel de. *Homo Vivens: Incorruptibilité et divinisation de l'homme selon Irénée de Lyon*. Paris: Augustiniennes, 1986.

———. "La Résurrection de la chair selon les Valentiniens et Irénée de Lyon." *Quatres Fleuves* 15/16 (1982): 59–70.

Appleby, Joyce, Lynn Hunt, and Margaret Jacob. *Telling the Truth about History*. New York: W. W. Norton, 2004.

Asmussen, Jes P. "Der apokryphe dritte Korintherbief in der armenischen Tradition." *Acta Orientalia* 35(1973): 51–55.

Assmann, Aleida. *Erinnerungsräume: Formen und Wandlungen des kulturellen Gedächtnisses*. München: C. H. Beck, 1999.

———. "The Religious Roots of Cultural Memory." *Norsk teologisk tidsskrift* 109(2008): 270–292.

Assmann, Aleida, Jan Assmann, and Christof Hardmeier, eds. *Schrift und Gedächtnis: Beitrage zur Archäologie der literarische Kommunikation*. Munich: Fink, 1983.

Assmann, Aleida, and Dietrich Harth, eds. *Mnemosyne: Formen und Funktionen der kulturellen Erinnerung*. Frankfurt am Main: Fischer Taschenbuch Verlag, 1991.

Assmann, Jan. "Form as a Mnemonic Device: Cultural Texts and Cultural Memory." Pages 67–82 in *Performing the Gospel: Orality, Memory and Mark*. Edited by Richard A. Horsley, Jonathan A. Draper, and John Miles Foley. Minneapolis: Fortress Press, 2006.

———. *Das kulturelle Gedächtnis: Schrift, Erinnerung, und politische Identität in frühen Hochkulturen*. Munich: C. H. Beck, 1992.

———. *Religion and Cultural Memory: Ten Studies*. Translated by Rodney Livingstone. Cultural Memory in the Present. Stanford, CA: Stanford University Press, 2006 [2000].

Attridge, Harold W. "The Gospel of Truth as an Exoteric Text." Pages 239–255 in *Nag Hammadi, Gnosticism, & Early Christianity*. Edited by Charles W. Hedrick and Robert Hodgson, Jr. Peabody, MA: Hendrickson, 1986.

Avemarie, Friedrich, and Hermann Lichtenberger, eds. *Auferstehung = Resurrection: the Fourth Durham-Tübingen Research Symposium: "Resurrection, Transfiguration and Exaltation in Old Testament, Ancient Judaism and Early Christianity" (Tübingen, September, 1999)*. Wissenschaftliche Untersuchungen zum Neuen Testament 135. Tübingen: Mohr Siebeck, 2001.

Babcock, William S., ed. *Paul and the Legacies of Paul*. Dallas: Southern Methodist University Press, 1990.

Backhaus, Knut. "Der Hebräerbrief und die Paulus–Schule." *Biblische Zeitschrift* 37(1993): 183–208.

———. "'Mitteilhaber des Evangeliums' (1 Kor 9,23): Zur christologischen Grundlegung einer 'Paulus–Schule' bei Paulus." Pages 44–71 in *Christologie in der Paulus-Schule: zur Rezeptionsgeschichte des paulinischen Evangeliums*. Edited by Klaus Scholtissek. Stuttgarter Bibelstudien 181. Stuttgart: Verlag Katholisches Bibelwerk, 2000.

Badiou, Alain. *Saint Paul: The Foundation of Universalism*. Translated by Ray Brassier. Cultural Memory in the Present. Stanford, CA: Stanford University Press, 2003 [1997].

Balás, David L. "Marcion Revisited: A 'Post–Harnack' Perspective." Pages 95–108 in *Texts and Testaments: Critical Essays on the Bible and Early Church Fathers*. Edited by W. E. March. San Antonio, TX: Trinity University Press, 1980.

———. "The Use and Interpretation of Paul in Irenaeus's Five Books *Adversus Haereses*." *Second Century: A Journal of Early Christian Studies* 9(1992): 27–39.

Bandstra, Andrew J. "Paul and an Ancient Interpreter: a Comparison of the Teaching of Redemption in Paul and Irenaeus." *Calvin Theological Journal* 5(1970): 43–63.

Barnett, Albert E. *Paul Becomes a Literary Influence*. Chicago: University of Chicago Press, 1941.

Barrett, Charles K. "Pauline Controversies in the Post–Pauline Period." *New Testament Studies* 20(1974): 229–245.

Barrier, Jeremy W. *The Acts of Paul and Thecla: a Critical Introduction and Commentary*. Wissenschaftliche Untersuchungen zum Neuen Testament 2.270. Tübingen: Mohr Siebeck, 2009.

Barth, Carola. *Die Interpretation des Neuen Testaments in der Valentinianischen Gnosis*. Texte und Untersuchungen zur Geschichte der altchristlichen Literatur 37, 3. Leipzig: Hinrichs, 1911.

Bartlett, Frederic C. *Remembering: A Study in Experimental and Social Psychology*. Cambridge: Cambridge University Press, 1932.

Barton, John. "Marcion Revisited." Pages 295–320 in *The Canon Debate*. Edited by Lee Martin McDonald and James A. Sanders. Peabody, MA: Hendrickson, 2002.

Barton, Stephen C., Loren T. Stuckenbruck, and Benjamin G. Wold, eds. *Memory in the Bible and Antiquity: the Fifth Durham-Tübingen Research Symposium (Durham, September 2004)*. Wissenschaftliche Untersuchungen zum Neuen Testament 212. Tübingen: Mohr Siebeck, 2007.

Bassler, Jouette M. "A Response to Jeffrey Bingham and Susan Graham: Networks and Noah's Sons." Pages 133–151 in *Early Patristic Readings of Romans*. Edited by Kathy L. Gaca and L. L. Welborn. New York: T&T Clark, 2005.

Bauckham, Richard. *Jesus and the Eyewitnesses: The Gospels as Eyewitness Testimony*. Grand Rapids, MI: Eerdmans, 2006.

———. *Jude, 2 Peter*. Word Biblical Commentary 50. Waco, TX: Word Books, 1983.

Bauer, Bruno. *Kritik der paulinischen Briefe*. 3 vols. Berlin: Hempel, 1850–1852.

Bauer, Walter. *Orthodoxy and Heresy in Earliest Christianity*. Philadelphia: Fortress Press, 1971.

Baum, Armin Daniel. *Pseudepigraphie und literarische Fälschung im frühen Christentum*. Wissenschaftliche Untersuchungen zum Neuen Testament 2.138. Tübingen: Mohr Siebeck, 2001.

Baur, Ferdinand Christian. "Die Christuspartie in der Corinthischen Gemeinde." *Zeitschrift für Theologie* 4(1831): 61–206.

———. *The Church History of the First Three Centuries*. 2 vols. Translated by Allan Menzies. 3rd ed. Theological Translation Fund Library. London: Williams and Norgate, 1878–1879 [1853–1860].

———. *Die Epochen der kirchlichen Geschichtsschreibung*. Tübingen: L. F. Fues, 1852.

———. *Der Gegensatz des Katholicismus und Protestantismus nach den Principien und Hauptdogmen der beiden Lehrbegriffe. Mit besonderer Rücksicht auf Herrn Dr. Möhler's Symbolik*. Tübingen, 1834.

———. *Paul the Apostle of Jesus Christ: His Life and Works, His Epistles and Teachings*. 2 vol. Translated by A. Menzies. Peabody, MA: Hendrickson, 2003 [1845].

———. *Die sogenannten Pastoralbriefe des Apostles Paulus aufs neue kritisch untersucht*. Stuttgart and Tübingen, 1835.

Beatrice, Pier Franco. "Der Presbyter des Irenäus, Polycarp von Smyrna und der Brief an Diognet." Pages 179–202 in *Pléroma Salus Carnis. Homenaje a Antonio Orbe, S.J.* Edited by Eugenio Romero-Pose. Santiago de Compostella, 1990.

Becker, Eve-Marie. "Marcion und die Korintherbriefe nach Tertullian, Adversus Marcionem V." Pages 95–109 in *Marcion und seine kirchengeschichtliche Wirkung*. Edited by Gerhard May and Katharina Greschat. Berlin: Walter de Gruyter, 2002.

Becker, Eve-Marie, and Peter Pilhofer, eds. *Biographie und Persönlichkeit des Paulus*. Wissenschaftliche Untersuchungen zum Neuen Testament 187. Tübingen: Mohr Siebeck, 2005.

Becker, Jürgen. *Die Auferstehung Jesu Christi nach dem Neuen Testament: Ostererfahrung und Osterverständnis im Urchristentum*. Tübingen: Mohr Siebeck, 2007.

Beiser, Frederick C. "Hegel and Ranke: A Re–examination." Pages 332–350 in *A Companion to Hegel*. Edited by Stephen Houlgate and Michael Baur. Blackwell Companions to Philosophy. West Sussex, UK: Wiley-Blackwell, 2011.

Beker, J. Christiaan. *Heirs of Paul: Paul's Legacy in the New Testament and in the Church Today*. Grand Rapids, MI: Eerdmans, 1996 [1991].

———. *Paul the Apostle: the Triumph of God in Life and Thought*. Philadelphia: Fortress Press, 1980.

Bengsch, Alfred. *Heilsgeschichte und Heilswissen: Eine Untersuchung zur Struktur und Entfaltung des Theologischen Denkens im Werk "Adversus Haereses" des Hl. Irenäus von Lyon*. Erfurter theologische Studien 3. Leipzig: St. Benno Verlag, 1957.

Benoit, André. "Ecriture et tradition chez Saint Irénée." *Revue d'histoire et de philosophie religieuses* 40(1960): 32–43.

———. *Saint Irénée: Introduction à l'étude de sa théologie*. Études d'histoire et de philosophie religieuses 52. Paris: Presses Universitaires de France, 1960.

Bentivegna, J. "Pauline Elements in the Anthropology of St. Irenaeus." *Studia evangelica* 5(1968): 229–233.

Benz, Ernst. "Das Paulusverständnis in der morgenländischen und abendländischen Kirche." *Zeitschrift für Religions- und Geistesgeschichte* 3(1951): 289–309.

Berding, Kenneth. "John or Paul? Who was Polycarp's Mentor?" *Tyndale Bulletin* 59(2008): 135–143.

———. *Polycarp and Paul: an Analysis of Their Literary and Theological Relationship in Light of Polycarp's Use of Biblical and Extra-Biblical Literature*. Supplements to Vigiliae christianae 62. Leiden: Brill, 2002.

Berger, Peter L., and Thomas Luckmann. *The Social Construction of Reality: A Treatise in the Sociology of Knowledge*. New York: Doubleday, 1966.

Bernstein, Richard J. "The Constellation of Hermeneutics, Critical Theory, and Deconstruction." Pages 267–282 in *The Cambridge Companion to Gadamer*. Edited by Robert J. Dostal. Cambridge: Cambridge University Press, 2002.

Betz, Hans Dieter. "The Concept of the 'Inner Human Being' (ὁ ἔσω ἄνθρωπος) in the Anthropology of Paul." *New Testament Studies* 46(2000): 315–324.

———. *Galatians: a Commentary on Paul's Letter to the Churches in Galatia*. Hermeneia. Philadelphia: Fortress Press, 1979.

Betz, Monika. "Die betörenden Worte des fremden Mannes: zur Funktion der Paulusbeschreibung in den Theklaakten." *New Testament Studies* 53(2007): 130–145.

Bianchi, Ugo. "Marcion: theologien biblique ou docteur gnostique?" *Vigiliae christianae* 21(1967): 141–149.

Bingham, D. Jeffrey. "Irenaeus Reads Romans 8: Resurrection and Renovation." Pages 114–132 in *Early Patristic Readings of Romans*. Edited by Kathy L. Gaca and L. L. Welborn. New York: T&T Clark, 2005.

Bird, Michael F., and Joseph R. Dodson, eds. *Paul and the Second Century*. Library of New Testament Studies 412. New York: T&T Clark, 2011.

Blackman, Edwin Cyril. *Marcion and His Influence*. London: SPCK, 1948.

Blackwell, Ben C. *Christosis: Pauline Soteriology in Light of Deification in Irenaeus and Cyril of Alexandria*. Wissenschaftliche Untersuchungen zum Neuen Testatement 2.314. Tübingen: Mohr Siebeck, 2011.

Blasi, Anthony J. *Making Charisma: The Social Construction of Paul's Public Image*. New Brunswick, NJ: Transaction Pubishers, 1991.

Bloch, Marc. *The Historian's Craft*. Translated by Peter Putnam. New York: Alfred A. Knopf, 1953.

Bockmuehl, Markus. *The Remembered Peter: in Ancient Reception and Modern Debate*. Wissenschaftliche Untersuchungen zum Neuen Testament 262. Tübingen: Mohr Siebeck, 2010.

———. *Seeing the Word: Refocusing New Testament Study*. Studies in Theological Interpretation. Grand Rapids, MI: Baker Academic, 2006.

———. *Simon Peter in Scripture and Memory: The New Testament Apostle in the Early Church*. Grand Rapids, MI: Baker Academic, 2012.

Bodnar, John. *Remaking America: Public Memory, Commemoration, and Patriotism in the Twentieth Century*. Princeton, NJ: Princeton University Press, 1993.

Bollok, Janos. "The Description of Paul in the *Acta Pauli*." Pages 1–15 in *The Apocryphal Acts of Paul and Thecla*. Edited by Jan N. Bremmer. Kampen: Kok Pharos, 1996.

Borg, Marcus J., and John Dominic Crossan. *The First Paul: Reclaiming the Radical Visionary Behind the Church's Conservative Icon*. New York: HarperCollins, 2009.

Bousset, Wilhelm. *Kyrios Christos*. Translated by John E. Steely. Nashville, TN: Abingdon Press, 1970 [1913].

Bovon, François. "The Canonical Structure of Gospel and Apostle." Pages 516–527 in *The Canon Debate*. Edited by Lee Martin McDonald and James A. Sanders. Peabody, MA: Hendrickson, 2002.

———. "Paul comme Document et Paul comme Monument." Pages 54–65 in *Chrétiens en conflit. L'Épître de Paul aux Galates*. Edited by J. Allaz. Essais bibliques 13. Genève: Labor et Fides, 1987.

Boyarin, Daniel. *A Radical Jew: Paul and the Politics of Identity*. Contraversions 1. Berkeley: University of California Press, 1994.

Boyarin, Jonathan, ed. *Remapping Memory: The Politics of TimeSpace*. Minneapolis: University of Minnesota Press, 1994.

————. "Space, Time, and the Politics of Memory." Pages 1–26 in *Remapping Memory: The Politics of TimeSpace*. Edited by Jonathan Boyarin. Minneapolis: University of Minnesota, 1994.

Brakke, David. *The Gnostics: Myth, Ritual and Diversity in Early Christianity*. Cambridge, MA: Harvard University Press, 2011.

Braun, Willi. "Physiotherapy of Femininity in the *Acts of Thecla*." Pages 209–230 in *Text and Artifact in the Religions of Mediterranean Antiquity: Essays in Honor of Peter Richardson*. Edited by Michel Desjardins and Stephen G. Wilson. Studies in Christianity and Judaism 9. Waterloo, ON: Wilfrid Laurier University Press, 2000.

Bremmer, Jan N., ed. *The Apocryphal Acts of Paul and Thecla*. Studies on the Apocryphal Acts of the Apostles 2. Kampen: Kok Pharos, 1996.

Bremmer, Jan N., and István Czachesz, eds. *The Visio Pauli and the Gnostic Apocalypse of Paul*. Studies on Early Christian Apocrypha 9. Leuven: Peeters, 2007.

Brennecke, H.-C. "Die Anfänge einer Paulus Verehrung." Pages 295–305 in *Biographie und Persönlichkeit des Paulus*. Edited by Eve-Marie Becker and Peter Pilhofer. Tübingen: Mohr Siebeck, 2005.

Brent, Allen. *Ignatius of Antioch and the Second Sophistic: a Study of an Early Christian Transformation of Pagan Culture*. Studien und Texte zu Antike und Christentum 36. Tübingen: Mohr Siebeck, 2006.

Brown, Delwin. "Limitation and Ingenuity: Radical Historicism and the Nature of Tradition." Pages 213–228 in *Tradition and Tradition Theories*. Edited by Thorsten Larbig and Siegfried Wiedenhofer. Berlin: LIT Verlag, 2006.

Brox, Norbert. *Falsche Verfasserangaben: Zur Erklärung der frühchristlichen Pseudepigraphie*. Stuttgart: KBW Verlag, 1975.

————. "Zum Problemstand in der Erforschung der altchristlichen Pseudepigraphie." *Kairos* 15(1973): 10–23.

Bruce, F. F. "St. Luke's Portrait of St. Paul." Pages 181–191 in *Aksum–Thyateira: FS Archbishop Methodius of Thyateira and Great Britain*. Edited by George Dragas. London: Thyateira House, 1985.

Bruns, Gerald L. "Tradition and the Terror of History: Christianity, the Holocaust, and the Jewish Theological Dilemma." Pages 19–38 in *The Force of Tradition*. Edited by Donald G. Marshall. Lanham, MD: Rowman & Littlefield, 2005.

Budick, Sanford. *The Western Theory of Tradition: Terms and Paradigms of the Cultural Sublime*. New Haven, CT: Yale University Press, 2000.

Bultmann, Rudolf. "Ignatius und Paulus." Pages 400–411 in *Exegetica: Aufsätze zur Erforschung des Neuen Testaments*. Edited by Erich Dinkler. Tübingen: J. C. B. Mohr (Paul Siebeck), 1967.

Bultmann, Rudolf. *Theology of the New Testament*. Translated by K. Grobel. New York: Charles Scribner's Sons, 1951.

Bundy, David. "The Pseudo-Ephremian *Commentary on Third Corinthians*: a Study in Exegesis and Anti–Bardaisanite Polemic." Pages 51–63 in *After Bardaisan:*

Studies on Continuity and Change in Syriac Christianity in Honour of Professor Han J. W. Drijvers. Edited by Gerrit J. Reinink and Alexander Cornelis Klugkist. Orientalia lovaniensia analecta 89. Louvain: Peeters, 1999.

Burkert, Walter. "Towards Plato and Paul: The 'Inner' Human Being." Pages 59–82 in *Ancient and Modern Perspectives on the Bible and Culture: Essays in Honor of Hans Dieter Betz.* Edited by Adela Yarbro Collins. Scholars Press Homage Series 22. Atlanta, GA: Scholars Press, 1998.

Burrus, Virginia. *Chastity as Autonomy: Women in the Stories of Apocryphal Acts.* Lewiston, NY: Edwin Mellen Press, 1987.

Byrskog, Samuel. "A New Quest for the *Sitz im Leben*: Social Memory, the Jesus Tradition and the Gospel of Matthew." *New Testament Studies* 52 (2006): 319–336.

———. *Story as History—History as Story: The Gospel Tradition in the Context of Ancient Oral History.* Leiden: Brill, 2002 [2000].

Cameron, Averil. *Christianity and the Rhetoric of Empire: The Development of Christian Discourse.* Sather Classical Lectures 55. Berkeley: University of California Press, 1991.

Campbell, Douglas. *The Deliverance of God: an Apocalyptic Rereading of Justification in Paul.* Grand Rapids, MI: Eerdmans, 2009.

Campenhausen, Hans Freiherr von. *The Formation of the Christian Bible.* Translated by J. A. Baker. Philadelphia: Fortress Press, 1972.

———. "Irenäus und das Neue Testament." *Theologische Literaturzeitung* 90(1965): 1–8.

———. "Polykarp von Smyrna und die Pastoralbriefe." Pages 197–301 in *Aus der Frühzeit des Christentums: Studien zur Kirchengeschichte des ersten und zweiten Jahrhunderts.* Tübingen: J. C. B. Mohr (Paul Siebeck), 1963.

Carr, Edward Hallett. *What is History?: The George Macaulay Trevelyan Lectures Delivered in the University of Cambridge, January–March 1961.* New York: Alfred A. Knopf, 1962.

Carruthers, Mary J. *The Book of Memory: a Study of Memory in Medieval Culture.* 2nd ed. Cambridge Studies in Medieval Literature. Cambridge: Cambridge University Press, 2008 [1990].

Casey, Robert Pierce. *The Excerpta ex Theodoto of Clement of Alexandria.* Studies and Documents 1. London: Christophers, 1934.

Castelli, Elizabeth A. *Martyrdom and Memory: Early Christian Culture Making.* Gender, Theory, and Religion. New York: Columbia University Press, 2004.

Certeau, Michel de. "History: Science and Fiction." Pages 199–221 in *Heterologies: Discourse on the Other.* Theory and History of Literature 17. Minneapolis: University of Minnesota Press, 1986.

———. *The Writing of History.* Translated by Tom Conley. New York: Columbia University Press, 1988.

Childs, Brevard S. *The Church's Guide for Reading Paul: the Canonical Shaping of the Pauline Corpus.* Grand Rapids, MI: Eerdmans, 2008.

Clabeaux, John J. *A Lost Edition of the Letters of Paul: A Reassessment of the Text of the Pauline Corpus Attested by Marcion.* Catholic Biblical Quarterly Monograph Series 21. Washington, DC: Catholic Biblical Association of America, 1989.

Clapin, Hugh, Phillip Staines, and Peter Slezak, eds. *Representation in Mind: New Approaches to Mental Representation.* Perspectives on Cognitive Science 1. Amsterdam: Elsevier, 2004.

Clark, Elizabeth A. *History, Theory, Text: Historians and the Linguistic Turn.* Cambridge, MA: Harvard University Press, 2004.

Clifford, James. *The Predicament of Culture: Twentieth-Century Ethnography, Literature, and Art.* Cambridge, MA: Harvard University Press, 1988.

———. "Traditional Futures." Pages 152–170 in *Questions of Tradition.* Edited by Mark Salber Phillips and Gordon Schochet. Toronto: University of Toronto Press, 2004.

Cohen, Gillian, George Kiss, and Martin E. Le Voi. *Memory: Current Issues.* Open Guides to Psychology. Philadelphia: Open University Press, 1993.

Collingwood, R. G. *The Idea of History.* Oxford: Oxford University Press, 1946.

Collins, Raymond F. *First Corinthians.* Sacra Pagina 7. Collegeville, MN: The Liturgical Press, 1999.

———. "The Image of Paul in the Pastorals." *Laval theologique et philosophique* 31(1975): 147–73.

Connerton, Paul. *How Societies Remember.* Cambridge: Cambridge University Press, 1989.

Conzelmann, Hans. *1 Corinthians: A Commentary on the First Epistle to the Corinthians.* Hermeneia. Philadelphia: Fortress Press, 1975 [1969].

———. "Paulus und die Weisheit." *New Testament Studies* 12(1966): 231–244.

———. "Die Schule des Paulus." Pages 85–96 in *Theologia Crucis—Signum Crucis: Festschrift für Erich Dinkler zum 70. Geburtstag.* Edited by Carl Andresen and Günter Klein. Tübingen: J. C. B. Mohr (Paul Siebeck), 1979.

Coolidge, John S. "The Pauline Basis of the Concept of Scriptural Form in Irenaeus." Pages 1–16 in *The Center for Hermeneutical Studies in Hellenistic and Modern Culture.* Edited by Wilhelm Wuellner. Berkeley, CA: The Center, 1973.

Cornoldi, Cesare, Robert H. Logie, Maria A. Brandimonte, Geir Kaufmann, and Daniel Reisberg. *Stretching the Imagination: Representation and Transformation in Mental Imagery.* Counterpoints: Cognition, Memory, & Language. Oxford: Oxford University Press, 1996.

Cosgrove, Charles H. "A Response to Ruth Clements and Sze-kar Wan: Will the Real Paul Please Stand Up!" Pages 195–205 in *Early Patristic Readings of Romans.* Edited by Kathy L. Gaca and L. L. Welborn. New York: T&T Clark, 2005.

Costa, G. "Principi ermeneutici gnostici nella lettura di Paolo (Lettera ai galati) secondo lo *Adv. Haer.* di Ireneo." *Rivista biblica* 34(1986): 615–637.

Cowe, S. Peter. "Text Critical Investigation of the Armenian Version of *Third Corinthians.*" Pages 91–102 in *Apocryphes arméniens: transmission–traduction–creation–iconographie.* Edited by Valentina Calzolari Bouvier, Jean-Daniel Kaestli, and

Bernard Outtier. Publications de l'Institut romand des sciences bibliques 1. Lausanne: Éditions du Zèbra, 1999.

Cox, Patricia. *Biography in Late Antiquity: A Quest for the Holy Man.* The Transformation of the Classical Heritage 5. Berkeley: University of California Press, 1983.

Cranfield, C. E. B. *Critical and Exegetical Commentary on the Epistle to the Romans.* 2 vols. International Critical Commentary. London: T&T Clark, 1979.

Credner, Karl A. *Beiträge zur Einleitung in die biblischen Schriften.* 2 vols. Halle: Buchhandlung des Waisenhauses, 1832–1838.

Danker, Frederick W., ed. *A Greek-English Lexicon of the New Testament and Other Early Christian Literature.* 3rd ed. Chicago: University of Chicago Press, 2000.

D'Anna, Alberto. *Terza lettera ai Corinzi: La risurrezione.* Letture cristiane del primo millenio 44. Milan: Pauline, 2009.

Dassmann, Ernst. "Archaeological Traces of Early Christian Veneration of Paul." Pages 281–306 in *Paul and the Legacies of Paul.* Edited by William S. Babcock. Dallas: Southern Methodist University Press, 1990.

———. "Paulus in der Gnosis." *Jahrbuch für Antike und Christentum* 22(1979): 123–138.

———. *Der Stachel im Fleisch: Paulus in der frühchristlichen Literatur bis Irenäus.* Münster: Aschendorff, 1979.

———. "Zum Paulusverständnis in der östlichen Kirche." *Jahrbuch für Antike und Christentum* 29(1986): 27–39.

Davidson, Arnold I., ed. *Foucault and His Interlocutors.* Chicago: University of Chicago Press, 1998.

Davies, John Gordon. "Factors Leading to the Emergence of Belief in the Resurrection of the Flesh." *Journal of Theological Studies* 23(1972): 448–455.

Davies, Stevan L. *The Revolt of the Widows: The Social World of the Apocryphal Acts.* Carbondale: Southern Illinois University Press, 1980.

———. "Women, Tertullian and the *Acts of Paul.*" *Semeia* 38 (1986): 139–143.

Davies, W. D., and Dale C. Allison, Jr. *A Critical and Exegetical Commentary on the Gospel According to Saint Matthew.* 3 vols. International Critical Commentary. Edinburgh: T&T Clark, 1997.

Davis, Stephen J. *The Cult of Saint Thecla: A Tradition of Women's Piety in Late Antiquity.* Oxford Early Christian Studies. Oxford: Oxford University Press, 2001.

———. "A 'Pauline' Defense of Women's Right to Baptize? Intertextuality and Apostolic Authority in the *Acts of Paul.*" *Journal of Early Christian Studies* 8(2000): 453–459.

Dawson, David. *Allegorical Readers and Cultural Revision in Ancient Alexandria.* Berkeley: University of California Press, 1992.

De Boer, Martinus C. "Images of Paul in the Post–Apostolic Period." *Catholic Biblical Quarterly* 42(1980): 359–380.

———. "Which Paul?" Pages 45–54 in *Paul and the Legacies of Paul.* Edited by William S. Babcock. Dallas: Southern Methodist University Press, 1990.

Dehandschutter, Boudewijn. "Ignatius, *Letter to the Magnesians* 8:2 Once Again." Pages 89–99 in *Jesus, Paul, and Early Christianity: Studies in Honour of Henk Jan de Jonge*. Edited by Rieuwerd Buitenwerf, Harm W. Hollander, and Johannes Tromp. Novum Testamentum Supplements 130. Leiden: Brill, 2008.

———. "Polycarp's Epistle to the Philippians: an Early Example of 'Reception.'" Pages 275–291 in *The New Testament in Early Christianity*. Edited by Jean-Marie Sevrin. Louvain: Leuven University Press, 1989.

Detering, Hermann. "The Dutch Radical Approach to the Pauline Epistles." *Journal of Higher Criticism* 3(1996): 163–193.

Detmers, Achim. "Interpretation der Israel–Lehre Marcions im ersten Drittel des 20. Jahrhunderts: theologischen Voraussetzungen und zeitgeschichtlicher Kontext." Pages 275–292 in *Marcion und seine kirchengeschichtliche Wirkung*. Edited by Gerhard May and Katharina Greschat. Berlin: Walter de Gruyter, 2002.

Dibelius, Martin, and Hans Conzelmann. *The Pastoral Epistles: a Commentary on the Pastoral Epistles*. Translated by P. Buttolph and Adela Yarbro. 4th ed. Hermeneia. Philadelphia: Fortress Press, 1972.

Dillon, John M. *The Middle Platonists: A Study of Platonism, 80 B.C. to A.D. 220*. Ithaca, NY: Cornell University Press, 1977.

Donovan, Mary A. "Irenaeus in Recent Scholarship." *Second Century: A Journal of Early Christian Studies* 4(1984): 219–241.

———. *One Right Reading?: A Guide to Irenaeus*. Collegeville, MN: Liturgical Press, 1997.

Dostal, Robert J. *The Cambridge Companion to Gadamer*. Cambridge Companions to Philosophy. Cambridge: Cambridge University Press, 2002.

Droysen, Johann Gustav. *Historik: Vorlesungen über Enzyklopadie und Methodologie der Geschichte*. Edited by Rudolf Hübner. München: R. Oldenbourg, 1937.

Dubois, Jean-Daniel. "L'utilisation gnostique du centon biblique cité en 1 Corinthiens 2,9." Pages 371–379 in κατὰ τούς o: *Selon les Septante: Trente études sur la Bible grecque des Septante: En Hommage à Marguerite Harl*. Edited by Gilles Dorival and Olivier Munnich. Paris: Editions du Cerf, 1995.

Dubowy, Ernst. *Klemens von Rom über die Reise Pauli nach Spanien*. Freiburg: Herder, 1914.

Duff, Jeremy. "P[46] and the Pastorals: A Misleading Consensus?" *New Testament Studies* 44(1998): 578–590.

———. "A Reconsideration of Pseudepigraphy in Early Christianity." Ph.D. diss., Oxford University, 1998.

Dulière, W. L. "Le Canon néotestamentaire et les écrits chrétiens approuvés par Irénée." *La nouvelle Clio* 6(1954): 199–224.

Dunderberg, Ismo. *Beyond Gnosticism: Myth, Lifestyle, and Society in the School of Valentinus*. New York: Columbia University Press, 2008.

———. "The School of Valentinus." Pages 64–99 in *A Companion to Second-Century Christian "Heretics."* Edited by Antii Marjanen and Petri Luomanen. Leiden: Brill, 2008.

Dunn, James D. G., ed. *The Cambridge Companion to St. Paul*. Cambridge Companions to Religion. Cambridge: Cambridge University Press, 2003.

———. *Jesus Remembered*. Christianity in the Making 1. Grand Rapids, MI: Eerdmans, 2003.

———. ed. *The New Perspective on Paul*. Rev. ed. Grand Rapids, MI: Eerdmans, 2007.

———. *Romans*. 2 vol. Word Biblical Commentary. Waco, TX: Word Books, 1988.

———. "Social Memory and the Oral Jesus Tradition." Pages 179–194 in *Memory in the Bible and Antiquity: the Fifth Durham-Tübingen Research Symposium (Durham, September 2004)*. Edited by Loren T. Stuckenbruck, Stephen C. Barton, and Benjamin G. Wold. Wissenschaftliche Untersuchungen zum Neuen Testament 212. Tübingen: Mohr Siebeck, 2007.

———. *The Theology of Paul the Apostle*. Grand Rapids, MI: Eerdmans, 1998.

Dunn, Peter W. "The *Acts of Paul* and the Pauline Legacy in the Second Century." Ph.D. diss., Cambridge University, 1996.

———. "The Influence of 1 Corinthians on the *Acts of Paul*." *Society of Biblical Literature Seminar Papers* 35(1996): 438–454.

———. "L'image de Paul dans les 'Actes de Paul.'" *Foi et vie* 94(1995): 75–85.

———. "Testing Pauline Pseudonymity: *3 Corinthians* and the Pastoral Epistles Compared." *Proceedings—Eastern Great Lakes and Midwest Biblical Societies* 20(2000): 63–70.

Dunning, Benjamin H. *Specters of Paul: Sexual Difference in Early Christian Thought*. Divinations: Rereading Late Ancient Religion. Philadelphia: University of Pennsylvania Press, 2011.

Eastman, David L. *Paul the Martyr: The Cult of the Apostle in the Latin West*. Writings from the Greco-Roman World Supplements 4. Atlanta: Society of Biblical Literature, 2011.

Ebner, Martin. *Aus Liebe zu Paulus? Die Akte Thekla neu aufgerollt*. Stuttgarter Bibelstudien 206. Stuttgart: Katholisches Bibelwerk, 2005.

Eco, Umberto. *Postscript to "The Name of the Rose."* Translated by W. Weaver. San Diego: Harcourt Brace Jovanovich, 1984.

Edwards, Mark. "Simon Magus, the Bad Samaritan." Pages 69–91 in *Portraits: Biographical Representation in the Greek and Latin Literature of the Roman Empire*. Edited by M. J. Edwards and S. Swain. Oxford: Clarenden Press, 1997.

Ehrman, Bart D., ed. *The Apostolic Fathers*. 2 vols. Loeb Classical Library 24–25. Cambridge, MA: Harvard University Press, 2003.

———. *Forgery and Counterforgery: The Use of Literary Deceit in Early Christian Polemics*. New York: Oxford University Press, 2012.

———. *Lost Scriptures: Books that Did Not Make it into the New Testament*. Oxford: Oxford University Press, 2003.

———. *The New Testament: a Historical Introduction to the Early Christian Writings*. 3rd ed. New York: Oxford University Press, 2004.

Eijk, A. H. C. van. "The *Gospel of Philip* and Clement of Alexandria: Gnostic and Ecclesiastical Theology on the Resurrection and the Eucharist." *Vigiliae christianae* 25(1971): 94–120.

———. "Resurrection–Language: Its Various Meanings in Early Christian Literature." *Studia patristica* 12(1975): 271–276.

Eisenstadt, Samuel N. "Some Comparative Reflections on the Continual Reconstruction of Tradition." Pages 6–25 in *Tradition and Tradition Theories*. Edited by Thorsten Larbig and Siegfried Wiedenhofer. Berlin: LIT Verlag, 2006.

———. *Tradition, Change and Modernity*. New York: Wiley, 1973.

Elliott, J.K., ed. *The Apocryphal New Testament: a Collection of Apocryphal Christian Literature in an English Translation Based on M. R. James*. Oxford: Clarendon Press, 1993.

Emmel, Stephen. "Exploring the Pathway that Leads from Paul to Gnosticism: What is the Genre of The Interpretation of Knowledge (NHC XI,1)?" Pages 257–276 in *Weisheit—Ursprünge und Rezeption: Festschrift für Karl Löning zum 65. Geburtstag*. Edited by Karl Lönig, Martin Fassnacht, Andreas Leinhäupl-Wilke, and Stefan Lücking. Neutestamenliche Abhandlungen 44. Münster: Aschendorff, 2003.

Engberg-Pedersen, Troels. "Complete and Incomplete Transformation in Paul: a Philosophical Reading of Paul on Body and Spirit." Pages 123–146 in *Metamorphoses: Resurrection, Body and Transformative Practices in Early Christianity*. Edited by Turid Karlsen Seim and Jorunn Økland. Berlin: Walter de Gruyter, 2009.

———. *Cosmology and Self in the Apostle Paul: The Material Spirit*. New York: Oxford University Press, 2011.

Engelhardt, Mortiz von. *Das Christenthum Justins des Märtyrers*. Erlangen: Deichert, 1878.

Epp, Eldon Jay. "Issues in the Interrelation of New Testament Textual Criticism and Canon." Pages 485–515 in *The Canon Debate*. Edited by Lee Martin McDonald and James A. Sanders. Peabody, MA: Hendrickson, 2002.

Eriksson, Anders. *Traditions as Rhetorical Proof: Pauline Argumentation in 1 Corinthians*. Coniectanea biblica: New Testament Series 29. Stockholm: Almqvist & Wiksell International, 1998.

Erll, Astrid, Ansgar Nünning, and Sara B. Young, eds. *Cultural Memory Studies: an International and Interdisciplinary Handbook*. Media and Cultural Memory 8. Berlin: Walter de Gruyter, 2008.

Esch-Wermeling, Elisabeth. *Thekla—Paulusschülerin wider Willen? Strategien der Leserlenkung in den Theklaakten*. Neutestamentliche Abhandlungen 53. Münster: Aschendorff, 2008.

Evans, Craig A., Robert L. Webb, and Richard A. Wiebe, eds. *Nag Hammadi Texts and the New Testament: a Synopsis and Index*. New Testament Tools and Studies 18. Leiden: Brill, 1993.

Evans, Ernest. *Tertullian: Adversus Marcionem*. Oxford: Oxford University Press, 1972.
———. *Tertullian's Homily on Baptism*. London: SPCK, 1964.
Evans, Richard J. *In Defence of History*. London: Granta Books, 1997.
Fantino, Jacques. *L'Homme image de Dieu chez S. Irénée de Lyon*. Paris: Éditions du Cerf, 1986.
———. *La théologie d'Irénée: lecture des Écritures en réponse à l'exégèse gnostique: une approche trinitaire*. Cogitatio fidei. Paris: Editions du Cerf, 1994.
Farkasfalvy, Denis. "Theology of Scripture in St. Irenaeus." *Revue bénédictine* 78(1968): 319–333.
Fee, Gordon D. *The First Epistle to the Corinthians*. New International Commentary on the New Testament. Grand Rapids, MI: Eerdmans, 1987.
Fentress, James, and Chris Wickham. *Social Memory*. Oxford: Blackwell, 1992.
Ferreiro, Alberto. *Simon Magus in Patristic, Medieval and Early Modern Traditions*. Studies in the History of Christian Traditions 125. Leiden: Brill, 2005.
Fishbane, Michael. *Biblical Interpretation in Ancient Israel*. Oxford: Clarendon Press, 1985.
Fitzer, Joseph. *Moehler and Baur in Controversy, 1832–38: Romantic-Idealist Assessment of the Reformation and Counter-Reformation*. American Academy of Religion Studies in Religion 7. Tallahassee, FL: American Academy of Religion, 1974.
Fitzmyer, Joseph A. *The Acts of the Apostles: a New Translation with Introduction and Commentary*. Anchor Bible 31. New York: Doubleday, 1998.
———. *First Corinthians: a New Translation with Introduction and Commentary*. The Anchor Yale Bible 32. New Haven, CT: Yale University Press, 2008.
Flusser, David. "Paul's Jewish-Christian Opponents in the *Didache*." Pages 71–90 in *Gilgul: Essays on Transformation, Revolution and Permanence in the History of Religions*. Edited by S. Shaked, D. Shulman, and Guy Stroumsa. Studies in the History of Religions 50. Leiden: Brill, 1987.
Foster, Paul. "The Epistles of Ignatius of Antioch and the Writings that later formed the New Testament." Pages 159–186 in *The Reception of the New Testament in the Apostolic Fathers*. Edited by Andrew F. Gregory and Christopher M. Tuckett. Oxford: Oxford University Press, 2005.
Foster, Paul, and Sara Parvis, eds. *Irenaeus: Life, Scripture, Legacy*. Minneapolis: Fortress Press, 2012.
Foucault, Michel. *The Archaeology of Knowledge and The Discourse on Language*. Trans. A. M. Sheridan Smith. New York: Pantheon Books, 1972 [1969].
———. *The Order of Things: An Archaeology of the Human Sciences*. New York: Vintage Books, 1994 [1966].
———. *Power/Knowledge: Selected Interviews & Other Writings—1972–1977*. Edited by Colin Gordon. Translated by Colin Gordon, Leo Marshall, John Mepham, and Kate Soper. New York: Pantheon Books, 1980.
Fredriksen, Paula. "Vile Bodies: Paul and Augustine on the Resurrection of the Flesh." Pages 75–82 in *Biblical Hermeneutics in Historical Perspective: Studies in Honor of Karlfried Froehlich on His Sixtieth Birthday*. Edited by M. S. Burrows and P. Rorem. Grand Rapids, MI: Eerdmans, 1991.

Frey, Jörg. "The Notion of 'Flesh' in 4QInstruction and the Background of Pauline Usage." Pages 197–226 in *Sapiential, Liturgical and Poetical Texts from Qumran: Proceedings of the Third Meeting of the International Organization for Qumran Studies, Published in Memory of Maurice Baillet.* Edited by Daniel K. Falk, F. Garcia Martinez, and Eileen M. Schuller. Studies on the Texts of the Desert of Judah 35. Leiden: Brill, 2000.

Frey, Jörg, Jens Herzer, Martina Janßen, and Clare K. Rothschild, eds. *Pseudepigraphie und Verfasserfiktion in frühchristlichen Briefen.* Wissenschaftliche Untersuchungen zum Neuen Testament 246. Tübingen: Mohr Siebeck, 2009.

Friese, Heidrun, and Aleida Assmann, eds. *Identities: Time, Difference, and Boundaries.* Making Sense of History 2. New York: Berghahn Books, 2002.

Frisius, Mark A. "Interpretive Method and Theological Controversy: Tertullian's Use of the Pastoral Epistles, Hebrews, James, 1 and 2 Peter, and Jude." Ph.D. diss, The Catholic University of America, 2009.

Froehlich, Karlfried. "Which Paul? Observations on the Image of the Apostle in the History of Biblical Exegesis." Pages 279–299 in *New Perspectives on Historical Theology: Essays in Memory of John Meyendorff.* Edited by Bradley Nassif. Grand Rapids, MI: Eerdmans, 1996.

Fuchs, Rüdiger. *Unerwartete Unterschiede: müssen wir unsere Ansichten über "die" Pastoralbriefe revidieren?* Bibelwissenschaftliche Monographien 12. Wuppertal: R. Brockhaus, 2003.

Gaca, Kathy L., and L. L. Welborn, eds. *Early Patristic Readings of Romans.* Romans through History and Cultures: Receptions and Critical Interpretations 1. New York: T&T Clark, 2005.

Gadamer, Hans-Georg. *Truth and Method.* Translated by Joel Weinsheimer and Donald G. Marshall. 2nd rev. ed. New York: Crossroad, 1989 [1960] .

Gaddis, John Lewis. *The Landscape of History: How Historians Map the Past.* Oxford: Oxford University Press, 2002.

Gager, John. "Marcion and Philosophy." *Vigiliae christianae* 26(1972): 53–59.

Gamble, Harry Y. *Books and Readers in the Early Church: a History of Early Christian Texts.* New Haven, CT: Yale University Press, 1995.

———. "The New Testament Canon: Recent Research and the Status Quaestionis." Pages 267–294 in *The Canon Debate.* Edited by Lee Martin McDonald and James A. Sanders. Peabody, MA: Hendrickson, 2002.

———. "The Redaction of the Pauline Letters and the Formation of the Pauline Corpus." *Journal of Biblical Literature* 94(1975): 403–418.

Gaventa, Beverly R. "The Overthrown Enemy: Luke's Portrait of Paul." *Society of Biblical Literature Seminar Papers* 24(1985): 439–449.

Geertz, Clifford. *The Interpretation of Cultures: Selected Essays.* New York: Basic Books, 1973.

Geiger, Wolfgang. *Spekulation und Kritik: Die Geschichtstheologie Ferdinand Christian Baurs.* Forschungen zur Geschichte und Lehre des Protestantismus 10.28. Munich: Chr. Kaiser Verlag, 1964.

Genette, Gérard. *Palimpsests: Literature in the Second Degree*. Translated by Channa Newman and Claude Doubinsky. Lincoln: University of Nebraska Press, 1997 [1982].

Genette, Gérard. *Paratexts: Thresholds of Interpretation*. Translated by Jane E. Lewin. Literature, Culture, Theory 20. Cambridge: Cambridge University Press, 1997 [1987].

Georgi, Dieter. "Hebrews and the Heritage of Paul." Pages 239–244 in *Hebrews: Contemporary Methods—New Insights*. Edited by G. Gelardini. Biblical Interpretation 75. Leiden: Brill, 2005.

———. "Irenaeus's and Origen's Treatment of Paul's Epistle to the Romans: An Assessment." Pages 206–212 in *Early Patristic Readings of Romans*. Edited by Kathy L. Gaca and L. L. Welborn. New York: T&T Clark, 2005.

Gilliard, Frank D. "The Apostolicity of Gallic Churches." *Harvard Theological Review* 68(1975): 17–33.

Gillis, John R., ed. *Commemorations: The Politics of National Identity*. Princeton, NJ: Princeton University Press, 1994.

———. "Memory and Identity: the History of a Relationship." Pages 3–24 in *Commemorations: The Politics of National Identity*. Edited by John R. Gillis. Princeton, NJ: Princeton University Press, 1996.

Glenny, W. Edward. "1 Corinthians 7:29–31 and the Teaching of Continence in *The Acts of Paul and Thecla*." *Grace Theological Journal* 11(1990): 53–70.

Gnilka, Joachim. "Das Paulusbild im Kolosser– und Epheserbrief." Pages 179–193 in *Kontinuität und Einheit: für Franz Mussner*. Edited by Paul-Gerhard Müller and Werner Stenger. Freiburg: Herder, 1981.

Goode, William J. *The Celebration of Heroes: Prestige as a Social Control System*. Berkeley: University of California Press, 1978.

Goodspeed, E. J. *The Formation of the New Testament*. Chicago: University of Chicago Press, 1926.

Goody, Jack. *The Domestication of the Savage Mind*. Cambridge: Cambridge University Press, 1977.

———. *The Interface between the Written and the Oral*. Cambridge: Cambridge University Press, 1987.

Grant, Robert M. "The Description of Paul in the Acts of Paul and Thecla." *Vigiliae christianae* 36(1982): 1–4.

———. *Irenaeus of Lyons*. The Early Christian Fathers. London: Routledge, 1997.

———. *The Letter and the Spirit*. London: SPCK, 1957.

———. "Marcion and the Critical Method." Pages 207–215 in *From Jesus to Paul: Studies in Honour of Francis Wright Beare*. Edited by Peter Richardson and John C. Hurd. Waterloo: Wilfred Laurier University Press, 1984.

———. "Scripture and Tradition in St Ignatius of Antioch." *Catholic Biblical Quarterly* 25(1963): 322–335.

Grappe, Christian. "De quelques images de Paul et de la manière dont elles se déploient au cours des deux premiers siècles." *Foi et vie* 94(1995): 49–59.

Gregory, Andrew F. "*1 Clement* and the Writings that later formed the New Testament." Pages 129–158 in *The Reception of the New Testament in the Apostolic Fathers.* Edited by Andrew F. Gregory and Christopher M. Tuckett. Oxford: Oxford University Press, 2005.

———. *The Reception of Luke and Acts in the Period Before Irenaeus: Looking for Luke in the Second Century.* Wissenschaftliche Untersuchungen zum Neuen Testament 169. Tübingen: J. C. B. Mohr, 2003.

Gregory, Andrew F., and Christopher M. Tuckett. "Reflections on Method: What constitutes the Use of the Writings that later formed the New Testament in the Apostolic Fathers?" Pages 61–82 in *The Reception of the New Testament in the Apostolic Fathers.* Edited by Andrew F. Gregory and Christopher M. Tuckett. Oxford: Oxford University Press, 2005.

———, eds. *The Reception of the New Testament in the Apostolic Fathers.* The New Testament and the Apostolic Fathers 1. Oxford: Oxford University Press, 2005.

———, eds. *Trajectories through the New Testament and the Apostolic Fathers.* The New Testament and the Apostolic Fathers 2. Oxford: Oxford University Press, 2005.

Gross, David. *The Past in Ruins: Tradition and the Critique of Modernity.* Critical Perspectives on Modern Culture. Amherst: The University of Massachusetts Press, 1992.

Gundry, Robert H. *Sōma in Biblical Theology: with Emphasis on Pauline Anthropology.* Society for New Testament Studies Monograph Series 29. Cambridge: Cambridge University Press, 1976.

Haar, Stephen. *Simon Magus: the First Gnostic?* Beihefte zur Zeitschrift für die neutestamentliche Wissenschaft 119. Berlin: Walter de Gruyter, 2003.

Haenchen, Ernst. *The Acts of the Apostles: a Commentary.* Translated by Bernard Noble and Gerald Shinn. Oxford: Basil Blackwell, 1971 [1959].

Häfner, Gerd. "Das Corpus Pastorale als literarisches Konstrukt." *Theologische Quartalschrift* 187(2007): 258–273.

Hagner, Donald A. *The Use of the Old and New Testaments in Clement of Rome.* Novum Testamentum Supplements 34. Leiden: Brill, 1973.

Halbwachs, Maurice. *The Collective Memory.* Translated by Francis J. Ditter, Jr. and Vida Yazdi Ditter. New York: Harper Colophon, 1980 [1950].

———. *On Collective Memory.* Edited by Donald N. Levine. Translated by Lewis A. Coser. The Heritage of Sociology. Chicago: University of Chicago Press, 1992.

Hällström, Gunnar af. *Carnis Resurrectio: The Interpretation of a Credal Formula.* Commentations Humanarum Litterarum 86. Helsinki: Societas Scientiarum Fennica, 1988.

Hammond Bammel, Caroline P. "Origen's Pauline Prefaces and the Chronology of his *Pauline Commentaries.*" Pages 495–513 in *Origeniana Sexta: Origene et la Bible/Origen and the Bible.* Edited by G. Dorival and Alain Le Boulluec. Bibliotheca Ephemeridum Theologicarum Lovaniensium 118. Leuven: Leuven University Press, 1995.

Hanson, Anthony T. "The Domestication of Paul: a Study in the Development of Early Christian Theology." *Bulletin of the John Rylands University Library of Manchester* 63(1981): 402–418.

Harnack, Adolf von. *Apocrypha IV: Die apokryphen Briefe des Paulus an die Laodicener und Korinther.* Berlin: Walter de Gruyter, 1931.

———. *History of Dogma.* 7 vols. Translated by Neil Buchanan. Boston: Little, Brown, and Company, 1901 [1885].

———. *Lehrbuch der Dogmengeschichte.* 3 vols. 4th ed. Darmstadt: Wissenschaftliche Buchgesellschaft, 1964 [1909].

———. *Marcion: das Evangelium vom fremden Gott: eine Monographie zur Geschichte der Grundlegung der katholischen Kirche.* Bibliothek klassischer Texte. Darmstadt: Wissenschaftliche Buchgesellschaft, 1996.

———. *Marcion: Der moderne Gläubige des 2. Jahrhunderts, der erste Reformator; die Dorpater Preisschrift (1870); kritische Edition des handschriftlichen Exemplars mit einem Anhang.* Edited by Friedemann Steck. Texte und Untersuchungen zur Geschichte der altchristlichen Literatur 149. Berlin: Walter de Gruyter, 2003 [1870].

———. *Marcion: The Gospel of the Alien God.* Translated by John E. Steely and Lyle D. Bierma. Durham, NC: Labyrinth Press, 1990 [1921].

———. "Der Presbyter-Prediger des Irenäus (IV,27,1–IV,32,1). Bruchstücke und Nachklänge der ältesten exegetisch–polemischen Homilieen." Pages 1–37 in *Philotesia: Paul Kleinert zum LXX Geburtstag.* Edited by Adolf von Harnack. Berlin: Trowitzsch & Sohn, 1907.

———. "Theophilus von Antiochien und das Neue Testament." *Zeitschrift für Kirchengeschichte* 11(1890): 1–21.

Harris, Horton. *The Tübingen School: a Historical and Theological Investigation of the School of F. C. Baur.* Leicester: Apollos, 1990 [1975].

Harrison, Jim. "In Quest of the Third Heaven: Paul and His Apocalyptic Imitators." *Vigiliae christianae* 58(2004): 24–55.

Hartog, Paul. *Polycarp and the New Testament: the Occasion, Rhetoric, Theme, and Unity of the Epistle to the Philippians and its Allusions to New Testament Literature.* Wissenschaftliche Untersuchungen zum Neuen Testament 2.134. Tübingen: Mohr Siebeck, 2002.

———. "Polycarp, Ephesians, and 'Scripture.'" *Westminster Theological Journal* 70 (2008): 255–275.

Harvey, W. Wigan. *Sancti Irenaei Episcopi Lugdunensis: Libros quinque adversus haereses.* 2 vols. Cambridge: Cambridge University Press, 1857.

Hearon, Holly E. "The Art of Biblical Interpretation: Re-membering the Past into the Present." *Encounter* 66(2005): 189–197.

———. "The Construction of Social Memory in Biblical Interpretation." *Encounter* 67(2006): 343–359.

Heckel, Theo K. "Body and Soul in Saint Paul." Pages 117–132 in *Psyche and Soma.* Edited by John P. Wright and Paul Potter. Oxford: Clarendon Press, 2000.

————. *Der Innere Mensch: Die paulinische Verarbeitung eines platonischen Motivs.* Wissenschaftliche Untersuchungen zum Neuen Testament 2.53. Tübingen: J. C. B. Mohr (Paul Siebeck), 1993.

Hefner, Philip J. "Saint Irenaeus and the Hypothesis of Faith." *Dialog* 2(1963): 300–306.

———— "Theological Methodology and St. Irenaeus." *Journal of Religion* 44(1964): 294–309.

Heimgartner, Martin. *Pseudojustin–Über die Auferstehung: Text und Studie.* Patristische Texte und Studien 54. Berlin: Walter de Gruyter, 2001.

Heine, Ronald E. *The Commentaries of Origen and Jerome on St Paul's Epistle to the Ephesians.* Oxford Early Christian Studies. Oxford: Oxford University Press, 2002.

Heinrici, Georg. *Die Valentinianische Gnosis und die heilige Schrift: eine Studie.* Berlin: Wiegandt und Grieben, 1871.

Helbig, Jörg. *Intertextualität und Markierung: Untersuchungen zur Systematik und Funktion der Signalisierung von Intertextualität.* Beiträge zur neueren Literaturgeschichte 3.141. Heidelberg: Universitätsverlag C. Winter, 1996.

Hembold, William. *Plutarch's Moralia, Vol. 6.* Loeb Classical Library 337. Cambridge, MA: Harvard University Press, 1962.

Hengel, Martin. "Der Jakobusbrief als antipaulinische Polemik." Pages 248–278 in *Tradition and Interpretation in the New Testament.* Edited by Gerald F. Hawthorne and Otto Betz. Grand Rapids, MI: Eerdmans, 1987.

Herzer, Jens. "Abschied vom Konses?: Die Pseudepigraphie der Pastoralbriefe als Herausforderung an die neutestamentliche Wissenschaft." *Theologische Literaturzeitung* 129(2004): 1267–1282.

Hester, Carl. "Gedanken zu Ferdinand Christian Baurs Entwicklung als Historiker anhand zweier unbekannter Briefe." *Zeitschrift für Kirchengeschichte* 84(1973): 249–269.

Hickling, C. J. A. "The Portrait of Paul in Acts 26." Pages 499–503 in *Les Actes des Apôtres: traditions, rédaction, théologie.* Edited by J. Kremer. Bibliotheca Ephemeridum Theologicarum Lovaniensium 48. Gembloux: J. Duculot, 1979.

Hilgenfeld, Adolf. *Der Kanon und die Kritik des Neuen Testaments in ihrer geschichtlichen Ausbildung und Gestaltung.* Halle: Pfeffer, 1863.

————. "Zur Geschichte des Unions–Paulinismus." *Zeitschrift für wissenschaftliche Theologie* 15(1872): 469–509.

Hilhorst, A. "Tertullian on the Acts of Paul." Pages 150–162 in *The Apocryphal Acts of Paul and Thecla.* Edited by Jan N. Bremmer. Kampen: Kok Pharos Publishing, 1996.

Hill, Charles E. "The *Epistula Apostolorum*: An Asian Tract from the Time of Polycarp." *Journal of Early Christian Studies* 7(1999): 416–438.

————. *From the Lost Teaching of Polycarp: Identifying Irenaeus' Apostolic Presbyter and the Author of Ad Diognetum.* Wissenschaftliche Untersuchungen zum Neuen Testament 186. Tübingen: Mohr Siebeck, 2006.

Hitchcock, F. R. Montgomery. *Irenaeus of Lugdunum: a Study of His Teaching.* Cambridge: Cambridge University Press, 1914.

Hobsbawm, Eric. *On History.* London: Weidenfeld & Nicolson, 1997.

Hobsbawm, Eric, and Terence Ranger, eds. *The Invention of Tradition.* Past and Present Publications. Cambridge: Cambridge University Press, 1983.

Hodgson, Peter C., ed. and trans. *Ferdinand Christian Baur on the Writing of Church History.* A Library of Protestant Thought. Oxford: Oxford University Press, 1968.

———. *The Formation of Historical Theology: A Study of Ferdinand Christian Baur.* Makers of Modern Theology. New York: Harper & Row, 1966.

Hoehner, Harold. "Did Paul Write Galatians?" Pages 150–169 in *History and Exegesis: New Testament Essays in Honor of Dr. E. Earle Ellis for his 80th Birthday.* Edited by Sang-Won (Aaron) Son. New York: T&T Clark, 2006.

Hoffmann, R. Joseph. "How Then Know this Troublous Teacher? Further Reflections on Marcion and His Church." *Second Century: A Journal of Early Christian Studies* 6 (1987–1988): 173–191.

———. *Marcion: On the Restitution of Christianity: An Essay on the Development of Radical Paulinist Theology in the Second Century.* American Academy of Religion: Academy Series 46. Chico, CA: Scholars Press, 1984.

Hoh, J. *Die Lehre des Hl. Irenäus über das Neue Testament.* Neutestamentliche Abhandlungen 7. Münster: Aschendorff, 1919.

Holmes, Michael. "Polycarp's *Letter to the Philippians* and the Writings that later formed the New Testament." Pages 187–228 in *The Reception of the New Testament in the Apostolic Fathers.* Edited by Andrew F. Gregory and Christopher M. Tuckett. Oxford: Oxford University Press, 2005.

Hooker, Morna D., and Stephen G. Wilson, eds. *Paul and Paulinism: Essays in Honor of C. K. Barrett.* London: SPCK, 1982.

Horkheimer, Max, and Theodor W. Adorno. *Dialectic of Enlightenment.* Translated by J. Cumming. New York: Herder and Herder, 1972 [1944].

Horn, Friedrich Wilhelm, ed. *Das Ende des Paulus: historische, theologische und literaturgeschichtliche Aspekte.* Beihefte zur Zeitschrift für die neutestamentliche Wissenschaft 106. Berlin: Walter de Gruyter, 2001.

Hovhanessian, Vahan. *Third Corinthians: Reclaiming Paul for Christian Orthodoxy.* Studies in Biblical Literature 18. New York: Peter Lang, 2000.

Howe, E. Margaret. "Interpretations of Paul in *The Acts of Paul and Thecla.*" Pages 33–49 in *Pauline Studies: Essays Presented to F. F. Bruce on his 70th Birthday.* Edited by Donald A. Hagner and Murray J. Harris. Grand Rapids, MI: Eerdmans, 1980.

Hutton, Patrick. *History as an Art of Memory.* Hanover, NH: University Press of New England, 1993.

Iggers, Georg, and James Powell, eds. *Leopold von Ranke and the Shaping of the Historical Discipline.* Syracuse, NY: Syracuse University Press, 1990.

Janßen, Martina. *Unter falschem Namen: Eine kritische Forschungsbilanz früchristlicher Pseudepigraphie.* Arbeiten zur Religion und Geschichte des Urchristentums 14. Frankfurt: Peter Lang, 2003.

Jewett, Robert. *Paul's Anthropological Terms: A Study of Their Use in Conflict Settings.* Arbeiten zur Geschichte des antiken Judentums und des Urchristentums 10. Leiden: Brill, 1971.

———. "The Redaction of 1 Corinthians and the Trajectory of the Pauline School." *Journal of the American Academy of Religion Supplements* 46(1978): 389–444.

John, J. P. H. "The Importance of St. Paul and the Pauline Epistles in Second Century Gnosticism (apart from Marcion)." Ph.D. diss., Oxford University, 1984.

Johnson, Andy. "On Removing a Trump Card: Flesh and Blood and the Reign of God." *Bulletin for Biblical Research* 13(2003): 175–192.

Johnson, Luke Timothy. *The First and Second Letters to Timothy: a New Translation with Introduction and Commentary.* Anchor Bible 35A. New York: Doubleday, 2001.

———. *Letters to Paul's Delegates: 1 Timothy, 2 Timothy, Titus.* Valley Forge, PA: Trinity Press International, 1996.

Johnson, Michael P., ed. *Abraham Lincoln, Slavery, and the Civil War: Selected Writings and Speeches.* Bedford Series in History and Culture. Boston: Bedford Press, 2001.

Johnston, Steve. "La Correspondance apocryphe entre Paul et les Corinthiens: Problèmes relies à l'identification des adversaires." Pages 187–230 in *Colloque international. "L'évangile selon Thomas et les textes de Nag Hammadi." Québec, 29–31 mai 2003.* Edited by Louis Painchaud and Paul-Hubert Poirier. Bibliothèque copte de Nag Hammadi: Études 8. Québec: Presses de l'Université Laval, 2007.

———. "La Correspondance apocryphe entre Paul et les Corinthiens: un pseudépigraphe Paulinien au service de la polémique anti–gnostique de la fin du IIE siècle." M.A. thesis, l'Université Laval, 2004.

Johnston, Steve, and Paul-Hubert Poirier. "Nouvelles citations chez Éphrem et Aphraate de la correspondence entre Paul et les Corinthiens." *Apocrypha* 16(2005): 137–147.

Jonas, Hans. *The Gnostic Religion: The Message of the Alien God and the Beginnings of Christianity.* 2nd ed. Boston: Beacon Press, 1963 [1958].

Jones, F. Stanley. *An Ancient Jewish Christian Source on the History of Christianity: Pseudo-Clementine Recognitions 1.21–71.* Society of Biblical Literature Texts and Translations 37. Atlanta, GA: Scholars Press, 1995.

Joppich, Godehard. *Salus carnis: Eine Untersuchung in der Theologie des hl. Irenäus von Lyon.* Münsterschwarzacher Studien 1. Münsterschwarzach: Vier-Türme, 1965.

Kaler, Michael. "Contextualizing the *Apocalypse of Paul.*" *Laval théologique et philosophique* 61(2005): 233–246.

———. *Flora Tells a Story: the Apocalypse of Paul and its Contexts.* Studies in Christianity and Judaism. Waterloo, ON: Wilfrid Laurier University Press, 2008.

———. "The Prayer of the Apostle Paul in the Context of Nag Hammadi Codex 1." *Journal of Early Christian Studies* 16(2008): 319–339.

Kaler, Michael. "Those Sneaky Valentinians." Pages 231–250 in *Colloque interna-tional: "L'évangile selon Thomas et les textes de Nag Hammadi," Québec, 29–31 mai 2003*. Edited by Louis Painchaud and Paul-Hubert Poirier. Bibliothèque copte de Nag Hammadi: Études 8. Québec: Presses de l'Université Laval, 2007.

———. "Towards an Expanded Understanding of Nag Hammadi Paulinism." *Stud-ies in Religion/Sciences religieuses* 33(2004): 301–317.

Kaler, Michael, Louis Painchaud, and Marie-Pierre Bussières. "The *Coptic Apoca-lypse of Paul*, Irenaeus' *Adversus haereses* 2.30.7, and the Second-Century Battle for Paul's Legacy." *Journal of Early Christian Studies* 12(2004): 173–193.

Kannengiesser, Charles. *Handbook of Patristic Exegesis: The Bible in Early Christian-ity*. 2 vols. Leiden: Brill, 2004.

Kasemann, Ernst. "Paul and Early Catholicism." Pages 236–251 in *New Testament Questions of Today*. Translated by W. J. Montague. Philadelphia: Fortress Press, 1969.

Keck, Leander E. "Images of Paul in New Testament." *Interpretation* 43(1989): 341–351.

Kelber, Werner. "The Case of the Gospels: Memory's Desire and the Limits of His-torical Criticism." *Oral Tradition* 17(2002): 55–86.

———. *The Oral and the Written Gospel: Hermeneutics of Speaking and Writing in the Synoptic Tradition, Mark, Paul and Q*. Philadelphia: Fortress Press, 1983.

Kelber, Werner, and Samuel Byrskog, eds. *Jesus in Memory: Traditions in Oral and Scribal Perspectives*. Waco, TX: Baylor University Press, 2009.

Kelly, J. N. D. *The Epistles of Peter and of Jude*. Harper's New Testament Commentar-ies. New York: Harper and Row, 1969.

Kertelge, Karl, ed. *Paulus in den neutestamentlichen Spätschriften: zur Paulusrezeption im Neuen Testament*. Quaestiones disputatae 89. Freiburg: Herder, 1981.

Kim, Dai S. "The Doctrine of Man in Irenaeus of Lyons." Ph.D. diss., Boston Uni-versity, 1969.

King, Karen. *What is Gnosticism?* Cambridge, MA: Harvard University Press, 2003.

Kinzig, Wolfram. "Ein Ketzer und sein Konstrukteur: Harnacks Marcion." Pages 253–274 in *Marcion und seine kirchengeschichtliche Wirkung*. Edited by Gerhard May and Katharina Greschat. Berlin: Walter de Gruyter, 2002.

———. *Harnack, Marcion und das Judentum: Nebst einer kommentierten Edition des Briefwechsels Adolf von Harnacks mit Houston Stewart Chamberlain*. Arbeiten zur Kirchen- und Theologiegeschichte 13. Leipzig: Evangelische Verlagsanstalt, 2004.

Kirk, Alan. "The Memory of Violence and the Death of Jesus in Q." Pages 191–206 in *Memory, Tradition, and Text: Uses of the Past in Early Christianity*. Edited by Alan Kirk and Tom Thatcher. Atlanta, GA: Society of Biblical Literature, 2005.

———. "Social and Cultural Memory." Pages 1–24 in *Memory, Tradition, and Text: Uses of the Past in Early Christianity*. Edited by Alan Kirk and Tom Thatcher. At-lanta, GA: Society of Biblical Literature, 2005.

─────. "Tradition and Memory in the *Gospel of Peter*." Pages 135–158 in *Evangelium nach Petrus: Text, Kontexte, Intertexte*. Edited by Tobias Nicklas and Thomas Kraus. Texte und Untersuchungen zur Geschichte der altchristlichen Literatur 158. Berlin: Walter de Gruyter, 2007.

Kirk, Alan, and Tom Thatcher, eds. *Memory, Tradition, and Text: Uses of the Past in Early Christianity*. Semeia Studies 52. Atlanta, GA: Society of Biblical Literature, 2005.

Klauck, Hans-Josef. "Die Himmelfahrt des Paulus (2 Kor. 12.2–4) in der koptischen Paulusapokalypse aus Nag Hammadi (NHC V/2)." *Studien zum Neuen Testament und seiner Umwelt* 10(1985): 151–190.

Klebba, Ernst. *Die Anthropologie des hl. Irenaeus: eine dogmenhistorische Studie*. Kirchengeschichtliche Studien Bd. 2, Heft 3. Münster: H. Schöningh, 1894.

Klijn, A. F. J. "Apocryphal Correspondence between Paul and the Corinthians." *Vigiliae christianae* 17(1963): 2–23.

Klijn, A. F. J., and G. J. Reinink, eds. *Patristic Evidence for Jewish-Christian Sects*. Novum Testamentum Supplements 36. Leiden: Brill, 1973.

Knoch, Otto. "Petrus und Paulus in den Schriften der Apostolischen Väter." Pages 240–260 in *Kontinuität und Einheit: für Franz Mussner*. Edited by Paul-Gerhard Müller and Werner Stenger. Freiburg: Herder, 1981.

Knox, John. *Marcion and the New Testament: an Essay in the Early History of the Canon*. Chicago: University of Chicago Press, 1942.

Knuth, Hans Christian. "Ferdinand Christian Baurs 'Paulus' und sein Verhältnis zu Hegel in der Spätzeit." Pages 227–244 in *Paulus, Apostel Jeus Christi: Festschrift für Günter Klein zum 70. Geburtstag*. Edited by Michael Trowitzsch. Tübingen: Mohr Siebeck, 1998.

Koester, Helmut. *Introduction to the New Testament*. 2 vols. 2nd ed. Berlin: Walter de Gruyter, 1995–2000 [1982].

Koschorke, Klaus. "Paulus in den Nag-Hammadi-Texten: ein Beitrag zur Geschichte der Paulusrezeption im frühen Christentum." *Zeitschrift für Theologie und Kirche* 78(1981): 177–205.

Kosslyn, Stephen M., William L. Thompson, and Giorgio Ganis. *The Case for Mental Imagery*. Oxford Psychology Series. Oxford: Oxford University Press, 2006.

Krajewski, Bruce, ed. *Gadamer's Repercussions: Reconsidering Philosophical Hermeneutics*. Berkeley: University of California Press, 2004.

Kuhn, K.G. "Πειρασμός–Ἁμαρτία–Σάρξ im Neuen Testament und die damit zusammenhängenden Vorstellungen." *Zeitschrift für Theologie und Kirche* 49(1952): 200–222.

Kuhn, Thomas. *The Structure of Scientific Revolutions*. Chicago: University of Chicago Press, 1962.

Kunzendorf, Robert G., ed. *Mental Imagery*. New York: Plenum Press, 1991.

Kuss, Otto. *Paulus: Die Rolle des Apostels in der theologischen Entwicklung der Urkirche*. 2nd ed. Regensberg: Pustet, 1976 [1971].

Labahn, Michael. "Paulus–ein homo honestus et iustus: das lukanische Paulusportrait von Act 27–28 im Lichte ausgewählter antiker Parallelen." Pages 75–106
in *Das Ende des Paulus*. Edited by Friedrich Wilhelm Horn. Berlin: Walter de
Gruyter, 2001.

Lalleman, Pieter. "The resurrection in the Acts of Paul." Pages 126–141 in *The Apocryphal Acts of Paul and Thecla*. Edited by Jan N. Bremmer. Kampen: Kok Pharos,
1996.

Lampe, Peter. *From Paul to Valentinus: Christians at Rome in the First Two Centuries.*
Translated by Michael Steinhauser. Minneapolis: Fortress Press, 2003 [1989].

Lang, Gladys Engel, and Kurt Lang. "Recognition and Renown: The Survival of Artistic Reputation." *The American Journal of Sociology* 94(1988): 79–109.

Larbig, Thorsten, and Siegfried Wiedenhofer, eds. *Tradition and Tradition Theories:
An International Discussion.* Studien zur Traditionstheorie/Studies in Tradition
Theory. Berlin: LIT Verlag, 2006.

Lawson, John. *The Biblical Theology of Saint Irenaeus.* London: Epworth Press, 1948.

Layton, Bentley. *The Gnostic Scriptures.* Anchor Bible Reference Library. New York:
Doubleday, 1987.

———. *The Gnostic Treatise on Resurrection from Nag Hammadi.* Harvard Dissertations in Religion 12. Missoula, MT: Scholars Press, 1979.

———. "Prolegomena to the Study of Ancient Gnosticism." Pages 334–350 in *The
Social World of the First Christians: Essays in Honor of Wayne A. Meeks.* Edited by
L. Michael White and O. Larry Yarborough. Minneapolis: Fortress Press, 1995.

———. "Vision and Revision: a Gnostic View of Resurrection." Pages 190–217 in
Colloque International sur les textes de Nag Hammadi. Edited by Bernard Barc. Bibliothèque copte de Nag Hammadi 1. Québec: Presses de L'Université Laval, 1981.

Layton, Richard A. "Origen as a Reader of Paul: A Study of the *Commentary on Ephesians.*" Ph.D. diss., University of Virginia, 1996.

———. "Recovering Origin's Pauline Exegesis: Exegesis and Eschatology in the
Commentary on Ephesians." *Journal of Early Christian Studies* 8(2000): 373–411.

Le Boulluec, Alain. "The Bible in Use among the Marginally Orthodox in the Second
and Third Centuries." Pages 197–216 in *The Bible in Greek Christian Antiquity.*
Edited by Paul M. Blowers. The Bible Through the Ages 1. Notre Dame: University of Notre Dame Press, 1997 [1984].

———. "Exégèse et polémique antignostique chez Irénée et Clément d'Alexandrie:
l'example du centon." *Studia patristica* 17(1982): 707–713.

Le Donne, Anthony. *The Historiographical Jesus: Memory, Typology, and the Son of
David.* Waco, TX: Baylor University Press, 2009.

———. "Theological Memory Distortion in the Jesus Tradition: a Study in Social
Memory Theory." Pages 163–177 in *Memory in the Bible and Antiquity: the Fifth
Durham-Tübingen Research Symposium (Durham, September 2004).* Edited by
Loren T. Stuckenbruck, Stephen C. Barton, and Benjamin G. Wold. Wissen-
schaftliche Untersuchungen zum Neuen Testament 212. Tübingen: Mohr Sie-
beck, 2007.

Le Goff, Jacques. *History and Memory*. New York: Columbia University Press, 1992.

Lehtipuu, Outi. "'Flesh and Blood Cannot Inherit the Kingdom of God': The Transformation of the Flesh in the Early Christian Debates." Pages 147–168 in *Metamorphoses: Resurrection, Body and Transformative Practices in Early Christianity*. Edited by Turid Karlsen Seim and Jorunn Økland. Berlin: Walter de Gruyter, 2009.

Lentz, John C., Jr. *Luke's Portrait of Paul*. Society for New Testament Studies Monograph Series 77. Cambridge: Cambridge University Press, 1993.

Lerner, Robert, Althea K. Nagai, and Stanley Rothman. *Molding the Good Citizen: The Politics of High School History Texts*. Westport, CT: Praeger, 1995.

Liddell, H. G., and R. Scott, eds. *A Greek-English Lexicon*. 9th ed. Oxford: Clarendon Press, 1996 [1897].

Liebing, Heinz. "Historical-Critical Theology: In Commemoration of the One Hundredth Anniversary of the Death of Ferdinand Christian Baur, December 2, 1960." Pages 55–69 in *Distinctive Protestant and Catholic Themes Reconsidered*. Edited by Ernst Käsemann, et al. Journal for Theology and the Church 3. Tübingen: J. C. B. Mohr (Paul Siebeck), 1967.

Lieu, Judith. "'As much my apostle as Christ is mine': The Dispute over Paul between Tertullian and Marcion." *Early Christianity* 1(2010): 41–59.

———. "The Battle for Paul in the Second Century." *Irish Theological Quarterly* 75(2010): 3–14.

Lightfoot, J. B. *The Apostolic Fathers: Clement, Ignatius, and Polycarp*. 5 vols. Peabody, MA: Hendrickson, 1989 [1889–90].

———. *St Paul's Epistle to the Galatians*. 3rd ed. London: Macmillan, 1869 [1865].

Liljeström, Kenneth, ed. *The Early Reception of Paul*. Publications of the Finnish Exegetical Society 99. Helsinki: Finnish Exegetical Society, 2011.

Lind, Michael. *What Lincoln Believed: The Values and Convictions of America's Greatest President*. New York: Doubleday, 2005.

Lindemann, Andreas. "Der Apostel Paulus im 2 Jahrhundert." Pages 39–67 in *The New Testament in Early Christianity*. Edited by Jean-Marie Sevrin. Louvain: Leuven University Press, 1989.

———. *Die Clemensbriefe*. Handbuch zum Neuen Testament. Tübingen: J. C. B. Mohr (Paul Siebeck), 1992.

———. "Die Sammlung der Paulusbriefe im 1. und 2. Jahrhundert." Pages 321–351 in *The Biblical Canons*. Edited by Jeanne-Marie Auwers and Henk Jan DeJonge. Bibliotheca Ephemeridum Theologicarum Lovaniensium 163. Leuven: Leuven University Press, 2003.

———. "Paul in the Writings of the Apostolic Fathers." Pages 25–45 in *Paul and the Legacies of Paul*. Edited by William S. Babcock. Dallas: Southern Methodist University Press, 1990.

———. "Paulinische Theologie im Brief an Diognet." Pages 337–350 in *Kerygma und Logos: Beiträge zu den geistesgeschichtlichen Beziehungen zwischen Antike und Christentum (Festschrift für Carl Andresen zum 70. Geburtstag)*. Edited by Adolf Martin Ritter. Göttingen: Vandenhoeck & Ruprecht, 1979.

Lindemann, Andreas. *Paulus, Apostel und Lehrer der Kirche: Studien zu Paulus und zum frühen Paulusverständnis.* Tübingen: J. C. B. Mohr (Paul Siebeck), 1999.

———. *Paulus im ältesten Christentum: Das Bild des Apostels und die Rezeption der paulinischen Theologie in der frühchristlichen Literatur bis Marcion.* Beiträge zur historischen Theologie 58. Tübingen: J. C. B. Mohr (Paul Siebeck), 1979.

———. "Paul's Influence on 'Clement' and Ignatius." Pages 9–24 in *Trajectories Through the New Testament and the Apostolic Fathers.* Edited by Andrew F. Gregory and Christopher M. Tuckett. Oxford: Oxford University Press, 2005.

Lipsius, Richard A., ed. *Acta Petri–Acta Pauli–Acta Petri et Pauli–Acta Pauli et Theclae–Acta Thaddaei.* Acta Apostolorum Apocrypha 1. Hildeshiem: Georg Olms, 1990 [1891].

Loewen, James. *Lies My Teacher Told Me: Everything Your American History Textbook Got Wrong.* New York: New Press, 1995.

Loftus, Elizabeth F. *Eyewitness Testimony.* Cambridge, MA: Harvard University Press, 1979.

Löhr, Dieter. "Did Marcion Distinguish Between a Just God and a Good God?" Pages 131–146 in *Marcion und seine kirchengeschichtliche Wirkung.* Edited by Gerhard May and Katharina Greschat. Berlin: Walter de Gruyter, 2002.

Löhr, Hermut. "Zur Paulus–Notiz in 1 Clem 5,5–7." Pages 197–213 in *Das Ende des Paulus.* Edited by Friedrich Wilhelm Horn. Berlin: Walter de Gruyter, 2001.

Lona, Horacio E. *Der erste Clemensbrief.* Kommentare zum Apostolischen Väter. Göttingen: Vandenhoeck & Ruprecht, 1998.

———. *Über die Auferstehung des Fleisches: Studien zur frühchristlichen Eschatologie.* Beiheft zur Zeitschrift für die neutestamentliche Wissenschaft und die Kunde der älteren Kirche 66. Berlin: Walter de Gruyter, 1993.

Long, A. A., and D. N. Sedley. *The Hellenistic Philosophers.* 2 vols. Cambridge: Cambridge University Press, 1987.

Long, William R. "The *Paulusbild* in the Trial of Paul in Acts." *Society of Biblical Literature Seminar Papers* 22(1983): 87–105.

Loofs, F. *Theophilus von Antiochien "Adversus Marcionem" und die anderen theologischen Quellen bei Irenaeus.* Texte und Untersuchungen zur Geschichte der altchristlichen Literatur 46.2. Leipzig: J. C. Hinrichs, 1930.

Looks, Carsten. *Das Anvertraute bewahren: die Rezeption der Pastoralbriefe im 2. Jahrhundert.* Münchner Theologische Beiträge 3. Munich: Herbert Utz Verlag, 1999.

Lovering, E. H., Jr. "The Collection, Redaction, and Early Circulation of the Corpus Paulinum." Ph.D. diss., Southern Methodist University, 1988.

Lowenthal, David. *The Past is a Foreign Country.* Cambridge: Cambridge University Press, 1985.

Lüdemann, Gerd. "The Acts of the Apostles and the Beginnings of Simonian Gnosis." *New Testament Studies* 33(1987): 420–426.

———. *Opposition to Paul in Jewish Christianity.* Translated by M. Eugene Boring. Minneapolis: Fortress Press, 1989.

Lundhaug, Hugo. "'These are the Symbols and Likenesses of the Resurrection': Conceptualizations of Death and Transformation in the *Treatise on the Resurrection* (NHC I, 4)." Pages 187–205 in *Metamorphoses: Resurrection, Body and Transformative Practices in Early Christianity*. Edited by Turid Karlsen Seim and Jorunn Økland. Berlin: Walter de Gruyter, 2009.

Luppe, W. "Rückseitentitel auf Papyrusrollen." *Zeitschrift für Papyrologie und Epigraphik* 27(1977): 89–99.

Luttikhuizen, Gerard. "The Apocryphal Correspondence with the Corinthians and the *Acts of Paul*." Pages 75–91 in *The Apocryphal Acts of Paul and Thecla*. Edited by Jan N. Bremmer. Kampen: Kok Pharos, 1996.

MacDonald, Dennis R. "Apocryphal and Canonical Narratives About Paul." Pages 55–70 in *Paul and the Legacies of Paul*. Edited by William S. Babcock. Dallas: Southern Methodist Press, 1990.

———. *The Legend and the Apostle: The Battle for Paul in Story and Canon*. Philadelphia: Westminster Press, 1983.

MacDonald, Margaret Y. *The Pauline Churches: A Socio-Historical Study of Institutionalization in the Pauline and Deutero-Pauline Writings*. Society for New Testament Studies Monograph Series 60. Cambridge: Cambridge University Press, 1988.

———. "Rereading Paul: Early Interpreters of Paul on Women and Gender." Pages 236–253 in *Women & Christian Origins*. Edited by Ross Shephard Kraemer and Mary Rose D'Angelo. New York: Oxford University Press, 1999.

MacIntyre, Alasdair. *After Virtue: a Study in Moral Theory*. Notre Dame, IN: Notre Dame University Press, 1981.

Mackay, Thomas W. "Content and Style in Two Pseudo-Pauline Epistles (3 Corinthians and the Epistle to the Laodiceans)." Pages 215–240 in *Apocryphal Writings of the Latter-day Saints*. Edited by C. W. Griggs. The Religious Studies Monograph Series 13. Provo, UT: Religious Studies Center, BYU, 1986.

———. "Observations on P. Bodmer X (Apocryphal Correspondence Between Paul and the Corinthian Saints)." *Papyrologica Bruxellensia* 18(1979): 119–128.

Maier, Harry O. "The Politics and Rhetoric of Discord and Concord in Paul and Ignatius." Pages 307–324 in *Trajectories through the New Testament and the Apostolic Fathers*. Edited by Andrew F. Gregory and Christopher M. Tuckett. Oxford: Oxford University Press, 2005.

Malherbe, Abraham J. "A Physical Description of Paul." *Harvard Theological Review* 79(1986): 170–175.

Malina, Bruce J., and Jerome H. Neyrey. *Portraits of Paul: an Archaeology of Ancient Personality*. Louisville, KY: Westminster John Knox, 1996.

Mannheim, Karl. *Essays on the Sociology of Knowledge*. New York: Oxford University Press, 1952.

———. *Ideology and Utopia: An Introduction to the Sociology of Knowledge*. Routledge Sociology Classics. London: Routledge, 1991 [1929].

Marguerat, Daniel. "L'Image de Paul dans les Actes des Apôtres." Pages 121–154 in *Les Actes des Apôtres: histoire, récit, théologie. XXᵉ congrès de l'Association catholique française pour l'étude de la Bible (Angers, 2003)*. Edited by M. Berder. Lectio divina 199. Paris: Éditions du Cerf, 2005.

———. "Paul après Paul: une histoire de réception." *New Testament Studies* 54(2008): 317–337.

Markschies, Christoph. "Die platonische Metapher vom 'inneren Menschen': Eine Brücke zwischen antiker Philosophie und altchristlicher Theologie." *Zeitschrift für Kirchengeschichte* 105(1994): 1–17.

———. "Die valentinische Gnosis und Marcion — einige neue Perspektiven." Pages 159–176 in *Marcion und seine kirchengeschichtliche Wirkung*. Edited by Gerhard May and Katharina Greschat. Berlin: Walter de Gruyter, 2002.

———. "A Response to Jeffrey Bingham and Susan Graham." Pages 152–158 in *Early Patristic Readings of Romans*. Edited by Kathy L. Gaca and L. L. Welborn. New York: T&T Clark, 2005.

———. *Valentinus Gnosticus?* Wissenschaftliche Untersuchungen zum Neuen Testament 65. Tübingen: J. C. B. Mohr (Paul Siebeck), 1992.

Marshall, Donald G., ed. *The Force of Tradition: Response and Resistance in Literature, Religion, and Cultural Studies*. Lanham, MD: Rowman & Littlefield Publishers, 2005.

Marshall, I. Howard. *A Critical and Exegetical Commentary on the Pastoral Epistles*. International Critical Commentary. Edinburgh: T&T Clark, 1999.

Martin, Dale. *The Corinthian Body*. New Haven, CT: Yale University Press, 1995.

Martyn, J. Louis. *Galatians: a New Translation with Introduction and Commentary*. Anchor Bible 33A. New York: Doubleday, 1997.

Marx, Karl. *The 18th Brumaire of Louis Bonaparte*. New York: International Publishers, 1963 [1852].

———. *On Religion*. New York: Schocken Books, 1964.

Mascellani, Elisa. *Prudens dispensator verbi: Romani 5:12–21 nell'esegesi di Clemente Alessandrino e Origene*. Florence: Nuova Italia, 1990.

Mason, Elliott J. "The Position of Hebrews in the Pauline Corpus in the Light of Chester Beatty Papyrus II." Ph.D. diss, University of Southern California, 1968.

Matthews, Shelly. "Thinking of Thecla: Issues in Feminist Historiography." *Journal of Feminist Studies in Religion* 17(2002): 39–65.

May, Gerhard. "Der Streit zwischen Petrus und Paulus in Antiochien bei Markion." Pages 204–211 in *Von Wittenberg nach Memphis: Festschrift für Reinhard Schwarz*. Edited by Reinhard Schwartz, Walter Homolka, and Otto Ziegelmeier. Arbeiten zur Religionspädagogik. Göttingen: Vandenhoeck & Ruprecht, 1989.

———. "Marcion in Contemporary Views: Results and Open Questions." *Second Century: A Journal of Early Christian Studies* 6(1988): 129–151.

———. "Marcion ohne Harnack." Pages 1–7 in *Marcion und seine kirchengeschichtliche Wirkung*. Edited by Gerhard May and Katharina Greschat. Berlin: Walter de Gruyter, 2002.

————. *Markion: Gesammelte Aufsätze.* Edited by Katharina Greschat and Martin Meiser. Veröffentlichungen des Instituts für Europäische Geschichte Mainz 68. Mainz: Philipp von Zabern, 2005.

May, Gerhard, and Katharina Greschat, eds. *Marcion und seine kirchengeschichtliche Wirkung = Marcion and His Impact on Church History: Vortrage der Internationalen Fachkonferenz zu Marcion, gehalten vom 15.–18. August 2001 in Mainz.* Texte und Untersuchungen zur Geschichte der altchristlichen Literatur 150. Berlin: Walter de Gruyter, 2002.

Mayer, Herbert T. "Clement of Rome and His Use of Scripture." *Concordia Theological Monthly* 42(1971): 536–540.

McDonald, Lee Martin. *The Biblical Canon: Its Origin, Transmission, and Authority.* Rev. and exp. ed. Peabody, MA: Hendrickson, 2007 [1995].

McDonald, Lee Martin, and James A. Sanders, eds. *The Canon Debate.* Peabody, MA: Hendrickson, 2002.

McGowan, Andrew. "Marcion's Love of Creation." *Journal of Early Christian Studies* 9(2001): 295–311.

McHugh, John. "A Reconsideration of Ephesians 1:10b in the Light of Irenaeus." Pages 302–309 in *Paul and Paulinism: Essays in Honor of C. K. Barrett.* Edited by Morna D. Hooker and Stephen G. Wilson. London: SPCK, 1982.

McKeon, Michael. "Tacit Knowledge: Tradition and Its Aftermath." Pages 171–202 in *Questions of Tradition.* Edited by Mark Salber Phillips and Gordon Schochet. Toronto: University of Toronto Press, 2004.

Mead, George Herbert. *Mind, Self & Society from the Standpoint of a Social Behaviorist.* Chicago: University of Chicago Press, 1934.

Means, Stewart. *Saint Paul and the Ante-Nicene Church: An Unwritten Chapter of Church History.* London: Black, 1903.

Meeks, Wayne A. *Christ is the Question.* Louisville, KY: Westminster John Knox, 2006.

————. "The Christian Proteus." Pages 689–694 in *The Writings of St. Paul: Annotated Texts, Reception and Criticism.* Edited by Wayne A. Meeks and John T. Fitzgerald. Norton Critical Editions in the History of Ideas. New York: W. W. Norton & Company, 2007 [1972].

Mellink, Osger. "Ignatius' Road to Rome: From Failure to Success or In the Footsteps of Paul?" Pages 127–165 in *Recycling Biblical Figures: Papers Read at a NOSTER Colloquium in Amsterdam, 12–3 May 1997.* Edited by Athalya Brenner and Jan Willem van Henten. Studies in Theology and Religion 1. Leiden: Deo, 1999.

Ménard, Jacques É. *L'évangile de Vérité.* Leiden: Brill, 1972.

Mendels, Doron. *Memory in Jewish, Pagan and Christian Societies of the Graeco-Roman World: Fragmented Memory–Comprehensive Memory–Collective Memory.* Library of Second Temple Studies. London: T&T Clark, 2004.

Merk, August. "Der Text des Neuen Testaments beim hl. Irenaeus." *Zeitschrift für katholische Theologie* 49(1925): 302–315.

Metzger, Bruce Manning. *The Canon of the New Testament: Its Origin, Development, and Significance.* Oxford: Clarendon Press, 1987.

Meunier, Bernard. "Paul et les pères grecs." *Recherches de science religieuse* 94(2006): 331–355.

Meyer, Arnold. "Religiöse Pseudepigraphie als ethisch–psychologisches Problem." *Zeitschrift für die neutestamentliche Wissenschaft und die Kunde der älteren Kirche* 35(1936): 262–279.

Middleton, David, and Derek Edwards, eds. *Collective Remembering*. Newbury Park, CA: Sage, 1990.

Miller, James D. *The Pastoral Letters as Composite Documents*. Society for New Testament Studies Monograph Series 93. Cambridge: Cambridge University Press, 1997.

Mills, Sara. *Discourse*. The New Critical Idiom. London: Routledge, 2004 [1997].

Minns, Denis. *Irenaeus*. Outstanding Christian Thinkers. London: Geoffrey Chapman, 1994.

———. *Irenaeus: An Introduction*. London: T&T Clark, 2010.

Mitchell, Margaret M. *The Heavenly Trumpet: John Chrysostom and the Art of Pauline Interpretation*. Louisville, KY: Westminster John Knox, 2002 [2000].

———. "The Letter of James as a Document of Paulinism?" Pages 75–98 in *Reading James with New Eyes: Methodological Reassessments of the Letter of James*. Edited by Robert L. Webb and John S. Kloppenborg. Library of New Testament Studies 342. New York: T&T Clark, 2007.

Mitchell, Matthew W. "In the Footsteps of Paul: Scriptural and Apostolic Authority in Ignatius of Antioch." *Journal of Early Christian Studies* 14(2006): 27–45.

Mitchell, W. J. T. *Iconology: Image, Text, Ideology*. Chicago: University of Chicago Press, 1986.

———, ed. *The Language of Images*. Chicago: University of Chicago Press, 1980.

Moffitt, David M. "Affirming the 'Creed': The Extent of Paul's Citation of an Early Christian Formula in 1 Cor 15, 3b – 7." *Zeitschrift für die neutestamentliche Wissenschaft und die Kunde der älteren Kirche* 99 (2008): 49–73.

Moll, Sebastian. *The Arch-Heretic Marcion*. Wissenschaftliche Untersuchungen zum Neuen Testament 250. Tübingen: Mohr Siebeck, 2010.

———. "Three Against Tertullian: the Second Tradition about Marcion's Life." *Journal of Theological Studies* 59(2008): 169–180.

Morgan, Robert. "Ferdinand Christian Baur." Pages 261–289 in *Nineteenth Century Religious Thought in the West, Vol. 1*. 3 vols. Edited by Ninian Smart, James Clayton, Steven Katz, and Patrick Sherry. Cambridge: Cambridge University Press, 1985.

———. "Paul's Enduring Legacy." Pages 242–255 in *The Cambridge Companion to St. Paul*. Edited by James D. G. Dunn. Cambridge: Cambridge University Press, 2003.

———. "The Significance of 'Paulinism.'" Pages 320–338 in *Paul and Paulinism*. Edited by Morna D. Hooker and Stephen G. Wilson. London: SPCK, 1982.

Mortley, Raoul. "Mirror and I Cor 13:12 in the Epistemology of Clement of Alexandria." *Vigiliae christianae* 30(1976): 109–120.

Motzkin, Gabriel. "Tradition, Time, and Memory." Pages 174–187 in *Tradition and Tradition Theories*. Edited by Thorsten Larbig and Siegfried Wiedenhofer. Berlin: LIT Verlag, 2006.

Mounce, William D. *Pastoral Epistles*. Word Bible Commentary. Nashville, TN: Thomas Nelson, 2000.

Mühlenberg, Ekkehard. "Marcion's Jealous God." Pages 93–113 in *Disciplina Nostra: Essays in Honor of Robert F. Evans*. Edited by Donald F. Winslow. Patristic Monograph Series 6. Philadelphia: Catholic University of America Press, 1979.

Müller, Peter. *Anfänge der Paulusschule: Dargestellt am zweiten Thessalonicherbrief und am Kolosserbrief.* Abhandlungen zur Theologie des Alten und Neuen Testaments 74. Zürich: Theologischer Verlag, 1988.

Munsterberg, Hugo. *On the Witness Stand: Essays on Psychology and Crime*. New York: Doubleday, Page & Co., 1908.

Murphy-O'Connor, Jerome. "2 Timothy Contrasted with 1 Timothy and Titus." *Revue biblique* 98(1991): 403–418.

Nautin, Pierre. "Irénée et la canonicité des Epîtres pauliniennes." *Revue de l'histoire des religions* 182(1972): 113–130.

Nielsen, Charles Merritt. "Polycarp, Paul and the Scriptures." *Anglican Theological Review* 47 (1965): 199–216.

Nielsen, Jan Tjeerd. *Adam and Christ in the Theology of Irenaeus of Lyons*. Van Gorcum's Theologische Bibliotheek 40. Assen, Netherlands: Van Gorcum, 1968.

Nietzsche, Friedrich. "On Truth and Lies in a Nonmoral Sense." Pages 79–91 in *Philosophy and Truth: Selections from Nietzsche's Notebooks of the Early 1870's*. Edited by Daniel Breazeale. Atlantic Highlands, NJ: Humanities Press, 1979.

Noormann, Rolf. "Himmelsbürger auf Erden: Anmerkungen zum Weltverhältnis und zum 'Paulinismus' des Auctor ad Diognetum." Pages 199–229 in *Die Weltlichkeit des Glaubens in der Alten Kirche: Festschrift für Ulrich Wickert zum siebzigsten Gerburtstag*. Edited by D. Wyrwa, et al. Beihefte zur Zeitschrift für die neutestamentlich Wissenschaft 85. Berlin: Walter de Gruyter, 1997.

———. *Irenäus als Paulusinterpret: zur Rezeption und Wirkung der paulinischen und deuteropaulinischen Briefe im Werk des Irenäus von Lyon*. Wissenschaftliche Untersuchungen zum Neuen Testament 2.66. Tübingen: J. C. B. Mohr (Paul Siebeck), 1994.

Nora, Pierre. "Between Memory and History: Les Lieux de Mémoire." *Representations* 26(1989): 7–25.

———, ed. *Realms of Memory: Rethinking the French Past*. 3 vols. European Perspectives. New York: Columbia University Press, 1996 [1984–1992].

Norelli, Enrico. "Marcion: ein christlicher Philosoph oder ein Christ gegen die Philosophie?" Pages 113–130 in *Marcion und seine kirchengeschichtliche Wirkung*. Edited by Gerhard May and Katharina Greschat. Berlin: Walter de Gruyter, 2002.

Norris, Richard A. "Irenaeus' Use of Paul in His Polemic Against the Gnostics." Pages 79–98 in *Paul and the Legacies of Paul*. Edited by William S. Babcock. Dallas: Southern Methodist University Press, 1990.

Oakes, Peter. "Leadership and Suffering in the Letters of Polycarp and Paul to the Philippians." Pages 353–374 in *Trajectories through the New Testament and the Apostolic Fathers*. Edited by Andrew F. Gregory and Christopher M. Tuckett. Oxford: Oxford University Press, 2005.

Økland, Jorunn. "Genealogies of the Self: Materiality, Personal Identity, and the Body in Paul's Letters to the Corinthians." Pages 83–108 in *Metamorphoses: Resurrection, Body and Transformative Practices in Early Christianity*. Edited by Turid Karlsen Seim and Jorunn Økland. Berlin: Walter de Gruyter, 2009.

Olick, Jeffrey K., and Joyce Robbins. "Social Memory Studies: From 'Collective Memory' to the Historical Sociology of Mnemonic Practices." *Annual Review of Sociology* 24(1998): 105–140.

Oliver, R. P. "The First Medicean MS of Tacitus and the Titulature of Ancient Books." *Transactions of the American Philological Association* 82(1951): 232–261.

Ollrog, Wolf-Henning. *Paulus und seine Mitarbeiter: Untersuchungen zu Theorie und Praxis der paulinischen Mission*. Wissenschaftliche Monographien zum Alten und Neuen Testament 50. Neukirchen-Vluyn: Neukirchener, 1979.

Olrik, Axel. "Epic Laws of Folk Narrative." Pages 131–141 in *The Study of Folklore*. Edited by Alan Dundes. Engelwood Cliffs, NJ: Prentice-Hall, 1965.

Olson, Mark J. *Irenaeus, the Valentinian Gnostics, and the Kingdom of God: The Debate about 1 Corinthians 15:50*. Lewiston, NY: Mellen Biblical Press, 1995.

Olson, S. Douglas. *The Learned Banqueters, 2: Books III.106e–V*. Loeb Classical Library 208. Cambridge, MA: Harvard University Press, 2006.

Omerzu, Heike. "The Portrayal of Paul's Outer Appearance in the *Acts of Paul and Thecla*: Reconsidering the Correspondence between the Body and Personality in Ancient Literature." *Religion & Theology/Religie & teologie* 15(2008): 252–279.

Ong, Walter. *Orality and Literacy: The Technologizing of the Word*. 2nd ed. London: Routledge, 2002 [1982].

Orbe, Antonio. "Adversarios anónimos de la Salus carnis." *Gregorianum* 60(1979): 9–53.

———. *Antropologia de San Ireneo*. Biblioteca de autores cristianos 286. Madrid: Ed Católica, 1969.

———. "La definición del hombre en la teología del s IIo." *Gregorianum* 48(1967): 522–576.

———. "San Ireneo y la creación de la materia." *Gregorianum* 59(1978): 71–127.

———. "San Ireneo y la doctrina de la reconciliación." *Gregorianum* 61(1980): 5–50.

———. *Teologia de san Ireneo: commentario al Libro V del Adversus haereses*. 3 vols. Biblioteca de autores cristianos: Maior 25, 29, 33. Madrid: La Editorial Catolica, 1985.

Ory, Georges. *Marcion*. Paris: Cercle Ernest-Renan, 1980.

Osborn, Eric F. *Irenaeus of Lyons*. Cambridge: Cambridge University Press, 2001.

Otto, Johann C. T. "Bezeihungen auf Paulinische Briefe bei Justin dem Märtyrer und dem Verfasser des Briefes an Diognet." *Zeitschrift für historische Theologie* 12(1842): 41–57.

———. "Nachträglisches über den Gebrauch Neutestamentlicher Schriften bei Justin dem Märtyrer und dem Verfasser des Briefes an Diognet." *Zeitschrift für historische Theologie* 13(1843): 34–45.

Overbeck, Franz. *Über die Auffassung des Streits des Paulus mit Petrus in Antiochien (Gal. 2, 11 ff.) bei den Kirchenvätern.* Libelli 183. Darmstadt: Wissenschaftliche Buchgesellschaft, 1968 [1877].

———. "Über das Verhältniss Justins des Märtyrers zur Apostelgeschichte." *Zeitschrift für wissenschaftliche Theologie* 15(1872): 305–349.

Oxford Society of Historical Theology. *The New Testament in the Apostolic Fathers.* Oxford: Clarendon Press, 1905.

Padovese, L. "L'antipaulinisme chrétien au IIᵉ siècle." *Recherches de science religieuse* 90(2002): 390–422.

Pagels, Elaine H. *The Gnostic Paul.* Philadelphia: Fortress Press, 1975.

———. "Mystery of the Resurrection: a Gnostic Reading of 1 Corinthians 15." *Journal of Biblical Literature* 93(1974): 276–288.

———. "Valentinian Claim to Esoteric Exegesis of Romans as Basis for Anthropological Theory." *Vigiliae christianae* 26(1972): 241–258.

Paget, James Carleton. *The Epistle of Barnabas: Outlook and Background.* Wissenschaftliche Untersuchungen zum Neuen Testament 2.64. Tübingen: J. C. B. Mohr (Paul Siebeck), 1994.

———. "The *Epistle of Barnabas* and the Writings that later formed the New Testament." Pages 229–250 in *The Reception of the New Testament in the Apostolic Fathers.* Edited by Andrew F. Gregory and Christopher M. Tuckett. Oxford: Oxford University Press, 2005.

———. "Paul and the Epistle of Barnabas." *Novum Testamentum* 38(1996): 359–381.

Pahl, P.D. "The Use of Scripture in *1 Clement.*" *Australian Theological Review* 27(1957): 107–111.

Painchaud, Louis. "The Use of Scripture in Gnostic Literature." *Journal of Early Christian Studies* 4(1996): 129–146.

Painchaud, Louis, and Michael Kaler. "From the *Prayer of the Apostle Paul* to the *Three Steles of Seth*: Codices I, XI, and VII from Nag Hammadi Viewed as a Collection." *Vigiliae christianae* 61 (2007): 445–469.

Parris, David Paul. *Reception History and Biblical Hermeneutics.* Princeton Theological Monograph Series. Eugene, OR: Pickwick, 2009.

Patsch, Hermann. "The Fear of Deutero-Paulinism: The Reception of Friedrich Schleiermacher's 'Critical Open Letter' Concerning 1 Timothy." Translated by Darrell J. Doughty. *Journal of Higher Criticism* 6(1993): 3–31.

Payne, Philip B. "Fuldensis, Sigla for Variants in Vaticanus, and 1 Cor 14.34–5." *New Testament Studies* 41 (1995): 240–262.

———. "Ms. 88 as Evidence for a Text without 1 Cor 14:34–35" *New Testament Studies* 44(1998): 152–158.

Payne, Philip B. "The Text-Critical Function of the Umlauts in Vaticanus, with Special Attention to 1 Corinthians 14.34–35: a Response to J. Edward Miller." *Journal for the Study of the New Testament* 27 (2004): 105–112.

Pearson, Birger. *Ancient Gnosticism: Traditions and Literature*. Minneapolis: Fortress Press, 2007.

Peel, Malcolm Lee. "Gnostic Eschatology and the New Testament." *Novum Testamentum* 12(1970): 141–165.

Pelikan, Jaroslav. *Obedient Rebels: Catholic Substance and Protestant Principle in Luther's Reformation*. New York: Harper and Row, 1964.

———. *The Vindication of Tradition*. New Haven, CT: Yale University Press, 1984.

Penny, Donald N. "The Pseudo-Pauline Letters of the First Two Centuries." Ph.D. diss., Emory University, 1979.

Penzel, Klaus. "Will the Real Ferdinand Christian Baur Please Stand Up?" *Journal of Religion* 48(1968): 310–323.

Peretto, Elio. *La Lettera ai Romani, cc 1–8, nell' Adversus Haereses d'Ireneo*. Quaderni di Vetera christianorum 6. Bari: Università di Bari (Istituto di Letteratura Cristiana Antica), 1971.

Perkins, Pheme. "Gnosticism and the Christian Bible." Pages 355–371 in *The Canon Debate*. Edited by Lee Martin McDonald and James A. Sanders. Peabody, MA: Hendrickson, 2002.

Pervo, Richard I. *The Making of Paul: Constructions of the Apostle in Early Christianity*. Minneapolis: Fortress Press, 2010.

Pfleiderer, Otto. *Paulinism: A Contribution to the History of Primitive Christian Theology*. Translated by Edward Peters. 2 vols. London: Williams & Norgate, 1877 [1873].

Phillips, Mark Salber. "What Is Tradition When It Is Not 'Invented'? A Historiographical Introduction." Pages 3–29 in *Questions of Tradition*. Edited by Mark Salber Phillips and Gordon Schochet. Toronto: University of Toronto Press, 2004.

Phillips, Mark Salber, and Gordon Schochet, eds. *Questions of Tradition*. Toronto: University of Toronto Press, 2004.

Phillips, Thomas E. "Narrative Characterizations of Peter and Paul in Early Christianity." *ARC: Journal of the Faculty of Religious Studies, McGill University* 30(2002): 139–157.

Pieper, Josef. *Tradition: Concept and Claim*. Translated by E. Christian Kopff. Crosscurrents. Wilmington, DE: ISI Books, 2008 [1970].

Pink, K. "Die pseudopaulinische Briefe." *Biblica* 6 (1925).

Piovanelli, Pierluigi. "*La Prière et apocalypse de Paul* au sein de la littérature apocryphe d'attribution Paulinienne." *Apocrypha* 15(2004): 31–40.

———. "The Miraculous Discovery of the Hidden Manuscript, or the Paratextual Function of the Prologue to the *Apocalypse of Paul*." Pages 23–49 in *The Visio Pauli and the Gnostic Apocalypse of Paul*. Edited by Jan N. Bremmer and István Czachesz. Leuven: Peeters, 2007.

Polanyi, Michael. *Science, Faith, and Society*. Chicago: University of Chicago Press, 1964.

———. *The Tacit Dimension*. London: Routledge, 1966.

Popper, Karl. *The Logic of Scientific Discovery*. London: Hutchinson, 1959.

Porter, Stanley E. *The Pauline Canon*. Pauline Studies 1. Leiden: Brill, 2004.

———. "When and How Was the Pauline Canon Compiled? An Assessment of Theories." Pages 95–127 in *The Pauline Canon*. Edited by Stanley Porter. Leiden: Brill, 2004.

Potter, Paul. "St Irenaeus and 'Recapitulation.'" *Dominican Studies* 4(1951): 192–200.

Price, Robert M. "The Evolution of the Pauline Canon." *Hervormde teologiese studies* 53(1997): 36–67.

Prior, Michael. *Paul the Letter Writer and the Second Letter to Timothy*. Journal for the Study of the New Testament: Supplement Series 23. Sheffield: Sheffield Academic Press, 1989.

Quinn, Jerome D. "P⁴⁶ – the Pauline Canon?" *Catholic Biblical Quarterly* 36(1974): 379–385.

———. "'Seven Times He Wore Chains' (*1 Clem* 5.6)." *Journal of Biblical Literature* 97(1978): 574–576.

Quispel, Gilles. "Marcion and the Text of the New Testament." *Vigiliae christianae* 52(1998): 349–360.

Räisänen, Heikki. "Marcion." Pages 100–124 in *A Companion to Second-Century Christian "Heretics."* Edited by Antii Marjanen and Petri Luomanen. Leiden: Brill, 2008.

Ranke, Leopold von. *Geschichte der romanischen und germanischen Völker von 1494 bis 1514*. Leipzig: Weimer, 1824.

Rathke, Heinrich. *Ignatius von Antiochien und die Paulusbriefe*. Texte und Untersuchungen zur Geschichte der altchristlichen Literatur 99. Berlin: Akademie-Verlag, 1967.

Rebell, Walter. "Das Leidensverständnis bei Paulus und Ignatius von Antiochien." *New Testament Studies* 32(1986): 457–465.

Redman, Judith C. S. "How Accurate Are Eyewitnesses? Bauckham and the Eyewitnesses in the Light of Psychological Research." *Journal of Biblical Literature* 129(2010): 177–197.

Reis, David M. "Following in Paul's Footsteps: *Mimesis* and Power in Ignatius." Pages 287–305 in *Trajectories through the New Testament and the Apostolic Fathers*. Edited by Andrew F. Gregory and Christopher M. Tuckett. Oxford: Oxford University Press, 2005.

Reisberg, D., D. G. Pearson, and S. M. Kosslyn. "Intuitions and Introspections about Imagery: The Role of Imagery Experience in Shaping an Investigator's Theoretical Views." *Applied Cognitive Psychology* 17(2003): 147–160.

Renan, Ernest. *Histoire des origins du christianisme*. 7 vols. Paris: Lévy, 1861–1893.

Rensberger, David K. "As the Apostle Teaches: The Development of the Use of Paul's Letters in Second-Century Christianity." Ph.D. diss., Yale University, 1981.

Richards, William A. *Difference and Distance in Post-Pauline Christianity: an Episto-lary Analysis of the Pastorals*. Studies in Biblical Literature 44. Bern: Peter Lang, 2002.

Richardson, John T. E. *Mental Imagery and Human Memory*. New York: St. Martins, 1980.

Ricoeur, Paul. *Memory, History, Forgetting*. Translated by Kathleen Blamey and David Pellauer. Chicago: Univeristy of Chicago Press, 2004.

Rinck, Wilhelm Friedrich. *Das Sendschreiben der Korinther an den Apostel Paulus und das dritte Sendschreiben Pauli an die Korinther*. Heidelberg: E. I. Winter, 1823.

Rist, Martin. "III Corinthians as a Pseudepigraphic Refutation of Marcionism." *Iliff Review* 26(1969): 49–58.

———. "Pseudepigraphic Refutations of Marcionism." *Journal of Religion* 22(1942): 39–62.

Ritschl, Albrecht. *Die Entstehung der altkatholischen Kirche*. 2nd ed. Bonn: Marcus, 1857.

Roberts, Alexander, and James Donaldson, eds. *The Ante-Nicene Fathers*. Grand Rapids, MI: Eerdmans, 1985 [1885–1887].

Roberts, David, ed. *Reconstructing Theory: Gadamer, Habermas, Luhmann*. Melbourne: Melbourne University Press, 1995.

Robinson, James M., and Helmut Koester. *Trajectories through Early Christianity*. Philadelphia: Fortress Press, 1971.

Rodriguez, Rafael. *Structuring Early Christian Memory: Jesus in Tradition, Performance and Text*. Library of New Testament Studies 407. London: T&T Clark, 2010.

Roetzel, Calvin J. *Paul: the Man and the Myth*. Minneapolis: Fortress Press, 1999 [1997].

———. "Paul in the Second Century." Pages 227–241 in *The Cambridge Companion to St Paul*. Edited by James D. G. Dunn. Cambridge: Cambridge University Press, 2003.

Rollins, Mark. *Mental Imagery: On the Limits of Cognitive Science*. New Haven, CT: Yale University Press, 1989.

Rollmann, Hans. "From Baur to Wrede: The quest for a historical method." *Studies in Religion* 17(1988): 443–454.

Rordorf, Willy. "Actes de Paul." In Vol. 1 of *Écrits apocryphes chrétiens*. Edited by François Bovon and Pierre Geoltrain. Paris: Gallimard, 1997.

———. "Hérésie et orthodoxie selon la Correspondance apocryphe entre les Corin-thiens et l'Apôtre Paul." Pages 21–63 in *Orthodoxie et hérésie dans l'Eglise ancienne*. Edited by H.-D. Altendorf, et al. Cahiers de la Revue de théologie et de philoso-phie 17. Lausanne: Revue de théologie et de philosophie, 1993.

———. "In welchem Verhältnis stehen die apokryphen Paulusakten zur kanon-ischen Apostelgeschichte und zu den Pastoralbriefen?" Pages 225–241 in *Text and Testimony: Essays on New Testament and Apocryphal Literature in Honour of A. F. J. Klijn*. Edited by Tjitze Baarda. Kampen: Uitgeversmaatschappij J. H. Kok, 1988.

————. "Nochmals: Paulusakten und Pastoralbriefe." Pages 319–327 in *Tradition and Interpretation in the New Testament: Essays in Honor of E. Earle Ellis for his 60th Birthday*. Edited by Gerald F. Hawthorne and Otto Betz. Grand Rapids, MI: Eerdmans, 1987.

————. "Tradition and Composition in the *Acts of Thecla*: the State of the Question." *Semeia* 38(1986): 43–52.

————. "Was wissen wire über Plan und Absicht der Paulusakten?" Pages 71–82 in *Oecumenica et Patristica: Festschrift für Wilhelm Schneemelcher*. Edited by Damaskinos Papandreou, Wolfgang A. Bienert, and Knut Schäferdiek. Stuttgart: Verlag W. Kohlhammer, 1989.

Rordorf, Willy, and Peter W. Dunn. "Paul's Conversion in the Canonical Acts and in the *Acts of Paul*." *Semeia* 80(1997): 137–144.

Rosenblatt, Marie Eloise. *Paul the Accused: His Portrait in the Acts of the Apostles*. Zacchaeus Studies: New Testament. Collegeville, MN: Liturgical Press, 1995.

Rosensweig, Roy, and David Thelen. *The Presence of the Past: Popular Uses of History in American Life*. New York: Columbia University Press, 1998.

Ross, G. R. T. *Aristotle: De sensu and De memoria*. Cambridge: Cambridge University Press, 1906.

Roth, Dieter T. "Marcion's Gospel and Luke: The History of Research in Current Debate." *Journal of Biblical Literature* 127(2008): 513–527.

Rothschild, Clare K. *Hebrews as Pseudepigraphon: the History and Significance of the Pauline Attribution of Hebrews*. Wissenschaftliche Untersuchungen zum Neuen Testament 235. Tübingen: Mohr Siebeck, 2009.

Roukema, Riemer. *De uitleg van Paulus' eerste brief aan de Corinthiërs in de tweede en derde eeuw*. Kampen: Kok, 1996.

Rousseau, Adelin, and Louis Doutreleau, eds. *Irénée de Lyon: Contre les Hérésies*. 5 vols. Sources chrétiennes. Paris: Éditions du Cerf, 1965–1982.

Rubin, David C., ed. *Remembering our Past: Studies in Autobiographical Memory*. Cambridge: Cambridge University Press, 1996.

Rudolf, Kurt. *Gnosis: The Nature & History of Gnosticism*. Translated by R. M. Wilson. San Francisco: Harper, 1984 [1977].

Salles, A. "La diatribe anti–paulinienne dans le 'Roman Pseudo–Clémentin' et l'origine des 'Kérygmes de Pierre.'" *Revue biblique* 64(1957): 516–551.

Sand, Alexander. "Überlieferung und Sammlung der Paulusbriefe." Pages 11–24 in *Paulus in den neutestamentlichen Spätschriften*. Edited by Karl Kertelge. Freiburg: Herder, 1981.

Satran, David. "Fingernails and Hair: Anatomy and Exegesis in Tertullian." *Journal of Theological Studies* 40(1989): 116–120.

Scarborough, Jason M. "The Making of an Apostle: Second and Third Century Interpretations of the Writings of Paul." Ph.D. diss., Union Theological Seminary, 2007.

Schacter, Daniel L., ed. *Memory Distortion: How Minds, Brains, and Societies Reconstruct the Past*. Cambridge, MA: Harvard University Press, 1997.

Schacter, Daniel L., ed. *The Seven Sins of Memory: How the Mind Forgets and Remembers*. Boston: Houghton Mifflin, 2001.

Schäfer, Karl T. "Die Zitate in der lateinischen Irenäusübersetzung und ihr Wert für die Textgeschichte des Neuen Testamentes." Pages 50–59 in *Vom Wort des Lebens: Festschrift für Max Meinertz des 70. Lebensjahres 19. Dezember 1950, dargeboten von seinen Freunden, Kollegen und Schülern*. Edited by Nikolaus Adler. Neutestamentliche Abhandlungen 1. Münster: Aschendorff, 1951.

Scharl, E. *Recapitulatio mundi: Der Rekapitulationsbegriff des Hl. Irenäus und seine Anwendung auf die Körperwelt*. Freiburger theologische Studien 60. Freiburg: Herder, 1941.

Scharlemann, Martin H. "Third Corinthians." *Concordia Theological Monthly* 26(1955): 518–529.

Scheibler, Ingrid. *Gadamer: Between Heidegger and Habermas*. Lanham, MD: Rowman & Littlefield, 2000.

Schenke, Hans-Martin. "Das Weiterwirken des Paulus und die Pflege seines Erbes durch die paulus–Schule." *New Testament Studies* 21 (1974–1975): 505–518.

Scherbenske, Eric W. *Canonizing Paul: Ancient Editorial Practice and the Corpus Paulinum*. New York: Oxford University Press, 2013.

Schille, Gottfried. *Das älteste Paulus-Bild: Beobachtungen zur lukanischen und zur deuteropaulinischen Paulus-Darstellung*. Berlin: Evangelische Verlagsanstalt, 1979.

Schleiermacher, Friedrich. *Über den sogenannten ersten Brief des Paulus an den Timotheos. Ein kritisches Sendschreiben an J. C. Gass*. Berlin: Realschulbuch, 1807.

Schmeller, Thomas. *Schulen im Neuen Testament? Zur Stellung des Urchristentums in der Bildungswelt seiner Zeit*. Herders biblische Studien 30. Freiburg: Herder, 2001.

Schmid, Ulrich. *Marcion und sein Apostolos: Rekonstruktion und historische Einordnung der marcionitischen Paulusbriefausgabe*. Arbeiten zur neutestamentlichen Textforschung 25. Berlin: Walter de Gruyter, 1995.

———. "Marcions Evangelium und die neutestamentlichen Evangelien – Rückfragen zur Geschichte und Kanonisierung der Evangelienüberlieferung." Pages 67–78 in *Marcion und seine kirchengeschichtliche Wirkung*. Edited by Gerhard May and Katharina Greschat. Berlin: Walter de Gruyter, 2002.

Schmidt, Carl. *Acta Pauli: Aus der Heidelberger Koptischen Papyrushandschrift Nr. 1*. Hildesheim: G. Olms, 1965 [1905].

Schmidt, Carl, and Wilhelm Schubart. ΠΡΑΞΕΙΣ ΠΑΥΛΟΥ. *Acta Pauli*. Glückstadt: J. J. Augustin, 1936.

Schmithals, Walter. *Das kirchliche Apostelamt: Eine historische Untersuchung*. Forschungen zur Religion und Literatur des Alten und Neuen Testaments 19. Göttingen: Vandenhoeck and Ruprecht, 1961.

Schneemelcher, Wilhelm, ed. *New Testament Apocrypha*. 2 vols. Louisville, KY: Westminster John Knox, 1992 [1989].

———. "Paulus in der griechischen Kirche des zweite Jahrhunderts." *Zeitschrift für Kirchengeschichte* 75(1964): 1–20.

Schochet, Gordon. "Tradition as Politics and the Politics of Tradition." Pages 296–322 in *Questions of Tradition*. Edited by Mark Salber Phillips and Gordon Schochet. Toronto: University of Toronto Press, 2004.

Schoedel, William R. *Ignatius of Antioch: A Commentary on the Letters of Ignatius of Antioch*. Hermeneia. Minneapolis: Fortress Press, 1985.

Scholder, Klaus. "Ferdinand Christian Baur als Historiker." *Evangelische Theologie* 21(1961): 435–458.

Schröter, Jens. *Erinnerung an Jesu Worte: Studien zur Rezeption der Logienüberlieferung in Markus, Q und Thomas*. Wissenschaftliche Monographien zum Alten und Neuen Testament 76. Neukirchen-Vluyn: Neukirchener, 1997.

———. "The Gospels of Eyewitness Testimony? A Critical Examination of Richard Bauckham's *Jesus and the Eyewitnesses*." *Journal for the Study of the New Testament* 31(2008): 195–209.

———. "Kirche im Anschluss an Paulus: Aspekte der Paulusrezeption in der Apostelgeschichte und in den Pastoralbriefen." *Zeitschrift für die neutestamentliche Wissenschaft und die Kunde der älteren Kirche* 98(2007): 77–104.

Schudson, Michael. "The Present in the Past Versus the Past in the Present." *Communication* 11(1989): 105–113.

Schwartz, Barry. *Abraham Lincoln and the Forge of National Memory*. Chicago: University of Chicago Press, 2000.

———. *Abraham Lincoln in the Post-Heroic Era: History and Memory in Late Twentieth-Century America*. Chicago: University of Chicago Press, 2008.

———. "Christian Origins: Historical Truth and Social Memory." Pages 43–56 in *Memory, Tradition, and Text: Uses of the Past in Early Christianity*. Edited by Alan Kirk and Tom Thatcher. Atlanta, GA: Society of Biblical Literature, 2005.

———. "The Social Context of Commemoration: A Study in Collective Memory." *Social Forces* 61(1982): 374–402.

Scornaienchi, Lorenzo. *Sarx und Soma bei Paulus: Der Mensch zwischen Destruktivität und Konstruktivität*. Novum Testamentum et Orbis Antiquus/Studien zur Umwelt des Neuen Testaments 67. Göttingen: Vandenhoeck & Ruprecht, 2008.

Scott, James C. *Domination and the Arts of Resistance: Hidden Transcripts*. New Haven, CT: Yale University Press, 1990.

Seesengood, Robert P. *Paul: A Brief History*. Blackwell Brief Histories of Religion. Chichester: Wiley-Blackwell, 2010.

Seim, Turid Karlsen, and Jorunn Økland, eds. *Metamorphoses: Resurrection, Body and Transformative Practices in Early Christianity*. Ekstasis 1. Berlin: Walter de Gruyter, 2009.

Sellin, Gerhard. *Der Streit um die Auferstehung der Toten: Eine religionsgeschichtliche und exegetische Untersuchung von 1 Kor 15*. Forschungen zur Religion und Literatur des Alten und Neuen Testaments 138. Göttingen: Vandenhoeck & Ruprecht, 1986.

Semisch, Carl. *Justin der Märtyrer: Eine kirchen- und dogmengeschichtliche Monographie*. 2 vols. Breslau: Schulz, 1842.

Setzer, Claudia. *Resurrection of the Body in Early Judaism and Early Christianity: Doctrine, Community, and Self-Definition.* Leiden: Brill, 2004.

Sevrin, Jean-Marie, ed. *The New Testament in Early Christianity–La réception des écrits néotestamentaires dans le christianisme primitif.* Bibliotheca Ephemeridum Theologicarum Lovaniensium 86. Louvain: Peeters, 1989.

Sharples, R. W. *Stoics, Epicureans and Sceptics: an Introduction to Hellenistic Philosophy.* London: Routledge, 1996.

Shils, Edward. *Tradition.* Chicago: University of Chicago, 1981.

Sider, Robert D. "Literary Artifice and the Figure of Paul in the Writings of Tertullian." Pages 99–120 in *Paul and the Legacies of Paul.* Edited by William S. Babcock. Dallas: Southern Methodist University Press, 1990.

Slenczka, Notger. "Die Einheit der Kirche und die Wahrheit der Reformation: Theologiegeschichtliche Errinnerungen an die Kontroverse zwischen J. A. Möhler und F. C. Baur angesichts der aktuellen Situation der Ökumene." *Kerygma und Dogma* 48(2002): 172–196.

Small, Jocelyn. *Wax Tablets of the Mind: Cognitive Studies of Memory and Literacy in Classical Antiquity.* London: Routledge, 1997.

Snyder, Glenn E. *Acts of Paul: The Formation of a Pauline Corpus.* Wissenschaftliche Untersuchungen zum Neuen Testament 2.352. Tübingen: Mohr Siebeck, 2013.

Snyder, Graydon F. "The Continuity of Early Christianity. A Study of Ignatius in Relation to Paul." Ph.D. diss., Princeton Theological Seminary, 1961.

Souter, Alexander. "The New Testament Text of Irenaeus." Pages cxii–clxx in *Novum Testamentum sancti Irenaei episcopi Lugdunensis.* Edited by William Sanday and Cuthbert Hamilton Turner. Old-Latin Biblical Texts 7. Oxford: Clarendon, 1923.

Speyer, Wolfgang. *Die literarische Fälschung im hiednischen und christlichen Altertum: Ein Versuch ihrer Deutung.* Handbuch der Altertumswissenschaft I/2. München: Beck, 1971.

Staden, Heinrich von. "Body, Soul, and Nerves: Epicurus, Herophilus, Erasistratus, the Stoics, and Galen." Pages 96–105 in *Psyche and Soma.* Edited by John P. Wright and Paul Potter. Oxford: Clarendon Press, 2000.

Standhartinger, Angela. "Colossians and the Pauline School." *New Testament Studies* 50(2004): 572–593.

Sterling, Gregory E. "From Apostle to the Gentiles to Apostle of the Church: Images of Paul at the End of the First Century." *Zeitschrift für die neutestamentliche Wissenschaft und die Kunde der älteren Kirche* 99(2008): 74–98.

Stewart-Sykes, A. "The Asian Context of the New Prophecy and of the *Epistula Apostolorum.*" *Vigiliae christianae* 51(1997): 416–438.

Still, Todd D., and David E. Wilhite. *Tertullian & Paul.* Pauline and Patristic Scholars in Debate. New York: Bloomsbury T&T Clark, 2013.

Stock, Brian. *Listening for the Text: On the Uses of the Past.* Parallax: Re-Visions of Culture and Society. Baltimore, MD: Johns Hopkins University Press, 1990.

Stoops, Robert F., Jr. "If I Suffer . . . Epistolary Authority in Ignatius of Antioch." *Harvard Theological Review* 80(1987): 161–178.

Story, Geoffrey L. "The Valentinian (Gnostic) Use of the Letters of Paul." Ph.D. diss., Northwestern University, 1968.

Stowers, Stanley K. "Text as Interpretation: Paul and Ancient Readings of Paul." Pages 17–27 in *Judaic and Christian Interpretation of Texts: Contents and Contexts*. Edited by Jacob Neusner and Ernest S. Frerichs. New Perspectives on Ancient Judaism. Lanham, MD: University Press of America, 1987.

———. "What Does *Unpauline* Mean?" Pages 70–78 in *Paul and the Legacies of Paul*. Edited by William S. Babcock. Dallas: Southern Methodist University Press, 1990.

Strecker, Georg. *Das Judenchristentum in den Pseudoklementinen*. Texte und Untersuchungen zur Geschichte der altchristlichen Literatur 70. Berlin: Akademie-Verlag, 1958.

———. "Paulus in Nachpaulinischer Zeit." *Kairos* 12(1970): 208–216.

Streete, Gail P. C. "Authority and Authorship: the *Acts of Paul and Thecla* as a Disputed Pauline Text." *Lexington Theological Quarterly* 40(2005): 265–276.

Stroud, William J. "New Testament Quotations in the Nag Hammadi Gospel of Philip." *Society of Biblical Literature Seminar Papers* 29(1990): 68–81.

Stuckwisch, D. Richard. "Saint Polycarp of Smyrna: Johannine or Pauline Figure?" *Concordia Theological Quarterly* 61(1997): 113–125.

Stuhlhofer, Franz. *Der Gebrauch der Bibel von Jesus bis Euseb: Eine statistische Untersuchung zur Kanongeschichte*. Monographien und Studienbücher 335. Wuppertal: Brockhaus, 1988.

Swete, H. B. "The Resurrection of the Flesh." *Journal of Theological Studies* 18(1917): 135–141.

Tanner, Kathryn. "Tradition and Theological Judgment in Light of Postmodern Cultural Criticism." Pages 229–246 in *Tradition and Tradition Theories*. Edited by Thorsten Larbig and Siegfried Wiedenhofer. Berlin: LIT Verlag, 2006.

Taubes, Jacob. *The Political Theology of Paul*. Edited by Aleida Assmann with Jan Assmann. Translated by Dana Hollander. Cultural Memory in the Present. Stanford, CA: Stanford University Press, 2004 [1993].

Teigas, Demetrius. *Knowledge and Hermeneutic Understanding: A Study of the Habermas-Gadamer Debate*. Lewisburg, PA: Bucknell University Press, 1995.

Testuz, Michel. *Papyrus Bodmer X-XII: Manuscrit du IIIe siècle*. Cologne: Bibliotheca Bodmeriana, 1959.

Thatcher, Tom. "John's Memory Theater: The Fourth Gospel and Ancient Mnemo-Rhetoric." *Catholic Biblical Quarterly* 69(2007): 487–505.

———. *Why John Wrote a Gospel: Jesus–Memory–History*. Louisville, KY: Westminster John Knox, 2006.

Thistleton, Anthony C. *The First Epistle to the Corinthians*. New International Greek Testament Commentary. Grand Rapids, MI: Eerdmans, 2000.

Thistleton, Anthony C. *New Horizons in Hermeneutics: The Theory and Practice of Transforming Biblical Reading*. Grand Rapids, MI: Zondervan, 1992.

Thoma, Albrecht. "Justins literarishes Verhältnis zu Paulus und zum Johannes–Evangelium." *Zeitschrift für wissenschaftliche Theologie* 18(1875): 385–412.

Thomassen, Einar. "Orthodoxy and Heresy in Second-Century Rome." *Harvard Theological Review* 97(2004): 241–256.

———. *The Spiritual Seed: The Church of the "Valentinians."* Leiden: Brill, 2008 [2006].

———. "Valentinian Ideas About Salvation as Transformation." Pages 169–186 in *Metamorphoses: Resurrection, Body and Transformative Practices in Early Christianity*. Edited by Turid Karlsen Seim and Jorunn Økland. Berlin: Walter de Gruyter, 2009.

Towner, Philip. "The Portrait of Paul and the Theology of 2 Timothy: the Closing Chapter of the Pauline Story." *Horizons in Biblical Theology* 21(1999): 151–170.

Trebilco, Paul. "Christian Communities in Western Asia Minor into the Early Second Century: Ignatius and Others as Witnesses against Bauer." *Journal of the Evangelical Theological Society* 49(2006): 17–44.

Trevett, Christine. *A Study of Ignatius of Antioch in Syria and Asia*. Studies in the Bible and Early Christianity 29. Lewiston, NY: Edwin Mellen Press, 1992.

Trobisch, David. *Die Entstehung der Paulusbriefsammlung: Studien zu den Anfängen christlicher Publizistik*. Novum Testamentum et Orbis Antiquus 10. Fribourg: Universitätsverlag, 1989.

———. *The First Edition of the New Testament*. Oxford: Oxford University Press, 2000.

———. *Paul's Letter Collection: Tracing the Origins*. Minneapolis: Augsburg Fortress Press, 1994.

Turner, Stephen. *The Social Theory of Practices: Tradition, Tacit Knowledge, and Presuppositions*. Chicago: University of Chicago Press, 1994.

Unger, Dominic J. *St. Irenaeus of Lyons: Against the Heresies*. Ancient Christian Writers 55. New York: Paulist Press, 1992.

Unnik, Willem Cornelis van. "The 'Gospel of Truth' and the New Testament." Pages 81–129 in *The Jung Codex: A Newly Recovered Gnostic Papyrus*. Edited by Frank L. Cross. London: A. R. Mowbray, 1955.

Uro, Risto. "*Thomas* and the Oral Gospel Tradition." Pages 8–32 in *Thomas at the Crossroads: Essays on the Gospel of Thomas*. Edited by Risto Uro. Edinburgh: T&T Clark, 1998.

Vallée, Gérard. *A Study in Anti-Gnostic Polemics: Irenaeus, Hippolytus and Epiphanius*. Studies in Christianity and Judaism 1. Waterloo, ON: Wilfrid Laurier University Press, 1981.

Van Kooten, George H. *Cosmic Christology in Paul and the Pauline School: Colossians and Ephesians in the Context of Graeco-Roman Cosmology, with a New Synopsis of the Greek Texts*. Wissenschaftliche Untersuchungen zum Neuen Testament 2.171. Tübingen: Mohr Siebeck, 2003.

————. *Paul's Anthropology in Context: The Image of God, Assimilation to God, and Tripartite Man in Ancient Judaism, Ancient Philosophy and Early Christianity.* Wissenschaftliche Untersuchungen zum Neuen Testament 232. Tübingen: Mohr Siebeck, 2008.

Vansina, Jan. *Oral Tradition as History.* Madison: University of Wisconsin Press, 1985.

Vetter, Paul. *Der apokryphe dritte Korintherbrief.* Vienna: Mechitharisten-Buchdruckerei, 1894.

Veyne, Paul. "Foucault Revolutionizes History." Pages 146–182 in *Foucault and His Interlocutors.* Edited by Arnold I. Davidson. Chicago: University of Chicago Press, 1998.

Vielhauer, Philipp. "On the 'Paulinism' of Acts." Pages 33–50 in *Studies in Luke-Acts: Essays Presented in Honor of Paul Schubert.* Edited by Leander Keck. Nashville, TN: Abingdon, 1966.

Vinzent, Markus. "Christ's Resurrection: the Pauline Basis for Marcion's Teaching." *Studia patristica* 31(1997): 225–233.

Völker, Walter, ed. *Quellen zur Geschichte der christlichen Gnosis.* Sammlung ausgewählter kirchen- und dogmengeschichtlicher Quellenschriften 5. Tübingen: J. C. B. Mohr, 1932.

Vorster, Johannes N. "Construction of Culture Through the Construction of Person: The Construction of Thecla in the *Acts of Thecla.*" Pages 98–117 in *A Feminist Companion to the New Testament Apocrypha.* Edited by Amy-Jill Levine and Maria Mayo Robbins. Feminist Companion to the New Testament and Early Christian Writings 11. London: T&T Clark International, 2006.

Vouaux, L. *Les Actes de Paul et ses lettres apocryphes.* Paris: Librairie Letouzey et Ané, 1913.

Wagenmann, Julius. *Die Stellung des Apostels Paulus neben den Zwölf in den ersten zwei Jahrhunderten.* Beihefte zur Zeitschrift für die neutestamentlich Wissenschaft 3. Gießen: Töpelmann, 1926.

Wagner, Peter, ed. *Icons–Texts–Iconotexts: Essays on Ekphrasis and Intermediality.* European Cultures 6. Berlin: Walter de Gruyter, 1996.

Walker, William O. "Interpolations in the Pauline Letters." Pages 189–235 in *The Pauline Canon.* Edited by Stanley Porter. Leiden: Brill, 2004.

Walton, Steve. *Leadership and Lifestyle: the Portrait of Paul in the Miletus Speech and I Thessalonians.* Society for New Testament Studies Monograph Series 108. Cambridge: Cambridge University Press, 2000.

Warren, David H. "The Text of the Apostle in the Second Century: A Contribution to the History of its Reception." Th.D. diss., Harvard University, 2001.

Wasserman, Emma. "The Death of the Soul in Romans 7: Revisiting Paul's Anthropology in Light of Hellenistic Moral Psychology." *Journal of Biblical Literature* 126(2007): 793–816.

Weber, Max. *Economy and Society: an Outline of Interpretive Sociology.* 2 vols. Berkeley: University of California Press, 1978.

Webb, Ruth. *Ekphrasis, Imagination and Persuasion in Ancient Rhetorical Theory and Practice*. Burlington, VT: Ashgate Publishing, 2009.

Wehn, Beate. "'Blessed are the bodies of those who are virgins': Reflections on the Image of Paul in the *Acts of Thecla*." *Journal for the Study of the New Testament* 79(2000): 149–164.

Weiss, Hans-Friedrich. *Frühes Christentum und Gnosis: eine rezeptionsgeschichtliche Studie*. Wissenschaftliche Untersuchungen zum Neuen Testament 225. Tübingen: Mohr Siebeck, 2008.

———. "Paulus und die Häretiker: Zum Paulusverständnis in der Gnosis." Pages 116–128 in *Christentum und Gnosis*. Edited by Walther Eltester. Beihafte zur Zeitschrift für die neutestamentliche Wissenschaft und die Kunde der älteren Kirche 37. Berlin: Töpelmann, 1969.

Welborn, L. L. "The Soteriology of Romans in Clement of Alexandria, *Stromateis 2*: Faith, Fear, and Assimilation to God." Pages 66–83 in *Early Patristic Readings of Romans*. Edited by Kathy L. Gaca and L. L. Welborn. New York: T&T Clark International, 2005.

Weldon, Mary Susan. "Remembering as a Social Process." *The Psychology of Learning and Motivation: Advances in Research and Theory* 40(2000): 67–120.

Wells, Gary L., and Elizabeth F. Loftus, eds. *Eyewitness Testimony: Psychological Perspectives*. New York: Cambridge University Press, 1984.

Werline, Rodney. "The Transformation of Pauline Arguments in Justin Martyr's *Dialogue with Trypho*." *Harvard Theological Review* 92(1999): 79–93.

Werner, Johannes. *Der Paulinismus des Irenaeus: Eine kirchen- und dogmengeschichtliche Untersuchung über das Verhältnis des Irenaeus zu der paulinischen Briefsammlung und Theologie*. Texte und Untersuchungen zur Geschichte der Altchristlichen Literatur 6.2. Leipzig: J. C. Hinrichs, 1889.

Westerholm, Stephen. *Perspectives Old and New on Paul: The "Lutheran" Paul and His Critics*. Grand Rapids, MI: Eerdmans, 2003.

Whiston, William. *A Collection of Authentick Records Belonging to the Old and New Testament, Part II*. London, 1728.

White, Benjamin L. "How to Read a Book: Irenaeus and the Pastoral Epistles Reconsidered." *Vigiliae christianae* 65(2011): 125–149.

———. "Reclaiming Paul?: Reconfiguration as Reclamation in *3 Corinthians*." *Journal of Early Christian Studies* 17(2009): 497–523.

White, Hayden. *The Content of the Form: Narrative Discourse and Historical Representation*. Baltimore, MD: Johns Hopkins University Press, 1987.

———. *Figural Realism: Studies in the Mimesis Effect*. Baltimore, MD: Johns Hopkins University Press, 1999.

———. *Metahistory: The Historical Imagination in Nineteenth-Century Europe*. Baltimore, MD: Johns Hopkins University Press, 1973.

———. "The Politics of Historical Interpretation: Discipline and De–Sublimation." Pages 119–143 in *The Politics of Interpretation*. Edited by W. J. T. Mitchell. Chicago: University of Chicago Press, 1983.

————. "Response to Arthur Marwick." *Journal of Contemporary History* 30(1995): 233–246.

————. "Rhetoric and History." Pages 3–24 in *Theories of History: Papers Read at a Clark Library Seminar, March 6, 1976*. Edited by Hayden White and Frank E. Manuel. Los Angeles: William Andrews Clark Memorial Library, 1978.

————. *Tropics of Discourse: Essays in Cultural Criticism*. Baltimore, MD: Johns Hopkins University Press, 1978.

White, Ronald C., Jr. *The Eloquent President: A Portrait of Lincoln through His Words*. New York: Random House, 2005.

Wiedenhofer, Siegfried. "Tradition – History – Memory: Why Do We Need a Comprehensive Theory of Tradition?" Pages 375–398 in *Tradition and Tradition Theories*. Edited by Thorsten Larbig and Siegfried Wiedenhofer. Berlin: LIT Verlag, 2006.

Wild, Robert A. "The Image of Paul in the Pastoral Letters." *The Bible Today* 23(1985): 239–245.

Wilder, Terry L. *Pseudonymity, the New Testament, and Deception: An Inquiry Into Intention and Reception*. Lanham, MD: University Press of America, 2004.

Wiles, Maurice F. *The Divine Apostle: The Interpretation of St. Paul's Epistles in the Early Church*. Cambridge: Cambridge University Press, 1967.

Williams, David Salter. "Reconsidering Marcion's Gospel." *Journal of Biblical Literature* 108(1989): 477–496.

Williams, Jacqueline A. *Biblical Interpretation in the Gnostic Gospel of Truth from Nag Hammadi*. Society of Biblical Literature Dissertation Series 79. Atlanta, GA: Scholars Press, 1988.

Williams, Michael. *Rethinking "Gnosticism": an Argument for Dismantling a Dubious Category*. Princeton, NJ: Princeton University Press, 1996.

Wilson, Robert McL. *The Gospel of Philip*. New York: Harper, 1962.

————. "The New Testament in the Nag Hammadi *Gospel of Philip*." *New Testament Studies* 9(1963): 291–294.

Wilson, Stephen G. "The Portrait of Paul in Acts and the Pastorals." *Society of Biblical Literature Seminar Papers* 15(1976): 397–411.

Wingren, Gustaf. *Man and the Incarnation: A Study in the Biblical Theology of Irenaeus*. Translated by Ross Mackenzie. Edinburgh: Oliver & Boyd, 1959 [1947].

Witherington, Ben, III. *Conflict & Community at Corinth: A Socio-Rhetorical Commentary on 1 and 2 Corinthians*. Grand Rapids, MI: Eerdmans, 1995.

Wittgenstein, Ludwig. *Tractatus Logico-Philosophicus*. Translated by D. G. Pears and B. F. McGuinness. London: Routledge & Kegan Paul, 1961 [1921].

Wolfson, Harry Austryn. "Immortality and Resurrection in the Philosophy of the Church Fathers." *Harvard Divinity School Bulletin* 22(1957): 5–40.

Wright, John P., and Paul Potter, eds. *Psyche and Soma: Physicians and Metaphysicians on the Mind-Body Problem from Antiquity to Enlightenment*. Oxford: Clarendon Press, 2000.

Yerushalmi, Yosef Hayim. *Zakhor: Jewish History and Jewish Memory*. The Samuel and Althea Stroum Lectures in Jewish Studies. Seattle: University of Washington Press, 1996 [1982].

Zahn, Theodor. *Geschichte des Neutestamentlichen Kanons*. 2 vols. Hildesheim: Georg Olms Verlag, 1975 [1888–1892].

Zelizer, Barbie. "Reading the Past Against the Grain: The Shape of Memory Studies." *Critical Studies in Mass Communication* 12(1995): 214–239.

Zerubavel, Eviatar. "Social Memories: Steps to a Sociology of the Past." *Quantitative Sociology* 19(1996): 283–299.

Zerubavel, Yael. "The Historic, the Legendary, and the Incredible: Invented Tradition and Collective Memory in Israel." Pages 105–123 in *Commemorations: The Politics of National Identity*. Edited by John R. Gillis. Princeton, NJ: Princeton University Press, 1994.

———. *Recovered Roots: Collective Memory and the Making of Israeli National Tradition*. Chicago: University of Chicago Press, 1995.

Zetterholm, Magnus. *Approaches to Paul: a Student's Guide to Recent Scholarship*. Minneapolis: Fortress Press, 2009.

Zhang, Tong, and Barry Schwartz. "Confucius and the Cultural Revolution: A Study in Collective Memory." *International Journal of Politics, Culture and Society* 11(1997): 189–212.

Ziman, John. *Reliable Knowledge: An Exploration of the Grounds for Belief in Science*. Canto Originals. Cambridge: Cambridge University Press, 1991 [1978].

Žižek, Slavoj. *The Fragile Absolute: Or, Why is the Christian Legacy Worth Fighting For?* Wo es War. London: Verso, 2000.

———. *The Puppet and the Dwarf: The Perverse Core of Christianity*. Short Circuits. Cambridge, MA: MIT Press, 2003.

———. *The Ticklish Subject: The Absent Center of Political Ontology*. Woe es War. London: Verso, 1999.

Zuntz, Günther. *The Text of the Epistles: A Disquisition upon the Corpus Paulinum*. Oxford: Oxford University Press, 1953.

Index of Ancient Sources

General references to whole texts and ancient authors can be found in the Index of Subjects. This index provides references to specific passages within those texts.

Index of Subjects

General references to ancient authors and texts are included as subjects here. Additional references to specific passages within these texts can be found in the Index of Ancient Sources. References to modern scholars can be found in the Index of Modern Scholars.

Index of Modern Scholars

CPSIA information can be obtained
at www.ICGtesting.com
Printed in the USA
BVOW03s0736070217
475486BV00002B/7/P